AF757795

ALCHEMISTS OF HUMAN NATURE: PSYCHOLOGICAL UTOPIANISM IN GROSS, JUNG, REICH AND FROMM

ALCHEMISTS OF HUMAN NATURE: PSYCHOLOGICAL UTOPIANISM IN GROSS, JUNG, REICH AND FROMM

BY

Petteri Pietikainen

Routledge
Taylor & Francis Group
LONDON AND NEW YORK

First published 2007 by Pickering & Chatto (Publishers) Limited

Published 2016 by Routledge
2 Park Square, Milton Park, Abingdon, Oxfordshire OX14 4RN
711 Third Avenue, New York, NY 10017, USA

First issued in paperback 2015

Routledge is an imprint of the Taylor & Francis Group, an informa business

© Taylor & Francis 2007
© Petteri Pietikainen 2007

All rights reserved, including those of translation into foreign languages. No part of this book may be reprinted or reproduced or utilised in any form or by any electronic, mechanical, or other means, now known or hereafter invented, including photocopying and recording, or in any information storage or retrieval system, without permission in writing from the publishers.

Notice:
Product or corporate names may be trademarks or registered trademarks, and are used only for identification and explanation without intent to infringe.

BRITISH LIBRARY CATALOGUING IN PUBLICATION

Pietikainen, Petteri
Alchemists of human nature: psychological utopianism in Gross, Jung, Reich and Fromm
1. Gross, Otto, 1877–1920 2. Jung, C. G. (Carl Gustav), 1875–1961 3. Reich, Wilhelm, 1897–1957 4. Fromm, Erich, 1900–1980 5. Psychoanalysis – History 6. Utopias
I. Title
150.1'95'0922

ISBN-13: 978-1-138-66357-2 (pbk)
ISBN-13: 978-1-8519-6923-4 (hbk)

Typeset by Pickering & Chatto (Publishers) Limited

CONTENTS

ACKNOWLEDGEMENTS

There is a place called Utopia in Texas (http://www.utopiatexas.com/). Once I toyed with the silly idea of writing my book on utopia in Utopia. For practical reasons, I gave up the idea, but in my mind I still have an enduring image of myself sitting in a coffee-house in the centre of Utopia, sipping coffee, eating doughnuts and thinking utopian thoughts. Maybe next time ...

Meanwhile, this is what happened in a place called reality. During the different stages of this work I have been in contact with a great number of colleagues who have offered me assistance in one way or another, and many people and institutions who have made it possible for me to research and write this book. Grants from Ella and Georg Ehrnrooth's Foundation and Lehto Foundation helped me to get started with my research in Helsinki, and with the help of the the Academy of Finland's post-doctoral funding I was able to spend an academic year at the Department of Psychology, University College Dublin. Conversations with Adrian Brock and other historically-minded psychologists in Dublin stimulated my thought and increased my understanding of the critical questions in the history of psychology.

From Dublin I moved further to the west to Boston, where I spent another academic year as a Fulbright scholar at the Department of History, Massachusetts Institute of Technology. My friendly host at MIT was Bruce Mazlish, who offered encouragement and thoughtful comments at a time when I was trying to build a solid structure to my wandering ideas. A year in Boston also offered valuable time for further research, archival work and conversations with intellectual historians, psychoanalysts and scholars of psychology in various conferences, seminars and cosy little restaurants across the country, as well as in the nearby Cambridge area. I would like to express my gratitude especially to the late professor Paul Roazen, who was always willing to engage in long enthusiastic discussions with me (with anyone, basically) about the history of psychoanalysis and psychiatry.

Back in Europe, two travel grants from the Emil Öhmann Foundation supported my study trips to German-speaking Europe. In one of these trips, Rainer Funk from the Erich Fromm Archives in Tubingen showed me warm hospitality when I spent a few hectic days there going through Fromm's letters and other archival material.

My research took an important step forward when the Ax:son Johnson Foundation in Sweden decided to organize an international conference on psychological utopias. I was given an opportunity not only to invite speakers to the conference but also to act as the chairman of the meeting. This was almost like a psychological utopia to me – too good to be true. In lovely surroundings in Swedish countryside, I had a unique chance to exchange ideas with Swedish (Kay Glans, Olav Hammer, Inga Sanner, Lennart Warring), Finnish (Juhani Ihanus), British (Paul Bishop, Gottfried Heuer, Janet Stewart), Russian (Alexander Etkind) and American (Jonathan Beecher, Alan C. Elms, Bruce Mazlish) scholars and writers in a near-utopian setting. During this conference I learned much about Otto Gross, B. F. Skinner, Charles Fourier, C. G. Jung and other utopian authors. I am very grateful for the generous support that Vicky Ax:son Johnson and Kurt Almqvist from the Ax:son Johnson Foundation offered me during that year and also later. Indeed, in the early 2000s, I spent three years in Sweden working as a project leader in a historical project funded by the Foundation. This gave me an opportunity to write a number of articles on psychological utopianism, as well as to examine in depth the history of Swedish mental medicine and intellectual culture. After returning to Finland and the University of Helsinki, I was able to finish the manuscript for this book with the help of a grant from the Wihuri Foundation.

In the last decade I have been sustained and entertained intellectually and emotionally by a community of scholars and friends, who have made sure that my utopian energies have not been exhausted. For their support and their valuable ideas, I would like to thank Stephen Berger, Paul Bishop, Jaap Bos, John Burnham, David Clark, Raymond Fancher, Martin Green, Benjamin Harris, Ari Helo, Gottfried Heuer, Juhani Ihanus, Horst Junginger, Dave Park, Hans Pols, Markku Roinila and Juha Siltala. Particular thanks are due to Heikki Sarmaja and Janne Kivivuori, whose insights, humour and unconventional understanding of human nature have inspired me all these years.

Finally, I would like to thank my family: my wife Anne, our daughter Mona and our son Eero. They have taught me to give a satisfactory answer to the annoying question: 'what is the meaning of life?' Eero has also provided me with a motto I like to use when things get too serious and important: 'Hands up if I shoot you!'

INTRODUCTION

This is a study of utopian elements in the writings of four psychological authors: Otto Gross, Carl G. Jung, Wilhelm Reich and Erich Fromm. They were all psychoanalytic renegades in one way or another, for after a period of collaboration with Freud (Gross, Jung and Reich), or with the faithful guardians of the psychoanalytic doctrine (Fromm), they were renounced as revisionists or stigmatized as mentally disturbed by Freud and his loyal cadre of followers. Consequently, they either retreated from the nascent psychoanalytic movement voluntarily (as did Jung) or were more or less forced to leave it (as did Gross, Reich and Fromm). As this book demonstrates, these four authors started to display utopian propensities only after their break with Freudian psychoanalysis.

The purpose of this book is to be the first to analyse historically the utopian elements in the writings of these four authors, and to demonstrate that, while they saw themselves as healers, explorers of the unconscious and, at best, political activists and proponents of specific belief systems, their thought patterns included distinct visionary and prophetic elements that belong squarely to the Western tradition of utopian thought. It is quite understandable that they did not openly refer to their ideas as 'utopian' or place any of them within this tradition, because it did not exactly boost an author's professional and intellectual status if his ideas were identified as representing utopianism – that is, idle, 'non-scientific' dreaming.

I have chosen to examine the ideas of these particular authors because they exemplify psychodynamic[1] utopianism better than any other psychoanalysts or psychoanalytically-inspired philosophers. There have been psychodynamic authors (such as Alfred Adler or R. D. Laing) as well as non-medical authors inspired by psychoanalysis (such as Herbert Marcuse) who expressed utopian ideas in some of their writings, but the point of this book is not to compile an exhaustive catalogue of all psychodynamic texts where utopian elements are discernible, but to examine in a historical context the utopian elements in the ideas of four authors, whose propensity to psychoutopian visions characterizes not only a certain publication or a certain period of their lives, but their very approach to questions concerning the self, morality, society, culture and the good life.

While psychological utopianism cannot be associated only with the psychoutopian thinkers discussed in this book, these four men cannot be excluded from any study that purports to say something essential about utopianism in the psychodynamic tradition. On the more general level, this books elucidates the thought patterns of four highly original psychological thinkers, some of whom have had a visible impact on twentieth-century psychology and intellectual culture (especially Jung and Fromm), while others are only now emerging from obscurity and oblivion (especially Gross).

The rationale for writing this book was my conviction that a historical study of utopian elements in psychological and psychodynamic thinking can fundamentally increase our understanding of the nature of modern utopianism on the one hand, and the nature of modern psychological thinking on the other. A historical analysis of utopianism in psychology can also provide important insights into the mechanisms behind the changing conceptions of morality, personhood and the malleability of human nature. Thus my ambition has been not only to contribute to the historical scholarship on psychology and utopian thought, but also to illustrate and analyse general aspects of Western intellectual history, as well as to raise broad comparative questions concerning basic assumptions about the human condition in the modern age.

I believe that utopianism or the utopian impulse – the desire for a different kind of modernity – played a major historical role during the twentieth century. In the confluence of psychoanalytic, intellectual (especially Marxist, but also anarchist and 'humanist') and utopian ideas we can see how the educated classes and the psychomedical experts tried to answer questions concerning the future of social institutions and forms of human bonding (marriage, the family, sexuality, comradeship, etc.), and how they related the destiny of the individual to larger, often violent and disruptive sociocultural and political forces. Thus a historical study of key representatives of modern utopianism can provide a valuable contribution to international scholarship on the ways in which Western intellectual culture in the twentieth century responded, and contributed, to changes in politics, culture and world-views. This book shows how our perception of human nature and our understanding of the nature of problems confronting humanity are inextricably interwoven, and nowhere more so than in the psychological utopianism of Gross, Jung, Reich and Fromm. I argue in this book that if we fail to recognize utopian elements in their thought patterns, we do not fully understand their fundamental ambitions.

There are no book-length studies of psychological utopianism. Closest to the theme of my book is Frank and Fritzie P. Manuel's massive *Utopian Thought in the Western World* (1979), where the authors dedicate one of their chapters to the psychological utopias of Reich, Fromm and Herbert Marcuse.[2] The Manuels may be credited with being the first to examine psychological utopianism, but their perspective on this issue is narrow and somewhat distorted: they associate psychological utopianism with so-called Freudo-Marxism, although the utopian propensities of Marxist psychoanalysts became much more pronounced only after they had abandoned their doctrinaire belief in Marx and Freud. Utopian elements in psychoanalysis, behaviourism and cognitive psychology have also been examined in articles by Jill Morawski,[3] Emanuel Berman[4] and Michael Barclay,[5] and in Alexander Etkind's historical study of psychoanalysis in the Soviet Union.[6] There are of course many studies on the individual authors discussed in this book, and in some of them their ideas are characterized as utopian. This is true especially of Richard Noll's two books on Jung,[7] Gottfried Heuer's unpublished dissertation on Otto Gross[8] and Paul A. Robinson's study on Freudo-Marxism.[9] But in all these works a more detailed analysis of the utopian inclinations of these thinkers is lacking.

To study psychological utopianism is not tantamount to studying utopias from the psychological (psychoanalytic, Jungian, Lacanian, 'Freudo-Marxist', etc.) perspective. In this book, I do not apply psychologizing categories to unmask the purported hidden motivations of psychoutopian authors, or explain their thinking from the psychohistorical perspective on childhood. I do not examine utopianism as, for example, a product of so-called unresolved Oedipal conflicts,[10] because it is my firm belief that to interpret the utopian world as representing an immature fantasy of total power, motivated by a wish to return to an infantile state of union and safety with the mother, is itself a form of psychoanalytic fantasy – or irrelevant psychobabble.

Whereas psychoanalytic interpretations of utopianism tend to be unilluminating and unhelpful, intellectual history provides valid methodological tools for an examination of utopian texts. In this book, I have been influenced especially by the 'behavioural science of ideas' of R. G. Collingwood and Quentin Skinner, two major historical thinkers of the twentieth century.[11] Collingwood viewed history as the history of thinking, as the mind's self-knowledge of itself. To understand how people think, said Collingwood, one has to conceive of thinking as a set of answers to questions that preoccupy people. In order to find out what people mean when they say something, we have to know the questions they are trying to answer. Collingwood emphasized that an essential aspect of historical scholarship is posing the right questions. This, as he knew very well, is quite difficult, because the questions that occupied people's minds in the past are not necessarily the same as those of today. Besides, authors did not explicate the question to which they gave answers in their texts, because they usually wrote to their contemporaries, who were interested in the same question and who understood the specific context without the author having to spell it out explicitly.

The questions that are asked are determined by tacit assumptions or presuppositions (a term used by Collingwood) which remain more or less hidden in the text. When presuppositions are different, so too are the questions that occupy people's minds. To understand the process of question and answer is to 're-enact', which in Collingwood's view is the goal of historical scholarship.[12]

For Quentin Skinner, a historian of political ideas inspired by Collingwood, texts are acts; in the philosopher J. L. Austin's meaning of the term they are 'speech acts'.[13] Skinner has studied the complicated question of the relationship between the intentions of historical agents and meanings in their texts. This relationship is complicated, because texts may have meanings that the author did not intend to convey. Thus Skinner urges historians to 'focus not just on the text to be interpreted but on the prevailing conventions governing the treatment of the issues or themes with which the text is concerned'.[14] An interpretation of a particular text requires not only the identification of intentions, but also of beliefs, and as these beliefs are something that authors typically take for granted and do not articulate – they may not be aware of all of their beliefs – these beliefs can be seen as presuppositions in Collingwood's sense. An intellectual historian, who tries to identify and describe particular beliefs, interprets them in a wider 'network of beliefs' or mentality, which refers to beliefs that were commonplace and typical at a given time. What is called 'contextualization' is a search for *connections* between intentions and (often) unarticulated beliefs. This search requires that, to use Skinner's terms, a historian tries to recapture the prevailing beliefs that 'govern the treatment' of a particular issue in a particular time and place. The foremost task of an intellectual historian is to identify and describe beliefs (Skinner) or presuppositions (Collingwood), and the starting-point of this inquiry is to find out what the historical agents *themselves* have possibly said about their beliefs.

Like Skinner, I believe in the importance of situational factors in historical explanations, and I also share his view that, in social explanation, human agency should be privileged over structure. A study of individual thinkers should not be seen merely as a preliminary stage to a more 'scientific' or otherwise essential study of 'structures' or 'institutions'. Through a proper study of historical agents we can understand the intellectual contexts out of which particular beliefs, ideas and arguments arose. For me, this is the ultimate goal of historical scholarship. While we cannot discover the true reality of the past, we can uncover not only the reasons why individual thinkers held certain beliefs, but also why it was rationally or morally acceptable or uncontroversial to hold these beliefs in a particular time and place. To accuse late nineteenth-century thinkers of racism, for example, may be an edifying exercise in moral reading, but it does not help us understand why these thinkers (Darwin or Marx, for instance) thought it rational to hold beliefs we now think of as racist, sexist or prejudiced, or what they may have intended or meant in their texts or utterances.

In this book, I try to practise what I preach, and uncover the beliefs and intentions of Gross, Jung, Reich and Fromm concerning the utopian regeneration of human life and of sociocultural reality. Following Skinner and Wittgenstein, I endorse the statement (made by Wittgenstein in his *Philosophical Investigations*) that 'words are also deeds' – we are always doing something as well as saying something.[15] With regard to our four protagonists, who made sweeping statements about politics, morality and human psychology, this argument about the performativity of texts is, I believe, incontestable.

I devote separate chapters to each author, but I start by examining the nature of psychological utopianism in Chapter 1, focusing on the clarification of the basic assumptions of such a utopianism. I also tentatively compare the professional identities and basic beliefs of Gross, Jung, Reich and Fromm. In Chapter 2, I give an outline of the early history of psychoanalysis in the Soviet Union, because for a decade or so after the Russian Revolution the Bolshevik authorities took a relatively benign attitude towards psychoanalysis. It was regarded as a useful psychological tool for both analysing and changing the structure of the personality, so that the ignorant, poor and superstitious Russian peasant might be transformed into the 'New Soviet Man' who would embody the scientific Marxist-Leninist values of the Bolsheviks. I illustrate how, in the early days of the Soviet Union, the utopian implications of psychoanalysis came to the fore and inspired both behavioural experts and the authorities, especially Trotsky.

The rest of the book is dedicated to the ideas of Gross, Jung, Reich and Fromm. I start with Otto Gross, for decades a forgotten figure in the history of psychoanalysis and European intellectual culture, who was the first of our quartet to develop psychoutopian ideas (in the 1910s). The chapter on Gross is the longest in the book, and the reason I 'favour' him in this regard is that he was the most explicitly utopian of all psychological thinkers fascinated with the idea of inner transformation and its potential significance for changing the very foundation of society. Moreover, compared to the three other protagonists in this book, Gross's life and work are much less familiar to most readers, and for this reason alone a more detailed study of his utopian ideas is in order. I also examine his relationship with Freud and especially Jung, who was not only his colleague, but also his physician and analyst at the Burghölzli mental hospital in 1908, when Jung diagnosed him as schizophrenic. In this context, I discuss the issues of marginalization and stigmatization, which clarify the reasons why Gross became all but a forgotten figure in the history of psychoanalysis, psychiatry and European intellectual culture.

Chapter 4 is devoted to Jung, who created the psychoutopian idea of individuation in the 1910s, while his theory of archetypes conveyed the notion that we all carry a psychic treasure within the deepest structure of the unconscious. In this chapter, I analyse how his utopia of authenticity assumed a more political outlook in the early 1930s when, for a few years, he believed that the 'German revolution of 1933' may have arisen from the deep archetypal layer of the human psyche, and that something like 'national individuation' was taking place in the Third Reich. Towards the end of the 1930s, Jung became disillusioned with National Socialism and ceased to believe that Germany was truly regenerating itself. Late in his life, Jung all but turned his back on sociopolitical reality, burying himself in alchemical and religious treatises which articulated, in his view, the perennial psychological dilemmas of humanity in a symbolic language.

In Chapter 5, I focus on the ideas as well as on the tumultuous and ultimately tragic life of Wilhelm Reich, a dissident psychoanalyst, social activist and 'functional scientist' who was harassed by the authorities both in Europe and in the United States. After giving an overview of his life and work, I examine first Reich's beliefs and intentions during his 'sexual-political' period in Austria, Germany and Norway (*c.* 1927–39). I then turn to his American phase (1939–57) and to the utopian elements in his 'Orgonomic Functionalism'. I discuss his transformation from a radical Marxist social activist, mental hygienist and sexual liberator in the late 1920s and 1930s to a utopian author who thought he had discovered the basic energy of the universe, and who then wrote a number of treatises in which he discussed the social, psychological and therapeutic implications of this so-called Orgone Energy.

In Chapter 6, I turn to Erich Fromm, who proclaimed from the mid-1950s onwards that the life we live, and the society we live in, is sick, alienated and inadequate. The solution he offered for this sick society was Socialist Humanism, a fusion of Marxist, psychoanalytic and Messianic doctrines that would provide a viable political and existential alternative to state socialism and bureaucratic capitalism – a 'third way'. In this chapter, I focus on the utopian aspects of Fromm's Socialist Humanism from the mid-1950s to the late 1960s, when he was one of the most popular public intellectuals in the United States.

In the short concluding chapter, I take up the issues of positive illusion, ideology and Second Reality, and relate them to psychological utopianism. In telling this story of psychological utopianism, which nobody else has yet done, my deeper ambition is to highlight an essential aspect of modernity, namely the desire to alter human nature and to create a society where people identify with their so-called Authentic Self (the original unspoiled source of good). Gross's Matriarchal Communism, Jung's Archetypal Cosmos, Reich's Orgonomic Functionalism and Fromm's Socialist Humanism were all utopian solutions to the problems of despair, alienation and neurosis which they saw as torturing modern man. In their desire to save humanity by changing the way people think, feel and act, they were utopians. This book is, then, a study of hope, but, as the reader will notice, it is also a study of folly.

1 THE NATURE OF PSYCHOLOGICAL UTOPIANISM

The *urtext* of utopian thought is Thomas More's *Utopia*, written in Latin and published in 1516. More, who was Lord Chancellor of England as well as a scholar and a humanist, formed the term 'utopia' from a combination of Greek root words that could be read in two ways. Utopia was *u-topia*, no-place, but it was also *eu-topia*, the good place.[1] This ambiguity was fundamental to More's purposes, for he wanted to say that his utopia was a good place that might *never* exist.[2] *Utopia* was translated during the sixteenth century into all the major European languages, and there are now well over one hundred editions of the book. *Utopia* is of paradigmatic importance, to say the least, for it set the pattern for Western utopia and launched a whole tradition of utopian thinking in the Western world. In the wake of *Utopia*, utopian literature flourished especially between the mid-sixteenth and mid-seventeenth centuries, when Andreae, Campanella, Francis Bacon and a host of other authors wrote 'classic' utopian novels. Utopian tradition is therefore as old as the Reformation – it may even be older than Christianity, if we also regard Plato's *Republic* and various myths of religious paradise as utopias.[3]

In the early nineteenth century, there was another remarkable outburst of utopian thought, when utopias became closely attached to forms of political thought later called socialism and anarchism. Later in the century, Marx famously warned against writing 'recipes for the cook-shops of the future',[4] and he consciously created and organized his ideas in opposition to what he regarded as socialist utopianism (Owen, Fourier, Saint-Simon), bourgeois (anarchist) individualism (Stirner) and anti-organizational socialism (Bakunin). But contrary to his own presentation of his political philosophy, there is a utopian streak in Marx's complex system, and much of utopian literature in the nineteenth and early twentieth centuries was explicitly socialist in orientation. Compared with the great nineteenth-century socialist utopias and anarchist exhortations of 'natural comradeship', there were relatively few outstanding utopian authors in the twentieth century. Utopian energies appeared to be exhausted during the century which the historian Eric Hobsbawm has characterized as a 'slaughter bench' (the term is from Hegel).[5] Instead of utopian fiction, authors such as Orwell, Huxley and Zamyatin produced suggestive visions of a bleak future for the human condition, which are now an essential part of the established canon of dystopias, the counter-images of utopias.

Far from being extinguished, however, utopianism merely assumed new, less explicit, forms in the twentieth century. One modern offshoot of utopianism found inspiration in evolutionary theories and various individualized, non-organizational forms of spirituality, while another looked into the depths of the human psyche and found the unconscious, the great no-place (*u-topos*). This book focuses on the psychological no-place, but evolutionary utopias also merit a few words. A good representative of modern evolutionary utopianism is the famous zoologist and sociobiologist E. O. Wilson, who believes that human evolution could in principle be speeded up so as to match the progress of cultural evolution. Wilson tried to convince people that his book, *Sociobiology*, was meant as a long-term scheme for saving humankind, while in *The Promethean Fire* he developed an explicit programme of social engineering, not unlike that of the neo-behaviourist B. F. Skinner's in his *Beyond Freedom and Dignity*. Wilson attributed to evolutionary biology an implicit moral function and looked for moral messages in nature by emphasizing the altruistic tendencies in animals and humans, and by looking for instances of the ideal of 'nobility' in nature. Another biologist, W. M. Wheeler, explicitly believed in the anarchist Peter Kropotkin's utopian-evolutionary idea of mutual aid.[6] The suggestion that humans are 'by nature' social, co-operative and (potentially) altruistic has tremendous utopian implications, and, as we shall see, we can find this idea in the writings of Gross, Jung, Reich and Fromm. Psychological and evolutionary forms of utopianism testify to the power of utopian thought in the twentieth century, as do feminist, ecological and recent offshoots of technological utopianism (new, freer forms of connection via cyberspace, the notions of global village and virtual realities, the utopian implications of genetic engineering, etc.) and the already established literary genre of science fiction.[7]

To talk about tradition in the context of utopian thought does not mean that there is a continuous thematic link, or a necessary connection, from one utopian text to another. There is little sense in tracing utopian 'unit ideas' or interpreting individual writers' views on 'perennial issues', simply because they answered different sets of questions. These were questions which were considered relevant in a specific time and place, and which were usually addressed with a specific audience in mind. As Quentin Skinner, a champion of a 'situationist' analysis of history, argues,

> the classic texts, especially in moral, social and political theory, can help us to reveal – if we let them – not the essential sameness but rather the variety of viable moral assumptions and political commitments.[8]

This does not mean there are no continuities between issues taken up for discussion in utopian texts, for it is evident that utopian treatises have been written because authors have been inspired, or irritated, by the utopian visions of their predecessors. More's *Utopia* has probably inspired most utopian authors, while Edward Bellamy's state-socialist utopia, *Looking Backward* (1888), irritated another socialist, William Morris, and prompted him to envisage a different kind of socialism in *News from Nowhere* (1890).

Despite the versatility of utopian thought from Thomas More to Erich Fromm, the common feature of all forms of utopian thought is that they combine either an explicit or an implicit critique of the prevailing social order with a vision of a world where the fundamental problems of existing societies have been successfully solved. Thus utopias are, to a varying degree, mixtures of social critique and description of human flourishing in a society or community quite unlike any other. More had launched this tradition with *Utopia*, in which the unhappy state of Tudor England, and European society as a whole, is contrasted with an ideal country, where happy people live in a perfectly organized society. But what makes a particular text utopian is not self-evident, because our understanding of utopia depends on the way the word is defined, and our own definition of the term is our guiding assumption when we start reading and analysing texts. Utopias are commonly held to be fictive narrations of a better life either in an imaginary place or imaginary time, or both, and their appeal to our imagination has been attributed to their way of representing radical visions of the *telos* or end to which social life aims.[9]

Utopia is decidedly not a reality-oriented theory of social reformism in the manner of twentieth-century social democracy, but a suggestive picture of a world where the fundamental social structures and human social relationships are transformed for the better. Utopian authors are engaged in a thought experiment (*Gedankenexperiment*) in which alternative images of human life are presented and new principles of social organization are propounded. These images and principles aim to offer a positive alternative to prevailing reality and to stress the necessity of a massive reorientation of human values. Utopia offers nothing less than a final solution to the alleged dilemmas of humanity. This is most obvious in utopian novels, which play freely with the notion of a better world, but the idea(l) of the final solution is visible also in specific social theories and political ideologies. For example, the ultimate goal of Marxism is a classless society where not only capitalist economy and bourgeois values are abandoned, but even the state has withered away. Although the means adopted to reach this goal were allegedly 'scientific' and anti-utopian, dismissing the possibility of building a utopia within a pre-Communist world, the goal was utopian.[10]

Modern Utopian Thought

I argue that, in the utopian thought of the last two hundred years, four essential ideas have become intertwined. First of all, the idea of the malleability and, thereby, the perfectibility of humans has been at the very centre of utopian thought from the beginning. In most cases, utopias have not been descriptions of a *perfect* world, but without the notion of perfectibility there would not be utopianism.[11] The changing conception of human nature in the modern age has brought to the fore John Locke's empiricist idea of the human mind as a blank slate or *tabula rasa*, which tallied well with the utopian idea that humans can be changed for the better. In its modern, secular version, this notion of the perfectibility of humans dates back to the Enlightenment, and especially to the French Enlightenment, where the idea of a 'New Man' found more resonance than, for example, among the more sceptically-minded Scottish thinkers.

A note to the reader might be in order here: I use the gender-specific term 'man' occasionally in the book to refer to humans, human beings and people, because this singular noun conveys the utopian dimension in the author's conception of the essence of humanity better than other concepts – besides, the term 'man' (and 'New Man') was used by the authors themselves when they wrote in English. Therefore I use this term only in its generic sense to refer to human beings and do not intend to give vent to male chauvinism.

The empiricist idea that human life is largely determined by social structures and cultural factors (environmental or cultural determinism) has influenced twentieth-century utopianism, the human sciences and Western intellectual culture. This doctrine discounts or belittles the inherent activity of the human mind (innateness) and maintains instead that the sociocultural environment determines much if not all of human life, and that genetically inherited mental dispositions are negligible if they exist at all. Environmental determinism proposes that there is no such thing as universal human nature, and that the human mind is like Locke's blank slate, produced and shaped by sociocultural factors. This sort of environmentalism, which stresses the mental faculty of learning and the mechanisms of social conditioning, took off during the early twentieth century, as can be seen in the breakthrough of behaviourism, cultural anthropology and so-called anti-reductionist sociology. Until the 1920s and 1930s, social scientists and humanist scholars had no trouble seeing biology in general and evolutionary theories (not necessarily Darwinian) in particular as necessary ingredients in theoretical constructions that purported to give a scientific account of social and cultural life.[12] But the moral and intellectual bankruptcy of the biological ideology of National Socialism, as well as the increasingly suspicious academic attitude towards cultural evolutionists and evolutionary models, paved the way for doctrines and beliefs revolving around environmental determinism, which stressed the variety of culturally specific behaviour patterns and mentalities.[13]

In the early twentieth century, a stress on environmental, sociocultural factors gave new impetus to utopianism, because the message it implied was that through education, social engineering and the overall manipulation of environmental conditions behaviour and deeply engrained mental structures could be changed. Environmentalism also opened unheard-of ideological vistas to the authorities and intellectuals who wanted their own values and beliefs to become the values and beliefs of all. If one holds that humans are almost infinitely malleable, then one can logically infer that, through carefully executed sociopolitical engineering, utopia is a distinct possibility and not just a pipe-dream or a thought experiment. Not surprisingly, in the early years of the Soviet Union some of the leading Bolsheviks had great expectations of constructing a new edition of the human species, *homo sovieticus*, which would signal the beginning of a socialist utopia where all citizens would be both equal and free. However, it was not only in the Soviet Union or among left-wing intellectuals in the West where environmentalist beliefs were to a large extent adopted as a tacit assumption or presupposition. Environmentalism was also well suited to the capitalist ethos, which was prone to treat the workers as human material that can be controlled and manipulated according to the needs of the market economy and the Taylorian technology of work efficiency.[14]

The idea that utopia was not to be found in some remote corner of the world but in the future became commonplace in modern utopian literature. Thomas More and his humanist contemporaries in the sixteenth century, as well as the authors of ancient Greece and Rome, placed their ideal societies either in imaginary places or in the past. According to the latter option, the golden age is not ahead of us but behind us. By contrast, in temporal utopias, exemplified by Louis-Sebastien Mercier's *L'An 2440* (1771), the golden age glimmers on the horizon of future. In temporal utopias, utopia transcends historical time, because it is not the product of historical laws or metaphysical necessity actualizing itself in history. However, as the utopian scholar Cosimo Quarta argues, in human aspirations to attain the unattainable, utopia functions as history's motive force, as the project of history. Hence, the 'end of history' would mean the 'end of utopia', because 'there can be no history without projects'.[15] History and utopia are thus interrelated: people in a given society are motivated by the utopian goals which they see in the future, but which are at the same time immanent in history. The socialist realism of Stalin's era, for example, can be seen as a vision of a utopia towards which the Soviet Union was heading, and which was designed to empower Russians to have faith, even in a time of crisis (such as the Great Patriotic War against Nazi Germany), in the emergence of a new Communist society and the 'New Soviet Man'. Utopia needs history in order to make its message accessible to the people, and history needs utopia in order to mobilize people's sentiments and dreams. Simultaneously, utopia seeks emancipation from the tyranny of time, which destroys illusions and clips the wings of those who believe they can fly above the contingencies of historical time. Hegel, that great worshipper of history, noted in his *Lectures on the Philosophy of History* that human history is the 'slaughter bench' of happiness.[16]

The fourth main component in modern utopianism is value monism, which was already a central part of the first great 'state utopia', Plato's *Republic*. In utopia, everyone holds the same values, and in this sense there are no dissidents in utopia. If, for some reason, there were people in utopia who failed to internalize the true values, they would necessarily be perceived as deviant individuals who must be either re-educated or excluded from society. Most utopias do not resemble pluralist liberal-democratic societies where different ideologies and values can freely contend. In fact, there is no *need* for value pluralism in a society where there exists a harmony of needs and values. In utopia, values are objective, and therefore valid everywhere. They are also in principle knowable to all, which means that a science of values is possible in utopian societies.

The Utopian Impulse in Psychoanalysis

All authors under discussion in this book originally found inspiration in Freudian psychoanalysis, only to go beyond the sceptical world-view of Freud to create doctrines of partial or total salvation. Freud, who was interested in cultural issues and the psychological mechanism behind cultural evolution, wrote in his famous essay *Civilisation and its Discontents* (1930) that

> Our possibilities of happiness are already restricted by our constitution. Unhappiness is much less difficult to experience. We are threatened with suffering from three directions: from our own body, which is doomed to decay and dissolution and which cannot even do without pain and anxiety as warning signals; from the external world, which may rage against us with overwhelming and merciless forces of destruction; and finally from our relations to other men. The suffering which comes from this last source is perhaps more painful to us than any other.[17]

Freud's fundamental message is: society and the individual are unavoidably in conflict, because the stability of society necessitates the repression of individual drives and desires. Due to his conviction of the anti-social nature of our instinctual apparatus, it is difficult to find utopian elements in Freud's thought. As he stated in a letter to Romain Rolland, 'a great part of my life's work has been spent [trying to] destroy illusions of my own and those of mankind'.[18] *Civilization and its Discontents* challenged radicals such as Wilhelm Reich, who wanted to use psychoanalysis to bring about political or cultural revolution. Freud's warning against linking psychoanalysis with political radicalism was at least partly a response to Marxist psychoanalysts in general, and Reich in particular. Indeed, Reich himself claimed that Freud wrote his essay as a rebuttal to Reich's call for psychopolitical activism.[19] What is indisputable is that Freud's *Civilization* became the frame of reference for almost all subsequent psychoanalytic cultural analysis. It is arguably the one great anti-utopian text of the twentieth century that was not narrated as a fiction – although the case could be made that, like all of Freud's works, *Civilization* represents imaginative psychology-fiction rather than science based on empirical evidence.

The only text in which Freud gave vent to utopianism is *The Future of an Illusion* (1927), where he spoke in favour of the 'rational operation of the intellect' and expressed 'hope for the future': 'Perhaps there is a treasure to be dug up capable of enriching civilization and ... it is worth making the experiment of an irreligious education'.[20] But this call for Enlightenment secularism is just about all you can find of 'social experiment' in Freud's oeuvre. Whereas Freud was content with analysing the allegedly neurotic mentality of modern people, some of his closest colleagues and disciples (such as Carl Jung, Alfred Adler and Otto Rank) were more inclined to leave the consultation room and develop doctrines that would not only analyse individuals and human culture but, more importantly, would have an impact on culture and the general world-view (*Weltanschauung*).

There is a remarkable discontinuity between Freud's own texts and those of political Freudians. While Freud himself was, if anything, an anti-utopian thinker, the movement that was built around his psychodynamic theories and his status as the founding father included utopian elements. This paradox can be explained by the fact that, as the sociologist Yiannis Gabriel has observed, 'psychoanalysis, while claiming to be the ultimate critique of all utopias, has become a launching platform of utopian inspiration'.[21] Indeed, despite its adherence to a seemingly anti-utopian, realistic *Weltanschauung*, Freudian psychoanalysis offers theoretical tools for authors who, first of all, want to produce nothing less than a total theory of human nature (Utopia of Omniscience); second, want to think of unrepressed sexuality and the free flow of Eros as the ultimate source of well-being and equality between men and women (Utopia of Eros), and, third, want to read into the unconscious all that they regard as good and desirable, such as innate altruism, solidarity and creativity (Utopia of Authenticity). It is only because psychoanalysts have been reluctant to discern and acknowledge the utopian or salvational strain in their complex intellectual system that they have been disinclined to see themselves as moralists, prophets or advocates of true values. Instead, the self-image they have cultivated has been one of a dispassionate physician, therapist and master of hidden psychic reality.

But psychoanalysis differed from other psychomedical theories in its implicit promise of deep insight if not secular salvation. The psychoanalytic message was: by freely associating psychoanalytically on the couch, you can learn to know your inner self in general and the relations between your emotions and your instinctual nature in particular. Psychoanalytic self-knowledge thus implied that through getting to know your innermost wishes, drives and motivations you could simultaneously minimize the psychic conflicts within yourself and learn to interpret other people's psychological symptoms and to unmask the purported hidden motivations behind their overt conduct and behaviour. This was considered possible simply because everyone has a 'Freudian' psyche, and so self-knowledge entailed a universal knowledge of the 'cunning of unreason'. Freud's mythical self-analysis of the mid-1890s was the foundation upon which the psychoanalytic double-strategy of providing tools for both increasing one's self-knowledge ('education to reality') and interpreting the hidden selves of others was successfully built.

Paradoxically, while psychoanalysis has attributed inner depths to humans, it has tried to make this inner self transparent and predictable. Psychoanalysis has thereby contributed to the psychocultural practice of making the private and intimate dimension of life an object of mental hygiene and of the rhetoric of mental health ideology ('tyranny of intimacy').[22] This has given psychoanalysis predictive power over people who might otherwise be reluctant to think of themselves as transparent subjects of (clinical) observation. As the French psychoanalysts Janine Chasseguet-Smirgel and Béla Grunberger self-assuredly tell us, psychoanalysis

> claims to be not only a key to understanding humanity, but the key which unlocks the doors to knowledge of the species, in all aspects of our behaviour and activities.[23]

This psychoanalytic technique of making the inner lives of others transparent can be traced back to Nietzsche's questioning of the authenticity of human ideals, which appeared in his writings in the form of *entlarvende Psychologie*, the psychology of unmasking. Nietzsche was perhaps the first thinker who discerned the 'true motivations' and drives hidden behind the facade of ego consciousness and who saw 'what we truly are'. He even envisaged the role of the 'unmasker' for intellectuals:

> Theoretical man, whom I take to be the intellectual, takes delight in the cast [off] garments and finds his highest satisfaction in the unveiling process itself which proves to him his own power.[24]

Psychoanalysis, which unmasks our purported hidden motivations and gives explanations for them, is greatly indebted to Nietzsche's *entlarvende Psychologie*, but the psychology of unmasking also has 'family resemblances' to the language of Marxism. Indeed, as the philosopher Paul Ricoeur has noted, all the leading members of the 'School of Suspicion' (Marx, Nietzsche and Freud) looked on the whole of consciousness primarily as 'false' consciousness.[25]

Utopianism in Psychology

Although Freud was not the originator of the idea of the unconscious, he was instrumental in launching not only a major intellectual and therapeutic movement but also a form of utopianism that was founded on the psychological notion of inner transformation as a prerequisite for social change. In the mid-1960s, a historian of utopian thought, Frank E. Manuel, observed that 'eupsychia'[26] was a characteristic form of twentieth-century utopia, and he referred to several authors who propagated the spiritualization of humankind and the attainment of a 'good state of consciousness'.[27] He suggested that, by advocating the abolition of instinctual repression and the ensuing liberation of the libido, Wilhelm Reich, Erich Fromm and Herbert Marcuse were 'Freudo-Marxist' utopians. In a massive 1979 study on utopian thought which he undertook with his wife, Manuel devoted one chapter to psychological utopias, where he again discussed the ideas of Reich, Fromm and Marcuse.[28] Some other scholars of utopianism, however, have been less convinced than Manuel that 'psychological utopia' is a valid concept. Sociologist Krishan Kumar admits that Reich, Fromm and Marcuse were indeed concerned with psychological well-being, but he also emphasizes, first, that these thinkers were also socialists and, second, that 'utopia is essentially a form of social thought'.[29] In two recently published anthologies of utopian texts (*The Utopia Reader* and *The Faber Book of Utopias*), the editors of each book have included excerpts from roughly one hundred treatises, many of them from the twentieth century, and only one of them (B. F. Skinner's *Walden Two*) is explicitly psychological. In the scholarly journal *Utopian Studies*, there are very few references to modern psychologists.[30] On the other hand, sociologist Ruth Levitas has argued that the 'pursuit of a better way of being does not always involve the alteration of external conditions, but may mean the pursuance of spiritual or psychological states'.[31] I agree with Levitas, even if I think that we should distinguish between those authors who pursue a good state of consciousness *per se*, without relating their pursuit to the public sphere, and those who make such a relation between the private and the public sphere explicit. It is this latter group of thinkers whom I study in this book, because they did not exclude society and/or culture from their vision of the good life.

As Frank and Fritzie P. Manuel's *magnum opus* testifies, the idea of psychological utopia is commonly associated with a group of thinkers loosely grouped together under the banner of Freudo-Marxism.[32] As Marxists (at some point in their lives), Wilhelm Reich, Siegfried Bernfeld, Erich Fromm and Herbert Marcuse had strong faith in the social utility of their own theories, which they combined with faith in the ability of psychoanalysis to explain scientifically the objective 'psychic determinants' of subjective inner life (e.g., why the proletariat does not have sufficiently strong class consciousness). They gave Freudian interpretations of Marx's thesis that in the ideal socialist society all human activities derive directly – that is, naturally – from human nature, and that in his or her most individual mode of being a person would at the same time be a social being (*Gemeinwesen)*. In their psychological utopianism, human nature is both socialized and essentially good, because humans are not alienated from their true nature, as is the case in the present capitalist society. Like their behaviourist colleagues across the Atlantic Ocean, European Freudo-Marxists were seduced by the perspectives thrown open for a thorough transformation of human nature.[33]

Freudo-Marxists have not been the only group of psychological thinkers whose ideas have been characterized as utopian. Psychologist J. G. Morawski has shown that, between 1915 and 1930, a number of leading American psychologists wrote utopias that are now 'all but forgotten'. She has examined the publications of G. Stanley Hall, William McDougall, Hugo Münsterberg and John B. Watson, who presented psychology in their texts as 'instrumental to human welfare' and as 'absolutely essential to improving society'.[34] In contrast to these 'psychoutopians', who for the most part lived and worked in the United States, European psychodynamic authors did not give concrete 'speaking-picture' descriptions of an ideal society in their writings. There is no psychodynamic equivalent to Skinner's behaviourist utopia *Walden Two*. Rather than 'utopia', it is the term 'utopianism' that is more applicable to the ideas of dynamic psychologists. In his important article on the concept of utopia, Lyman Tower Sargent defines utopianism as 'social dreaming' which expresses quasi-eternal truths about the human condition, whereas utopia denotes a 'nonexistent society described in detail and normally located in time and place'.[35]

In my own definition of *psychological* utopianism, the concept refers to a form of social dreaming in which the attainment of an ideal state of consciousness requires the employment of psychological insights and methods that are effective in transforming the human personality and, thereby, the whole of society or culture. This means that those whose utopian visions are characteristically psychological have both a definite view of the human psyche and a vision of a world that would offer an ideal matrix for psychological well-being. Authors who display psychoutopian propensities do not have to be psychologists themselves, but they must have either adopted – and possibly modified – some particular theoretical conception of the psyche already in existence, or developed their own conceptual framework for explaining the mind. The distinguishing characteristic of psychodynamic utopianism is that it revolved around the possibility of transforming society through a peculiar psychopolitical therapy, in most cases through the employment of psychodynamic theories and ideas for a variety of ideological purposes, from the radical and society-oriented to the more conservative and culture-oriented.

What I argue in this book is that Gross, Jung, Reich and Fromm incorporated utopian elements in their writings without offering complete utopian blueprints. They were all original thinkers who worked in the field of mental medicine; who had an ambition to analyse not only their patients but also the sociocultural reality; who articulated their profound dissatisfaction with certain aspects of the modern world in their writings; and, lastly, who manifested the desire to transform human beings and, thereby, the whole society or culture. They were social dreamers who wanted to contribute to the emergence of a new *Menschentyp*, a human being who would be authentic, natural, loving, altruistic, empathic, spontaneous, sincere, co-operative, just and courageous – in a word, a more 'humane' human being.

Basic Assumptions of Psychodynamic Utopianism

In addition to the scarcity of studies on utopian thought in psychology, the few studies that we have do not offer a systematic analysis of this issue. For Frank and Fritzie P. Manuel, psychological utopia refers to a 'good state of mind that could be induced virtually in any place and at any time by an adept',[36] while for clinical psychologist Michael Barclay, utopianism manifests itself negatively as an impulse towards totalizing explanations in behaviourism and cognitive psychology.[37] Psychoanalyst Emanuel Berman proposes in turn that

> the proneness of psychoanalysts and psychotherapists to develop utopian visions stems from a central ingredient in the unconscious motivation to become an analyst or a therapist in the first place: namely, from our rescue fantasy.[38]

While all these perspectives illustrate one particular aspect of psychological utopianism, they address inadequately what I myself aspire to clarify in this book, namely the very idea of the role and function of utopianism in psychology.

Throughout this book, I propose that psychodynamic utopianism is characterized by a set of taken-for-granted assumptions or beliefs that the writers do not spell out. But before I turn to these assumptions, I need to highlight the one absolutely crucial ingredient in psychodynamic utopianism, namely the notion of the unconscious (*das Unbewusste*). In utopian terms, the unconscious is the great no-place (*u-topos*) that could also be a good place (*eu-topos*) – the seeds of utopia are to be found in the deepest structures of the psyche. Psychological utopianism without the idea of the unconscious as *eu-topos* is of course quite possible – Skinner's behaviourist utopia has no room for inner mental processes – but for psychodynamic utopianism the unconscious is as indispensable as 'operant conditioning' is for B. F. Skinner. The four psychodynamic authors examined in this book 'visited' the unconscious in the way Raphael Hythlodaeus visited the island of Utopia in Thomas More's novel. All these visitors knew what it was like to be in *u-topos/eu-topos*: Hythlodaeus described the laws and customs in Utopia in detail for outsiders (e.g., 'In Utopia they have a six-hour working day'[39]), while psychoutopians described in detail for outsiders the laws and customs of the unconscious (e.g., the 'Unconscious is the Whole Man'[40]). Like Hythlodaeus, psychoutopians had knowledge, gained through experience, which others did not have. It is true, in principle, that everyone has an access to their unconscious at least when they are dreaming, but without necessary skills one can never actually explore the landscape of the unconscious and draw a reliable map of it.

The unconscious is the indispensable matrix of psychodynamic utopianism, the cornerstone of all subsequent theoretical and ideological constructions. In addition to seeing the idea of the unconscious as the necessary requirement for psychodynamic utopianism, I argue that there are four basic assumptions regarding the relationship between self and society which characterize this mode of thinking. First, psychodynamic authors emphasize the social and cultural significance of an 'inner transformation'. According to this key assumption, humans can only liberate themselves socially through the liberation of their inner selves, a transformation of personality being a prerequisite for a transformation of society. With this program of 'turning inward', they transformed the classic point of departure of utopian thinking, in which ideas of change were conceived in the functional context of social and political activity, and in which the institutions of utopians were not the creation but the creator of their good qualities. Hence the model for the classic utopian picture of a person is *animal laborans* or *homo faber*, an active agent who is constantly fabricating material and political tools in order to shape the environment and collective consciousness. In contrast to classical utopian thought, in psychological utopianism humans are united not by the forms of their external activities, but by the structure of their psyche which, as 'the unconscious', 'the Collective Unconscious', 'the self', 'the true self', 'inner nature' or some other form of inner force, operates as an agent of change against the distorted or outright pathogenic structures of society.

The psychoutopian key notion of the liberated inner self contains a very suggestive moral vision, according to which the only kind of moral order worth embracing is the one which finds personal resonance in us. Inner transformation is not a religious conversion, but rather a psychological and philosophical insight or conviction which prompts us to comprehend human life and the order of reality in a new way, and to act in accordance with our insight. Henceforth, what we say and do corresponds to what we truly believe – we live in sincerity. Needless to say, one essential consequence of inner transformation is that one is no longer tormented by anxiety, depression or neurosis, and that one can cope with the petty demands of everyday life without succumbing to mental strain or stress. A good state of consciousness means liberation, partial or total, from the shackles of the empirical self with its socially-determined discontent, alienation and unhappiness, which constitute the burden of modern man.

The idea of inner transformation is ancient, and in a religious context it can be found in the thought-systems of many pre-modern thinkers, such as Augustine. The secular tradition of 'innerness' (*Innerlichkeit*) has its roots in Romanticism, and it is probably Nietzsche who is the most important single proponent of the idea that humans could be altered from within. His radical call for the re-examination of all values, together with his romantic concept of the *Übermensch* and his suspicion of 'Little Men' (who prefer comfort and security to risk-taking and adventure), makes him an important philosophical advocate of inner transformation, and a source of inspiration for two of our psychoutopian authors, Gross and Jung. Gross, who constantly discussed Nietzsche in cafés, was stimulated by Nietzsche's philosophical contempt for the philistine and the petty democrat, as well as by Nietzsche's assault on Christian 'slave morality', while Jung's whole approach to the unconscious, culture and *Wissenschaft* has in it a strong Nietzschean streak.[41]

The second basic assumption of psychological utopianism is the belief in an interconnection between the structure of the personality and the structure of society. (The latter structure refers to forms of government, disciplinary and educational institutions, religion, morality, the family, law, and the nature of economic and social hierarchy). The appeal of this assumption can be explained by its predictive and ordering power: if there is a strong reciprocal link between self and society, then we could in principle change society by changing the structure of the personality, provided that we have discovered the social and psychological determinants that constitute this link. A belief in this assumption thus enables psychoutopians to interpret the human condition using a neat and simple conceptual category, which is useful for making historical and cross-cultural comparisons. Moreover, it can be employed in producing quasi-nomothetic predictions based on investigations of the pattern of change either in social structures or, as is the case with psychoutopians, in the deep structure of the human personality. The assumed interconnection between the structure of the personality and the structure of society has also been asserted, for example, by the social philosopher Theodor Adorno and his colleagues and, more recently, by the German-English sociologist Norbert Elias.[42]

Third, psychoutopians claim that individual psychopathologies reflect the pathogenicity of Western society. When the social, political and moral order becomes corrupt, not only individuals, but whole societies can fall into a pathological state. This claim concerning the sick society is based on an anthropological or holistic conception of illness, which asserts that sociocultural factors play a major role in the aetiology of mental disorders, which in turn means that to restore the mental health of single individuals is not enough; what is needed is to restore the health of the whole of society so that people would feel a natural inclination to live according to their true values and principles – that is, in authenticity. Typically, psychoutopian authors referred to hidden populations, and exaggerated the number of the sick (neurotic, alienated, psychotic) as if to emphasize the urgency of psychopolitical measures against the pathogenicity of society (Wilhelm Reich estimated that as many as 90 per cent of all women and 70 to 80 per cent of all men were neurotic!). By promoting an anthropological conception of illness, psychoutopians became therapeutic politicians, who translated social critique into clinical language and gave their sociocultural interpretations a distinct diagnostic stamp. Instead of employing traditional moral, legal, theological or philosophical categories, they tended to view modern culture and society in the medical terms of sickness and health. Seeing emotional wrongs in general and the repression of 'inner nature' – the source of truth and beauty – in particular as the most fundamental pathogenic factors in modern society, they saw themselves both as unmaskers of the social determinants of psychopathologies and as visionaries who knew what was good and what was bad for us.

Fourth, much of psychodynamic utopianism is characterized by an antagonistic if not outright hostile attitude towards history and 'profane time'. While all utopias are transcendent in the sense that they look far beyond the confines of a given social reality, psychological utopianism signified a profoundly anti-historical perspective on questions regarding the basic constituents of human life and the improvement of the human condition. Psychoutopians were transcendentalists in their questioning of historical progress, namely the idea that cultural evolution equals technological, social and moral betterment. For the universalist psychoutopians, humans cannot be reduced to their historical conditions, for through their inner nature they are in direct contact with the timeless sphere of humanity, which in its historical representations changes through time and yet retains its basic identity. To our authors, human nature is not so much influenced by history or external nature as by the universal structures of the psyche, which in its creative fusion of biology and spirit is relatively immune to the oppression of historical contingency.

I shall argue throughout this book that psychological utopianism is based on these four assumptions (inner transformation, an interrelationship between the structure of society and the structure of the personality, an anthropological conception of illness and an anti-historical mentality), all of which stress the interdependence of mind and body, psyche and soma, self and society, external and inner nature. Consequently, all our psychoutopian authors propagated total therapy and the reconstitution of the harmony between culture and inner nature.

Family at the Centre of Psychoutopian Attention

Among social institutions, it was the family that most interested psychoutopians. It was with the dynamics and constellations within the family, as well as with the role of the family in instilling sociocultural norms and values in its members, that the psychodynamic authors were most preoccupied. That their eyes were fixed on this particular social unit, at the expense of other institutions, is easily explained: they were mostly physicians by training and education, and while they were socialized at medical school into looking at the individual in terms of sickness and health, such a medical gaze also normally included the wider context of the family. This medical stress on the family became even more pronounced when they were converted to psychoanalysis, which is concerned with the psychological dynamics in the family. All versions of dynamic psychology (even, to some extent, that of Jung) affirmed the idea that the human personality develops through an interaction with family members, sexual partners and other significant persons in the individual's environment. Reich and Fromm were convinced that early childhood determines to a large extent the development of character, and in their belief in childhood determinism they did not deviate from orthodox psychoanalytic theories. And when three of them (all but Jung) became inspired by Marxism and/or Communism, they adopted the predominantly negative view of the 'bourgeois' family prevalent among the left-wing intellectuals in Europe.

Small wonder, then, that three of our psychoutopians – Gross, Reich and Fromm – tended to see the family as the locus of both social and individual pathology. The family almost became an institution of which the analysis explained all other institutions, such as education, economy, political system and religion. According to the way these authors saw it, an analysis of the inner conflicts of the individual led the analyst to the wider context of the family, which in turn led to the even larger context of politics, economy and morality. But they hardly ever even tried to analyse this larger sociocultural context; hence the links they forged between what they thought they knew very well – the individual psyche and the family dynamics – and what they did not know very well at all – the function of social structures – remained weak, because these links were forged by assertions, convictions and casual observations rather than by careful empirical analyses of relevant economic, political and moral issues. While they diagnosed society or culture as sick, they did not become engaged in any detailed study of the pathology of social evils. But then again, this is one of the main reasons why they were social dreamers and not sociologists: their strength was not their empirical investigative bent, but their imaginative ability to conjure up startling correlations, suggestive metaphors and new associations between seemingly unconnected phenomena. As we shall see, Gross, Reich and Fromm saw the transformation of the family structure as the key to social and psychological change.

In addition to discussing the family as the principal social institution responsible for much that was wrong in the modern world, our authors were all inspired by the myth of matriarchy as originally developed by J. J. Bachofen in his 1861 study of the 'Mother Right' (*das Mutterrecht*).[43] Bachofen's theory of matriarchy and its historical place in cultural evolution encouraged them to discuss matriarchy as an early cultural stage, the significance of the mother for the individual's destiny, and the archetypal aspects of the mother, the great mother and the eternally female (anima).

Jung differed from the other protagonists in this book in his relative neglect of childhood and family dynamics in general. He preferred discussing the inherent tendency of humans to realize their inner, archetypal potentialities during the second stage of life (starting around the age of thirty-eight). Far from being a theorist of childhood development, Jung was a theorist of the development of personality in the mature age. Thus it is only in the chapter on Jung that I can restrain myself from discussing the fascinating myth of matriarchy.

Gross, Jung, Reich and Fromm: Some Comparative Remarks

Our psychoutopian quartet was from German-speaking Europe: Fromm was German, Jung Swiss, and Gross and Reich were from Austria(-Hungary). Roughly speaking, they represent two generations: Gross and Jung were born in the 1870s, Reich in 1897 and Fromm in 1900. What they all shared was their European (upper) middle-class background, and their class-related disdain for lower middle-class culture and lifestyle. Of these four, all but Fromm were psychiatrists and psychoanalysts by education and training, and even Fromm, who acquired a degree in sociology, became a lay analyst in his late twenties.

As for their religious background, Reich and Fromm were Jews, Jung a Protestant and Gross a Catholic, but none of them practised religion in the conventional sense of the term. Jung and Fromm had a much more positive attitude towards religiosity than did Reich and Gross, but even the later Reich developed doctrines that contained strong religious elements. Jung devoted much of his time to the study of religions from the psychodynamic perspective, while Fromm incorporated Messianic ideas into his Socialist Humanism. Gross is the only author in this book who was not particularly interested in religion. It is no coincidence that religion played a role in psychodynamic utopianism: as scholars of utopian thought have suggested, religion and utopianism are interconnected. Krishan Kumar notes that, although utopia is a form of secular fiction, religion is the '"unconscious of utopia", the subterranean source of much of its emotional force and dynamism'.[44] In a similar vein, Lyman Tower Sargent points out that, although for many Christians utopianism is heretical, 'Christianity provided the basis for much Western utopianism'.[45] In the case of psychodynamic utopianism, non-confessional religiosity could very well form part of the good life to Jung and Fromm, and even Gross and Reich did not consider it to be a problem that could be solved by extinguishing religious feelings and practices.

What about the personal relations of the four authors? As we shall see, Gross and Jung knew each other personally, as did Reich and Fromm. But, with the exception of Jung's psychoanalytic treatment of Gross, they did not have much to do with one another. Gross died in 1920, so he did not witness the early career of his younger colleagues Reich and Fromm. He probably would have had much to say about the young Reich's theories, which were often surprisingly close to Gross's own ideas. Oddly enough, Reich never referred to Gross in his published writings, but it is highly unlikely that he had never heard of Gross, or that he was not inspired by Gross's theories. Jung was interested in the early work of Gross, his somewhat younger colleague, whose typological ideas influenced him when he created his own theory of psychological types. But after his treatment of Gross – which was actually a 'mutual analysis' – Jung's comments on Gross became more negative, and even decades later he would reminiscence about Gross in unflattering terms (see Chapter 3). Of Reich and Fromm, Jung never said anything in his writings or in his published seminars and letters. Presumably, he could not have cared less about the work of young Freudian analysts, such as Reich. Reich, who remained silent about Gross, referred to Jung positively a few times in his early career, but over time his comments became increasingly critical, even hostile, culminating in his statement that Jung was a fascist.[46] Reich and Fromm moved in the same psychoanalytic circles in Berlin in the early 1930s but, although they were both sociologically-oriented Marxist analysts, they never collaborated, and in later years they made predominantly negative comments about each other: Reich accused Fromm of watering down the radical implications of psychoanalysis, especially the emphasis on the power of sexuality, while Fromm characterized Reich as misguided in his association of sexual emancipation with political radicalism. Fromm's views on Jung were also mostly critical, and after Jung's death he called Jung a 'necrophilous' character – that is, a person who loves death. But he also gave some credit to Jung for his understanding of dreams, symbols and the overall creative function of the unconscious.

Thus, we can hardly call our quartet a 'gang of four' or four musketeers; they were more like four cocks strutting around and pecking at rivals whom they thought of as having encroached on their territory. They were rather ill-equipped to work on equal terms with their professional peers, let alone to submit to the intellectual authority of anyone, not even Freud. They all had a prophetic streak in them, and a high regard of their own capacity to divine the inner thoughts of others; to understand what other people and the whole of culture truly needed;

to see the timeless sphere of truth and beauty beyond the everyday world of appearances and historical contingencies; and, ultimately, to heal sick humanity. Their kindred spirits were other visionaries and prophets – Old Testament prophets, Jesus, Buddha, Lao-Tze, Meister Eckhardt, Giordano Bruno, Goethe, Marx, Nietzsche and Albert Schweitzer – rather than their professional peers. Nonetheless, such visionaries were addressing questions that are intelligible only if we contextualize them historically by analysing the relationships between their beliefs and intentions. Each age creates its own 'perennial problems', and the leading idea of this book is that both the problems and the solutions put forward by these authors can only be explained if we understand the ways in which morality, psychology, science and politics became intertwined in Western intellectual culture from the late nineteenth century onwards.

Most European psychoutopians were socialists, but there was one remarkable exception to this: Jung. He was a conservative Swiss republican, who detested socialism and was deeply suspicious of the democratic rule of the 'masses'. In stark contrast to Jung, Gross, Reich and Fromm were all socialists at some point in their lives. Nevertheless, their utopian ideas cannot be characterized as Freudo-Marxist, even if Reich was a Marxist psychoanalyst for about a decade (*c.* 1927–37). However, even before he emigrated to the United States in 1939 he had distanced himself from Marxism, declaring himself 'apolitical'. Fromm remained a Marxist humanist and a democratic socialist until the end of his life, but in his utopianism there were also important elements of Messianism and 'humanist ethics'. Gross in turn was mainly inspired by turn-of-the-century anarchism, and he socialized with anarchists, artists, writers and other bohemians and iconoclasts who represented a counter-culture to bourgeois respectability.

None of the four authors were typical armchair intellectuals, for they all – even Jung – went through a period when they were politically and socially active. And what should be kept in mind when one examines their utopianism is that they all led active and eventful lives, which included fierce debates with critics and enemies, travels in Africa and Asia, best-selling books, countless therapy sessions, political persecution, forced emigrations and expulsions, periods in custody and mental asylums, drug addiction, various illnesses, near-psychotic episodes, prison sentences, involvement with espionage, extramarital sexual liaisons, and experiments with spiritual seances, parapsychology and nuclear energy. In this sense, they were anything but Nietzsche's 'Little Men' who avoided risk-taking and adventure.

Gross, Jung, Reich and Fromm were not involved in setting up any utopian communities, but none of them was a prototypical detached academic either, although they all had academic degrees and were affiliated with academic institutions at some point in their careers. But their involvement with academia was rather sporadic and of little consequence to their intellectual activity, and the fact that they did not spend their lives within the relatively safe confines of a university probably made it easier for them to propound ideas and theories that were considered eccentric or unacceptable by academics. Of course, it also meant that, unlike academics, whose ideas and theories constantly receive critical feedback from their peers, our authors did not have to worry too much about the reception of their ideas at the institutions of higher learning. In short, they were academic outsiders, who could quite freely speculate and construct theories not formally submitted to the critical scrutiny of other specialists in their field. If, for example, Jung and Reich had become professors of psychiatry in their thirties or forties, I wonder whether they would have ever 'discovered' the 'Collective Unconscious' or 'Orgone Energy'. Instead of establishing safe careers in academia, they became psychotherapists, psychopoliticians, social critics and productive writers, who discussed the life experiences of countless individuals and, at times, appeared to explain everything under the sun in psychodynamic terms.

The earliest publications (those of Gross and Jung) which I discuss in this book date from the very beginning of the twentieth century, while the latest publications (those of Fromm) are from the late 1970s. This means that the literary activity of these four authors spans about eighty years, which is a long time indeed. Moreover, they created their utopian ideas in widely differing social and cultural milieux: Gross in Germany, Austria and Switzerland; Jung in Switzerland; and Fromm and Reich first in Germany and/or Austria and then on the East Coast of the United States (and, in Fromm's case, also in Mexico). What has made my task somewhat less intimidating than it might otherwise have been is that these four authors also had many things in common. First of all, they were all originally from German-speaking parts of Europe; second, they had a rather similar socioeconomic background; third, they were all trained as psychiatrists or psychoanalysts; fourth, they worked as psychotherapists and often supported their ideas by referring to 'clinical evidence'; and, fifth, they were all critics of the modern world, who also aspired to tell people what were the necessary ingredients of a radically better world – in brief, they were all psychoutopians.

The Meaning of Authenticity

The institutional marginality and need for intellectual independence which characterized the four authors discussed in this book may have strengthened their inclination to fuse moral and scientific explanatory categories. As a result, their ideas were suffused with the naturalistic fallacy, which means that they routinely deduced a value from a fact by presenting what they considered to be natural (i.e. sexuality or spirituality) as also being intrinsically good. This inference is logically incorrect, because 'is' does not imply 'ought' – one *cannot* logically derive judgments of value from statements of facts, as philosophers David Hume and G. E. Moore pointed out in the late eighteenth (Hume) and early twentieth (Moore) centuries. Although Hume's and Moore's ideas were well known in academia, at least in the Anglo-American world, our psychoutopian authors seemed to be unaware of what the concept of naturalistic fallacy is all about. And even if they had become acquainted with this concept, it is extremely doubtful whether they would have taken it to heart and tried to avoid carelessly mixing value judgments with statements concerning matters of fact. Hence they did not reflect on the argument that 'no matter how convincingly you show that something is true, it never follows logically that it *ought* to be true'.[47] But it was not only that they believed that what happens in nature is intrinsically good, they also affirmed its converse, the moralistic fallacy which psychologist Steven Pinker formulates succinctly as follows: 'If a trait is moral, it must be found in nature'.[48] Thus, when Fromm wrote that humans are altruistic by nature, and that they feel natural solidarity towards fellow humans, he succumbed to a moralistic fallacy: he inferred a statement of fact from a judgment of value (if X is good, it is true). In a similar vein, Jung, Gross and Reich thought that what they perceived as moral traits (wisdom, goodness, justice, disobedience, etc.) were natural and therefore intrinsic to human nature.

Of course, instances of naturalistic and moralistic fallacy are not hard to find in the writings of most thinkers, including those who eschewed moral statements. There simply would not be any utopian literature without the phenomenon of naturalistic fallacy. Such moralistic and naturalistic fallacies are hard to avoid if you believe, as our psychoutopians did, in the myth of inner nature (or the 'Beautiful People' myth). Our authors were inclined to believe that humans in their alleged natural state were authentic, mentally and sexually untroubled, wise, egalitarian, spiritual and spontaneous – if also primitive, uninhibited and cognitively not fully developed. Gross, Reich and Fromm all supported one version of the Beautiful People Myth, according to which humankind once lived in (matriarchal) harmony with nature before the 'blessings' of (patriarchal) civilization destroyed this harmony. Patriarchy, large-scale industry, the division of labour, capitalism and a Christian anti-sexual value system are chiefly to be blamed for the disappearance of Beautiful People and the emergence of a new type of character structure, which was greedier, more selfish and more aggressive – in short, more destructive in every possible way. Utopians as they were, all these authors believed that we can re-establish contact with our inner nature and become again like the mythical Beautiful People, who were whole and true to themselves.

Jung differed from other psychoutopians in that he combined a belief in the authenticity of inner nature with an equally strong belief in the evolution of consciousness, which prompted him to differentiate between 'primitive' and developed mentalities, the latter term being more or less synonymous with 'western mentality'.[49] In his racial prejudices regarding non-European ethnic groups, Jung belongs to a period in Western history when racialist language was employed as naturally as it is avoided today. Indeed, most psychoanalysts and psychologists in the early twentieth century held views that are today rightly considered racist.[50] Reich and Fromm, who were born a generation later than Jung, were not affected by racial doctrines as strongly as Jung was, and we cannot find openly racist remarks in their writings – but neither can we find in them public gestures of support for the rights of the oppressed 'racial' minorities, such as African-Americans in the United States. While objecting to the prejudiced mentality of the common (white) man in general, they did not raise their voices to attack the white man's racial prejudices and discriminatory politics in particular.

They addressed their message mainly to an educated (white) middle-class audience, and did not critically examine the sociocultural parameters of their own assumptions, but their visions of the good life included the whole of humanity and not just certain groups of people living in the West. Jung's initial infatuation with the 'archetypal' dynamics in National Socialism is an exception to the universalist outlook of psychological utopianism, and in my chapter on Jung I shall discuss his utopian ideas regarding Nazi Germany. But his early enthusiasm towards the 'archetypal' aspects of National Socialism notwithstanding, it was Jung more than anybody else who was convinced about the psychic unity of humankind; he saw the Collective Unconscious as a psychic bond uniting all people regardless of race, colour or creed. At the same time, Jung and the other three protagonists of this book deliberated on the plight of modern man in their own cultural sphere, the relatively prosperous western Europe (and the United States). Thus they formulated the main problem facing people as one of authenticity and inauthenticity rather than, say, one of poverty and affluence, or political rights. Such a preoccupation with authenticity in Western culture has produced a vast number of publications that deal with our more or less problematic relationship with our identity or 'true self'. The psychocultural 'triumph of the therapeutic'[51] has influenced the way we conceive of our 'inner self' as well as the basic frameworks that constitute the good life for us. People living in western societies have been taught by self-help guidebooks, therapists and pop-psychologists to have faith in the possibility of becoming 'authentic', to realize all the mental and spiritual potentialities that are inherent in us and to become 'what we truly are'. In the twentieth century, there emerged philosophical (*Lebensphilosophie*, existentialism), religious (e.g., anthroposophy, New Age religion) and psychological forms of authenticity-seeking.

The rhetoric of authenticity is easy to ridicule as another manifestation of simple-minded pop-psychology or the quasi-profound wordplay of anguished existentialists, but there is more to it than trivial therapeutic 'growth'-ideology or obsolete philosophical angst. The quest for authenticity did not appear out of thin air, but has historical roots that go back to the era of Romanticism, if not before. Perhaps the principal legacy of Romanticism, a tremendous internalization of the 'soft' imperatives of self-realization ('you shall become what you really are') took place in the Western cultural sphere. The need to realize oneself, to find fulfilment in the expression of the virtuous or otherwise valuable aspects of one's personality, is one of the main features of modern culture. This need has typically manifested itself in a commitment to political ideologies, but it has also been closely connected with a more broadly conceived notion of expressive fulfilment and originality, which were first idealized by the Romantic authors.[52] In the nineteenth century, utopian and anarchist writers were increasingly seeking a social order that emphasized individualism, self-expression and self-fulfilment. Even the young Marx glorified the self-actualization of the individual, as can be seen in his *Economic and Philosophic Manuscripts of 1844*.

For historians and philosophers of world-views and *Menschenbild* (views of man), an exclusive concern with the self and innerness is one of the most distinctive features of the modern age.[53] This tradition of 'inwardness' has several sources, such as the Christian emphasis on inwardness, Cartesian philosophy and the Rousseauean and Romantic glorification of inner nature (the myth of the noble savage). Concurrently with this inward turn there was a development towards modern utilitarian rationalism. The Enlightenment emphasis on the utility and applicability of reason paved the way for a new conception of humans, which was founded on the normative notion that we are in control of ourselves; that our behaviour is shaped by appropriate rational standards that cannot be subjugated by random impulses and urges. A paradigmatic modern example of such an attitude can be found in B. F. Skinner's book *Beyond Freedom and Dignity* (1972), where this famous neo-behaviourist writes that 'the evolution of a culture is a gigantic exercise in self-control'.[54] As a behaviourist, Skinner was pleased with this development, because it guaranteed to him that the environment that determines our destiny functions rationally.

In contrast to Skinner's Enlightenment mentality, psychological utopianism is an heir to the broad Romantic mentality in its concern with expressive fulfilment and authenticity, and with its location of the source or matrix of authenticity in the inner self. It was the unconscious, the Collective Unconscious, *das Eigene* (the own), inner nature or some other form of 'innerness' which represented in the psychoutopian texts the original unspoiled source of good. The concept of inner nature functions as the organizing principle in the utopian thinking of Gross, Jung, Reich and Fromm. For these authors, inner nature is something that the philosopher Charles Taylor has termed 'constitutive good': it is a moral source, a 'something the love of which empowers us to do and be good'.[55] In Taylor's account of constitutive goods, one finds God, reason (our rational powers) and nature (both external and inner nature). These are the goods of the higher order, for they are not only more substantial than other goods (such as work, family, money and so forth), but also more fundamental in the sense that they constitute the standpoint from which these other, lesser goods are evaluated. With regard to nature as a constitutive good, we can say that there are Enlightenment and Romantic versions of nature as an ultimate moral source. Scientific naturalism – exemplified in evolutionary biology – is a paradigmatic representative of the Enlightenment as it derives its power from disengaged reason, and is committed to progress by scientific means, whereas the constitutive good in the Romantic version of nature or its modernist successor visions, of which Jung's analytical psychology is a prime example, is subjective fulfilment. The important point Taylor makes in his *Sources of the Self* is that the 'inner nature' of Romanticism is a constitutive good and, as such, a fundamental moral source.

As we shall see, our psychodynamic authors founded their utopianism on the ideal of inner nature as constitutive good – a source of subjective fulfilment and self-realization. In their understanding of inner nature as the authentic part of human nature, they rejected the environmentalist suggestion that the mind is a blank slate, even if Reich and Fromm asserted during their Freudo-Marxist period that the human personality – one's 'social character' – is to a large extent determined by socioeconomic factors and the prevailing ideology. But when they started to display utopian propensities, their mode of thinking became more universalist and teleological, and, simultaneously, less culture-specific and ideological. Rather than deny the existence of universal human nature, they maintained that cultural evolution in the West has produced a specific type of *Kulturmensch*, a rather wretched being who is alienated from his or her true nature. They talked about neuroses, evil secondary drives, the authoritarian (or, anal, necrophilous, compulsive, etc.) character, the false identification with one's social role (persona) and the dichotomy between the own and the strange, in order to refer to the psychological and biological results of such an alienation or 'de-naturalization' of (Western) man. It was their ambition to reconnect ourselves with our inner nature that made the psychoutopian approach to human nature Rousseauean-Romantic rather than Darwinian-Naturalist.

In his study of classical anarchism, George Crowder gives an insightful account of the role of authenticity in Western intellectual culture. He suggests that anarchists promoted the idea that true freedom means 'a freedom to act in accordance not with the empirical self but with the authentic self, with that part of my personality which identifies me most fundamentally'.[56] Crowder sees rationality and virtue as the two elements of the authentic self which in classical anarchist thought guaranteed that there would be a moral order in a society without government. In anarchist thought, humans would obey moral rules in a free society not because they fear the sanctions awaiting norm-breakers, nor because they calculate that such obedience is useful in the procedural, utilitarian sense, but rather because they believe, intuitively or otherwise, that human flourishing requires a commitment to objectively valid moral imperatives that guide our thoughts and behaviour. And the reason people in a free society would be spontaneously committed to such a moral order is that their 'positive freedom' renders possible the actualization of their authentic selves, the two elements of which are virtue and rationality.

Crowder's interpretation of the role of authenticity in classical anarchism clarifies its meaning in the context of psychological utopianism. Although psychoutopians identified complete self-knowledge, a sense of connectedness with all living things, innate morality, wholeness of being (etc.), rather than rationality or virtue, as the elements of the authentic self, they too believed that there is such a thing as 'natural law', and that human flourishing is predicated on our natural obedience to this imperative, which resides within ourselves. This is the morality of inner nature, from which most people have become estranged due to the unfortunate vicissitudes of history. And it was the restoration of this crucial connection with the authentic part of our personality that Gross, Jung, Reich and Fromm saw as their ultimate goal, because it would mean the full realization of human nature. There is, then, a burning moral vision in their utopian glorification of authenticity: as modern-day psychoalchemists, they wanted to ennoble the base substances of human nature and produce a new, improved edition of man. This was the philosopher's stone they searched for, and even if they died (Gross), ended up in a haze of mental confusion (Reich) or became disillusioned with the capability of man to change for the better (Jung and Fromm), their utopian imagination merits consideration. They had a dream that was destined to clash with reality, but to imagine a world without dreams is to imagine an anti-utopia.

2 THE NEW SOVIET MAN: PSYCHOANALYSIS AND THE CONQUEST OF THE UNCONSCIOUS IN THE EARLY DAYS OF THE SOVIET UNION

We can find the first adherents of modern dynamic psychology among the educated members of the Central European middle class. The same bourgeoisie that was at the receiving end of contempt and hatred from both the left and the right in the early twentieth century was also participating in the feverish quest for the 'self'. This idea of the self fashioning itself was partly a result of the precarious social position of the bourgeoisie: as its members were making money and/or occupied key positions in governmental institutions, they were perceived by one group (the extreme left) as the class enemy and by the other (the extreme right) as greedy materialists. It was this social group, once it fell under the spell of Marxism on the one hand and dynamic psychology on the other, which attempted to redefine its position vis-à-vis other social groups. Among bourgeois citizens, this led to conversions to Marxism as well as to right-wing ideologies but also to psychological 'identity crises', self-doubt and a yearning for individual and cultural wholeness. The incessant self-scrutiny of the early twentieth-century bourgeoisie and the success story of dynamic psychology are inescapably intertwined.

In addition to psychoanalysis, it was Marxism that provided light in the darkness for many intellectuals in the post-World War I West. The Russian Revolution of 1917 rekindled hopes for progress and emancipation, and the Soviet Union seemed to represent the first necessary step towards the future utopia. As the Marxist historian Eric Hobsbawm notes in his autobiography, 'in the Vienna of the late 1920s, one acquired political consciousness as naturally as sexual awareness'.[1] And by 'political consciousness' he means Marxism and socialism. Hobsbawm also explains that Marxism appealed to the younger generation of educated Central Europeans because of its comprehensiveness:

> 'Dialectical materialism' provided, if not a 'theory of everything', then at least a 'framework for everything', linking inorganic and organic nature with human affairs, collective and individual, and providing a guide to the nature of all interactions in a world in constant flux.[2]

For Western Communists in the interwar years, the Russian Revolution had a massive political and symbolic significance. Among other things, the Revolution appeared to demonstrate that people could invent themselves, that they could both make their history and be aware of the future implications of their doings – the hidden face of history was revealed in the Revolution. For many socialists, this revelation resulted in the deification of history, for it was history alone that would lead humanity to freedom.[3] At the same time, both Marxism and psychoanalysis fanned the spirit of suspicion and antagonism, the former in its declaration of war between social classes (in the public sphere) and the latter in its diagnoses of the psychic constellations in the family (in the private sphere). Whereas Marxists focused on the conflict between the bourgeoisie and the proletariat, declaring that the movement of history determines the overthrow of the former by the latter, psychoanalysis focused on the conflict between sons and fathers, children and parents, and, ultimately, between the outer self (the ego) and the inner self (the unconscious). Marxists saw bourgeois society as radically divided against itself and hence in conflict; Freudians saw human nature as radically divided against itself and hence in conflict. Psychoanalysis and Marxism were both closed, self-referential systems that promised quick, deep knowledge while sharply differentiating between the chosen ones (those with proletarian consciousness and those who are analysed) and the outsiders. And they both demanded irrational loyalty.[4]

In Europe after World War I, then, Marxism and psychoanalysis attracted people who were thirsting for (secular) faith in a world that was in a state of disintegration and instability. In one particular European country, these two belief systems were more conspicuously linked to the political system than anywhere else in the world. During the first decade of the Soviet Union, Marxism provided the basis for the only official ideology, while psychoanalysts managed to carve a small niche for themselves as pioneers in the psychological transformation of people. In this chapter, I shall examine the short history of psychoanalysis in the Soviet Union from the utopian perspective.

Freud goes East

There was an early interest in psychoanalysis in Tsarist Russia. A Russian translation of Freud's *Interpretation of Dreams*, 'the first to be made in any language', was published in 1904.[5] The man who was instrumental in introducing psychoanalysis to Russia was Nikolai Osipov, a psychiatrist at the Moscow Psychiatric Clinic. In 1908, Osipov visited Jung (and the neurologist Paul Dubois) in Zurich and Freud in Vienna. On returning to Moscow he organized a small discussion group at his clinic and opened an outpatient facility for 'neurotics', where psychoanalytic methods were first used in Russia. His 1909 article 'On Anxiety Neurosis' was the first psychoanalytic case study published in Russia. Soon other Russian psychiatrists started to write about psychoanalytic topics, and a psychoanalytic journal called *Psychotherapy* (*Psikhoterapiia*) was established in Russia in 1910, immediately after the founding of Freud's own journal, *Jahrbuch für psychoanalytische und psychopathologische Forschungen*. In addition, Freud's works began to appear in 1909 in Russian translation. Within a few years, five of Freud's works had been published in Russia and there was a group of psychiatrists who actively promoted psychoanalytic ideas and methods in Moscow.[6]

During World War I, the burgeoning psychoanalytic movement in Russia came to a halt, and *Psychotherapy*, in which Alfred Adler's influence was becoming more and more visible, ceased publication in 1914. But the Russian Revolution in 1917 changed the scene once again. By 1922, the ruling Communist Party had consolidated its power in Russia, and the country was officially renamed the Union of Soviet Socialist Republics (USSR). The small psychoanalytic community in post-revolutionary Soviet Russia was well aware that it could not survive without the approval of the Bolsheviks. Some psychiatrists did not even try to accommodate themselves to the new society, but decided to leave the country. Most importantly, Osipov emigrated to Prague in 1921. He kept his psychoanalytic practice there and also taught at the Charles University to physicians in training until his death in 1934.[7] The same year that Osipov left Russia, another important psychoanalyst, Tatiana Rosenthal, committed suicide at the age of thirty-six. Rosenthal had studied medicine in Zurich and was trained at the Burghölzli mental hospital, and she was also a member of the Vienna Psychoanalytic Society from 1911 until her death. After her return to Russia, she worked at Vladimir Bekhterev's famous Institute of Brain Pathology in Petrograd (St Petersburg), giving courses on psychoanalysis and treating patients psychoanalytically at the Institute's clinic.[8]

Osipov's emigration and Rosenthal's suicide were a heavy blow to the Russian psychoanalytic community, but these losses did not destroy the development of psychoanalysis in Soviet Russia. A psychoanalytic group was formed in Moscow in 1921, and, in early 1922, the Russian Psychoanalytic Society was founded. A second psychoanalytic society was soon formed in the provincial town of Kazan, where the *primus motor* was a young psychologist, Aleksandr Luria. The following year the Kazan group of Freudians joined Moscow's Psychoanalytic Society. Then, in the autumn of 1922, the Institute for Psychoanalysis was founded in Moscow. After the establishment of Freudian institutes in Vienna and Berlin, it was the third psychoanalytic training centre in Europe (and in the world). In 1923, the Moscow Institute had thirty members, which made it a remarkably large national group in the International Psychoanalytic Association. One of the most distinguished members of the institute was Sabina Spielrein, a Russian-Jewish psychiatrist who had originally been an analytic patient of Jung at the

Burghölzli in Zurich. After attaining her medical degree, she became a full member of the Vienna Psychoanalytic Institute in 1911. In 1923, she moved from Lausanne, Switzerland, to Moscow and, together with Moshe Wulff, another psychiatrist who had undergone training analysis in Europe (in Berlin), she became a training analyst and the director of a clinical program at the Moscow Institute. Under Wulff's direction, the institute opened an outpatient clinic, where patients were treated psychoanalytically. Wulff, who refused to yield to the ideological demands of the Communist Party, emigrated to Berlin in 1927 and, after the Nazis came to power in 1933, to Palestine, where he helped establish the Israeli Psychoanalytic Society together with Max Eitingon.[9]

The most original project at the Moscow Institute was the founding in 1921 of the Psychoanalytic Orphanage Laboratory, a psychoanalytic clinical institution for children (the original name of the institute is peculiar, for children at the institute were not actually orphans). The school, which changed its name to Psychoanalytic Kindergarten 'International Solidarity' in 1923, was run by Vera Schmidt according to anti-authoritarian principles. Schmidt, a teacher by profession, and her staff paid great attention to the sexual life of the children, who were between the ages of one and five years. Most children at the 'orphanage-laboratory' were sons and daughters of high-ranking Party officials who apparently did not have time to raise their children themselves. Schmidt's own son was taken care of at the institute, and Stalin's son Vasily, who was born in 1921, probably also went there.[10] The children of the new elite in the Soviet Russia were looked after by teachers who employed psychoanalytic methods and who were obliged in principle to undergo training analysis themselves (this was a pipe-dream that was never realized). In 1923, certain changes were introduced at the Psychoanalytic Kindergarten, initiated by the authorities, and the number of working-class children there was increased.

The publication of Russian translations of works by Freud and his followers was also undertaken, starting with *Introductory Lectures on Psychoanalysis*, which appeared in 1922. During the 1920s, fifteen of the projected thirty-two volumes of psychoanalytic literature were published, 'all of them sponsored and financed under the imprint of the State Publishing House'.[11] The director of the State Publishing House between 1921 and 1924 was the prominent mathematician and famous polar explorer Otto Schmidt, who was Vera Schmidt's husband and an officer of the Moscow Psychoanalytic Society. An interesting detail in the history of the State Psychoanalytic Institute is that it was partly financed by a German trade union.[12]

The Bolshevik Interest in the Conquest of the Unconscious

A re-emergence of psychoanalysis in Russia in the early 1920s would have been impossible without the approval and active support of the Communist authorities. As historian Martin A. Miller points out,

> no government was ever responsible for supporting psychoanalysis to such extent, before or after ... Nowhere else were the institutions of psychoanalysis supported by a national government whose legitimacy was rooted in the enforcement of ideological doctrine.[13]

While psychoanalysis was enjoying its short-lived golden age in the Soviet Union, an official Marxist approach to philosophy and psychology was being formulated, which meant that Soviet psychoanalysts started to direct their attention towards the kind of research required by the new society. Being in a precarious position, in which their activities were financed and monitored by the state, psychoanalysts had no choice but to meet the political demands and requirements of the Communist Party. One such requirement was the formation of the 'New Man'.

When the Moscow Institute of Psychoanalysis was established and became the State Psychoanalytic Institute, it had three main objectives: first, to psychoanalyse adults and children; second, to teach psychoanalysis to future college teachers and researchers; and third, to find scientific solutions to political problems.[14] This last objective introduced an explicit utopian element to psychoanalysis in the Soviet Union. Soviet psychoanalysts, who attempted to legitimate Freudian theory by interpreting it within a Marxist ideological framework, started to investigate the influence of social structures on personality formation. Trying to be as faithful as possible to Marxist doctrines, psychoanalytic researchers centred on the possibility of transforming society through social therapy. Consequently, they began to 'discover changes in [the] personality that the new regime *wanted* them to find'.[15] Marxist doctrinarians increasingly dictated the alleged scientific analysis of the psyche.

Psychoanalysis attained a certain level of success among the highest echelons of political and administrative power in the new Soviet Union. A key figure in the official recognition of psychoanalysis was Leon Trotsky, who was one of the most powerful Bolshevik leaders in the early 1920s and by far the most influential patron of psychoanalysis in the Soviet Union (until 1927).[16] Unlike Lenin, who was apparently quite indifferent to Freudian theories, Trotsky supported psychoanalysis, primarily because he believed in its social utility. He was not the only high-ranking party official who was well-disposed towards psychoanalysis, for his interest was shared by Stanislav Shatskii – leader of the government's pedagogical section – and Otto Schmidt, among others. In a letter of 1923 to

Ivan Pavlov, Trotsky wrote: 'During my years in Vienna, I came in[to] rather close contact with the Freudians, read their work and even attended their meetings'.[17] In 1908, Trotsky had met Adolf Joffe in Vienna, and together they edited the Viennese *Pravda*. Ten years later, Joffe was one of the central figures of the Russian Revolution and worked as Soviet ambassador in several countries in the 1920s. But in pre-war Vienna, he had been a young revolutionary and a patient of Alfred Adler's on account of his neurotic symptoms.[18] Trotsky occasionally met the well-known socialist Adler, who had a Russian wife. So he knew about psychoanalysis when the psychoanalytic movement in post-revolutionary Soviet Russia was established.

Trotsky was a leader of a huge nation, but his ambition to transform Russians and the whole of humankind with the help of applied psychoanalysis was not at all peculiar to him; many leftist intellectuals, including sociologist Karl Mannheim and Freudo-Marxists such as Wilhelm Reich and Siegfried Bernfeld, toyed with the utopian idea of using psychoanalysis to change the mental structure of people. Ideology-driven Trotsky thought of psychoanalysis as a technical means of invading the unconscious and controlling spontaneous emotions, feelings and thoughts – anything that was unpredictable in human behaviour. He held that this unpredictable part of the human mind – the unconscious – had to be subjected to conscious control, because that was the 'place' where spontaneous human nature resided. Therefore, the greatest research efforts and creative initiatives of Marxist science should be directed towards the psychological (i.e. ideological) superstructure, just as Marxist science had already forced the unpredictable elements out of the socioeconomic structure. The task of Communism, proclaimed Trotsky, was to 'publish a new, improved edition'[19] of man:

> Man will look for the first time at himself as if at raw material, or at best, as at a half-finished product, and say, 'I've finally got you, my dear *homo sapiens*; now I can get to work on you, friend!'[20]

This task, utopian as it was, was topical in post-revolutionary Soviet Russia for the simple reason that Russians were not exactly enamoured of the new authorities, and were quite reluctant to live in a Communist society. There was popular discontent, especially in the countryside, which in the long run could not be simply suppressed. This was a dilemma that needed to be solved somehow. Lenin's New Economic Policy (1921–8) was one way of seeking a solution to the situation through the strategic relegalization of private small-scale manufacturing;[21] Stalin's merciless policy of repression in the 1930s was another.

Trotsky, who at first supported the New Economic Policy, was thinking along lines that betrayed not only his utopian inclinations, but also his understanding of the crucial problem of how to force the minds of Russians to harmonize with Communist ideology. If people found it impossible to live in the new Communist society, then why not change the way people thought and felt? Why not change human nature? This was easier said than done, for, as Trotsky very well knew, Marxism was of little use in a situation where the historical process had to be speeded up, as it were. Something else had to be invented in order to find a solution, but what? An historian of Russian psychoanalysis, Alexander Etkind, writes:

> Reading Trotsky's works from the 1920s, it begins to seem as if the Kremlin dreamer sincerely believed that at any moment he would find the Philosopher's Stone among the latest scientific advances, some device that would make people happy in the society that he and his comrades had created.[22]

Trotsky's master plan was to unite Freudian psychoanalysis with Pavlov's physiology of conditioned reflexes, and for this purpose he wrote a letter to Pavlov in the autumn of 1923. Pavlov, the doyen of Russian science, was rather sympathetic towards Freud and did not believe that psychoanalysis and his physicalist reflexology were incompatible. Pavlov in turn was highly regarded by many Western psychoanalysts, who were interested in Pavlov's studies of experimental neuroses with animals. However, Pavlov probably never responded to Trotsky's letter. He was a pre-eminent scientist and a Nobel laureate, and did not have to grovel before the new Bolshevik authorities. Trotsky and perhaps other prestigious Bolsheviks may have entertained hopes of enlisting Pavlov in the great experiment of remaking human nature, but apparently the elderly physiologist was not interested (in the 1930s, however, the scientific patriarch became more accommodating to the political elite[23]).

The Fall of Psychoanalysis

After Lenin's death in January 1924, the intensifying battle for control of the Communist Party made the future of psychoanalysis in the Soviet Union extremely uncertain. In the mid-1920s, the ideological opponents of psychoanalysis began to attack in various ways what the Soviet authorities now referred to as 'Freudism' or 'Freudianism'. For example, I. D. Sapir wrote a critical article on 'Freudism and Marxism', which was published in the leading Bolshevik journal, *Under the Banner of Marxism*, while V. N. Voloshinov wrote a book-length Marxist critique of 'Freudianism' (his book is sometimes credited to Mikhail Bakhtin).[24]

The fact that Trotsky approved of psychoanalysis intensified opposition to 'Freudianism' after Trotsky's fall in the autumn of 1927. His gradual fall from grace after Lenin's death coincided with the decline in the psychoanalytic movement in the Soviet Union. In the late 1920s, Freud's teachings were condemned as representative of reactionary bourgeois idealism, and, as Etkind points out, in the ideological polemics of that time, 'psychoanalysts (and later pedologists as well) were often accused of Trotskyism'.[25] For example, in two articles published in the first issue of *Psikhologia* in 1932, the authors claimed to have identified a direct link between Trotskyism and psychoanalysis. In one of the articles, the author (psychologist A. Talankin) wrote that 'it had been Trotsky and no one else who had proposed the idea of uniting the theories of Freud and Pavlov as the basis of psychology'.[26] The message in these articles was clear: both Freud and Trotsky were anti-Marxist and anti-materialist, and all Marxist science should be cleansed of the filth of Trotskyism. Trotsky himself was first banished to Alma Ata – 3,000 kilometres from Moscow – in early 1928, and, then, a year later, deported from the country. He settled in Mexico, where he was murdered by a Spanish Communist in 1940. His daughter, Zinaida Volkova, who apparently suffered from depression, committed suicide in Berlin in 1933 – she had been treated by a Berlin psychoanalyst for a year before her suicide.[27] In the Soviet Union, Trotsky 'was dropped into what George Orwell called the "memory hole"',[28] and remained there until the era of Gorbachev.

In August 1925, the Greater Council of Ministers liquidated both the State Psychoanalytic Institute and the Psychoanalytic Kindergarten. In the latter half of the 1920s, the number of psychoanalytically-oriented clinical articles dwindled, and the last book on clinical psychoanalysis was published in 1927 (its author was I. A. Perepel). The regime still tolerated the practice of psychoanalytic psychotherapy, while denouncing Freudian theory as incompatible with Marxism. Within a few years, the political struggle against Trotsky and his ideological comrades had 'resulted in the removal of psychoanalysis from the nation's theoretical and practical knowledge'.[29] The Psychoanalytic Society had its last meetings in 1930. In early 1931, a series of meetings was held at the Academy of Communist Education, the purpose of which was to point out and discuss the 'ideological mistakes' of such behavioural scientists as Luria, Vygotsky (who had been interested in psychoanalysis in the 1920s) and Zalkind (see below). These scholars publicly confessed their past sins and regretted their 'political blindness', or at least deplored their 'uncritical' attitude towards Freud.

In the 1930s, any mention of psychoanalysis or any attempt to apply Freudian theory was perceived as illegal, dangerous and politically incorrect. This signified the end of psychoanalysis in the Soviet Union. Psychoanalysis was not the only psychological theory that was eliminated after 1925, by which time the era of relative openness, experimentation and tolerance was over, and the Communist Party started to look with growing suspicion at any theory or organization that could be seen as a potential threat to the official doctrine and the stability of the state apparatus. Later on in the 1930s, pedology – the behavioural science of childhood – and industrial psychology shared the fate of psychoanalysis. The authorities wanted to establish a Marxist psychology that would bear no marks of a bourgeois mentality and ideology. Psychoanalysis fared badly in this respect, for it was accused of being idealistic and therefore at odds with historical materialism. Psychoanalytic 'pessimism' and its non-dialectical focus on sexuality and its role in human psychology hastened its elimination, because sex was considered to be a far too individualistic and 'spontaneous' area of human life. Psychoanalysis was also 'reductionist' and 'biologistic' and therefore incompatible with environmental determinism as espoused by the Soviet regime. For the Bolshevik authorities, the Freudian individual was driven too much by sexuality and innate aggressiveness and too little influenced by social determinants. The reasoning behind such environmental determinism is the same as that found in Lysenkoism, which revived the erroneous Lamarckian theory of the inheritance of acquired characteristics and discredited Mendelian genetics in the Soviet Union.[30]

By the mid-1930s, the doctrines of the Communist Party had 'successfully permeated all levels of Soviet society',[31] which meant that there were no longer any scientific and medical activities or institutions that were not administered or monitored by party functionaries. The last shreds of pluralism in Soviet society had been torn apart during the 'great break' in the late 1920s and early 1930s, when the authorities started to pursue a more systematic policy of repression. Psychoanalysis was not completely wiped out, however, for a scattered group of people continued to give psychoanalytic therapy underground and discuss developments in psychoanalytic theory even after 1930. During the 1930s, there were even some conciliatory articles on psychoanalysis in official publications, such as the entry on 'Psychoanalysis' in volume 47 of the *Great Soviet Encyclopedia*. The article was co-authored by a psychologist who had once founded a Psychoanalytic Society in Kazan: Aleksandr Luria.[32]

Aron Zalkind and the Science of Pedology

One of the most ardent advocates of Marxist psychology was Aron Zalkind, a psychoanalytic physician and one of the founders of pedology in the Soviet Union.[33] Pedology was an interdisciplinary science of the child, which was founded by the American psychologist G. Stanley Hall in the early twentieth century. Pedology and psychoanalysis shared an interest in childhood, and, in the Soviet Union, the founders of pedology had gone through training in psychoanalysis. Whereas in the West pedology quickly lost its importance, in the Soviet Union the situation was completely different. By the early 1930s, psychoanalysis had been virtually stamped out, while pedology was undergoing a tremendous boom. Towards the end of 1930, Zalkind became director of the reformed Psychological Institute in Moscow, now renamed the Institute of Psychology, Pedology, and Industrial Psychology. He also became the editor of the journal *Pedology*. In the early and mid-1920s, Zalkind promoted psychoanalysis and, through his various organizational activities, tried to contribute to the formation of a Marxist psychology in which psychoanalysis would play a role.[34] One of the ways in which he tried to make psychoanalysis politically acceptable was to coin the term 'Freudism', which in the Soviet world of political 'isms' gave psychoanalysis an immediately recognizable outlook. But when the political winds changed in the Soviet Union, he turned from being an advocate of psychoanalysis to one of its official critics.

For the Soviet authorities, pedology was a promising method for changing individuals during childhood, and, as one of the leaders of pedology (Pavel Blonsky) stated, it is the 'study of the entire set of symptoms of the various eras, phases, and stages of childhood, their temporary consequences, and their dependence on a range of conditions'.[35] For Zalkind, pedology was nothing less than a universal science of human development. In 1930, he described the task of pedology as the 'mass construction of a new man'.[36] Zalkind's successor, Anton Makarenko, 'explained the goal of his "pedagogy" as instilling in the behaviour, the character, and the personality qualities that are necessary for the Soviet state'.[37] In practice, pedology was far less spectacular and groundbreaking than its chief advocates made it out to be, for it relied on the rather mundane method of mental testing, which was heavily used in schools by educational and child psychologists. Zalkind's own research in the 1920s centred on the so-called 'socioreactive neuropathy', or, as he wrote in 1925, an 'illness mediated by changes in the social orientation of the organism ... ideological frustrations'.[38]

Zalkind's descriptions of specific clinical cases in his pre-pedological phase illustrate the confluence of ideological and psychodynamic categories in the Soviet version of Marxist psychoanalysis. One medical protocol tells the story of a young woman who was a zealous member of the Russian Communist Party. During the Civil War, she had been captured near the front-line by a group of anti-Bolshevik Kazakhs, who had raped her. Now she suffered from mental disturbances, such as constant anguish, desperation, feelings of emptiness, nervous excitability, disturbed sleep, shivering, trembling and so forth. She had been expelled from the Communist Party as a 'useless element' and was about to leave for her home town.

What was Zalkind's diagnostic evaluation of the young woman? Quite extraordinary: he writes that

> [he] has met a minimum of ten party comrades who were raped in the process of bloody struggle with the enemy, and only F., and one other, reacted to that *as incurable disaster*. The other [comrades], in general rather sexually normal, possessors of healthy femininity ... related to that *in a revolutionary way* ... [and] did not live through any ideological crises after it. This is the best proof that *in case of correct, strongly social and class-conscious orientation* mere sexuality, even the most difficult,

> does not create psychoneurosis and plays only a secondary role *in service to the relationship with the social*.[39]

As psychologist Jaan Valsiner points out, Zalkind contends that

> the class-conscious revolutionary attitude of women comrades was expected to block their individual psychological reactions to rape in the social context of bringing about the revolution. Conversely, in cases where this did not happen, the outcome was diagnosed as indicating an insufficient revolutionary orientation.[40]

Thus the young woman who came to Zalkind for treatment was really suffering from ideological weakness rather than from the devastating experience of the rape. For Zalkind, the adoption of a correct ideology should function as a prophylactic against individual psychopathological reactions. He totally ideologized mental health and blamed the victim by dismissing the young woman's mental problems for political reasons – the woman had a too weakly-developed class consciousness. This kind of ideological mindset was typical of Marxist (-Leninist) scholars; for example, in his critical overview of 'Freudianism' of 1927, V. N. Voloshinov writes that

> 'content of the psyche' is ideological through and through; from the vaguest of thoughts and dimmest and most uncertain of desires all the way to philosophical systems and complex political institutions.[41]

When an eminent psychiatrist, V. A. Giliarovskii, had included 'Soviet exhaustion' (*iznoshennost*) among the problems created by urbanization, he was reproached by a former leader of the mental health movement (Subbotnik) with the following words:

> So-called 'Soviet exhaustion' does not exist in reality. What exists is merely a reactionary delusion [*bred*], by which they are trying to pit the proletariat against its revolutionary tempo, and by sowing fear of non-existent difficulties to hold back our movement forward. This whole theory of Professor Giliarovskii is a theory of bourgeois restoration.[42]

For dedicated Soviet scholars, consciousness was the mark of Marxist political maturity: a healthy worker was automatically a conscious one, while a mentally disordered worker exhibited false consciousness – his or her thinking was confused by a false ideology. As the historian David Joravsky so aptly puts it, 'by shouts of agreement, such lesser illnesses [as Soviet exhaustion] were cured'.[43]

In the Soviet Union, ideology was perceived as an omnipotent tool that could be used to change human behaviour and influence all areas of life, including work productivity and health. Such ideology-as-political-therapy could turn an ill person into a healthy one, and a healthy person into a pure-hearted comrade and a tireless builder of a new society (a true Stakhanovite). Obviously, Russian psychoanalysts were driven by their own illusory hopes and beliefs, and at first most of them did not appear to see any contradiction between psychoanalysis and the developing totalitarianism – or, if they did see contradictions, they prudently decided to keep quiet. Stalin and the rest of the Soviet regime appeared to have the transformation of its people as their utopian goal, and they wanted to use intellectuals and scientists to carry out this transformation. At a meeting with Soviet writers at Maxim Gorky's house in 1932, Stalin called them the 'engineers of the human soul',[44] and he established a new intellectual and artistic genre, Socialist Realism, the goal of which was to see both in the psyche and in the external world the traits of true socialism, and to portray these traits. Thus the idea of the 'New Soviet Man' became central as an ideal. A historian of Soviet psychology, John McLeish, gives the following list of the characteristic virtues of the New Soviet Man, who would be fundamentally different from the non-Soviet Man: collectivism, socialist humanism, patriotism, ideological approach to all questions, a sense of duty, Communist attitude to work and readiness to overcome difficulties and fight for Communism.[45]

Faith in the utopian vision of the 'New Man' requires a commitment to a specific anthropology. In his speech to the First Pedological Conference in 1927, Nikolai Bukharin, who was in charge of the political control of public education in the 1920s, reveals this Bolshevik anthropology:

> The question of social environment and its influence must be solved, in the sense that the influence of social environment is greater than usually supposed. Changes can take place much more quickly, and the profound reorganization that we call the cultural revolution has a sociobiological equivalent that reaches down to the very physiological nature of the [human] organism.[46]

On another occasion Bukharin expressed his environmentalist attitude more succinctly by characterizing the human personality as 'a sausage skin stuffed [with] environmental influences'.[47] According to the Bolshevik anthropology, humans are made of plastic material, and there is nothing in human nature that cannot in principle be altered. Bukharin expressed a similar environmental determinism to that adopted by the totalitarian government in Orwell's *Nineteen Eighty-Four*. As the government agent O'Brien, the fearsome representative of Big Brother in Orwell's dystopia, says to the captured 'dissident' Winston: 'We create human nature. Men are infinitely malleable.'[48]

In 1932, Zalkind himself became a victim of the ideologically-based institution of Soviet psychology which he had actively helped to build. He turned into a Bolshevik self-critic eager to publicly acknowledge his 'Freudian mistakes'. His public confessions of past sins were to no avail, for not only did he lose his institutional positions, but the whole of pedology was attacked as a pseudo-Marxist deviation from the Party line. In 1936, mental testing, the methodological backbone of pedology, was abolished in the school system by a decree of the Central Committee entitled 'On Pedological Distortions in the Soviet School System'. According to Alexander Etkind, Zalkind, who had already become a few years earlier a scientific non-entity, died of a heart attack after reading this decree.[49] At the same time as pedology was eliminated as a science, Isaac Spielrein, the leading industrial psychologist in the country (and Sabina Spielrein's brother), was arrested by the dreaded NKVD (People's Commissariat of Internal Affairs). He was executed in Stalin's gulag in 1937. His two brothers, Jan and Emil, both of them scientists with no interest in politics, shared his tragic fate.[50] It seems the leading industrial psychologists made the 'mistake' of seeing the optimum, not the maximum, workload as the ideal (i.e., there is a limit to the workers' endurance, which the authorities need to take into consideration in their labour policy).[51]

The Fate of the New Soviet Man

In 1936, all the prevailing psychological disciplines, including reflexology, Gestalt psychology, behaviourism, social psychology and forensic psychology, were condemned. The only research carried on after that was confined to educational psychology, psychophysiology, neurology, thinking and speech. Rather than being indifferent to psychological research, the Bolshevik demand for psychology was genuine and also dangerous to professionals working in the field.[52] The rigid application of Marxist methodology in psychology meant that the mind was seen as a reflection of the objective, external world. A privileged position was given to the reformulated Pavlovian physiology which on the conceptual level was made to harmonize with the dialectical materialist approach to the psyche.

Under Stalin's dictatorship, Trotsky's utopian dream for the transformation of humans was not extinguished as an ideal, but it is a matter of dispute whether the New Soviet Man ever materialized at all. This is what the historian Geoffrey Hosking writes about the clash of utopianism and *Realpolitik* in the Soviet Union:

> The function of ideology … had changed considerably since Lenin's time. Lenin had proclaimed that 'Marxism is all-powerful because it is *true*', and he had insisted on his own version of it because he wanted to *get things done*; his colleagues followed him (in spite of periodic doubts) because they wanted to 'change the world'. But as the utopian dream faded, and the real world became more intractable, the party leaders split into those who wanted to return to utopia by ever more coercive means (Trotsky and the left) and those who were prepared to recognize reality and to try to accommodate themselves to it (Bukharin and the right). Stalin took a third course, which was to consolidate the hold on power which was the Bolsheviks' one tangible achievement, abandoning the utopian dreams in practice, while still using the utopian myths,

> only now as a means, not of changing society, but of bolstering the existing power structure and inducting the population to accept it. The new-style ideology, then, was no longer a guide to action, but a system of stylized myths and fictions to which the population was required to render symbolic obeisance. Actual belief in the myths could now be subversive: what was demanded was the external acquiescence.[53]

Hosking's thesis is that, instead of attempting to create a 'new edition of Man', Stalin's regime of terror manufactured political myths in a way that has distinct resemblances with the constructivist methods of myth-making in Nazi Germany.[54] The function of such myths (of equality, an improved standard of living, 'enemies of the people', etc.) was to justify government policy, no matter how repressive and paranoid it was. But it would seem nevertheless that, under Stalin's dictatorship, the New Soviet Man (*homo sovieticus*) was more than an empty slogan or a political myth. In an e-mail message to the author on 26 April 2006, philosopher Dmitry Uzlaner from Moscow State University argues that the fall of psychoanalysis did not coincide with the end of utopia, and that behind the coercive ideology and propaganda there was a real belief in Marxism. Without any regard for the value of individual or human rights, Stalin's 'amoral' regime tried to implement the utopian ideals of the new society and the New Soviet Man by means of various psychological, propagandistic and educational (etc.) methods.[55]

Contrary to what Hosking argues, one could insist that, for the majority of Russians, such words as equality, an improved standard of living, full employment, even potential 'enemies of the people' (the kulak, the old bourgeois intelligentsia, the urban businessman and trader, the handful of dissidents and political opponents of Communism) were real entities, not just empty slogans. At the same time, Stalin's coercive ideology kept the dreams of the New Man within strict bounds, and an absolute obedience to the authorities remained the norm until the Gorbachev era. But in contemporary Russian social science, the term *homo sovieticus*, no matter how pejoratively it is regarded, denotes more than a myth. Compared to the cultural archetype of the average pre-revolutionary Russian – an ignorant, poor and superstitious peasant – *homo sovieticus* symbolized the tangible achievements of the Soviet Union, which within a few decades developed into a modern industrial nation and a political and technological superpower with a high level of primary and secondary education, nuclear arms, Sputniks and cosmonauts. Indeed, it would have been quite extraordinary if the mentality of Russians had *not* changed during the Soviet era, when the structures of society were radically transformed. *Homo sovieticus* can be seen as the result of the ultimately failed utopian attempt to reconstruct human nature. As Dmitry Uzlaner suggests in his e-mail message to the author on 28 April 2006, maybe the USSR was a utopia itself. When faith in Soviet utopia was lost, the USSR collapsed.[56]

As for psychoanalysis, it lived a more-or-less underground existence until the dissolution of the Soviet Union (although psychoanalysis was banned, hypnosis never lost its popularity as a form of psychotherapy). In the 1990s, it made a rather spectacular comeback in post-Communist Russia, and was fully legitimized in 1996 by a decree entitled 'Concerning the Rebirth of Philosophical, Clinical and Applied Psychoanalysis'. President Yeltsin's decree meant that psychoanalysis had come full circle: its first official recognition in 1921–2 was followed by half a century of suppression after 1930, then, in 1996, when the Soviet Union no longer existed, it was again officially recognized and made part of university education. Any half-literate Hegelian could see the law of dialectics in operation here. The 'pest'[57] is back in Russia, but this time without any explicit psychopolitical baggage.

3 ANARCHY, EROS AND THE MOTHER RIGHT: UTOPIANISM IN OTTO GROSS

> [Otto Gross] was the nearest approach to the romantic ideal of a genius I have ever met, and he also illustrated the supposed resemblance of genius to madness, for he was suffering from an unmistakable form of insanity that before my eyes culminated in murder, asylum, and suicide.
>
> Ernest Jones, 1959[1]

For more than half a century, Otto Gross (1877–1920) was a forgotten figure in the annals of mental medicine and intellectual culture. The man whose name and reputation had once been familiar to many professionals who worked in the fields of psychoanalysis and psychiatry in German-speaking Europe, and who had moved effortlessly in bohemian, anarchistic and counter-cultural circles, had become a non-entity at the time of the fiftieth anniversary of his death. Then, in 1974, the American literary scholar Martin Green published a study of the von Richthofen sisters Frieda and Else, both of whom had once been lovers and friends of Gross (one of them belonged to the Heidelberg circle of Max Weber, while the other married D. H. Lawrence).[2] It was in Green's book that the reading public first learnt about an eccentric psychoanalyst, anarchist and social dreamer who had socialized or worked with Sigmund Freud, Carl Jung, Emil Kraepelin, Wilhelm Stekel, Franz Werfel, Franz Kafka, Max Brod, Erich Mühsam and a number of other writers, many of whom were influenced and excited by Gross's provocative ideas and his extraordinary personality.

The publication of the correspondence between Freud and Jung in 1974 brought Gross's name to the attention of psychoanalysts and scholars interested in the history of psychoanalysis. In their correspondence, Freud and Jung made many references to their colleague who was also unsuccessfully treated by Jung at the Burghölzli mental hospital in 1908. It was now becoming clear to the scholarly community that someone called Otto Gross had once been a well-known psychiatrist and psychoanalyst who interacted with some of the leading figures in the field of mental medicine. Then, in the late 1970s, the first scholarly study devoted to Otto Gross was published. The author was the Swiss psychiatrist and psychoanalyst Emanuel Hurwitz, who examined the life and work of Gross from the perspective of the history of psychoanalysis. In his landmark study, Hurwitz used unpublished material, including the archival records of the Burghölzli mental hospital, and his book has become a standard historical work on Otto Gross. In the Anglo-Saxon world, the literary scholar Jennifer Michaels's 1983 book brought to the light another important aspect of Gross, namely his influence on German Expressionist writers (such as Leonard Frank, Franz Werfel, Max Brod and Franz Jung).

During the last two decades, scholarly interest in Gross has grown, and there is now an active international Otto Gross Society, which organizes congresses and publishes collections of articles by scholars interested in Gross.[3] Today, the life and work of Otto Gross are discussed not only by the handful of Gross scholars, but occasionally also by scholars who are doing research on other figures, especially Carl Jung.[4] But the fact that Gross's writings have not been published as edited volumes, and that only his early psychiatric articles have been translated into English[5] means that, even if he is talked about and referred to by scholars who acknowledge his importance, he is still very little read today.

A good example of a widespread neglect (especially in the English-speaking world) of what Gross actually said is Deirdre Bair's recent biography of Jung. In her well-researched book, the author devotes a chapter to Gross, but she presents him merely as an eccentric psychoanalytic renegade and as Jung's mental patient, who was addicted to cocaine and anarchism, who created wild ideas about sexual revolution and who had a bent for all kinds of excesses.[6] She does not discuss any of Gross's writings, even those that exerted a well-documented influence on Jung, the protagonist of her book, as if what Gross thought paled into insignificance next to what he did. But this neglect of Gross's writings is understandable: he was an author whose life was more exciting, outlandish and thrilling than anything he wrote – and he did make many extraordinary claims and radical suggestions in his texts. In contrast to a biographical approach to an author's life, in this chapter (as in the whole book) my focus is on what Gross (and Jung, Reich and Fromm) thought and wrote, not what they did, or how they acted and behaved. This is simply because they created utopian *ideas*, not utopian communities. However, before I focus on Gross's ideas, I shall give an outline of his tumultuous life and pay special attention to his difficult relationships with Jung and Freud.

An Experiment in Life: Gross's Road from Bourgeois Respectability to the Margins of Society

Otto Gross was born in the small Austrian village of Gniebing in Styria in 1877.[7] When he was still a small child, his family moved to Graz, one of the biggest towns in Austria. He was the only child of the famous criminologist Hans Gross and his wife Adele, who seemed to have been fully dedicated to the upbringing and education of their son, who at an early age showed signs of extraordinary talent. Although Hans Gross was an authoritarian law and order figure, there is no doubt that he was proud of his only child, who was first educated at home by private tutors, and who impressed everyone with his ability to learn and comprehend complex issues. His mother, a typical bourgeois *Hausfrau* in her submission to her husband's patriarchal authority, was devoted to her cerebral son, who was not allowed to socialize with children of his own age. In fact, Otto was a prototype of a 'spoiled child' whose every wish was granted, and who was effectively sheltered from the harsh reality. Small wonder, then, that by the time he graduated from a private *Gymnasium*, he was a shy and socially undeveloped young man who found it difficult to relate to his peers or to cope with the petty demands of everyday life (such as eating regularly, changing clothes or waking up in the morning). As his father noted in 1902, Otto was something of a child prodigy who easily learned Latin, Greek and mathematics, but who was almost totally helpless in practical life, to which he was adjusted less successfully than a six-year-old child.[8] This child-like helplessness would characterize Gross's life to the very end.

After graduating from the *Gymnasium*, Otto Gross began to study medicine at the University of Graz. This choice of profession delighted his father, who wanted to collaborate with his son in the developing field of criminology. Indeed, some of Otto Gross's early articles were published in his father's criminological journal, *Archiv für Kriminal-Anthropologie und Kriminalistik*, and Hans Gross referred to his son's writings in his own works. Hans Gross was particularly interested in the medical and psychological aspects of criminal behaviour, and his ambition was to apply the latest psychomedical discoveries and theories to the study of criminals, whom he regarded as 'degenerate' individuals constitutionally disposed to antisocial behaviour. In the late nineteenth century, the doctrine of degenerationism was all the rage in European medicine, especially in psychiatry, and it was commonly held that, alongside hysteria, alcoholism, epilepsy, feeble-mindedness, mental illness and proneness to suicide, criminality was a manifestation of degeneration. With his vivid professional interest in all kinds of abnormal behaviour, Hans Gross wanted to create a science of criminology that would help the authorities ward off the dangers to the social order created by homosexuals, perverts, prostitutes, criminals, revolutionaries and other 'degenerate' groups who corrupted society and lowered the racial qualities of its people. In 1905, he went so far as to propose that degenerate people should be deported to designated colonies where they could only socialize with one another.[9]

Hans Gross obviously thought that he could easily categorize people into the good, the bad and the ugly. But, as the years went by, he must have felt frustrated in his attempt to keep his own son in the category of 'the good'. After Otto Gross had completed his medical studies in 1900, he was hired as a ship's doctor on the German steamship line, and he sailed all the way to South America, where he pursued his botanical interests. It was probably during this one-year trip as a naval doctor that Gross began to use drugs, especially cocaine and morphine. His addiction to drugs turned out to be the great catastrophe in his life, for it disturbed his social relations, confused his cognitive capacities and powers of judgment and, in the end, made him a social outcast dependent on the availability of drugs. But his abuse of drugs also gave him the energy he seemed to need in order to write and to have sexual encounters with many women, which was an essential part of his erotic life philosophy. In 1902, only one year after his return from his voyage to South America, he was admitted to the Burghölzli mental hospital to be cured of his narcomania. Later in his life, he received medical treatment a number of times for his addiction, most famously at the Burghölzli for the second time in 1908, when he was treated psychoanalytically by Jung (see below). It should be noted that Gross was everywhere treated as a first-class patient, and as such his institutional life was usually considerably more comfortable than that of less privileged patients.[10] He also received more medical attention and care than second- or third-class patients. Thus Gross was largely spared from the more brutal sides of institutional life in asylums and clinics.

As a young, bright doctor, Gross was tall and slender, his expression was boyish and lively, and his Roman nose made his friends compare his profile to a hawk. In later years he grew a beard, and his gentle and noble appearance was slowly ruined by his drug abuse. He started to look more and more like those 'degenerates' that his father abhorred and condemned. But his worrisome addiction notwithstanding, things were not that bad for Gross around 1900. After his sea voyage, he worked first as a psychiatric volunteer and assistant doctor in Munich, and then he went back to his home town, Graz, where he worked at the second most famous psychiatric clinic in Austria. The head of the clinic was Gabriel Anton, to whom Gross made several appreciative references in his early neuropsychiatric articles. It is not altogether clear why Gross decided to specialize in psychiatry, which at that time was at the bottom of the hierarchy of medical specialties. One reason for his interest in the workings of the psyche may have been his acquaintance with Freud's writings around 1900, but in his early career he was more influenced by the great German neuropsychiatrist Carl Wernicke, who had become world famous on the strength of his studies on sensory aphasia, and whose work on the system of psychiatry, published in three volumes between 1894 and 1900, exerted a great influence on German psychiatry at the time when Gross was studying medicine.[11] Wernicke was 'anti-psychological' in his approach to mental illnesses, for he was convinced that mental disorders were disorders of the brain ('Geisteskrankheiten sind Gehirnkrankheiten'). The young Gross largely adopted the prevailing neurophysiological approach to mental illness[12] and, like most of his peers, adhered to the psychophysiological monism, according to which psychological and physiological phenomena are but two aspects of the same unified whole.[13]

Already in his early career Gross became interested in the larger context of mental illness.[14] Although trained as a neuropsychiatrist, he incorporated psychological elements in his work almost right from the start: his early article on the 'socially repressive images' (1901) focuses on psychic processes and discusses psychological aspects of antisocial tendencies, images of fear and moral indignation.[15] In this paper, published in his father's journal *Archiv für Kriminal-Anthropologie und Kriminalistik*, his criminological views were still in line with those of his father, for he writes that

> the punishment of criminals is a sacrifice of the individual for the general well being, and it is justified in that the general well being stands above that of an individual, whether innocent or guilty.[16]

In what was probably his most cited publication – a small book entitled *Die cerebrale Sekundärfunktion* ('The Cerebral Second Function', 1902) – Gross states that 'the greatest value of psychiatry is that it gives us pictures that comprise an individual psychology'.[17] The parameters of his scientific thinking were also provided by biology and evolutionary theories, since his way of approaching the question of moral emotions (e.g., 'demand for retribution') and ethics was built on the theory of biological drives and instincts.[18]

The young Gross already had an ambition to develop a theory of ethics based on scientific, biological foundation (see below).[19] He also constructed a theory of mental functions (which influenced Jung when he was creating his theory of psychological types) and a theory of psychosis (dementia sejunctiva), which was indebted to the psychiatric ideas of Carl Wernicke, Eugen Bleuler and Emil Kraepelin. He began to refer to Freud (and Jung) in 1904, and after moving to Munich in 1906 to work at the psychiatric clinic headed by the formidable Emil Kraepelin, he was committed to the psychoanalytic cause, and had high hopes of psychoanalysis leading psychiatry into new, more promising paths. He also began to use psychoanalysis as a method of treatment.[20] Still, even if psychoanalysis, and especially the fundamental Freudian idea of 'psychic conflict', became a central part of his 'mindscape', he never was a true disciple of Freud. I believe he valued intellectual and psychological independence too much to be able to submit to anyone's intellectual authority. On the contrary, like Jung later on, he himself had an ambition to become an intellectual leader and a prophet of the new age.

When he lived and worked in Graz, Gross married Frieda Schloffer, the daughter of a local impoverished attorney. Frieda had become friends with the von Richthofen sisters in Germany, and a few years after their marriage Gross had an affair with both sisters (Else Jaffé and Frieda Weekley). When he was still a student and a young doctor in Graz, he was not known to be a womanizer, but his father later revealed that Otto had had intimate relationships with several women before he met Frieda, and that he had to extricate his son from these annoying 'Weibergeschichten'. The young couple did not feel at home in their conservative surroundings, and Gross's evolving social, philosophical and political thinking was given much fuel when he visited the countercultural colony Ascona by Lake Maggiore in Switzerland for the first time in 1905. Ascona was frequented by bohemians, artists, anarchists and various experimenters in new lifestyles, and Gross appeared to be immediately attracted to these people and their unconventional social behaviour. In the following years, he often travelled to Ascona and became one of the brightest stars of the colony.[21]

During those years (*c.* 1905–10), Gross led a double life, as it were, for while he was more and more attracted to the 'anti-bourgeois' lifestyle of his new bohemian friends, he also worked as a psychiatrist at Kraepelin's clinic. His post there was made possible when he attained the position of a lecturer (docent) in psychiatry at the University of Graz in 1906. When he moved to Munich together with his wife in the same year, he began to spend his evenings in coffee houses in Schwabing (especially in Café Stephanie), which was the artistic centre of Munich. He also became involved in the anarchist Tat Gruppe, becoming friends with Erich Mühsam and Johannes Nohl, the founders of the group. These smoke-filled coffee houses in Schwabing provided Gross with the proper scene for his evolving psychoutopian ideas, which took shape during his discussions with anarchists, architects, Nietzschean coffee-house intellectuals and philosophers, writers, painters, poets, models, musicians, religious and sexual enthusiasts, emancipated women and eternal students. In this company, Gross felt liberated from his suffocating bourgeois background and particularly from his father, from whom he was becoming increasingly alienated. During his years in Munich his relationship with Hans Gross became strained as he adopted a lifestyle and created ideas strongly disapproved of by his conservative father. Obviously, Otto Gross's new philosophy of 'nichts verdrängen' ('repress nothing') could not have been further removed from the world-view of his frustrated and agitated father.

In 1907, Frieda Gross gave birth to their son Peter, and it was also in this year that Otto had affairs with the von Richthofen sisters Else Jaffé and Frieda Weekley. Later in the same year, Else gave birth to their son, also named Peter (he died in 1915). This year was the pinnacle of Gross's love life: three extraordinary women had erotic relationships with Gross, whose enthusiasm over these amorous relationships is evident in the letters he wrote to these women.[22] He also had affairs with other women during these years, but it was his relationship with

Frieda Weekley (the future wife of D. H. Lawrence) that was most important for Gross, as their published correspondence demonstrates.

I shall not go into the biographical details of Gross's later life, which included incarceration against his will in 1913 (masterminded by his father, who wanted to control his erratic, unpredictable and self-destructive son), his increasing alienation not only from the psychiatric establishment but also from the nascent psychoanalytic movement, and his seemingly aimless drifting and wandering between Munich, Ascona, Vienna, Prague, Graz and Berlin, where he died in February 1920 after having collapsed in a dark alley of a Berlin warehouse, suffering from pneumonia and malnutrition. This is how his friend and collaborator Franz Jung described the last days of Otto Gross:

> [he was] pain-tormented, lonely man, crying out for love, who sought the truth about others and himself ... One could see on the streets of Berlin that winter (1919–20) a tattered and starving man, running through the snow, howling aloud in pain and then bending over to warm his fingers on his chest. People stopped to watch him and laugh.[23]

A man who was once hailed by Freud as one of the most promising young psychoanalysts had become a totally marginalized outcast, who was seen by the good people of Berlin as a poor old sot. His death did not make headlines in the press, hardly anyone in his former professional peer group made any public gestures when he died. The only true exception to the rule of 'remain silent about Gross' was the maverick psychoanalyst Wilhelm Stekel, who had treated Gross in 1914, and who wrote in his appreciative obituary of him that 'I am acquainted with no one who more terribly laid waste his powers, no one who might have done greater things'.[24]

Next, I shall turn to Gross's relationship with one of the four protagonists of this book, Carl G. Jung. My thesis is that this relationship, and the related 'unmaking' of Gross as a psychoanalytic authority by Jung and Freud, helps to clarify the process which resulted in Gross becoming a stigmatized outsider whose publications began to be infused with psychoutopian ideas.

'Twin Brothers' Gross and Jung: Colleagues, Analysts and Rivals

Gross developed his analytic skills more in cafés than in clinics. He never had a private practice, and after he quit Kraepelin's clinic he no longer made his living as a psychiatrist. In fact, he did not seem to have any steady income at all, and he was probably supported by his anxious father on the one hand, and by his circle of friends and admirers on the other. If he had been a more conventional psychoanalyst, I believe he could have easily become a respected and highly successful therapist, for there was one area of expertise in which he was exceptionally gifted: face-to-face interaction. Ernest Jones, a young Welsh-born neurologist eager to commit himself to the cause of psychoanalysis, met Gross in Munich in 1908, and he recalled late in his life how Gross became his 'first instructor in the practice of psychoanalysis and I used to be present during his treatment of a case'.[25] Jones, who quickly became a lifelong disciple of Freud, wrote of Gross half a century later that 'such penetrative power of divining the inner thoughts of others I was never to see again, nor is it a matter that lends itself to description'.[26]

In 1907, Gross met Jung at an important International Congress for Neurology and Psychiatry in Amsterdam. They were now colleagues, but five years earlier (1902) Gross had been a patient at the Burghölzli mental hospital, where Jung worked at that time as a junior physician. To have a doctor as a patient in an asylum was unusual, and being the son of a famous professor of criminology must have made Gross a very well-known patient at the Burghölzli. Jung probably did not personally treat Gross in 1902, as he was to do in 1908, when Gross was committed to the Burghölzli again. At the Amsterdam Congress, both Gross and Jung defended Freud's theories, and the correspondence between Freud and Jung documents how the two soul doctors evaluated Gross as a colleague and a person.

Jung mentioned Gross for the first time in a letter to Freud in June 1907, a few months before the Amsterdam Congress. After making some comments on Gross's slim book on Freud's theory (*Das Freudsche Ideogenitätsmoment*, 1907), Jung writes that Gross has an 'excellent mind'.[27] In his reply, Freud agrees with Jung's assessment of Gross's intelligence, but he also criticizes Gross's book for having 'too much theory and too little observation'. Gross also 'wallows in superlatives', which in Freud's view reveals the abnormality of Gross's affective life to which Jung had earlier referred.[28] After the Amsterdam Congress, Jung reports to Freud how energetically Gross defended Freud's ideas, and how Gross's own theory of secondary function has influenced psychologists. He repeats his former evaluation of Gross as 'very intelligent', but now he also begins in earnest the psychopathologization of Gross that would characterize both Jung's and Freud's subsequent comments on Gross in their correspondence: he writes that it is 'a pity that G.[ross] is such a psychopath'.[29] This was in fact an 'official diagnosis', for Gross was classified as a 'psychopath' when he was treated for drug addiction at the Burghölzli in 1902.[30] At the time when 'psychopathy' – referring to a pathological personality structure or 'constitution' – was routinely coupled with degeneration, Gross was branded as a (potential) degenerate with hereditary taint.[31]

Jung's divergence from Gross's understanding of analysis is revealed in an exemplary fashion in another letter he sent to Freud after the Amsterdam Congress. This is what he says about Gross in his letter:

> Dr Gross tells me that he puts a quick stop to the transference by turning people into sexual immoralists. He says the transference to the analyst and its persistent fixation are mere monogamy symbols and as such symptomatic of repression. The truly healthy state for the neurotic is sexual immorality. Hence he associates you with

> Nietzsche. It seems to me, however, that sexual repression is a very important and indispensable civilizing factor, even if pathogenic for many inferior people ... I feel Gross is going too far with the vogue for the sexual short circuit, which is neither intelligent, nor in good taste, but merely convenient, and therefore anything but a civilizing factor.[32]

To Jung, Gross was simply too extreme, an 'excellent' but 'abnormal' mind with little sense of proportion and decency. Gross was undoubtedly talented, but he was also too wild and unpredictable, which was a bit too much for Jung, who was a cultural conservative and an advocate of a middle-class morality of prudence and decency. Still, his 'abnormal mind' and 'psychopathy' notwithstanding, both Jung and Freud considered Gross a potentially important player in the psychoanalytic field. Freud's interest in Gross was partly motivated by the fact that Gross, like Jung, was a Gentile, and the son of a well-respected criminologist. As Freud wrote to Jung in February 1908, only Jung and 'perhaps' Gross are capable of making an original contribution to psychoanalysis. 'Unfortunately', Freud went on to write, Gross's 'health is poor'.[33]

To Freud, Gross in 1908 was a good catch, and he was welcomed to the Freudian circle when he was invited to attend the First Congress for Freudian Psychology in Salzburg in April 1908. Strangely, his name is not mentioned in the Congress report published three years later by Otto Rank, but Ernest Jones listed his name among the forty-two participants in his biography of Freud.[34] And Wilhelm Stekel later recalled that,

> attending the meeting was also the highly gifted Otto Gross. In his inspiring speech he compared Freud to Nietzsche and hailed him as a destroyer of old prejudices, an enlarger of psychological horizons, and a scientific revolutionary.[35]

Such talk, however, was not what Freud fully appreciated: as he told Gross after the latter's speech, 'we are physicians and physicians we wish to remain'.[36]

Indeed, it was in the role of physician that Freud and Jung continued their discussion of Gross. A week before the Salzburg Congress, Freud wrote to Jung that Gross urgently needed Jung's medical help: 'He is addicted to cocaine and probably in the early phase of toxic cocaine paranoia'. Freud, who himself used cocaine in the 1880s, felt genuine sympathy for his troubled younger colleague (Gross was only thirty-one years old then), calling him 'a gifted, resolute man'.[37] In his reply to Freud, Jung wrote that Hans Gross has asked him to take his son to the Burghölzli for treatment right after the Salzburg Congress.[38] This plan fell through, but in May Freud sent Jung the medical certificate for Gross. Apparently, Freud wanted Jung to treat Gross during the first phase when withdrawal symptoms require intensive care in a hospital. Freud himself would then continue analysing Gross in Vienna in the autumn. Gross was admitted to the Burghölzli in mid-May, and Jung immediately began his psychoanalytic treatment. His novel method of treatment had the blessing of Eugen Bleuler, the Burghölzli's chief physician. Bleuler was the first academic psychiatrist to (cautiously) apply psychoanalytic methods to mental illnesses, and for a short period of time he was a member of the newly-founded International Psychoanalytic Association (IPA).[39]

What happened between Jung and Gross at the Burghölzli in May and June 1908 is one of the most fascinating 'case studies' in the history of psychiatry (in his book, Hurwitz quotes extensively from Jung's medical record of Gross[40]). Jung's initial diagnosis of Gross was obsessional neurosis, a debilitating mental affliction but not a psychotic illness. Obviously, Gross's obsession manifested itself in his drug abuse. At first, Jung gave Gross a full ration of drugs 'so as not to upset the analysis by arousing feelings of privation'.[41] Then, Gross voluntarily reduced the dose to the half of the original amount of 6.0 grams per day. The truly remarkable thing about this doctor-patient relationship was that their respective roles became blurred and sometimes altogether reversed, as Jung confessed in his letter to Freud:

> I have let everything drop and have spent all my available time, day and night, on Gross, pushing on with his analysis ... Whenever I got stuck, he analysed me. In this way my own psychic health has benefited.[42]

Ernest Jones, who knew both Gross and Jung, wrote in his memoirs that Jung had told him that 'one day he worked unceasingly with Gross for twelve hours, until they were almost reduced to the condition of nodding automata'.[43] Jung was enthusiastic over the insights that their 'mutual analysis' had given to him, and in his letter to Freud he is optimistic about the prognosis ('psychically his condition has improved a lot'), as well as impressed by Gross's personality, characterizing him as an 'extraordinarily decent fellow with whom you can hit it off at once provided you can get your own complexes out of the way'. He also referred to 'scientifically valuable results which we shall try to formulate soon'.[44]

But things did not go as smoothly as Jung – and Freud – had planned. In the spring of 1908, Freud had entertained hopes that Jung and Gross, two young and talented Gentile psychiatrists, would collaborate with him and contribute to the development and academic legitimation of psychoanalytic theory (within parameters provided by Freud, of course).[45] But, in mid-June Jung wrote to Freud that 'I have sacrificed days and nights to him [Gross]. Under analysis he gave up *all* medication. The last three weeks we worked only with very early infantile material.' He went on to describe how Gross's 'infantile complexes' were 'overwhelmingly powerful', and how they drew their effects 'from inexhaustible depths'. After these descriptive statements he let the bomb fall, as it were: he wrote that Gross suffered from dementia praecox.[46] This diagnosis was the forerunner of today's schizophrenia diagnosis, and in 1908 it denoted a chronic mental illness that seriously impaired mental functioning and often ended in premature dementia and death.

In addition to illustrating Gross's 'complexes' as if they revealed a more serious underlying illness, Jung gave two more reasons for labelling Gross as psychotic: first, an anamnesis and a 'partial psychanalysis' of Frieda Gross, and, second, Gross's escape from the Burghölzli. On 17 June, Gross jumped over the garden wall and travelled first to Zurich and then back to Munich, having the 'delusion' that Jung had cured him. Ernest Jones met him in Munich and reported in his letter to Freud that he had escaped from the Burghölzli, and that 'he seems to be much worse, quite paranoiac – shut off from the outside world – and has already started taking cocaine again'.[47] What was more, Gross wanted to 'provoke a lawsuit to prove the value of psychoanalysis, to drag Kraepelin in and expose his ignorance [regarding psychoanalysis] before the world!!'[48] If this is true, it suggests that Jung had been unable to help Gross, but also that Gross had a high regard of the results of his and Jung's mutual psychoanalysis (otherwise he would not have come up with the idea of proving the value of psychoanalysis in court).

Jung in turn appeared to be sad and frustrated over what had happened, calling Gross his 'friend' and a 'very good and fine man with an unusual mind' in his letter to Freud. He continued:

> For me this experience is one of the harshest in my life, for in Gross I discovered many aspects of my own nature, so that he often seemed like my twin brother – but for the Dementia praecox. This is tragic. You can guess what powers I have summoned up in myself in order to cure him. But in spite of the sorrow of it, I would not have missed this experience for anything; for in the end it has given me, with the help of a unique personality, a unique insight into the nethermost depths of Dementia pr.[49]

Freud replied to Jung that he had no reason to doubt Jung's diagnosis, but he wondered whether Gross's condition could be 'another (obsessional) psychoneurosis, with negative transference caused by his hostility to his father'. Freud admitted that he knew too little about the mechanism of psychoses (dementia praecox and paranoia) as compared with neuroses (hysteria and obsession), and he emphasized to Jung how important Gross's 'case' was both to Jung and to psychoanalysis: 'You could never have learned so much from another case; and a further good result, I see, is that your views have once again come much closer to mine'.[50] Jung clearly wanted to further justify to Freud his diagnosis of Gross as psychotic. In a letter sent to Freud in late June he refers to Frieda Gross's 'latest report' to Eugen Bleuler, which gives an account of Gross's persecutory ideas and auditory hallucinations (a tell-tale sign of schizophrenia in modern psychiatry), which in Jung's view give evidence of Gross's paranoid state of mind. In this letter, he uses Bleuler's term 'schizophrenia' for the first time when he refers to the concepts dementia praecox, schizophrenia and paranoia, and argues for the incurability of dementia praecox.[51] At this crucial stage, Freud turns his back on Gross and declares in a letter to Jung that Gross 'is addicted and can only do great harm to our cause'.[52]

The diagnosis 'dementia praecox' was coined by Emil Kraepelin in 1893, and by 1908 it was widely used in the German psychiatric profession. There was a serious stigma attached to this diagnosis, for Kraepelin regarded patients suffering from dementia praecox not only as chronically ill, but also as 'psychopaths' and 'degenerated'; they were people whose will, emotional life and overall mental constitution was not only disturbed but also constitutionally inferior. This meant that their overt behaviour was often unacceptable to their social environment. As Kraepelin wrote in 1913, 'the patients sit about idle, trouble themselves about nothing, do not go to their work'. They also 'conduct themselves in a free and easy way, laugh on serious occasions, are rude and impertinent towards their superiors, challenge them to duels' etc.[53] In short, the Kraepelinian dementia praecox is a fatal illness which, while being a chronic psychosis usually ending in dementia and death, corrupts intellectual capacities and the moral sense, and results in various perversions.

What makes the question of Gross's alleged schizophrenia even more intriguing is, first, that he worked at Kraepelin's clinic in Munich as a psychiatrist; and, second, that he himself had coined the term 'dementia sejunctiva' in 1904 to replace Kraepelin's diagnosis, which he considered misleading. Gross argued that dementia praecox should be renamed 'dementia sejunctiva', because the main symptom of this illness is the splitting of consciousness (*Bewusstseinzerfall*), not the gradual deterioration of mental faculties, as Kraepelin claimed.[54] He did not pick the term from out of thin air: he was influenced by the most famous late nineteenth-century neuropsychiatrist Carl Wernicke, who had used the term 'sejunctiva' in his own clinical work (but not to describe the illness known as dementia praecox). Gross, who insisted on the diagnostic superiority of his dementia sejunctiva over Kraepelin's dementia praecox, also referred to Bleuler's ideas on the disturbances in the thought processes of people suffering from dementia praecox.[55] As it happened, Bleuler, the chief physician at the Burghölzli, was the one who coined the term 'schizophrenia' in the very same year (1908) as Jung diagnosed Gross's illness as dementia praecox. When Bleuler published his major work on schizophrenia in 1911, Gross reacted with anger – he claimed that Bleuler had stolen his term from him and only given it a Greek name.[56]

Jung and Freud made a few more references to Gross and his writings after the dramatic events surrounding Jung's and Gross's mutual analysis in 1908. Although some of Freud's comments were rather favourable,[57] it is evident that after Jung had given him the diagnosis dementia praecox Gross became a marginalized figure within psychoanalysis. He was not only addicted to drugs, which was bad enough; but he was also classified by Jung as mentally disturbed, and this effectively thwarted the prospect of Freud collaborating with Gross. And there is ample evidence of Gross going through cocaine-induced episodes of mental disorientation and confusion in his later years. His friend Erich Mühsam wrote in his diary in 1911:

> [Gross] had fallen into a state of complete madness. Again, he was hallucinating a lot, in a state of being half asleep he was smashing mirrors, lamps and other things, wiping his injured nose on anything at hand, like milk jars etc., and was totally mad and sick ... My wish for Otto Gross is that he should die before night falls.[58]

Fortunately, Gross's health improved after this particular bout of madness, but for the rest of his short life he kept on taking cocaine and destroying his health. Already as a young doctor he had noticed that cocaine improved his working capacity, and by 1911 he appeared to be incapable of doing *any* work (such as writing) without first taking drugs. I believe it is not too extravagant to say that his life course was largely determined by his drug abuse, which ultimately led to his premature death at the age of forty-two (but not to a 'premature dementia' à la dementia praecox).

Mutual Analysis, Madness and the Question of Expertise

What can be gathered from the clinical encounter between the two young psychiatrists at the Burghölzli is that the patient (Gross) exerted a more powerful influence on the doctor (Jung) than vice versa. At the time of their mutual analysis, Jung was in the midst of an entanglement with his former patient at the Burghölzli, Sabina Spielrein, who had an affair with Jung while studying medicine at the University of Zurich. Jung had a wife and children and, as a respected Swiss middle-class professional, he was keen on keeping up appearances in a society that placed a premium on the strict adherence to social norms.[59] Thus it was anything but easy for Jung to have an intimate relationship with another woman, especially if she was his former mental patient. Evidently Gross, a champion of polygamy, 'helped' Jung to overcome his inhibitions and break down the barriers of convention, for Sabina Spielrein wrote in her undated diary in 1908/9 that

> now he [Jung] arrives, beaming with pleasure, and tells me with strong emotion about Gross, about the great insight he has just received (i.e. about polygamy); he no longer wants to suppress his feeling for me, he admitted that I was his first dearest woman friend, etc. etc.[60]

Gross, whose relationship with his criminologist father was conflict-ridden, also analysed Jung's relationship to his late father, a Protestant pastor who had died when Jung was a medical student in Basel. Gross and Jung probably had plans of publishing their psychoanalytic discussions of the 'significance of the father for the destiny of the individual' in a joint article, but in fact it was Jung alone who wrote and published the paper in 1911. This infuriated Gross, who in April 1911 wrote Freud a letter to which he enclosed a communication that he wanted Freud to publish (The communication was entitled 'In Self-Defence. Concerning the So-Called Bleuler-Jung School'). In his communication, he claimed, first, that Bleuler had stolen the term 'dementia sejunctiva' from him (see above), and, second, that Jung's article on the 'significance of the father' was based on the ideas Gross had presented to Jung in the course of their mutual analysis in May–June 1908.[61] In the first published version of the article, Jung referred to experiences gained 'in an analysis carried out conjointly with Dr. Otto Gross', these experiences having 'impressed upon me the soundness of this view [i.e. the psychological influence of the father]'.[62] In later editions of this article, including the version published in *Collected Works*, Jung's reference to Gross was omitted.[63]

To Gross's dismay, Freud refused to publish his communication. Meanwhile, Jung reacted to Gross's accusations with indignation. In a letter to Freud, he calls Gross a 'complete nut, for whom Steinhof [a sanatorium near Vienna] is a fitting sinecure'. He claims that he and Gross agreed on the formula that would be used in the article (that is, Jung mentioned Gross's contribution in a passage in his article), and in his fury he compares Gross to a parasite.[64] No longer was Gross a fine man whom Jung regarded as a 'twin brother', except for his mental illness.

I agree with Emanuel Hurwitz, who has argued that Jung deliberately used a diagnosis that was harmful to Gross and his reputation as a physician. According to Hurwitz, who recently reviewed and evaluated all the available psychiatric documents concerning Gross's mental health after his 1908 stay at the Burghölzli, there is no reason to doubt that Gross was the victim of a mistaken diagnosis.[65] Another Gross scholar, Bernd Laska, goes so far as to suggest that Jung and Freud, who had begun to see Gross as a danger to the 'cause', did not even *want* Gross to regain his health.[66] To be declared mentally ill is a very serious matter to anyone, let alone to a young man who is a psychiatrist himself. Jung, who never retracted his diagnosis, made life difficult for Gross, because his diagnosis formed the basis for declaring Gross legally incompetent. This happened in late 1913 when Hans Gross manoeuvred the arrest and incarceration of his son in a mental asylum. For the rest of his life, Gross had to struggle to regain full citizen's rights. Jung may have earnestly believed in the validity of his diagnosis, but one cannot help but wonder why he did not choose a less stigmatizing diagnosis, such as obsession, because the choice of a diagnosis does not in itself have any effect on the possible cure – in fact, there was no cure for dementia praecox/schizophrenia in early 1900, nor is there a cure even today. In my mind, by preferring to label a drug addict such as Gross psychotic rather than neurotic, Jung behaved irresponsibly in his role as a physician, as if he wanted to punish Gross for his unacceptable behaviour.

Another reason for Jung's diagnostic preference may have been his professional ambition as a psychiatrist who studies and treats severe mental illnesses. Freud, his revered elder colleague and friend, was a neurosis specialist in private practice, and most of his patients were unhappy or nervous rather than mentally ill. Freud had very little experience of mental illnesses, and I believe it is a distinct possibility that Jung, who had published an acclaimed book on dementia praecox in late 1906,[67] wanted to show Freud how good he was in the difficult art of studying psychoses, of which Freud had no first-hand experience (except in his early career, when he worked for a period of time as *Sekundärarzt* at the Psychiatric Clinic of the General Hospital of Vienna). It was almost as if Jung was saying to Freud between the lines: 'you may very well be the master of neuroses and of various unconscious conflicts, but I treat severely ill people at a mental hospital, and as an expert in the field of psychoses I can tell the difference between a milder psychic disturbance and severe mental illness'. Ernest Jones, who himself spent several months studying with Jung at the Burghölzli, later claimed that Jung had 'the ambition of being the first to cure a case of schizophrenia', and the further ambition of being the first to effect a cure by using psychoanalytic methods.[68]

Furthermore, it seems to me that Jung was more concerned with the effects his treatment of Gross had on himself than with his former patient's wellbeing. In a letter to Freud in September 1908, he notes how Gross 'did me a world of good. In spite of his prickliness, talk with him is wonderfully stimulating.'[69] This was undoubtedly true, but Jung did not sacrifice a single thought to the question of whether Gross was happy with the way he was treated at the Burghölzli as a patient, or what possible consequences the dementia praecox diagnosis might have to the future professional career of Dr Gross. A year after the 'mutual analysis', Jung complained to Freud that both Gross and Spielrein 'are bitter experiences. To none of my patients have I extended so much friendship and from none have I reaped so much sorrow.'[70] It was as if these 'patients' should have showed gratitude and affection to Jung, instead of fleeing from him (Gross) or 'seeking revenge' after having failed in her attempt to 'seduce' him (Spielrein).

I also believe that Jung was fascinated with Gross's unconventional personality and his bohemian lifestyle, recognizing in Gross the wilder and darker side of his own personality.[71] But after the immediate effects of their mutual analysis started to wear off, Jung came to his senses, as it were, and realized that he was not like Gross: his place was not among the bohemians, anarchists and 'idle dreamers' of a new age, but in the clinic, in the lecture hall, in the secure surroundings of a comfortable house and in the ambience of bourgeois respectability. It would take a few more years before Jung could no longer ignore his own wilder side, which resulted in his partial retreat from social reality during his now-famous 'confrontation with the Unconscious' between 1913 and 1917/18.[72] But his 1908 'confrontation with his Twin Brother' may have confused and even scared him, and as he found it difficult to come to grips with what had happened to him in May and June 1908, he wanted to distance himself from Gross and everything he represented. I believe it is in this 'self-protective' light one can understand Jung's harsh words about Gross in a letter he wrote to Ernest Jones in May 1909:

> I believe that by openly advocating certain things one cuts off the branch on which culture rests ... In any case, the extreme attitude which Gross preaches is definitely wrong and dangerous to the whole cause [i.e., psychoanalysis] – Gross sterilises himself, and therefore his dangerousness will be reduced.[73]

A year earlier, when Gross went to the Burghölzli to be treated by Jung, Ernest Jones reported to Freud his observation that

> Jung does not find it easy to conceal his feelings and he has a pretty strong dislike to Gross; in addition there are some fundamental differences of opinion between them on moral questions.[74]

Decades later, in January 1936 (but dated January 1935), Jung sent a letter to the Freudian analyst Franz Wittels, who had asked him about Gross's life and work. In his letter, Jung refers to his treatment of Gross at the Burghölzli, claiming that he treated Gross both in 1902 and 1908 (the patient records indicate that the physician in charge of Gross in 1902 was not Jung). He gives a rather unflattering picture of Gross as a person and as a thinker. In his strong view, Gross did not show any signs of true ingenuity, but rather of brilliant instability which blinded many people. His other 'symptoms' of ingenuity were his know-all babble and problem-wallowing. He had conducted psychoanalysis in the most disgusting drinking holes, and the ensuing emotional entanglements ('transferences') usually resulted in illegitimate children. Jung recalls that Gross had mainly socialized with artists, writers, political fanatics and decadents of all shape and size, and revelled in repulsive orgies in the morass of Ascona. Gross was a megalomaniac who always thought he could treat psychically his doctors, and already back then he was physically, socially and morally declined and impoverished. Jung did not have a high regard for Gross's work either, with the exception of his theory of the secondary function, which had influenced Jung's own theory of psychological types. He also erroneously claims that Gross died of pneumonia before World War I.[75]

I would suggest that Jung's predominantly negative assessment of a colleague whose cognitive capacities he had once characterized as 'excellent' can be interpreted in the context of marginalization and stigmatization. As I believe that Gross's marginalization and stigmatization are an important part not only of his professional life, but also of his proneness to utopianism, I shall say a few words about these issues in the next section before I turn to the examination of his utopian ideas.

The Marginalization and Stigmatization of Gross

Gross held distinct positions in two different fields, one being professional and the other cultural and political. The professional field was that of psychiatry and psychoanalysis, while the cultural and political field comprised of a loosely-knit group of friends and like-minded people – writers, artists, bohemian experimenters in a new lifestyle – who often sought inspiration in the philosophy of anarchism, aestheticism and revolutionary socialism, and who partly made up what has been called the counter-culture of Ascona.[76] Over time, Gross's position in the professional field became increasingly invisible, while his position in the diffuse anarchist and literary field became more visible.[77] Concurrently, his sociocultural thinking became increasingly utopian, as his early criticism of the pathogenic effects of society on the individual[78] developed into a more radical vision that purported to offer an alternative to the prevailing hegemonic power of patriarchy.

That Gross became a marginalized figure within psychoanalysis and psychiatry is a standard claim, and in the previous sections of this chapter I have given an account of how Freud and Jung dissociated themselves from Gross during 1908–9. But I think we need to qualify the marginalization thesis, because we can easily distinguish between optimal or positive *marginality* and negative *stigmatization*. On one side there were 'renegade' analysts such as Jung, Fromm and R. D. Laing, whose marginalization (if Jung's position even during the years 1913–17/18 can be called marginal in any sense of the term) was optimal. Fromm's marginalization has been called optimal by sociologist Neil McLaughlin, who has argued that, while optimally marginal intellectuals have access to the creative core of an intellectual tradition, they are not bound by institutional restrictions. They are thus in an ideal position to transfer novel ideas from the margin to the core. While Fromm trumpeted his difference from academic psychiatry, psychology and psychoanalysis in the 1940s and 1950s, he possessed valuable connections to Freudian institutions and networks. Fromm's popular psychoanalytic and social philosophical writing shows how his marginal position outside the psychoanalytic mainstream could be utilized as a viable public face. That is why his kind of optimal marginality can be termed 'self-marginalization'.[79]

R. D. Laing is another analyst whose positioning vis-à-vis the centre and the margins can be termed optimal. When Laing played up his marginalization within his professional community in his popular books and public appearances in the 1960s, his voice found resonance among individuals and groups in the media and elsewhere who shared his critical views on the psychiatric establishment, and who could help him carve a high-profile niche for himself as a 'radical dissident thinker'. The point I am making here is that a construction of one's marginality can be an effective means to get positive publicity, and so-called 'ambitious outsiders' can get to the position in which it is precisely the presentation of their marginalization that is conducive to their professional career. To represent oneself (or others) as being 'marginalized' or an 'outsider' can be a rhetorical, manipulative strategy, a way to find a new and professionally profitable niche for oneself; to favourably contrast one's position from those conformists at or close to the centre who do not dare to show intellectual independence; and to win positive attention from groups that represent other centres. Thus, a marginalized place in the field of positions gives to those identified with the margins a set of symbolic resources that can indeed be most valuable.[80]

If Fromm and Laing were successful in positioning themselves at the margins of psychiatry and psychoanalysis, Gross was not. Rather than becoming a publicly-acknowledged, optimally marginalized dissident, his destiny was to become first a stigmatized outsider and then a non-entity. Stigmatization is about exercising the power of inclusion and exclusion, and specifically refers to how one party defines another party's identity *in terms* of exclusion. In his classic study of 'spoiled identity', sociologist Erving Goffman refers to the process in which, in the light of evidence, we begin to see a person

> possessing an attribute that makes him different from others in the category of persons available for him to be, and of a less desirable kind – in the extreme, a person who is quite thoroughly bad, or dangerous, or weak. He is thus reduced in our minds from a whole and usual person to a tainted, discounted one. Such an attribute is a stigma, especially when its discrediting effect is very extensive; sometimes it is also called a failing, a shortcoming, a handicap.[81]

I would suggest that Goffman's definition of stigma is readily applicable to Gross, whose identity became 'spoiled' in 1908 when he was not only perceived as a drug addict, but also diagnosed as schizophrenic. Moreover, Freud and Jung reacted to his ambition to apply psychoanalytic theories to sociocultural renewal with categorical disapproval. And the rather conservative psychiatric establishment, including Emil Kraepelin, hardly wanted to have any dealings with a doctor who in their eyes was an extremist convert to psychoanalysis, a misguided colleague who was bringing the whole psychiatric profession into disrepute.

The early career of Gross was certainly not that of a stigmatized outsider. On the contrary, he was publicly acknowledged as a competent player in the professional field. At the outset, Gross was in fact destined to make a name for himself in his profession, and his early writings easily fulfilled the standards of a sound, even innovative, psychiatric research. He was, after all, appointed to a post at

Emil Kraepelin's prestigious psychiatric clinic in Munich in 1906. But it soon became evident to all concerned that his unconventional way of filling his role as a physician broke too many rules, and he became anathema to the academic psychiatric establishment, including the rigidly conservative Kraepelin. It is not clear when exactly Gross left Kraepelin's clinic, but Kraepelin was probably glad to get rid of him.[82] In the dominant field of one's profession, there is no place for those who become stigmatized.

As early as 1902, Gross's future wife Frieda, who had just met him and fallen in love with him, made the following observation about him in a letter to Else von Richthofen: 'Perhaps too different from the others, too unpractical, removed from reality ... The "people" think he is crazy.'[83] In 1914, Gross himself raised the question whether his discontent with the prevailing social order was evidence of his mental disturbance. He pointed out that the answer to this question is determined by what is regarded as the criteria for mental health: 'If we assume that normality means an adjustment to the prevailing order, then we can see discontent with the prevailing order as a sign of mental disturbance'.[84] Gross himself, of course, was of the opposite opinion: it is the recognition of the inferiority of the social order, together with the affirmation of the complete fulfilment of innate potentialities of humans, which constitute the true criteria for mental health.[85]

It was precisely the question of Gross's own mental health, together with his self-destructive drug abuse and his radical anthropological conception of illness (patriarchal society makes us sick), that pushed him outside of his professional field. If a psychiatrist himself is repeatedly considered a mental case and branded by the professional peer group as a drug addict or schizophrenic or antisocial psychopath, there is no way he or she can be taken seriously even as a renegade psychiatrist and a marginalized thinker. While there is a constant dialogue between the marginalizer and the marginalized, because they are bound by a common understanding of what constitutes the mainstream, those who are excluded and stigmatized are no longer participants in the dominant discourse, and thus unable to attain a viable position of optimal marginality in their professional fields.

Within psychiatry and psychoanalysis, then, there occurred something like the unmaking of Gross as an authority.[86] He was pushed aside, because he did not follow the rules of the game, as a consequence of which he was considered a liability by those who were at or near the centre, including Freud and Jung during 1908 and 1909. There is something uncanny about the way in which psychoanalysts especially have remained silent about Gross. For example, Wilhelm Reich, himself a man who first (after 1933) lost his central position and then, by the early 1950s, even his marginal position within psychoanalysis and psychiatry, was able to write all his numerous books and articles without ever mentioning Gross. I find this silence vis-à-vis Gross peculiar, not least because Reich was most 'Grossian' of all psychoutopians in his focus on the coming 'sexual revolution'.[87] But, as we know for certain now, it was Gross who long before Reich used the term 'die sexuelle Revolution' in what was perhaps the last text he ever wrote.[88] Gross's friend Franz Jung, who became acquainted with Reich's works in the 1950s (probably already in the 1920s or 1930s), called Reich a 'direct copy' of Gross.[89] That his version of the 'sexual revolution' made Reich famous – and infamous – while Gross was silenced, says something about the strange consensus with regard to Gross that seemed to prevail among the members of the psychiatric and psychoanalytic profession in German-speaking Europe.

When the first decade of the twentieth century drew to a close, Gross had been dropped out of sight in mental medicine, and his terrain was no longer professional but cultural and political; he now moved in circles infused with large doses of anarchism, utopianism and expressive fulfilment, a desire to create art and make one's own life and lifestyle a form of art. In these circles, of course, Gross's influence and importance was acknowledged, even if he was evaluated negatively.[90] I believe the 'utopianization' of Gross's thinking during the last decade of his life was related to his stigmatization in his own professional field. He may have interpreted his professional predicament as a liberation from the shackles of *vaterrechtliche* authoritarianism, which simultaneously liberated his mind from the intellectual conventions created and shaped during the process of his institutional socialization into the medical profession. When he no longer attempted to fulfil the social role of a physician, he was free to pursue interests that nourished his imagination and prompted him to develop psychopolitical ideas directed at radical, so far unrealized, possibilities. He was now concerned not only with what is – matters of fact – but also with what ought to be. It was the transformation of society and human life which preoccupied his mind during the last ten years of his life.

Utopianism in Gross

There are a number of Gross scholars who have characterized his thinking as 'utopian', but, as far as I know, they have not undertaken a more detailed analysis of the elements that made up his utopianism.[91] For obvious reasons, Gross's social and political views are usually contextualized by referring to the anarchist circles in which he moved.

In Chapter 1, I presented my thesis that there are four basic assumptions that characterize utopianism in the psychodynamic tradition: the idea of inner transformation; a belief in the interconnection between the structure of personality and the structure of society; the anthropological conception of illness; and an antagonistic attitude towards historical time. In Gross's thinking, we can easily find all these assumptions or beliefs. He held that humans are able to change their understanding of reality if they are given a chance to discard false values and false modes of thinking and acting. As a firm believer in the ideas of innate morality and the original harmony of drives, he was convinced that there is an authentic or true self that is altruistic, co-operative and prone to relate to others on an equal, reciprocal basis (*Wille zur Beziehung*). And he also believed that only self-knowledge and true understanding of human nature can lead into changes in society and culture. Conversely, patriarchal social structures mould people's personality and socialize them into a moral universe that is deeply flawed in its ideological sustaining of rigid hierarchies, a near-total rule of men over women and children, and pathological suppression of Eros, by which he meant not only sexuality but relatedness in a psychological and anthropological sense.

Gross was a psychodynamic utopian also in his belief that individual psychopathologies should be analysed and healed in the larger context of society and culture. He forcefully advocated the view that the pathogenic patriarchal society breeds illnesses and creates mental habits that are detrimental to human flourishing. Like most psychoutopians, he held the family to be principally responsible for instilling false values and modes of thinking into children, who in their early life have to adopt a conventional pattern of behaviour and adjust to a social reality founded on inhuman principles of life. Thus it was not so much individual pathologies as the pathogenicity of the whole society that Gross considered the most urgent problem. Lastly, Gross discounted or rather ignored Marxist, degenerationist (etc.) notions of historical cum biological determinism, and promoted the profoundly utopian view that, far from historical contingencies shaping the innermost kernel of the human psyche, it is the universal and transhistorical constituent of the human condition that in the end will prevail and bring about a new society where true human needs and values are realized. Even if he supported Communism late in his life, he felt much more at home in anarchist circles, where the idea of the innately social nature of humans was typically connected with an understanding of social change and inner change which overlooked the preparatory work (the forces of ideology and historical analysis) in favour of the ultimate result of change (a society or community based on the full realization of an essentially good human nature).

Gross, like the other psychodynamic utopians portrayed in this book, did not only hold these four assumptions, but he also held context-bound beliefs that were unique to him. One crucial factor conducive to Gross's utopianism was that, around 1905, he began to socialize more and more with artists, political activists, writers and 'dreamers of a New Age', as Martin Green has called them.[92] His own major scene was no longer a clinic but a café, and I believe there is no doubt that the long nights he spent in coffee houses in Munich, Vienna and Berlin shaped his utopian visions. He was stimulated by drugs, but also by endless discussions he had with his friends, lovers and basically anyone who joined the group that gathered in these coffee houses, some of which were open all night. Ernest Jones writes in his memoirs that Gross's 'analytic treatments were all carried out at a table in the Café Passage, where Gross spent most of the twenty-four hours – the café had no closing time'.[93]

In a way, and I am not saying this to belittle Gross's utopian ideas, his type of utopianism can be called coffee-house utopianism. It seems to me that he needed constant face-to-face interactions with other dreamers in order to feel sufficiently inspired and driven to experiment with ideas. Keeping himself awake long nights with the help of cocaine, cigarettes and coffee, his utopian imagination was nourished by his appetite for free psychological analyses, monologues, dialogues, polyphonies, and for extraordinary life stories and anecdotes of eccentric bohemians whose company he sought, and who in turn were attracted to him. The founder of Dadaism, Hugo Ball, who frequented the same cafés in Munich where Gross spent most of his time, noted in a letter to his sister that the café is the place 'where my friends, newspapers, and new ideas are'. Ball even wrote an ode to the café: 'We can do without everything – except, of course, our coffee (enchanting olive ink, ringing the interior) and our café'.[94]

Gross clearly preferred an informal coffee-house setting to the professional doctor-patient interaction. He never had a private therapeutic practice, which indicates that he disapproved of such a formal medical setting, or that he was simply incapable of, or uninterested in, conducting a life that would revolve around schedules, appointments, self-control and the whole tedious regularity of a middle-class life. It has also been said that he did not want to be a therapist treating people (psycho)medically, because he believed he could change people through his teachings and through his influence as a moral and philosophical guide to a better life.[95]

One can even claim that it was better for all concerned that he did not treat patients on a regular basis after he left Kraepelin's clinic, or after he was ousted from his job there. Throughout his life, his treatment of his female companions was characterized by therapeutic irresponsibility, which resulted in the suicide of Lotte Hammer, the death of Sophie Benz and the callous treatment of another lover, Regina Ullmann. Sophie Benz's death in 1911 led to a police investigation and an arrest warrant, but Gross managed to escape the police first by voluntarily entering a sanatorium in Stenhof near Vienna, and then by travelling to Switzerland and France. The investigation was dropped when his father intervened and assured the authorities that his son's condition had improved.[96]

Another situationist factor in Gross's life which moulded his utopianism was his long-lasting struggle with patriarchal respectability in general and the paternal figure of his father in particular. When he developed the philosophy of 'repress nothing', his ideas were bound to clash with the 'philistine' values of his social environment, including with his father. Hans Gross went so far as to have him incarcerated and placed in a sanatorium against his will in late 1913, but I believe it would be unsound to see this seemingly brutal act as nothing but the wicked expression of an authoritarian father's will to control his son's life. True, in his last testament, Hans Gross had disinherited his son and declared that after his death his son should be placed under guardianship and sent to a mental institution. But he seemed to have believed in Jung's diagnostic verdict of his son, which prompted him to regard Otto as incurably insane. Hans Gross was also concerned with the plight of his grandson Peter, whom he had made his heir, and whom he wanted to take away from the custody of his biological parents Otto and Frieda Gross. Otto Gross was indeed made legally incompetent after he was arrested by the police in Berlin in November 1913, and even after his father's death in 1915 another guardian was appointed to him. Hans Gross died an embittered and disappointed man, and in his last will he wrote of his son that

> I can say here that my son is a highly gifted person, endowed with genius, but in him are to be found all the criteria of madness listed in Paragraph 773 of the Civil Code which defines madness.[97]

Gross never succeeded in attaining full citizen's rights again. This struggle with his father and the world he represented had an impact on almost everything Gross wrote during the last decade of his life, and even if the immediate conclusion one is inclined to draw from this fundamental conflict is that it made Gross's life difficult and troublesome, one could also assert that he needed a mighty opponent in the figure of his father in order to be fully convinced of the validity of his own ideas. In a way, Hans Gross was a perfect enemy to his son, and after the father's death the son lost the adversary who had haunted him, but who had also driven him to seek alternatives to the bourgeois order he detested so much. Emanuel Hurwitz, who knows about the relationship between the father and the son more than most Gross scholars, suggests that his father had become an important part of Otto Gross's self-understanding, and that the death of Hans Gross led into the disintegration of the son's identity.[98] There is no doubt that Hans Gross exerted an important negative influence on Otto Gross when the latter portrayed his dismal picture of the *vaterrechtliche* society. Hans Gross inspired his son to create utopian alternatives to his detestable anti-utopia.

I shall now take a closer look at the key issues in Gross's utopianism, starting with his contacts with German anarchists.

Anarchism and 'mutual aid'

Gross started to socialize with anarchists probably in 1905, when he met the writer Erich Mühsam in Ascona. Together with Gustav Landauer, Mühsam represented the most influential group of German anarchists, and he played a leading role in the Socialist Munich *Räterepublik* (the Council Republic) after World War I (he was murdered by Gestapo in 1934). As Gottfried Heuer suggests, it is probable that Gross was introduced to the anarchist theories of Max Stirner and Peter Kropotkin through Mühsam, one of the most important anarchist intellectuals in the German Reich, who became one of Gross's closest friends and comrades.[99] Together with the writer Johannes Nohl, Mühsam founded the anarchistic Tat-Gruppe ('Action Group') in Munich in 1909. Mühsam's group was affiliated with Gustav Landauer's *Sozialistischer Bund*, which was one of the few organized anarchist groups in the Wilhelmine Germany. Mühsam had plans of founding a journal together with Gross, who was involved in the activities of this small Tat-Gruppe, which from 1911 onwards also included Franz Jung.[100] When Jung, who became perhaps Gross's closest friend for the last ten years of his life, moved to Berlin, Gross followed him. When Gross was arrested by the police in Jung's flat and taken to a private mental institution in Austria under guard, it was Jung who initiated an international press campaign for the release of his friend in late 1913.[101]

In December 1913, when Gross, who was now a mental patient, was interviewed by psychiatrists on behalf of the district court (*Bezirksgericht*) in Tulln, he announced: 'I have only mixed with Anarchists and I declare myself to be an Anarchist'.[102] After this statement, he called himself a psychoanalyst who had learnt through experience that the prevailing order of the family was a bad one; that nobody could escape the (detrimental) influence of education; that he believed in innate morality that is in contact with innate sexuality; and that the only one who had made these observations was the national economist Kaspar Schmidt – that is, Max Stirner.

Max Stirner was a German political writer and a teacher whose main work, *Das Einzige und sein Eigentum* (*The Ego and His Own*, 1844) aroused the wrath of Karl Marx, who devoted much of his severe criticism of 'German ideology' to Stirner in *The German Ideology* (1845). Stirner was an outspoken radical theorist who (most probably) influenced Nietzsche, and who is now closely associated with anarchism, a political theory that opposes the state, the coercive rule of the government and bureaucratic organizations. Scholars of anarchism have emphasized that, as an extreme form of libertarian socialism, the classical anarchism of the nineteenth and early twentieth centuries was not advocating chaos or disorder; rather, William Godwin, Pierre-Joseph Proudhon, Michael Bakunin, Peter Kropotkin and other anarchist writers in the heyday of anarchism wanted to create a free society without the state, but not without an order.[103] In an anarchist society, coercive authority is replaced by its 'natural' substitute, comradeship, which is based on the belief in the capability of people to impose moral rules on themselves and to create closely-knit voluntary relationships. Thus, classical anarchism promoted a society held together by moral self-direction, which is manifested in voluntary relationships and organizations.

The basic ideas of perhaps the most important 'classical anarchists' were not identical, but they were all committed to the theory of freedom, which they regarded as inviolable, and which they wanted to validate with the help of science, especially biology and anthropology. The anthropological assumption of later anarchists (especially Bakunin and Kropotkin) has its roots in Aristotle's conception of the human being as a *zoon politikon*, a political animal. Bakunin and Kropotkin did not necessarily believe that people are naturally good, but they did believe that they are naturally *social*.[104] They emphasized reciprocity as the essence of justice and developed the (Rousseauean) idea of social contract to the direction where it was conceived of as an agreement between free individuals, and not between individuals and the potentially coercive state, or between the potentially usurping capitalist and the oppressed worker.[105] The point in their glorification of the free individual is that such an individual identifies with his or her rational and moral self, and regards social interdependence not only as unavoidable, but also desirable. As George Crowder has argued, their understanding of the authentic self has two elements, one being rationality and the other morality:

> I am free, for the anarchists, to the extent that I conscientiously govern my actions in accordance with moral rules. The good society is a realm neither of chaos nor of competition nor of purely procedural reason, but a moral order in which freedom implies virtue as part of its meaning.[106]

Thus the later classical anarchists saw freedom as a social virtue. Proudhon, Bakunin and Kropotkin were also secular, naturalist thinkers who placed high hopes in science, and Darwin's theory of evolution enabled Kropotkin and his contemporary anarchists to see natural laws as evolving through evolution. Conversely, they could argue that authoritarian political institutions were perverted outcomes of evolution, non-natural forms of social bonding. Kropotkin in particular had a Darwinian frame of mind, and his anarchist-evolutionary theory of 'mutual aid' had a great impact on the early twentieth-century anarchist thinking (see my discussion of 'mutual aid' below).[107] In the twentieth century, anarchist thinkers were more inspired by psychology than evolutionary theories (which by the turn of the century were hijacked by scientific racists of all shape and size), and Reich's and Fromm's psychopolitical theories appealed to some anarchists. One anarchist writer, Herbert Read, was inspired especially by Jung when he developed his educational ideas in the 1940s.[108] (Read was a member of the editorial committee which supervised the publication of Jung's *Collected Works*.)

Gross acquainted himself with anarchist tenets during the period of 'propaganda by deed' (about 1880 to 1910), when a number of terrorist acts were carried out in the name of anarchism. Although most anarchist writers repudiated violence and promoted moral change and education as the principal ways to create a free society, the more militant, often marginal anarchist groups were committed to 'direct action', and Gross was inspired both by the moral and the more directly subversive aspects of anarchism.[109] Kropotkin and Bakunin, who created the idea of 'propaganda by deed', both advocated revolutionary action, endorsing the belief that such an action is necessarily violent and demands victims. They were also fully aware of the inherent contradiction between revolutionary violence and their cherished notion of freedom as moral self-direction.[110] Their attempt to downplay the magnitude of interpersonal violence in the revolution reflects their difficulties in harmonizing the notion of the revolution with the notion of the moral order of a free society. Bakunin especially emphasized the need to heighten the revolutionary consciousness of the masses through armed struggle, whereas Kropotkin had a little more faith in the people's capacity for rational self-government. He believed that, when they are left to their own devices, 'the masses will act both efficiently and fairly' – they only need scientific education, which makes them more knowledgeable and virtuous.[111] Indeed, in their commitment to the secular science of ethics, Bakunin and Kropotkin believed that scientific knowledge is the only route to moral truths, and that a comprehension of moral truths is what makes one virtuous and authentic. This is a crucial part of their reasoning, because they needed to explain how a society without government could survive. If, as they claimed, people's natural inclinations are towards co-operation and voluntary relationships based on egalitarianism, then there would be nothing intrinsically utopian or unrealistic in their idea of social freedom. Yet, when it came to the integration of the violent revolution with this fundamental goal of moral self-direction, the dilemma remained unsolved. As George Crowder puts it, 'revolution is, in fact, unavoidably in conflict with those goals, less a structural component of their theory, as it is of Marxism, than a cry of frustration'.[112]

A central anarchistic tenet to which Gross adhered concerned morality: like Proudhon, Bakunin and especially Kropotkin, Gross believed that humans are naturally moral – to these anarchists, morality is not a cultural achievement but a human universal.[113] The central problem for anarchists was not only that all existing forms of government were coercive and therefore unjustified, but also that coercive institutions corrupted morality, including the sense of justice. Without an articulation of the core belief in the innately social nature of humans, anarchism would collapse as a political theory. If human societies attempted to attain the state of justice, stability and peace without a government, they would fail miserably (as Thomas Hobbes convincingly argued in his *Leviathan*, 1651), unless citizens were bound together by a voluntary contractual agreement based on natural comradeship. And to assume that there exists a natural comradeship is to assume that humans are innately or naturally moral. This is the basic ethical assumption of classical anarchism, and one can easily find it in Gross's texts: in the heart of Gross's vision there is the idea of the moral sense, which is buried under the pathological layers of patriarchal sociocultural evolution.

Gross was never what we would nowadays call a 'social constructivist' or cultural determinist – someone who believes that human psychology is wholly created by the historically specific sociocultural conditions. In his early work, Gross's psychiatric and psychological language is tinged with biological theories, concepts and assumptions, and he never abandoned his belief in a human nature that remains essentially the same throughout time. Already in his psychiatric writings, he was keenly interested in the biological aspects of morality, and he conjectured that the instinct to imitate others is the foundation of higher social feelings and concepts, such as empathy. The instinctual ability to imitate also explains the development of language, as he argues in a paper devoted to the 'biology of language apparatus'.[114]

In Gross's late utopianism, humans would help each other because they have a natural inclination to do so. He referred to the Russian-English anarchist (and prince) Peter Kropotkin's notion of mutual aid when he discussed the social aspects of inborn ethics.[115] Kropotkin was a naturalist who was inspired by Darwin's evolutionary theory, and who founded his idea of mutual aid, which in present-day evolutionary theory is called 'reciprocal altruism', on Darwinism.[116] (Darwin himself did not write much about moral emotions, but he thought that they were universal products of natural selection, that is, adaptations.) Before Kropotkin, the French anarchist Proudhon had used the term 'mutualism' to denote his understanding of anarchism. By mutualism, Proudhon referred to the voluntarist organization of society based on equal exchange, reciprocity and justice, and in its application of the principle of equilibrium in daily life, it is an expression of moral self-direction.

Gottfried Heuer has rightly emphasized the importance of Kropotkin's idea of mutual aid to Gross's thinking.[117] All I want to add to his discussion is that Kropotkin belongs to an intellectual tradition which advocates naturalist morality and locates the origins of moral ideas within universal human emotions. As George Crowder has observed,

> among Kropotkin's contemporaries the search for a scientific grounding for morality to compensate for the erosion of the traditional religious base was widely accepted as a legitimate and necessary enterprise.[118]

The evolutionary moral view promoted by Kropotkin is one in which social co-operation, and not only individualist competition ('struggle for survival'), is rooted in nature, both animal and human nature.[119] In his *Ethics*, he wrote that

> nature is the first ethical teacher of man … The social instinct, innate in men as well as in all the social animals … this is the origin of all ethical conceptions and all subsequent development of morality.[120]

Kropotkin's understanding of the 'struggle for survival' differed crucially from that of Social Darwinists in that he saw it as a 'struggle *against* adverse circumstances rather than between individuals of the same species'.[121] What made his evolutionary thinking essentially optimistic, if not utopian, was that he suggested a 'teleological progress to ever more natural cooperation'.[122] And when Gross discussed the implications of an inborn ethic for the establishment of a new social order based on the free flow of Eros, he was following along the same line of evolutionary thinking. He had first expressed this idea in one of his earliest publications in 1902, when he had claimed that 'the sense of justice is born out of primitive instinct'.[123]

For Gross, Kropotkin's key assumption about the 'instinct for mutual aid' provided the framework for his utopian vision of human flourishing in a free society where all true, authentic needs and desires are fulfilled. The notion of reciprocal altruism is not the only 'axiom' in Gross's moral thinking, since he also needs to make two substantial if only implicitly articulated claims about the realm of needs and desires. First, he claims that what is good is natural (this is called 'moralistic fallacy'), which means that he naturalizes the morality of 'mutual aid' (altruism, co-operation and solidarity) and presents this morality as rooted in human nature. Second, he needs to make the opposite claim, namely that what is bad is unnatural. Therefore, all that he subsumes under the category of *das Fremde* (the Strange) represent to him an unnatural mode of being. Will to power, for example, has its source in the perverted morality created and sustained by the *vaterrechtliche* social order. Indeed, the 'Father Right' itself corresponds to the unnatural state of humanity, while the preceding 'Mother Right' signifies to Gross a state of natural, good morality.

Inevitably, Gross's moral assumptions or 'axioms' governed the ways in which he treated social, political and psychological issues, and the elucidation of these assumptions can clarify and explain the basic characteristics of Gross's anarchist frame of mind. Following the ideals of classical anarchism, Gross and his friends defied the coercive government, created networks of voluntary relationships and dreamed of a society built on the principle of total freedom. To Gross and his anarchist friends, anarchism was appealing not only because it represented a radical form of socialism, but also and especially because it signified non-conformism and an anti-philistine attitude towards the bourgeois normality. At one point, Gross toyed with the idea of founding a school of anarchism at Ascona, one of the centres of 'bohemian anarchism' in Europe.[124] It was his embrace of bohemian-anarchist tenets, as well as his friendship with anarchists, which led Gross's way of thinking to more radical paths.

The Radicalization of Gross's Psychopolitical Thinking

True to his disdain of middle-class values that put a premium on stability and order, Gross remained a restless wanderer for the rest of his life, moving from one place to another. His move to Berlin in 1913 probably increased his inclination to (psycho)analyse society and to create ideas of a better world, for he wrote most of his psycho-political texts during the last seven years of his life (1913–20). In 1913 alone, he published five papers in the radical Berlin journal *Die Aktion*. When World War I broke out, he served in military hospitals in Austria, Hungary and Slovene, and for a while his condition improved. But, as Martin Green has noted, 'it was not in fact very long before Gross was again addicted; and in early 1917 he was judged incapable of medical service, either military or civil'.[125] In 1917 and 1918 he spent much of his time in Prague, Vienna and Graz. In autumn 1919, he returned to Berlin, where he had become involved in Berlin Dada together with Franz Jung. As Jennifer Michaels has noted, Berlin Dada was more political than Dada in Zurich,[126] and some of the leading members of this 'movement', such as Franz Jung, Raoul Haussmann, and Richard Oehring, were influenced by Gross's ideas on sexual revolution, liberation of instincts and inhibitions, and his basic bipolar conception of the 'Own' and the 'Strange' (*das Eigene und das Fremde*). It was no coincidence that the members of Berlin Dada were attracted to Gross's political and utopian ideas; the relations between Dada and contemporary anarchism were close, as Hubert van den Berg has demonstrated in his historical study of Dada in Zurich and Berlin.[127]

Gross's psycho-political manifesto, and a motto for his growing affinity with radical solutions, is the sentence he wrote at the beginning of his 1913 paper on the 'overcoming of cultural crisis': 'The psychology of the Unconscious is the philosophy of the revolution'. This sentence is a succinct expression of Gross's ambition to marry psychoanalysis to anarchist politics. He elaborates his motto as follows: psychoanalysis is the

> ferment of rebellion within the psyche, a liberation from individuality that is bound to one's own unconscious. Its calling is to make way for the freedom within – to prepare for the revolution.[128]

Gross envisaged psychoanalysis becoming a tool for the revaluation of all values, and he saw Nietzsche's ideas about the hidden recesses of the soul, combined with Freud's psychoanalytic technique, rendering possible for the first time the liberation of the unconscious as an object of empirical knowledge. To have access to the unconscious meant that it had now become possible to know oneself. This amounted to nothing less than the birth of a new ethic. But the serious problem with the construction of a new ethic based on Nietzsche's insights and Freud's technique is that psychoanalysts, including its founder, have rejected the revolutionary potentiality of their doctrine.[129] Therefore, a new kind of psychoanalysis is needed, a psychoanalysis that is put in the service of the revolution. Needless to say, Gross thought of himself as the creator of such a revolutionary psychoanalysis.

At the very end of his life, Gross elevated psychoanalysis as the means whereby the 'horrible process of the hardening of the soul, alienation and a systematic self-education to egoism'[130] could be followed and analysed. The darkest, most horrible experience for the psychologist of the unconscious, writes Gross, is the terrifying, secret fight of man against man where the ultimate prize is the exclusive right over women. Fortunately, 'the psychoanalyst knows the latent unconscious death wishes of a friend towards friend, a comrade towards comrade'.[131] It should be noted that it was neither Freud nor Jung whom Gross referred to in his psychopolitical texts. Rather, he took an important concept, will to power, from Alfred Adler, who in his psychoanalytic work was much more concerned with education, socialization and the dynamics of social relations than most psychoanalysts. Adler's 'ingenious' conceptualization of the will to power provided Gross with a sound theory of the psychological damage caused by the patriarchal society obsessed with power.[132]

In another text written just before his death in 1920, Gross gives a short, schematic outline of the 'themes of revolutionary psychology'. He ascribes to psychoanalytic psychology the ability to methodically solve the inner conflict by bringing into the light of consciousness the foreign psychic bodies, *Fremdkörper*, the inauthentic products of inner fragmentation. Such a psychological method illuminates the chains of unconsciously and consciously adopted authority in each and every one – even in those who are most free.[133] For Gross, then, self-knowledge through the psychology of the unconscious signifies the anarchist-ethical preparatory work (*Vorarbeit*), which he identifies as the 'inner understanding' of the revolution and its deepest meaning, universality. This is Gross's utopian will to relatedness (*Wille zur Beziehung*), which can only be constituted with the help of psychoanalysis. As a *Vorarbeit*, psychoanalysis is absolutely crucial for the attainment of a new society. As he wrote in 1914, 'the clinic of a psychoanalyst is preoccupied with the suffering humanity itself'[134] – psychoanalysts have to heal the whole of humanity, no less!

In Berlin, Gross's psycho-political ideas were promulgated in the journal *Die Freie Strasse*, which was founded in 1915 by people who were actively involved in Berlin Dada, three of whom were former members of Mühsam's Tat Gruppe (Franz Jung, Oskar Maria Graf and Georg Schrimpf). Franz Jung and some other key members of Berlin Dada who published in *Die Freie Strasse* believed that the radical psychoanalysis of Gross would provide ammunition to the fight against social evils, and, at the same time, provoke the philistines.

Gross himself published an article on *das Eigene und das Fremde* (the Own and the Strange) in the fourth issue of *Die Freie Strasse* in 1916.[135] In his text, he discusses what Erich Fromm would later call the 'pathology of normalcy', tracing such a pathology to childhood. However, rather than focusing on the psychosexual development and the Oedipus complex, like mainstream psychoanalysts used to do, he describes the fear of loneliness in children, a fear which prompts them to internalize the false values and attitudes of their parents.[136] Children cannot live without parental affection, and so they have to become like their nearest and dearest (parents, sisters, brothers, peers, etc.) in order to feel accepted and loved. The state of inauthenticity (*das Fremde*) in children is caused by authority figures who value obedience to them above anything else, and who require children to submit unconditionally to the social reality constructed by conformist adults. Dreading loneliness, children have no choice but to internalize authority and become conformists themselves, and so the vicious circle will not be broken. Tragically, the dictates of conformism require children to suppress their own true selves, which results in an inevitable inner conflict between *das Eigene* and *das Fremde:* 'Be alone or become what we are' is the only solution offered to the child by the parents.[137]

For Gross, who in his conceptualization of the Own and the Strange was probably inspired by Nietzsche,[138] *das Eigene* (the Own) was a major symbol representing the authentic unspoiled self, which is still alive and vibrant in children, while *das Fremde* (the Strange) denoted everything that contributed to the alienation and the 'spoiling' of one's true self. Thus, altruism, solidarity and comradeship were essential parts of *das Eigene*, while egoism, will to power and the authoritarian control of women, children and sexuality represented *das Fremde*. The components of the Strange were products of cultural evolution gone astray, while the Own signified the true humanity buried under the pathological layers of sick society.[139]

The Mother Right

When he still lived on and off in Munich and Ascona, Gross learned about a theory which argued that woman was the source of the first civilization. This theory stimulated his utopian frame of mind more than any other theory or idea, perhaps with the exception of the psychoanalytic unconscious. The theory was created by the Swiss private scholar J. J. Bachofen, who in 1861 published a book called *Das Mutterrecht* ('Mother Right'). The most remarkable thesis in his book is that the present patriarchal organization of the family (in the West) was preceded by a matriarchal family that had been prevalent in ancient times.

Bachofen, who was a philosopher of history rather than an empirical anthropologist or ethnologist, claims in his book that humanity passed through three cultural stages, the first being a stage of polygamy and sexual equality, the second being matriarchal, and the third and now prevailing stage patriarchal.[140]

Bachofen asserted that in the earliest history of humanity there was no organized society nor the institution of marriage, but people lived in a state of promiscuity and, like dogs, copulated in public (this stage is called 'hetaerism' or the 'tellurian stage' by Bachofen). This lowest stage of human existence was then replaced by the elementary form of society, matriarchy, in which women ruled in the family, in society and in the religious sphere. But, as the earliest stage of unregulated sexual relations was replaced by matriarchy, the matriarchal society (the 'lunar period') was replaced – when it degenerated to the lower form of Dionysian matriarchy – by patriarchy (the 'solar period'), which in Bachofen's evolutionist view represents a higher form of society than the earlier stage of the Mother Right.

Bachofen's engaging arguments are long on imaginative speculation and short on historical evidence. He based his theory on his interpretation of myths, accounts of cults and archaeological artefacts of feminine divinities and goddesses of ancient Egypt and pre-Hellenic peoples in ancient Greece, which allegedly gave evidence for the existence of matriarchy. He was not alone in arguing that matriarchal kinship patterns had prevailed in ancient societies: the pioneer American anthropologist Lewis Henry Morgan, who in the mid-1800s studied the Native Americans (especially the Iroquois Indians) living in the state of New York, classified the cultures of the world into progressive stages and was among the first scholars to develop a historical genealogy of the family.[141]

Bachofen's and Morgan's theories on matriarchy and the history of the family were first accepted by many scholars who were 'pioneering the new discipline of anthropology along evolutionary lines (including John Ferguson MacLennan, William Robertson Smith, Sir John Lubbock, Herbert Spencer [etc.])'.[142] However, by the early twentieth century these theories were discredited by most anthropologists and historians, partly because *all* theories of cultural evolution began to be criticized at that time by the younger generation of scholars, especially by American anthropologists (such as Franz Boas). The young Darwinian sociologist Edward Westermarck had attacked the theory of matriarchy in 1891 in his *History of Human Marriage*, and the growing dissatisfaction with the universalizing assumptions of evolutionary anthropology contributed to the rapid decline of Bachofen's and Morgan's theories. But, as we shall see, the theory continued to fascinate some Freudian and Jungian analysts, Wilhelm Reich, Erich Fromm and the Jungian analyst Erich Neumann[143] among them.

The theory of matriarchy had also caught the attention of Karl Marx, who late in his life had turned his attention to prehistory. Taking up where Marx had left this 'project', Friedrich Engels organized Marx's fragmentary notes and wrote *The Origin of the Family, Private Property, and the State,* which became an extremely influential book among Marxists who wanted anthropological, archaeological and classical studies to support their dialectical, materialist view on history and prehistory.[144] Engels based his observations on Bachofen's and Morgan's work, to which he made many positive references throughout the book. His point was to show that the patriarchal 'bourgeois' family, like private property, was a historical invention determined by new socioeconomic conditions that were conducive to the establishment of the institution of the 'modern' family. Engels's ideologically motivated affirmation of the theory of matriarchy gave it an explicitly political dimension, and 'it served to institutionalize the myth of matriarchal prehistory as a socialist origin story'.[145]

Although the theory of matriarchy began to be discredited by the academic community in the late nineteenth century, the scientific dismissal of the theory had little effect on the radical cultural and bohemian circles in Europe. On the contrary, Bachofen's historical myth stimulated diverse occult, neo-pagan and *völkisch* groups in German-speaking Europe, most notably the group called the Cosmic Circle, which was located in Munich-Schwabing and had connections with the bohemian colony in Ascona. Gross certainly knew and probably socialized with (some of those) people who were involved in this esoteric 'artistic mystery cult'. One of them was the Contessa Franziska ('Fanny') zu Reventlow, who moved effortlessly in artistic circles and inspired her famous lovers, including the poet Rainer Maria Rilke and the life philosopher and graphologist Ludwig Klages, who was a central figure in the Cosmic Circle.[146]

'Anti-bourgeois' people in German-speaking Europe were fascinated by Bachofen's theory, which appeared to demonstrate not only that the allegedly egalitarian matriarchal order of society constituted the 'original' form of the family, but also that there had been a 'pre-family' period in human history when both sexes lived freely in a state of promiscuity without any sexual inhibitions. In places like Ascona or Munich-Schwabing, there were artists, writers, occultists, life philosophers and others who rejected Judeo-Christian and Enlightenment traditions, worshipped Mother Earth and glorified the ostensibly primordial state of promiscuity, although Bachofen himself made it clear that matriarchy grew out of women's discontent with and resistance to the 'debasing state of hetaerism', when women were exploited and abused by men.[147] Bachofen's theory functioned in the minds of many enthusiasts as a 'good myth' in that it nourished their imagination, encouraged them to sexual and social experimentation, and made them realize that the masculine domination of women and children was not a natural fact but a result of the vicissitudes of history. In places such as Ascona, Bachofen's theory was put into practice when the 'original' state of formless, orderless (sexual) freedom was re-enacted in the form of orgies. In the early 1970s, the myth of matriarchy made a comeback of sorts in feminist circles, and it has adherents even today.[148]

Gross, whose understanding of Eros will be discussed later in this chapter, was one of the most dedicated adherents to the theory of *Mutterrecht* during the last ten years of his life, as his published writings amply demonstrate. Gross presented the theory of *Mutterrecht* as an anthropological fact, although by that time (the 1910s) it had already fallen into disrepute in academia. Bachofen's almost poetic rhapsodies about the 'lack of intestine strife and conflict' and about the 'air of tender humanity' in matriarchal societies must have found resonance in Gross, as did Bachofen's observation that the ancients 'regarded carnal and political emancipation as inseparable twin brothers'.[149] I believe Gross saw the earliest stage of human history as a utopian period of good-natured sexual anarchy, when, in the words of Bachofen, 'the only bond between creatures [was] that of Aphroditean desire'.[150] Following Bachofen, he saw matriarchy as a historical period when women enjoyed economic and thereby also sexual independence from men. In short, matriarchy represented to Gross the 'golden age and the paradise of the primordial time'.[151] As the historian of matriarchal myth Cynthia Eller has noted, it was the assumption about the harmony that existed between people and nature which appealed to many proponents of this myth.[152]

Gross conjectured that this paradisiacal period ended when the currently prevailing patriarchal order of the family was given a decisive impetus by the custom of the abduction of women by male warriors, who during war took women of the enemy camp as slaves (*Raubehe*). The institutionalization of the modern family has its roots in the abduction of women in the early history of humanity, which signified the origin of the patriarchal family. This assumption was very much in the air in the late nineteenth century, as Engels's book on the origins of the family testifies. In it, Engels refers to the British anthropologist J. F. MacLennan, who in the 1880s had argued that exogamy – the custom of marrying outside a specified group of people to which one belongs (e.g. family, clan or tribe) – was constituted by the abduction of women, because the scarcity of women obliged men to seek wives from other groups.[153] (In the early 1890s, the Darwinian sociologist Edward Westermarck proposed a theory which is now widely accepted by anthropologists: that exogamy arose in the aversion to marriage between blood relatives or near kin – horror of incest thus explains the custom of marrying outside one's own group.[154])

Taking MacLennan's theory about 'marriage by abduction' (*Raubehe*) as his (pre)historical point of reference, Gross claimed that the prevailing order of the family was founded on the exploitation of women, and that such an institutionally-sanctioned exploitation caused psychological damage to both men and women – the prevalence of the symbolism of rape and destruction in the human psyche gave evidence of the fact that 'inner conflict' determines or at least disturbs the lives of contemporary people to a large extent. The great tragedy inherent in the patriarchal family is that male sexual relation to women is basically a rape.[155] The patriarchal society of *Vaterrecht* (the 'Father Right') as portrayed by Gross is a veritable anti-utopia, a place where 'healthy' sexuality is suppressed, where women and children are the property of authoritarian husbands and fathers, and where alienation and inner conflict (between *das Eigene und das Fremde*) torments each and every soul. As he declared at the end of his 'classic' paper on the 'overcoming of cultural crisis': 'The coming revolution is the revolution for matriarchy'.[156] Regarding the coming revolution, Gross founded his optimism on the assumption that, all denials and distortions of this basic truth notwithstanding, humans are moral animals.

The Body Politic in Gross's Last Writings

Gross was a prolific writer during the last year of his life. A number of his articles were published in small, radical journals, and his last monograph (a collection of three essays on 'psychic conflict'), *Drei Aufsätze über den inneren Konflikt*, was published in Germany the year he died (1920). My suggestion that Gross's thought became increasingly utopian late in his life is based not only on these published texts, but also on two hitherto unknown texts which the Gross scholar Gottfried Heuer recently found in New York. Gross wrote these two texts, which are now published,[157] at the end of his life, and they are among the handful of writings where Gross truly pays attention to the wider social context, and not only to the family and the pathogenic nature of *das Vaterrecht*. These two texts are overtly political, as their titles indicate. In 'On the Problem of Solidarity in the Class Struggle' (*Zum Solidaritätsproblem im Klassenkampf*), Gross uses the terms 'capital' (*das Kapital*), 'economy' and 'economic order' (*wirtschaftliche Ordnung*), and refers to Lenin and Henry Ford. Anticipating Erich Fromm's critique of welfare socialism thirty to forty years later, he proclaims that, as Ford's automobile empire has demonstrated, it is possible for a capitalist to put an end to the class conflict 'as soon as he succeeds in bringing the families of all employees to the same economic level as that of the petty-bourgeois household'.[158]

Gross also points out that the class conflict will nevertheless persist, because the prevailing social order is profoundly unequal; the life-demands of the bourgeoisie are amply fulfilled in the capitalist society, while the *Lebensforderungen* of the proletariat remain unfulfilled. In a society where a segment of the working class has access to the basic goods in life, the class conflict will lose its revolutionary edge, because the divided workers, some of whom are materially privileged while the majority remains underprivileged, no longer have a shared sense of solidarity based on common will. It is obvious that Gross was no friend of reformist socialism, which sees the parliamentary step-by-step approach to a good society preferable to the revolution.[159] As a self-confessed anarchist who despised parliamentarism, he would not have applauded Swedish state-centred social democracy.

That Gross was not a mainstream Marxist revolutionary either becomes clear when one reads 'On the Problem of Solidarity in the Class Struggle' further. In it, he claims that, instead of fighting the owner of capital, the revolutionaries should fight a certain kind of personality that is driven by will to power (*der Wille zur Macht*). It is this power-mad *Typusmenschen* that all good revolutionaries should try to defeat, because as long as the principle of power dominates in a society, there is no fertile soil for Kropotkin's innate instinct for mutual aid, and the pure will to free relations (*der Wille zur freien Beziehung an sich*) will not be understood, let alone be taken seriously.[160] And as long as the power-mad *Menschenart* has hegemony, society is a battleground where fellow humans are regarded as enemies, and where even the most intimate human relationships are dictated by the authority of the most repulsive kind, that of men over women, and parents over children. This is of course the patriarchal familial order (*die Vaterrechtsfamilie*), the institutional matrix of the will to power. Nobody can escape the hegemony of the *Vaterrecht*, and so it is futile to place high hopes in the revolutionary fervour of the proletariat so long as both the bourgeoisie and the proletariat are under the all-encompassing hegemony of the will to power. Even the children of the working class are raised and educated according to the authoritarian principles of the *Vaterrechtsfamilie*.[161]

Gross's late utopianism comes to the fore in this short but remarkable text, where he declares that the precondition for liberation through revolution is the fundamental awareness that 'will to power is an unnatural result of an unnatural external influence, and that it absolutely violates the innate state and preformed design of the essence of humanity'.[162] Gross contends that this specific *Menschenart* is an unnatural creature, a sort of socioculturally determined freak or monster that has become dominant in a society alienated from the harmonious state of the primordial matriarchal society. This state of alienation is the result of the suppression of the authentic inner nature (*das Eigene*), which cannot make its natural plea for solidarity, co-operation and altruism heard in a society where men keep women on an economic leash. Women are under men's thumb economically, because working women lose their jobs, and thereby their economic security, when they get married and become mothers.

Here Gross raised an important issue, as historians of the modern family can easily confirm. At the time Gross wrote this text, very many Swedish women, for example, remained unmarried because they knew that once they got married and had children, the job market would become closed to them.[163] And that, in turn, meant that married women lost their relative autonomy by becoming dependent on other people, namely their husbands. Gross had a practical solution to this difficult dilemma women had to face: the establishment of maternal funds, *Mutterschaftskasse*. Maternal funds, which should be made as large as the German Communist Party itself, would make it possible for mothers to obtain economic security. Such funds would also guarantee that women could go back to their old jobs sometime after childbirth, because children would be collectively raised. While female comrades would have the right to motherhood, the party would assume the duties of the father. Gross wonders whether a new revolutionary leader would eventually arise from out of this *mutterrechtliche* spirit.[164]

Maternal funds and the ensuing practice of the collective upbringing of children might bring about a new social order where the patriarchal norm that holds women as the property of men would be abolished for good and replaced by a new norm, that of solidarity. Gross locates the naturally altruistic will to relatedness (*Wille zur Beziehung*) in the utopian state of *mutterrechtliche Kommunismus* that has once, in a primordial time à la Bachofen, existed as a real society.

I believe that, while the late Gross had little interest in theoretical Marxism, he favoured the Communists because they seemed to have a less patriarchal and paternalistic attitude towards women than other German parties had. Furthermore, the Russian Revolution appeared to signify the end of male dominance over women in one particular society. Women in the new Soviet Russia were clearly much more emancipated than women in capitalist societies, which prompted Gross late in his life to evaluate Communism and the revolutionary proletariat more positively. When the Communist journal *Sowjet* wrote an obituary of Gross in May 1920, the author of the obituary claimed that, right after the end of World War I, Gross had joined the Communist movement in Germany and volunteered to work as a physician in Russia, where he would have fought against the typhus epidemic there. Due to his ill health, his wish was not granted. Gross then decided to go to the Soviet Republic of Hungary, but by the time he reached the border the short-lived Communist rule in Hungary had collapsed.[165] Instead of participating in the concrete realization of Communism, Gross had to be content with preparing the way for his brand of Communism in Germany. As his *mutterrecthliche Kommunismus* revolved around the idea of emancipated Eros, I shall examine next his utopian ideas of sexuality.

The Two Sides of Eros

It was the woman, especially the woman as mother, who fascinated the psycho-utopian authors, even if, as in the case of Gross, it was the father and the patriarchal law and order principle – *das Vaterrecht* – that caused him trouble and provided him with a mighty opponent in the form of his father Hans Gross.[166] Gross and Jung were the two psychodynamic authors whose fascination with the feminine principle was most visible, Gross rhapsodizing about the emancipatory *Mutter-*

recht, while Jung theorized about the mighty archetype of the mother and the 'Great Mother'. As we shall see, Reich and Fromm were also attracted to the myth of primordial matriarchy and, like Gross before them, associated *Mutterrecht* with Eros, with unrepressed (genital) sexuality and egalitarianism in all spheres of life. The significance of sexuality to Gross's utopianism is plain to see: he was the first 'depth psychologist' who conceptualized the revolution as essentially the sexual revolution. According to his friend Franz Jung, he even wanted to revive the ancient matriarchal cult of Astarte and integrate it into contemporary life.[167] This interest in the cult of Astarte is the only indication of Gross having any interest in religion, except as an object of analysis (late in his life, he interpreted the 'Communist' symbols of paradise in Genesis[168]). And even in the case of Astarte, it was the powerful sexual element in this cult – especially the practice of orgies – that fascinated him.

I would suggest that there are two distinct yet interrelated elements in Gross's conception of the sexual revolution: sexuality is both a destroyer and a creator. But before I discuss these elements, I shall briefly refer to Gross's own sexual life. There is no doubt that he enjoyed the more carnal side of Eros, and had sexual intercourse with many women. He was obviously bright, good-looking, charming, a mesmerizing talker and psychologically extraordinarily 'profound'. Small wonder, then, that many women were attracted to Gross. He in turn loved women, and his use and abuse of cocaine makes sense from the perspective of male sexuality: it is a well-known fact that cocaine has a vitalizing effect on the genital sphere. I think this mundane aspect of Gross's utopianism has to be taken into account when one analyses his ideas. In a way, Gross lived a sexual life that many men dream about, but cannot ever live out. In other words, Gross dreamt of a new world where free sexual relationships would flourish, and where women could also have the kind of assertive and active sexual life they preferred.[169]

Gross not only enjoyed sex, he also elevated sexuality to a sacred principle and social force. Just like Reich from the late 1920s onward, Gross sacralized sexuality by seeing it not only as the ultimate well-spring for the good life, but also as a powerful medium of sociocultural transformation. However, whereas Reich was keen on conducting bioelectrical investigations into the physiology of orgasm and genital potency (sexuality without tears), Gross refrained from a crude medicalized approach to the sensual sphere of life, preferring to formulate Eros in a more mystifying if not poetic language, combining mystification with social-psychological and sociopolitical interpretations of free sexuality as a social adhesive if not panacea. And he wanted to differentiate his version of Eros from the reformist, more trivial and tame medical version, which stressed the importance of 'healthy' sexuality for human life in general and for marital bliss in particular. Compared to the Eros of most sexual enlightenment activists,

Gross's Eros was more dangerous, more unpredictable and more unrestrained – in a word, more Dionysian.

I contend that Gross's understanding of Eros was similar to that of Plato's in the 'state-utopian' *Republic*. In Plato's book, the role of Eros is that of a destabilizer and troublemaker: Eros disrupts the harmony of the soul, thereby threatening the stability and unity of Kallipolis (the 'Beautiful City'). As the philosopher David Roochnik has argued in his study of the *Republic*, it is precisely the authorities' failure to control sexual relations – Eros – that ruins the allegedly just city.[170] But the *Republic* is not about the necessity of controlling Eros in a society, for Plato's Socrates is aware that, since a philosopher is someone who desires wisdom and loves the sight of the true, philosophy *itself* is an erotic activity. Thus, philosophy enters the *Republic* with the introduction of Eros, which breeds factionalism, or dialogue between different kinds of human beings.

Inspired by Plato's depiction of Eros in the *Republic*, I believe Gross's conception of Eros is, like that of Plato, twofold. First, Eros is an 'anarchistic' destabilizer of the bourgeois order, a troublemaker and a destroyer of social control. Second, Eros or erotic activity connects human beings with one another on the deepest level of the psyche, thereby awakening the mystical sense of being at one with the whole of humanity (the dissolution of the conflict between *Eigenen und Fremden*). For Gross, then, the double role of Eros is that of the destabilizer of the profoundly inadequate social order and the creator of communicative connections between human beings. The role of Eros as the creator of human relations is in my view the more essential element in Gross's understanding of Eros, which he identified with Kropotkin's evolutionary-anarchist conceptualization of the instinct for mutual aid. The 'Kropotkinian' idea of relatedness (*Beziehung*) is a recurring theme in Gross's later writings, and I fully agree with Gottfried Heuer, who regards *Beziehung* as a key term for Gross.[171] Indeed, I would suggest that the will to relatedness (*der Wille zur Beziehung*) is at the centre of Gross's utopian vision, and that the importance of this principle helps us to understand the point he was trying to make with his exhortation of *das Mutterrecht* and matriarchal Communism as a remedy for alienation and deeply-felt loneliness that haunts all good people in a *vaterrechtliche* society.[172] In an important short paper on the 'functional mental education of a revolutionary' (1919), Gross stated that

> the will to relatedness in opposition to the will to power is unearthed as an elementary opposite of a revolutionary psyche to the well-adjusted – bourgeois – psyche, and indicated as the highest, most essential goal of the revolution.[173]

The significance of communicative connection, of being in touch with others on an equal level, intrigued and puzzled Gross right from the start. In his psychiatric article on 'affective rejection', he contended that

> no individual is capable of bearing a lack of contact over a long period of time; sooner or later he would join in a conversation with even his most hated enemy. One only needs to think of observations of prisoners in solitary confinement. Overvalued ideas are powerless in the long run against the most rudimentary social instinct, the drive to communicate.[174]

Also in an important article on dementia sejunctiva (1904), he referred to disturbances in communication to which physicians need to pay attention in their clinical work.[175] One might even say that his interest in Freud and psychoanalysis can be partly explained by his fascination with what he saw as the psychoanalytic concentration on the dialogue and on the symbolic significance of verbal utterances and body language. In his later writings, the role of Eros as the creator of connections brings a pronouncedly utopian element to his mode of thinking, in which true love and innate altruism are set against the tyranny of authority and selfishness.

Arguably, group sexual experiments that Gross may have been involved in at Ascona would have inspired him to conceive of sexuality in terms of comradeship, generosity and *gemeinschaftliche* happiness. As his friend Franz Jung noted, albeit in a mystifying and exaggerating tone, Gross built his ethics on the conception of sexual utopia which found one expression in the experience of orgy.[176] According to *Webster's Online Dictionary*,

> An orgy is a sexual activity in which four or more participants are present and involved in sexual activity with each other. In some cultures, it has been practiced as part of a communal ritual or religious practice ... Participation in an orgy is a common sexual fantasy. Most people have only seen an orgy in explicit films or pornography.[177]

The dictionary also refers to both 'technical' and psychological issues involved in an orgy:

> Practical difficulties in participating in an orgy include figuring out where all the arms and legs go, figuring out what positions work and in what complexity, and addressing in advance such issues as consent and jealousy. A 'drunken orgy' resulting from intoxication may leave the participants embarrassed and upset in the morning when the hangover strikes ... Figuratively, the word may also refer to acts of unrestrained indulgence, e.g. 'an orgy of destruction'.[178]

Orgy, then, seems to have characteristics both of group sexual activity and of religious ritual. This definition accords well with Gross's conception of Eros. In Franz Jung's view,

> the sexual revolution and utopia as orgy are an experience, the first conflict-free experience. Without ideas of possession, without judgement and without convention – it is nothing but liveliness, nothing but humane conscious existence.[179]

Gross's Eros, then, contains the 'anti-bourgeois' idea of an untamed collective form of sexuality – orgy – which binds humanity together in a manner that paves the way for the utopian state of the 'community of sexes' (*Geschlechtsgemeinschaft*), where nobody needs to suffer from loneliness.

For a sceptic, Gross's vision of collectivist, conflict-free sexuality with its sacralized element of relatedness demonstrates the extent to which his ideas were removed from the real world of sexual relationships with its endless discords, conflicts and competition. Unlike Darwin and Freud, who observed that sexuality is a battleground with winners and losers, Gross dreamed of a world where 'bourgeois' sexual jealousy and the competition for sexual partners would be replaced by the collective joy of sexual sharing, taking and giving. It would give full vent to polygamous sexuality which recognizes the anti-collectivist and potentially disruptive consequences of emotional attachments between two individuals. But in utopian communities that were established in North America in the late nineteenth and early twentieth centuries, it was the unwelcome phenomenon of sexual jealousy and sexual competition that brought serious discord to these communities and contributed to their downfall (this is what happened in the most well-known utopian community founded by a group of Finns in the late nineteenth century on the north-west coast of North America).[180] And Gross himself was not free from sexual jealousy, as the studies of his relationships with the important women in his life convincingly demonstrate.[181]

Gross's utopian motto of 'repress nothing' (*nichts verdrängen*) is hard to reconcile with social reality that constantly requires role-playing, conformity and various subtle forms of scheming, deception and self-deception – also, or rather *especially*, in the field of sexuality.[182] In a dialectical fashion that Plato himself might have appreciated, Gross's own construction of Eros the Creator is destabilized by Eros the Destroyer, albeit not the destroyer of social order, but rather the destroyer of precisely those human connections that Gross's own Eros ostensibly creates. Plato's lesson to Gross is that the latter's 'Beautiful City' is a stage, a dialectical moment in time (or, in conversation) that inevitably passes away.

Abolition of the Family

As I pointed out in Chapter 1, the family was the one and only social institution on which psychodynamic utopianism, unlike much of previous utopian thinking, truly reflected. Perhaps more than anyone else's, Gross's utopian critique was directed at the *vaterrechtliche* family, which he regarded almost as the source of all evil. In the early twentieth century, the medical and psycho-medical theoretical starting-point for the interest in the family varied from hereditarianism to environmentalism. Hereditarianism, in the form of degenerationism, for example, held sway until the 1920s, when more socially-oriented explanations began to gain ground in Western Europe. Gross originally endorsed the doctrine of degeneration that his famous father Hans Gross advocated so forcefully, even if his evaluation of the social value of degeneration was more positive than that of most of his peers.[183]

Late in his life, Gross addressed the elite of the proletariat in outspoken terms when he told them to put an end to their families.[184] His uncompromising opposition to the patriarchal family led him to propose a solution that would have amounted to the extinction of this fundamental social unit. It was as if he attributed all that was fake, distorted and sick to the patriarchal *Vaterrecht* of which he himself was a victim, while all that was true, authentic and beautiful had its source in the spirit of *Mutterrecht*. Such tendency to create binary oppositions is a characteristic feature in all utopian thought and, even beyond that, an essential element in Western intellectual tradition nourished by Christian and philosophical dualism (Descartes being the one thinker who gave the most substantial intellectual contribution to Western dualism).

Just like in the case of his conceptualization of the sexual revolution, Gross's way of presenting the family as solely a patriarchal instrument of oppression disregarded evidence that would have undermined his own position. He was not alone in evaluating the family as a historically determined rather than natural form of bonding. Most notably, Engels's theory-laden account of the history of the family was influential amongst the Marxist and radical intellectuals in Europe.[185] Psychoanalyst and socialist educator Siegfried Bernfeld, for example, presented the family as a reactionary institution that fosters egoism and obstructs social progress. Engels's account of the history of the family appeared to be much more appealing to the radical intelligentsia than, for example, Edward Westermarck's study of the history of human marriage, where Westermarck argues in a Darwinian-naturalist fashion that the family as a social unit has its roots in human nature, and that some version of the family is to be found in all known cultures in the world.[186] As we know today, Westermarck's theory of the family has been corroborated by modern anthropological and evolutionary studies, while the version that Engels – and Gross – propounded is evidently false.

Gross, of course, had ideological reasons for discounting the (patriarchal) family, but even if his observations were guided by his erroneous beliefs, one should not judge his views too harshly. At the time, the Western families were indeed deeply patriarchal, and women and children were more or less subordinated to the capricious will of the husband and the father. It was precisely this potentially oppressive dominance of men over women, and parents over children, which prompted the Zionist utopians and feminists in Palestine/Israel to think of alternatives to patriarchal families in the inter-war years.[187] The Israeli kibbutz movement was a social experiment in which the structures of the traditional family were abolished and children were raised collectively by professional caretakers in the utopian hope of creating a just and egalitarian society in the Promised Land. The published memoirs of kibbutz childhood testify to the bitter memories of lives damaged by the children's deprivation of parental affection and attention.[188] The ideology of raising children outside of the family unit ignored or disparaged the Darwinian view that the family is based on the universal sense of kinship between parents and their offspring. But the pioneers in Zionist utopia, while rigid and doctrinaire, had a desire to create a society quite unlike any other; a society where a gender-based inequality would be abolished forever. Even if their good intentions met with less-than-ideal results, one should be careful when judging the experiment itself with the benefit of hindsight. In a way, the collectively raised kibbutz children were guinea pigs in a failed social experiment, but the impetus for such an experiment grew in a society where women often experienced the family dynamics in ways that accorded with Engels's and Gross's conception of the family as a form of institutionalized despotism.

Gross opposed not only the patriarchal control of women, but also the almost total parental dominance of children. In his defence of the rights of children he clearly stood out from the majority of educated people of his time, including Freud. In 1908, he published a paper in which he described the plight of a nineteen-year-old young woman called Elisabeth Lang, who was his patient, but who was taken to a 'lunatic clinic' by her parents. Gross believed that the woman suffered from disturbed family dynamics, and that she was not mentally ill, only troubled by inner conflict caused by the parental influence. In his paper, Gross writes that the parents terminated the treatment that was going well, and that their decision to put their daughter in a clinic may have worsened her condition due to mental shock caused by the deprivation of her liberty.[189] As Gross revealed the true identity of his patient in his paper, it is probable that he did it in agreement with Elisabeth Lang, who may have wanted to publicize her own medical treatment in order to get out of the psychiatric clinic. Gross succeeded in his attempt to free her: his article won public attention and Ms Lang was eventually released from the clinic.[190]

This was not the only occasion on which Gross explicitly sided with children. His fundamental idea of the (inner) conflict between the Own and the Strange (*das Eigene und das Fremden*) had its psychological starting point in children's authoritarian milieu, which forces defenceless children to internalize 'psychic foreign bodies' (*seelische Fremdkörper*). These are elements of a foreign will, a will which in its absolute opposition to the child's own will brings about the first major inner conflict and, thereby, determines all future psychic phenomena derived from inner disintegration and the 'self-sabotage of the soul' (*Selbstsabotage der Seele*).[191] Gross saw the loneliness of children as the real cause of all neurotic anxiety and the ensuing formation of a specific character that is full of anxiety, despair and remorselessness.[192] He emphasized the simple and obvious truth that 'a child cannot live without love', a love that is absolutely unconditional, free from all parental demands and expectations. He also highlighted the significance of the mother for the wellbeing of her child: if the child's instinctual love for the mother remains unfulfilled, his or her little soul will die of psychic undernourishment.[193]

With all his exhortations about the dissolution of the traditional patriarchal family and his demands about bringing up children collectively, Gross, like the cultural conservatives, acknowledged and affirmed the crucial importance of the mother-child bond, and did not weigh the importance of the father-child bond. It seems he took it for granted that children are in need of maternal love rather than paternal love, and that, holding this truth to be self-evident, he expected mothers, not fathers, to be fully devoted to their children. Gross's emphasis on the traditional role of the mother tallies well with the ideals of contemporary 'bourgeois' families in many Western countries, where women were expected to sacrifice their own life in the public sphere (especially their careers) when they became mothers. But, as I hope has become crystal clear to the reader, Gross was a fierce opponent of the father's dominance in the family, and of the male rule in society as a whole, and his glorification of the mother can be partly explained by his commitment to the utopian belief that the ideal society is the matriarchal society. To Gross, the Mother Right was a symbol of utopia.

Conclusion: Revolution of the Unconscious

Over time, Gross's utopian inclinations did not show any signs of exhaustion – on the contrary, the years between the Russian Revolution and his death in February 1920 comprised a period of full-blown utopianism in his life. During this short period, Gross outlined his programme for the attainment of a classless matriarchal society free of restraints and inhibitions. What he regarded as a necessary means to achieve this ultimate goal was, first of all, the psychological analysis of the unconscious, which in its crucial contribution to the understanding of the sources and dynamics of the inner conflict is indispensable for the preparatory revolutionary work. But this was not enough, for what was also needed was the technique of psychological influence (propaganda and education), which must be employed to shape and activate the minds of the proletariat. What Gross especially had in mind were the elite groups of workers, those born revolutionaries who possess the inner strength to tear down the walls of patriarchal power, and to adopt a new attitude towards women, children and the social hierarchies.[194] Psychological analysis of all concerned needed to be conducted in order to see and explain the problem, while psychological influence on the key figures in the workers' movement had to be exerted in order to change their mode of thinking and, thereby, their whole understanding of reality.

As a 'revolutionary of the Unconscious', Gross had much to say about the psychological analysis of the inner conflict, but he said next to nothing about *how* to shape the workers' minds. This, of course, was what also puzzled Marx and Engels, who wanted to replace the 'false consciousness' of the workers with the revolutionary 'class consciousness'. They believed that as changes in the social order change the minds of men, it was crucially important to promote a radical sociopolitical change (Communist revolution) that would bring about a new kind of human being – a human being with a revolutionary class consciousness. Gross, on the other hand, was a psychoutopian in his belief that inner revolution is the prerequisite for the political revolution; that workers reared in patriarchy need to think, feel and act differently before they are capable of transforming society. As indicated by his many plans to establish journals devoted to the dissemination of anarchist and psychopolitical ideas, he seemed to believe that there are people in society who are in principle well-disposed to his basic message, it is only that this potential avant-garde needs encouragement and guidance from those who know what is good and what is bad for people.

With his psychopolitical idea of giving the 'functional education of the mind' (*funktionelle Geistesschulung*) a central position in the humanistic education,[195] Gross wanted not only to prevent the tragic development of inner conflict within children and youths; he also envisaged his psychoanalytic educational method to function as a transmitter of the contents of the unconscious to revolutionary consciousness. He did not give practical suggestions as to how to educate children in proper ways – should all children be psychoanalysed, for example? – but one can imagine that, with his psychodynamically-oriented anti-authoritarianism, his practical approach to education would have been similar to that of the British pedagogue A. S. Neill, who established an experimental school, Summerhill, in the early 1920s, and who was influenced by psychoanalysis and, from the 1930s onwards, by Wilhelm Reich's 'Grossian' views on upbringing and education.[196]

To change the mental habits of people is nothing short of difficult, and Gross's method of penetrating into the private sphere of his friends, comrades and patients, and inquiring about their most intimate secrets, was not always accepted. His friend Erich Mühsam recalled in 1929 that he broke off his analytic treatment with Gross 'when the physician [Gross] posed questions pertaining to the most secret issues of the erotic life and I replied with a brief explanation: "That's none of your business!"'.[197] (At that time, Mühsam was having a love affair – with Gross's blessing – with Gross's wife Frieda.)

Although a typical intellectual in his belief in the power of words, either spoken or written, Gross also differed from the majority of radical intellectuals (and psychoutopians) in his militant anarchism ('propaganda by deed'), which manifested itself in his willingness to create chaos in society by means of direct action, including sabotage. In the last paragraph of perhaps the last text he ever wrote, Gross refers to the sexual revolution and the ultimate goal in his utopian vision:

> The mission: to make individual cells of the social body an object of agitation and sabotage. To initiate a fight against the principle of the family, that is, against the prevailing family of the Father Right, on behalf of the Communist Mother Right.[198]

In the same uncompromising spirit, Gross had declared to the physicians who had interviewed him at the private sanatorium Tulln in 1913: 'As a matter of fact, I would like to live until my forty-fifth birthday; then I would like to perish [zugrunde gehen], preferably in an attempted anarchist assassination [bei einem anarchistischen Attentate]'.[199]

These are not the words of your mainstream socialist – they are in fact more radical and extreme statements than anything else I have come across in the field of psychological utopianism, perhaps with the exception of B. F. Skinner's radical vision of behavioural engineering in his utopian novel *Walden Two* (1948). Evidently, when Gross wrote these lines about the coming mission, he had nothing to lose, and he may have been well aware that he would not live long. In his own time, his psychoutopian vision remained a rather idiosyncratic, 'lonely' vision, and his utopian ideas failed to make a dent among his professional peers, including psychoanalysts.

While Gross was by far the most utopian of all psychoanalytically-oriented thinkers in his lifetime, he was not alone in speculating about matriarchal and patriarchal cultures and their respective configurations of complexes. Were there, for example, fewer neuroses and perversions in societies where people had a more tolerant attitude towards infantile sexuality? Many psychoanalysts, especially socialists, liked to think so. What they also suggested was that the so-called Western civilization, by contrast, suffered from neurosis due to the inordinate intensity of repression. The 'radical' Dutch psychoanalyst August Stärcke, for example, made a theory-laden observation that the period of industrialization in the West represents a regression to the anal stage, which according to the Freudian theory is the second pregenital stage of libido development.[200] The sombre message of social analysts such as Stärcke was that the sick society must confront its unconscious and acknowledge that its sickness is due to the repression of the natural flow of the libido. Following Freud, Stärcke believed that we will not become much happier with this knowledge about the culturally sanctioned control of sexuality, but at least the problem is brought to our awareness. We just have to stoically accept the fact that the life of a modern *Kulturmensch* is quite miserable. But Gross did not subscribe to this 'realistic' view of the human condition, and his understanding of psychoanalysis deviated radically from that of Freud and August Stärcke. He wanted not only to make psychoanalysis the scientific foundation of a new morality and a tool for diagnosing the sickness of society, but also a method to heal sick humanity and realize the utopian principle of hope – by force if necessary.

Gross's friends and lovers may have regarded his motto of 'repress nothing' as a beautiful manifesto of authenticity, freedom and sincerity, but in real life it led to all sorts of difficulties and emotional entanglements. To require others to reveal their inner life and live out their erotic and political fantasies is an impossible demand, because such a 'tyranny of intimacy' only institutes new norms in place of the old ones, and strives to destroy the boundaries between one's social roles and the private self.[201] If you are constantly asked to be authentic and spontaneous and put your emotions and intimate thoughts on display, it is not only extremely demanding and consuming, but may also be detrimental to your social relations and to the psychological need to remain at least to some extent unpredictable and opaque to others, especially when we feel threatened by the power of the predictive practices of others. Moral philosopher Alasdair MacIntyre has pointed out that we like to cling to the ideal of self-determination, which makes us reluctant to think of ourselves as subjects of external forces and as creations of others.[202]

Gross's ethic of absolute authenticity (repress *nothing*) is a testimony to his own alienation from reality. He was blind to psychological, social and political factors that to a certain extent mould our mental habits and require us to avoid speaking our minds and showing our true feelings on all occasions. Much of current psychological and evolutionary research suggests that, rather than displaying natural inclination to authenticity, we constantly deceive others and ourselves in subtle ways, and that this play-acting and lack of self-knowledge is part and parcel of our mental configuration that has slowly developed through millennia.[203] Gross's aspiration to change this configuration with his ethic of absolute authenticity was doomed to fail.

In 1917, the Austrian writer Max Brod met Gross in Prague, and the two men noticed that they had common interests in sexuality, psychology and anarchism. Together with Franz Kafka, who knew Gross especially through his many writings in the journal *Die Aktion*, they planned to publish a new journal with a Grossian title 'Bulletin for the Struggle Against the Will to Power' (*Blätter zur Bekämpfung des Machtwillens*).[204] This project came to nothing, but Brod wrote a novel, *Das grosse Wagnis* ('A Big Venture', 1918), which owes a great deal to the ideas of Gross. In his novel, Brod 'describes a bohemian community which is similar to the one in Ascona in its ideas, and the leader of the community, Dr Askonas, has traits of Gross'.[205] This bohemian community, called Liberia, appears to be a veritable utopia where everyone is equal and free, but below the harmonious surface there is friction and discord. Askonas's life philosophy is founded on the idea that everybody should give free rein to their instinctual urges and desires – repress nothing – but the protagonist of the novel, a musician, observes that Askonas's lust for women creates ill-feeling in the community. Askonas is married, but his love for another woman, Ruth, makes his own inner life conflict-ridden, because he can only make decisions that are detrimental either to his community or to himself. If he leaves Liberia with Ruth, who is marginalized in the colony, he betrays his life work, but if he decides to stay he has to repress his instincts – his love for Ruth. Askonas recognizes this unsolvable dilemma, and in despair he admits that 'you should think of the salvation of your fellow humans only after you have completed the difficult task of making your own life pure'.[206]

Askonas has founded the colony on the principle that a 'healthy society' can only be built on 'healthy relationships', but in the end he has to face the truth that, even though he himself has not experienced a healthy, sexually-fulfilling relationship that would be in harmony with one's instincts, he has tried to change the world. As Askonas cannot liberate himself, he cannot liberate others either, and so he knows that his utopian community is doomed. The narrator is sceptical towards Askonas's colony and his Messianic posture, but he is also fascinated by his ideas of salvation and *Gemeinshaft*. And although he dislikes the petty intrigues in the colony, the narrator attributes this problem not so much to Askonas but to the petty people gathered there.

It seems as if Brod wanted to show the inherent utopianism in any attempt to found a society on the tyranny of authentic emotional life: to elevate the liberation of the so-called instinctual urges to a norm and to a guiding principle is like building castles in the sand. The high-tide of reality will erode and eventually destroy the castle and ruin the lives of people who put their faith in a prophet whose eternal truths turned out to be pipe-dreams. Gross dreamed of a world where a 'healthy' instinctual life guarantees universal happiness, but his psycho-medical vision of a good life overlooks the possibility that what he regarded as 'natural' and 'healthy' is not necessarily the same as 'good' and 'desirable'. In his belief in the universal validity of his own cherished values, he was a true utopian. It is very fitting that perhaps the last words he wrote refer 'the Communist Mother Right',[207] a symbol of Gross's utopian society which would fully realize the principle of Eros and bring about the utopian state of reciprocal altruism, co-operation and solidarity. It is a message that still reverberates in the minds of those who believe that inner change can prepare the way for future happiness.

4 INDIVIDUATION AND 'NATIONAL INDIVIDUATION': UTOPIANISM IN CARL G. JUNG

> There are things that are not yet true today, perhaps we are not yet permitted to recognize them as true, although they may be true tomorrow. Therefore, every pioneer must take his own path ... Our age is seeking a new spring of life. I found one and drank of it and the water tasted good. That is all that I can or want to say.
>
> Jung, 1917[1]

Historian Sonu Shamdasani has noted that Carl Gustav Jung (1875–1961) has been called

> Occultist, Scientist, Prophet, Charlatan, Philosopher, Racist, Guru, Anti-Semite, Liberator of Women, Misogynist, Freudian Apostate, Gnostic, Post-Modernist, Polygamist, Healer, Poet, Con-Artist, Psychiatrist and Anti-Psychiatrist – what has Jung not been called?[2]

To Shamdasani's list, I would like to add that Jung has also been called *völkisch* scholar (by Richard Noll), pseudo-mythologist (by Herbert Marcuse), crypto-fascist (by Ernst Bloch), National Socialist (by Wilhelm Reich), sympathizer of Hitler and 'necrophilous character' – that is, a lover of death (by Erich Fromm)! As early as the 1930s, the German left-wing psychiatrist John Rittmeister accused Jung of 'archetypal mysticism', seeing 'in Jung's "ahistorical image-collectivism" the symptoms of the frightened and confused bourgeois response to the great social changes of the twentieth century'.[3] More recently, the German sociologist Heinz Gess connected Jungian psychology with neo-fascism and the New Age movements. Grounding his ideological critique on the critical theory of the Frankfurt School, Gess discounted Jung's archetypal theory as representing a legitimization of the capitalist society with its emphasis on the mythical, unchanging and eternal. In Jung's pursuit of organic, psychic wholeness, Gess detected distinct resemblances with Hitler's ambitions and, at the same time, a continuation of a fascist personality type.[4] Judging by these invectives, Jung must have been an abominable character indeed.

From the point of view of historical truth, how serious are these accusations hurled at Jung? Do they correspond to what we know about Jung's beliefs and intentions? Most importantly for our purposes, was his 'Utopia of Authenticity' addressed to only certain segments of society, such as pure Germans or the 'Aryan Race', with the exclusion of others, such as Jews or socialists? In order to answer these questions, I shall concentrate on Jung's writings, seminars and letters from the late 1920s to the end of World War II. I argue that this was a period during which Jung's ideas were most utopian and most political, since he envisaged something that I shall call 'national individuation' in Germany. But I shall not confine myself to a historical analysis of his utopian visions vis-à-vis Germany, partly because utopianism was an intrinsic part of his thinking irrespective of changing political situations in Germany or elsewhere, and partly because I argue that one cannot overlook his Swiss republican identity when his political, sociocultural and utopian ideas are under discussion.

Largely due to the fact that Jung was not a socialist nor a radical psychoanalyst, his psychoutopian ideas were not even recognized as a form of utopian thought until recently.[5] In stark contrast to the other psychoutopian authors discussed in this book, an examination of Jung's texts elucidates a mode of utopian thought that manifested neither socialist nor anarchist thought patterns but a conservative value system, which was prevalent among the German-speaking middle classes during the first decades of the twentieth century. Not only were Jung's theories suffused with psychological utopianism, it is this strong utopian strain in his thought that helps to explain why Jungian psychology has become relatively popular in recent decades. What most of all makes Jung a utopian writer is his imaginative application of his own archetypal theory to ideas that are related to personality transformation (individuation) and an ensuing cultural regeneration. But before I turn to his utopian ideas I shall give a short outline of his life and work.

From an Asylum Psychiatrist to the Wise Old Man: Jung's Life

Carl Gustav Jung was born in a little village (Kesswil) in canton Thurgau in eastern Switzerland in 1875.[6] His parents had come from Basle, and before Jung went to school, his family moved to the village of Klein-Hüningen, near Basle. His father, Paul Achilles Jung, was a highly-educated minister of the Protestant (but not Calvinist) Church, who had studied at the University of Göttingen and then abandoned his career as a philologist in order to become a member of the clergy. His mother, Emilie Preiswerk Jung, was herself the daughter of a clergyman, who was an expert on the Hebrew language and one of the first proponents of cultural Zionism. In 1884, Jung's sister, Johanna Gertrud ('Trudi') was born; she remained unmarried and, in her mature years, helped Jung with secretarial duties, and also took care of his children (she died unexpectedly during a 'routine' surgical operation in 1935).

Jung had a strong religious family background, for on his mother's side he had a total of six uncles who were members of the clergy. Unpublished interview materials and the first draft of Jung's memoirs indicate that his mother suffered from mental problems.[7] Emilie Jung was hospitalized for a few months when her son was about three years old, and she did not totally recover her health until her husband passed away in 1896 (Jung was then twenty-one years old). On all accounts, it seems that the marriage of Paul and Emilie Jung was not a success.[8]

In 1891, Jung went to the *Gymnasium* in Basle, and four years later he began to study medicine at the University of Basle, which for a long time had been the only university in Switzerland. By choosing to study medicine he followed in the footsteps of his famous paternal grandfather, Karl Gustav, who was of German origin. K. G. Jung became a professor of medicine (in 1822) and a rector of the University of Basle. He was a very well-known figure in Basle, a man of progressive ideas and a somewhat eccentric character.[9] Nevertheless, the younger Carl Gustav's decision to study medicine did not come easy, for he was also interested in the humanities, especially archaeology, and in natural sciences. This is how the Jung scholar Richard Noll describes the twenty-year-old medical student who was just beginning his adventures in the spirit world by participating in séances:

> He had already reached the commanding height and bulging weight that framed him throughout most of his life. His hair was cropped military short in the Prussian style. While youthful and unsure of himself, to most people he seemed stiff, perhaps a bit arrogant ... Girls were enthralled by his height and broad shoulders, his piercing intellect and delightful wit, his promise as a man and as a mate. And women who were a bit older than this wunderkind admired all this and more, for they sensed his acute emotional sensitivity, an alluring quality – almost an aura – that set him apart from most men.[10]

Later in his life, Jung's outward appearance gradually changed from the robust Prussian-style physical exuberance to the embodied wisdom of the 'Wise Old Man'. He seemed to radiate some sort of animal magnetism that was irresistible to many women. In Zurich, groups of (upper-class and upper-middle-class) women that gathered around him began to be called the Jungfrauen, the Vestal Virgins or the Valkyries by those (usually men) who looked at the female veneration of Jung with more sceptical or jaundiced eyes.[11]

Jung was at the end of his studies when he had to read a textbook of psychiatry for the state examination. The book was written by Richard Krafft-Ebing, whose *Psychopathia Sexualis* from 1886 has become a classic study on 'sexual pathologies'. According to Jung's own words, he had attended the lectures on psychiatry without any enthusiasm and was not thinking of specializing in the subject. Then, out of the blue, Krafft-Ebing's book turned out to be an 'illumination', as the author made him realize that in psychiatry the two great currents of Jung's interest, nature and spirit, could flow together and unite in a way that Jung found intriguing. After this unexpected reaction, Jung was determined to become a specialist in this 'obscure by-path' of medicine.[12]

After his graduation, Jung became an assistant at the Burghölzli mental hospital in Zurich in late 1900. Burghölzli, which, as we know, played a part in Otto Gross's life, was an internationally famous psychiatric institute, and its innovative director Eugen Bleuler was the first representative of academic psychiatry who encouraged his staff to cautiously apply the psychoanalytic methods of Freud to the treatment of mental patients. It was above all due to Bleuler's contribution that at the turn of the century the Burghölzli started to attract European and American psychiatrists who wanted to learn the new methods that Bleuler and his staff were employing there. Jung worked at the Burghölzli for eight years and acquired a solid psychiatric reputation with his studies on word association and schizophrenia (or dementia praecox), which led him to postulate a theory of complexes. In 1902, Jung earned his MD – the subject of his dissertation was his cousin's mediumistic fantasies[13] – and the following year he married Emma Rauschenbach, daughter of a wealthy industrialist. Two years later (1905) he became a lecturer (*Privatdozent*) in psychiatry at the University of Zurich and a senior physician at the Burghölzli. Of his two most famous patients at the Burghölzli, one was Otto Gross and the other was a young, bright Russian-Jewish woman, Sabina Spielrein. During Jung's psychotherapeutic treatment of Spielrein, who began to study medicine in Zurich, they gradually became attracted to each other. The discreet romantic relationship most probably prompted Jung to conceive the idea of 'countertransference' (the analyst develops strong feelings towards the patient), which has become part of standard psychoanalytic language. The relationship ended when Spielrein, disappointed at Jung's reluctance to leave his wife, as well as engrossed in her own career, moved to Munich and then to Vienna in 1911 after attaining her medical degree. Through most of his married life, however, Jung had (at least) two female companions: alongside his wife, he shared his intimate moments with Toni Wolff, a patient of Jung's who became 'a close friend and colleague' when his relationship with Spielrein was cooling off in 1910–11.[14]

In 1906, Jung sent his book 'Diagnostic Association Studies' (*Diagnostische Assoziationsstudien*) to Freud (who already owned the volume), and the two men started to correspond. The following year they met for the first time at Freud's home in Vienna.[15] This meeting sealed their friendship and Jung's conversion to psychoanalysis. In 1909, Jung left the Burghölzli in order to keep a full-time private practice as a (Freudian) psychotherapist, although he remained affiliated with the hospital as a volunteer doctor. It seems that one of the reasons for his resignation was the increasingly strained relationship between Jung and the chief physician Bleuler, who in a letter to Freud in 1911 claimed that he had evidence of Jung's hatred towards him.[16] It is true that, until the end of his life, Jung's comments on his former chief were mostly tinged with hostility and bitterness, which is difficult to understand in the light of what we know about Bleuler's rather benevolent attitude towards his gifted younger colleague at the Burghölzli. In 1909, Jung was perhaps disappointed that, unlike himself, Bleuler had not become an eager supporter of Freud's psychoanalysis (Bleuler would never become a 'Freudian', although he had a high regard for many of Freud's theories). But Jung's relationship with Freud would also deteriorate. When he left the Burghölzli, he was the second most important member of the nascent psychoanalytic movement, but after only a few more years – at the beginning of 1913 – his already-strained relation with Freud broke off. Within a year, Jung, who at that time was the president of the newly-founded International Psychoanalytic Association, left Freudian psychoanalysis for good.[17] The reasons for the break are complex, not least because the spheres of the professional and the personal were totally intertwined in their relationship. What we are able to say is that Jung was not willing to remain a mere pupil of Freud, and that in addition to theoretical differences, they had a remarkably conflicting view of the whole raison d'être of psychoanalysis. While Freud wanted to limit its domain to the analysis of modern man and modern culture, Jung had a far more extensive ambition: to make psychoanalysis a cultural force, a modern symbolic form par excellence which was to combine the strengths of religion (*telos*, meaning) and *Wissenschaft* (analysis, understanding).

When Jung left the psychoanalytic movement in the spring of 1914 at the age of thirty-nine, he also gave up his academic position as *Privatdozent* and became preoccupied with his own mental life. In his memoirs, Jung has given a vivid account of how he went through a period of inner uncertainty and crisis, which he called his 'confrontation with the Unconscious'.[18] If we look at his 'external' life in this period (*c.* 1913–17), we can see that he kept his practice, travelled and even published some papers. When the war broke out, Switzerland received refugees from all over Europe, and Zurich became a cosmopolitan city with a host of avant garde artists, writers and poets (e.g., Dadaists), who upset the bourgeois respectability of that commercial centre. Jung, however, was too preoccupied with his own psyche and with the consolidation of the Jungian movement to become more involved in what was happening in his hometown.

The first 'unofficial' Jungian organization, *Psychologischer Club*, was founded in Zurich in 1916 with the financial help of an immensely rich American, Edith Rockefeller McCormick, daughter of the founder of the Rockefeller dynasty. She underwent analysis with Jung and later became a Jungian analyst herself.[19] At least in outward appearances, Jung's life did not seem to be too dangerously threatened by his period of mental confusion. During World War I, Jung began to formulate his own psychological ideas, and the first major work to be published after his break with psychoanalysis was *Psychologische Typen* (1921), his famous study of 'introversion' and 'extraversion', which built on the typological ideas of a number of previous authors, Otto Gross among them.[20]

Beginning in the early 1920s, Jung divided his time between his practice (which he gradually abandoned after having a severe heart attack at the age of sixty-nine in 1944), his scholarly work – including reading, writing and lecturing – and travels. He had many foreign – and wealthy – patients, especially from the Anglo-Saxon countries; received many honorary doctorates and an honorary professorship in Zurich; became (like Freud) a member of the Royal Society; and visited North Africa, Pueblo Indians in North America, the Elgonyi people in Mount Elgon in East Africa, and a couple of universities in India. Between 1933 and 1951, he attended the annual Eranos conference in Ascona, Switzerland, very soon becoming the 'spiritual leader' of this meeting of international scholars, who were mainly humanists (orientalists, historians of religion and so forth). In the interwar years, a group of devoted disciples gathered around him, and he was beginning to be venerated as a psychological shaman and a wounded healer who had revealed mysteries of the inner universe. The growing Jung movement institutionalized itself officially in 1948, when the C. G. Jung Institute was founded in Zurich.[21]

During the last two decades of his life, Jung more or less dedicated himself to his own peculiar type of scholarly work. Beside his immense interest in alchemy, which materialized in two thick books, *Psychologie und Alchemie* (1944) and *Mysterium Coniunctionis* (1955), he discussed the archetype of the self, the Book of Job, synchronicity, UFOs and the 'cultural crisis' of the West. During his eighty-fifth year in 1961 he wrote his last essay, a 'primer of Jungian psychology', which appeared as one of five articles in the book he was then editing (*Man and His Symbols*, 1964). He died peacefully at his home in Küsnacht near Zurich in July 1961. In his old age, he was visited by a number of people from all over the world, many of them regarding Jung as the living embodiment of one of his central archetypes, the Wise Old Man.

Archetype, Memory and the Mysteries of Inheritance

The theory of archetypes and the Collective Unconscious is arguably Jung's most original contribution to twentieth-century intellectual culture.[22] Archetypes in Jung's theory are innate predispositions of the mental structure (the Collective Unconscious), which we all share regardless of nationality, ethnicity or cultural background.[23] Jung thought that the archetypal structure of the mind is biologically inherited, even if the outlook of archetypes varies between cultures. He was convinced that, since the deeper 'archetypal layers' of the human psyche are everywhere the same, people living in different cultures are united by these archetypes in the sense that there are universal human experiences that are structured by them. Jung, of course, has not been the only thinker who has argued for the fundamental identity of (unconscious) mental functioning, the so-called 'psychic unity of humankind', but he was unique in placing the idea of the Collective Unconscious at the very centre of a psychological theory.

Jung developed his archetypal theory after he broke off with Freud and Freudian psychoanalysis in 1913–14. When he still worked at the Burghölzli mental hospital, the chief physician Bleuler and his associates, including Jung, were especially interested in the mechanism of memory and its relation to mental disorders. They were inspired by the work of the biologist Richard Semon, who published his studies on memory in the first decade of the twentieth century.[24] Semon developed a theory of memory in which he 'attempted to unite the biological analysis of heredity with the psychological and physiological analysis of memory'.[25] He coined the term 'mneme' to refer to a process that links heredity and memory together; he conceived 'mneme' as an 'elemental elasticity of biological tissue that allows the effects of experience to be preserved over time'.[26] Semon argued not only that information is encoded into memory and that there are 'memory traces' (*engrams*) or after-effects of stimulation that conserve the changes in the nervous system, he also contended that these changes in the brain (that is, engrams) are inherited. Semon's mneme-theory fell into disrepute largely because in a Lamarckian fashion it proposed that memory units are passed from one generation to another. However, Semon emphasized not only heredity but also *ecphory*, or the process of retrieving a memory, and with this emphasis he was ahead of his time. Years before Semon, German psychophysiologist Ewald Hering had already claimed that 'organic memory' covered both the phenomena of human memory and heredity. Freud was enthusiastic about Hering's theory, while Jung and Bleuler were influenced by Semon.[27] In his later years, Jung wanted to distance himself from the disreputable notion of organic memory, but his theory of the Collective Unconscious relied on Semon's insights.[28]

Jung was initially fascinated with the idea that memory traces could be inheritable.[29] Inspired by Bleuler's theoretical work, he formulated a notion of 'complex' to account for the mechanism in which individual experiences have effects on emotions. He tried to verify his theory experimentally with his word-association test, which he developed to clarify the relationship between memory and emotion.[30] This work made him receptive to Freud's idea of repression, for it seemed plausible that complexes arise when a memory of an unpleasant or otherwise emotionally disturbing event is repressed by consciousness. Originally, he related complexes and inheritable memory traces to the *individual* unconscious. The idea of the Collective Unconscious only took shape after he had 'discovered' the phylogenetic unconscious and 'descended' into the unconscious himself. At the time he left the Burghölzli, he immersed himself with mythological studies, which led him to 'find' the collective nature of complexes. In his first major book, *Wandlungen und Symbole der Libido* (1912), he argued for the 'phylogenetic Unconscious', which connects modern individuals with their ancestors and with the psychology of the past peoples.

The collective aspect of the unconscious was at this stage of Jung's career still partly rooted in evolutionary biology, especially in the so-called 'recapitulation theory'. This theory was introduced by Ernst Haeckel, an influential German zoologist and popularizer of Darwin, who gave the theory the grand name 'Biogenetic Law'. The simplest formulation of the recapitulation theory is that 'ontogeny is a brief and imperfect recapitulation of phylogeny', which means that within the (embryonic) development of an individual human being, one can trace the development of the whole lineage on a miniature scale. As the late Stephen Jay Gould pointed out, palaeontologists and embryologists, for example, were

> obsessed with the idea of reconstructing evolutionary lineages, and all regarded recapitulation as the key to the question. The gill slits of an early human embryo represented an ancestral adult fish; at a later stage, the temporary tail revealed a reptilian or mammalian ancestor.[31]

At the turn of the twentieth century, recapitulation theory was one of the most influential scientific ideas. It fascinated biologists and depth psychologists, such as Jung and Freud, whose theory of the psychosexual stages (oral, anal and genital) follows Haeckel's Biogenetic Law.[32] Jung in turn asserted that an individual's early childhood represents the early state of unconsciousness in the whole humankind, and as children grow up, their *individual* consciousness develops until finally they attain the level of consciousness that characterizes the whole species.[33] The recapitulation theory was conclusively rejected after Mendelian studies of the genetic basis of heredity became widely known and accepted in the biological sciences during the first decades of the twentieth century, but the theory held its ground for some time as a general theory of life sciences in Continental Europe, especially in Germany.

As for Lamarckism, the German biologist August Weismann had already explained in 1885 why environment could not cause adaptive changes in hereditary material. Weismann's research on 'germ plasm' gave Lamarckism its deathblow, but it took decades before his rejection of 'soft inheritance' was universally accepted.[34] For Jung and Freud and some biologists, Lamarckism was still a credible theory, and in both Jung's and Freud's theories there are strong biological assumptions based on the Lamarckian theory of the inheritance of acquired characteristics.[35] Jung was a Lamarckian both in his understanding of the mechanism of heredity and in his belief that there is a natural tendency for each species to progress towards a higher form. Jung thought of evolution as a framework for the development of consciousness. In his 'Psycho-Lamarckian' view, the human mind contains the historical remnants of humanity's gradual coming to consciousness. Most importantly to Jung, evolution has a *goal*.[36]

Jung's early concept of the phylogenetic unconscious is also a racial concept. With the help of the recapitulation theory and the theory of organic memory, Jung was able to contend that he could find not only personal but also *racial* history within the individual. As collective history was visible in the unconscious psyche, one could decipher the whole evolutionary history of humanity by studying the individual unconscious. For a period of time after World War I, Jung advocated the idea of racial typologies based on the different 'archaeological layers' of the unconscious, such as 'animal ancestors', 'primeval ancestors', 'large group' (e.g., Europe) and 'nation'.[37] Most notably, he differentiated between the 'Aryan' and 'Semitic' unconscious, which unfortunately made his racial psychology somewhat compatible with National-Socialist doctrines in the 1930s.[38]

One additional component in Jung's archetypal theory is his personal 'confrontation with the Unconscious'. During the years 1913–17, he went through a confusing period of mental disorientation. He had many disturbing dreams and visions that he saw as impulses coming from the subliminal world, from the depths of the unconscious.[39] After this 'descent into the underworld', Jung started to proclaim that the human mind contains memories of past experiences of humankind and that the 'spirit' of our ancestors lives on at the deepest level of the psyche. He had direct experiences of the 'universal complexes' in the form of distinct personalities within his own mind. The two most notable intrapsychic figures were Salome (i.e., the archetype of 'Anima') and Philemon (the 'Wise Old Man'). He had discussions with Philemon in his garden and regarded him as a spiritual guide or guru. This particular guru, however, resided in his own head. These highly personal and dramatic experiences – at one point Jung thought he would go mad – strengthened his conviction about the existence of collective psychic universals. In his old age, Jung frankly acknowledged that his later psychological constructions, such as archetypal theory, stemmed from this experiential source. There is indeed a strong revelatory aspect in his psychology, for his visionary experiences were important to his theoretical language, as he himself admits in his memoirs.[40]

To recapitulate, there are four different 'archaeological layers' of Jung's archetypal theory: first, a theory of emotion-charged complexes; second, the idea of 'organic memory'; third, the Haeckelian notion of the phylogenetic unconscious; and, fourth, his personal 'descent into the underworld'. There were also other influences that I can only mention here, such as anthropologist Adolf Bastian's notion of 'elementary ideas', Goethe's notion of a 'primordial image', German *Völkerpsychologie* and the psychopathological tradition of French and the French-Swiss psychiatry and psychology.[41]

Archetype and Neo-Vitalism

At first, Jung called archetypes the 'primordial images', 'prototypes' and 'transpersonal dominants' before he introduced the term 'archetype' in 1919.[42] After finding the leading archetypes that repeated themselves frequently in phenomena like dreams, myths and art, Jung gave them names and short descriptions. Among these archetypes, there are figures (images or ideas) such as the Shadow, the Hero, the Wise Old Man, the Mother, the Child, Anima and Animus and the Self (archetype of wholeness and God). In addition, there are such 'biological norms of psychic activity' as birth, death, 'rebirth', initiation, love and religious and totemistic rituals, which all refer to archetypal situations and experiences. All archetypes are archaic and animate the primordial experiences of humankind. As 'psychic instincts' they correspond to biological instincts and have their own phylogenetic 'natural history', comparable to 'physical' evolution, which Jung saw as separate from 'psychic' evolution.

What makes archetypes so profoundly anti-biological is Jung's way of spiritualizing these 'psychic instincts'. As an advocate of the myth of the 'Ghost in the Machine', he made spirit or soul inherent to our biological constitution.[43] In contradistinction to Freud, who had naturalized the world of spirit and reduced even the loftiest of ideas to the level of elementary drives, Jung proposed that there are spiritual and ethical values that manifest themselves as drives. As he wrote in 1928,

> I must also emphasize that the spiritual principle does not, strictly speaking, conflict with instinct as such but only with blind instinctuality, which really amounts to an unjustified preponderance of the instinctual nature over the spiritual. *The spiritual appears in the psyche also as an instinct,* indeed as a real passion, 'a consuming fire', as Nietzsche once expressed it. [italics added][44]

To understand Jung's spiritualization of the mind, we have to know a little about his neo-vitalism. In the early twentieth century, there were only a few major biologists who advocated neo-vitalism, and among those were Hans Driesch. Neo-vitalists suggested that there is an inherent developmental disposition in the regulatory processes of the organism, which can only function through a complex of 'self-activities'. In their search for such activities or purposive forces, biologists such as Driesch formulated metaphysical postulates, including 'soul', 'psychoid' and Aristotelian 'entelechy'. These purposive forces have the capacity to change the direction of physico-chemical forces, thus – in Driesch's view – representing a true challenge to mechanical explanations.[45] Neo-vitalism did have implications concerning matters of fact, for the truth value of some vitalist arguments, such as 'the Life is the blood', could be empirically tested. However, neo-vitalism exemplifies confused thinking in which nature seems to have one law for the material organisms and another for the non-material soul/psychoid/entelechy. It is essentially a 'metaphysical doctrine in the sense that is formulated with a degree of vagueness sufficient to exempt it from empirical refutation'.[46] In biological sciences, the implausible vitalist theses about the independent formative forces or 'dominants' crumbled after World War I and, since then, vitalism 'has had no serious adherency'.[47]

With the collapse of neo-vitalism, idealistic metaphysics was expelled from biology – but not from dynamic psychology. Despite his objections, Jung's formulation of the 'spiritual principle' fits neatly with the neo-vitalist doctrine of the autonomy of the living organism. Jung remained a neo-vitalist all through his life, although as an 'empiricist' he tried to rhetorically distance himself from bankrupt vitalist doctrines. Like neo-vitalists, Jung firmly believed in the existence of a 'vital entity' that animates the organism and possesses 'some degree of autonomy with respect to the body it animates'.[48] These almost autonomous vital entities are those famous 'archetypes'. In addition to neo-vitalist theories in biology, Jung was influenced by the French philosopher Henri Bergson's speculative philosophical-vitalist notions of a collective biological memory and the principle of life force (*élan vital*).[49] Vitalism is hardly mentioned in the writings of most Jung scholars today, but Jung's contemporaries had no difficulty in discerning vitalist elements in his psychology.[50]

'Memories in the Blood'

The crucial question regarding archetypes is this: was Jung able to explain the mechanism whereby early humanity internalized the 'constitutive' psychological experiences so that they became psychic condensations of these primordial experiences and passed from one generation to another via genetic inheritance? The answer is no. Instead of evidence, he was always ready to give imaginative assertions:

> I have often been asked where the archetypes or primordial images come from. It seems to me that their origin can only be explained by assuming them to be deposits of the constantly repeated experiences of humanity ... The archetype is a kind of readiness to produce over and over again the same or similar mythical ideas. Hence it seems as though what is impressed upon the unconscious were exclusively the subjective fantasy-ideas aroused by the physical process. We may therefore assume that the archetypes are recurrent impressions made by subjective reactions ... Not only are the archetypes, apparently, impressions of ever-repeated typical experiences, but, at the same time, they behave empirically like agents that tend towards the repetition of these same experiences. For when an archetype appears in a dream, in a fantasy, or in life, it always brings with it a certain influence or power by virtue of which it either exercises a numinous or a fascinating effect, or impels to action.[51]

To give another example of the mature Jung's non-Darwinian archetypal psychology, this is what he uttered in his Visions seminar in 1933 (Jung is referring to the 'German revolution of 1933' here):

> The remains of ancestral life which are found in the unconscious [of the Germans] consist in what the ancestors have done; there are memories of riding in carts, of using weapons, so one must necessarily do something similar, in order to put those ancestral memories into practice.[52]

In a 1932 essay on Picasso, Jung proclaimed that 'the journey through the psychic history of mankind has as its object the restoration of the whole man, by awakening the memories in the blood'.[53] These statements about 'recurrent impressions', 'ancestral memories' and 'memories in the blood' are impregnated with Lamarckism, neo-vitalism and the theory of organic memory. They spring from the same theoretical foundation on which Jung built his holistic utopianism, a form of utopian thought that aspired to heal the fragmentary state of the modern world and to bring a state of wholeness both at the individual and collective (sociocultural) level.

The framework of Jung's mature evolutionary ideas can be traced back to early nineteenth-century German idealistic philosophy, especially to Hegel and speculative philosophy of nature (*Naturphilosophie*). Hegelian idealism characterizes Jung's approach to the development of consciousness not only in its absolute idealism but also in its 'dialectical' methodology, theology and philosophical anthropology.[54] Rather than building on the theoretical basis of Darwinism, Jung formulated an evolutionary theory of the spirit, of the vital archetypal entity that is subsumed under the 'compensatory law of the psyche'. He believed in the superior wisdom and prophetic function of the unconscious: for him, the Collective Unconscious 'works ahead' and 'knows ahead'.[55] Small wonder, then, that Jung is seen as a 'direct link between the esoteric traditions in German Romantic *Naturphilosophie* and the contemporary New Age movement'.[56] While the scientific status of Jung's theory is rather feeble, the very idea of an archetype has filtered into common usage and influenced popular psychology, especially growth-oriented therapeutic practices. Another, related idea of Jung's that has found favour among educated westerners is the idea of individuation, which is at the heart of Jung's psychological utopianism.

Even before conceptualizing the theory of archetypes, Jung had coined the term 'individuation' in 1916 to denote the process of self-realization.[57] In this archetypal process, which usually starts between the age of thirty-six and thirty-eight, at the threshold of the 'second part of life', we first become aware of the artificiality of our social self (the Persona) and encounter the infantile and inferior part of our personality. This is the Shadow, which denotes more or less the Freudian Unconscious. The next stage is reached when we acknowledge our contrasexual aspect, which is Anima in man and Animus in woman. For a man, Anima also signifies his relationship to his soul. These demanding encounters with the Persona, the Shadow and Anima/Animus pave the way for attaining a new understanding of life and gaining insight into our inner nature, represented by the Wise Old Man (or the Great Mother) and, at the end of our journey, the Self (*das Selbst*), an archetype of psychic totality and God.[58]

Proceeding from the premise of his own theory of archetypes, Jung's individuation promises a psychospiritual adventure, which has its most dramatic phase when one descends into the psychic underworld. In this 'night sea journey' (*Nekyia*), one has to confront archetypal entities in order to gain wisdom and self-understanding. After these 'numinous' confrontations, one can attain authenticity and find one's 'personal myth', something to live by. This individual process has a social meaning as well, for an 'individuated individual' is in a position to provide the necessary 'creative impulses' that culture needs for continuous development. Every progressive step in cultural evolution is psychologically an expansion of consciousness, a semi-divine act of becoming conscious (*Bewusst-Werdung*). As Jung stated in a broadcast talk for the BBC in late 1946,

> it [individuation] is a most difficult task, demanding a high degree of ethical responsibility. Only relatively few individuals can be expected to be capable of such an achievement, and they are not the political but the *moral* leaders of mankind. The maintenance and further development of civilisation depend on such individuals, for it is obvious enough that the consciousness of the masses has not advanced since the first World War.[59]

What Jung is saying here in the post-war mood of pessimism is that, in modern 'mass societies', there are only a limited number of exceptional individuals who in their individuation process can confront the archetypal figures to their moral and spiritual advantage. His attitude towards the universality of individuation was much more optimistic thirteen years earlier, when the political situation in Germany changed dramatically. As I shall argue in the sections that follow, Jung even envisioned individuation on a national level in the Third Reich, where the primordial contents of the Collective Unconscious were bursting out and the German people were possessed by those fascinating and awe-inspiring archetypes, especially by one Teutonic archetype called 'Wotan'.

'To jump farther, one must fall back': On Jung's Early Interpretation of the 'German Revolution'

In 1933, Jung became president of the reorganized International General Medical Society for Psychotherapy (*Überstaatliche allgemeine ärztliche Gesellschaft für Psychotherapie*), and the editor of its journal *Zentralblatt*. German psychotherapists, now under the sway of National Socialism, were by far the largest national group in the International Society, and held the main executive positions. Although Jung inserted a circular letter in the December 1934 issue of the *Zentralblatt*, in which he declared that the International Society was neutral in its politics and creed,[60] the official journal of the society published papers and reviews which praised Hitler and extolled National Socialism. It seems that Jung was exploited by the scheming German psychotherapists, who tried to take full advantage of Jung's fame and neutral citizenship in order to legitimize National Socialist ideology and policy.[61] These manipulations and organizational arrangements, together with Jung's questionable 'psychological profiles' of the Jews, written in the late 1920s and early 1930s, provoked legitimate criticism both during his life and after his death.[62]

I shall not discuss Jung's involvement in the German psychotherapeutic scene here, because it has already been done by a number of gifted scholars (especially Geoffrey Cocks), and there is nothing new or noteworthy that I could say about his relationship with German psychotherapists in the Nazi era. Instead, my leading idea is that Jung originally interpreted the developments in the Third Reich as a social equivalent to what he called individuation. In the 1930s, he expanded his psychoutopian idea of authenticity and wholeness to apply not only to individuals but also to nations. He formulated ideas that had their ultimate source in his belief that what he called the 'German revolution'[63] of 1933 might very well signify individuation writ large, or *national* individuation, a process whereby a whole nation attains a new spiritual and cultural level. I argue that it was this promise of a psychospiritual regeneration of Germany that attracted Jung to National Socialism in the early years of the Third Reich. What is more, it was this prospect for a national individuation that encouraged Jung to co-operate with the National Socialist Indologist Wilhelm Hauer, whom he first met in the late 1920s at Count Keyserling's School of Wisdom in Darmstadt.[64]

Jung and Hauer stayed in contact after National Socialism rose to power, and when Hauer began to put in practice his ideas of authentic, non-Christian German religiosity, Jung probably monitored his manoeuvres with mixed feelings of bewilderment, fascination and professional psychiatric interest in 'abnormal' phenomena. A few years after Hauer had established the neo-pagan German Faith Movement (*Die Deutsche Glaubensbewegung*) in 1933, Jung declared that Hauer and the other members of his movement were possessed by the ancient German pagan god, Wotan, which had reappeared in Germany as an archetype of the Collective Unconscious (Hauer himself denied that his movement had anything to do with Wotan).[65] In 1936, Jung devoted an (infamous) essay to the depth-psychological analysis of the Wotan archetype, stating that Wotan revealed more about National Socialism than political, economical or psychological explanations. This is what he said of the German Faith Movement in his essay:

> There are people in the German Faith Movement who are intelligent enough not only to *believe* but to *know* that the god of the *Germans* is Wotan and not the Christian God. This is a tragic experience and no disgrace ... We who stand outside judge the

> Germans far too much as if they were responsible agents, but perhaps it would be nearer the truth to regard them also as *victims*.[66]

By 'victims', Jung did not mean that the Germans were victims of National Socialist tyranny; what he meant rather was that they were victims of the archetypal forces of the Collective Unconscious. Hauer and the members of his Faith Movement were 'possessed' by the archetype of Wotan.

In his seminar on Nietzsche's *Zarathustra* in February 1936, Jung told his audience that

> I must say that I am very *grateful* to the Germans for their paganistic movement, at the head of which is my friend Professor Hauer who taught us the Tantric Yoga, and who has now become a savior of the fools. [italics added][67]

Why was Jung 'grateful' to the Germans? And what sort of archetype was the archetype of Wotan that Jung saw as responsible for the emerging psychospiritual revolution in Germany? To answer the latter question first, Jung's Wotan appeared to be a very formidable archetype indeed – an archetype which (or who?) would first bring about chaos and tumult, and then – after the storm – introduce a new and potentially regenerated or 'individuated' German nation. Was, then, this promise of a better future for Germany the reason why Jung was 'grateful' to the Germans for Hauer and his Faith Movement? Before answering this question, I shall examine the 'case of German revolution' a little further.

In May 1933, four months after Hitler was elected the new chancellor in Germany, Jung gave comments on the Third Reich in his *Visions* seminar. He saw the new situation there not as a preparation for a war. On the contrary, it appeared to Jung as 'a great feast of love':

> It is really an outburst of a new spirit which externally of course may have very disagreeable consequences. Whether you talk to the man in the street, or to the professors in a university, it is all the same; they are trying to get back to the roots of the nation, the psychological roots, and naturally for that purpose it is necessary to make a regression.[68]

In his Nietzsche seminar two years later, Jung interpreted the 'German revolution' in an even more symbolistic style, a style he was so fond of. This time he spent much time deliberating upon the psychic background of colour symbolism, zodiacal signs and national symbolism. He observed, first, how the Soviet-Russians had chosen as their national symbol the five-rayed star, which is the pentagram, the sign of evil magic: 'The Soviet star is not only five-rayed, it is also red, the color of blood, so it is an intensely evil sign'.[69] Second, he made a social statement based on astrology: 'One can really say there is a tremendous transformation going on throughout the world, and it is coincident with the approach of Aquarius'.[70] Third, he paid attention to the 'curious' fact that the swastika turns the wrong way, to the way of 'evil':

> Now, in choosing the black swastika turning to the left, the Germans have surely expressed the backward movement in many ways. First of all, the swastika is a pagan sun symbol in spite of the fact that it is found in early Christianity, in the catacombs for instance ... Then secondly, its backward movement, and thirdly, the black color, the color of evil. Those are regressions into archaism, into the path of the left hand which is the dark unconscious side. So one could say the sun is now transformed into a counter-sun, a sun which is not above but below, which is not bright but dark, which does not go clockwise but counterclockwise. It is a revolution against the old trend of things, and therefore progress is arrested: there is a regression.[71]

This looks like a rather negative assessment of National Socialism, unless one is aware that Jungian individuation begins with the insight that one's social role (Persona) is only the external side of one's personality, which is followed by the acknowledgment of the darker and inferior side of one's personality, an encounter with the archetype of the Shadow. In this same meeting, Jung said that

> there are plenty of people, foreigners, who have seen and praised what has happened in Germany, and even in Russia, as a higher tendency ... From one aspect things are positive, and from another, quite negative.[72]

Following this statement, a member of Jung's seminar provided Jung with the French phrase to which he would refer a year later when he wrote 'Wotan': 'Il faut reculer pour mieux sauter' ('to jump farther, one must fall back').[73] Jung commented on this phrase as follows:

> It depends upon whether we give credit to the vitality of the European race or not. There were certain *reculements* in history where no better jump followed, the Romans did not jump higher, after Rome had gone down. And think of Egypt, Babylonia, Assyria – all the great empires! But as long as there is vitality left in a race, the *reculer* is surely pour mieux sauter.[74]

In other words, if the 'European' (meaning 'German' in this context) race is vital enough, the regressive 'falling back' will be followed by a jump farther, which amounts to a sociocultural renewal. The following year, Jung concluded his essay on Wotan by referring to Wotan's reawakening in the form of National Socialism as a *reculer pour mieux sauter*; it is a stepping back into the past, but Jung's point is that such a regression is required before 'the water will overleap the obstacle. Then at last we shall know what Wotan is saying when he "murmurs with Mimir's head"'.[75] Thus, National Socialism is a collective equivalent to an individual encounter with the Shadow, which is truly an act of *reculer pour mieux sauter* both for the individual and the nation: you regress and take a step back in order to jump farther.

Historian Stanley Grossman has noted in his analysis of 'Wotan' that, in the original 1936 edition, Jung ended his essay with the positive note on 'water overleaping the obstacle', but added the supplementary, more sinister quotation from Voluspa (Poetic Edda) after World War II.[76] This is a detail which, as Grossman suggests, implies that dark future rather than cultural renewal is to be expected in Germany.[77] This minor gesture – which is not noted in the *Collected Works* edition – indicates a major change in Jung's attitude towards National Socialism between 1936 and 1945. His changed attitude prompted him to revise his essay on Wotan after the war in order to strike a more pessimistic note, which he expressed in his comments on individuation in a broadcast talk for the BBC in late 1946 (see above). A sceptic might say that it is easy to be wise after the event.

The Significance of Wotan

For Jung, the reappearance of the archetype of Wotan signalled the beginning of a national individuation in Germany. He admitted that Wotan's reawakening amounted to cultural regression, but he also believed that, after the Germans had overcome the first tumultuous effects of Wotan's resurgence, something more valuable and long-lasting would appear in Germany. Inspired by the Heraclitean principle of *enantiodromia* (running towards the opposite), Jung appeared to hold that through the inherently dialectical development of culture, Germany would perhaps enter into a new Golden Age after the initial spiritual regression. What Jung failed to make clear in this context was whether he saw the new Golden Age emerging as a later phase of the National Socialist 'revolution' or as a totally new, post-Nazi, era, although it can be inferred that a political turnover was *not* a prerequisite for a better future for Germany.

I would suggest that this is the main reason Jung became so interested in Wotan and German neo-paganism in the early 1930s: he believed that National Socialism had awakened the collective, primordial archetypal forces in the unconscious of the Germans, and that it was the archetype of Wotan that corresponded to the confused and regressed, but extremely vital state of the German unconscious psyche. In fact, he did not confine Wotan's sphere of activity to Germany: after expressing his gratefulness to Germans for their 'paganistic movement' (Hauer's *Glaubensbewegung*) in his Nietzsche seminar in February 1936, he proclaimed that

> Now Old Wotan is in the center of Europe; you can see all the psychological symptoms which he personifies, including his romantic character of the sorcerer, the god of mysteries – all that is living again. As far as the German mentality reaches in Europe – and it reaches, as you know, from the Urals to Spain – we see religion upset; in the most Catholic of all countries, Spain, the Church is completely overthrown. And that

> is old Wotan, you could not name it better, the wind came and blew the thing into bits. Fascism in Italy is old Wotan again; it is all Germanic blood down there, with no trace of the Romans; they are Langobards, and they all have that Germanic spirit. Of course Switzerland is still a little exception, you know! Oh, we have joined in but we were not so foolish as to say so.[78]

It is no coincidence that Jung focused on the ancient German pagan god when he tried to make sense of the 'German revolution', and of the political developments in Spain and Italy. In Jung's utopian vision of national regeneration, religion played an essential role as the symbolic outlet for the cataclysm caused by the social and political turmoil in these countries which in his view were affected by the 'German mentality'. Jung was in agreement with other religiously-oriented physicians when he announced that religions are psychotherapeutic systems, and that religiosity guarantees mental health better than any other 'mental hygienic' procedure. From the mental-hygienic and psychological perspective, it did not matter much which particular religion or creed one adhered to; the main thing was to experience the 'numinous', symbolic power of religion, which as a symbolic system was the most vital and expressive manifestation of the archetypal universe.[79] While embracing religiosity, Jung disliked organized religions, and in an unpublished letter to his Jewish disciple Jolande Jacobi (who contemplated converting to Catholicism), he wrote that he did not accept people who belong to the Church – he is for those who are *out* of the Church. In an interview, Jacobi went on to comment on Jung's letter by saying that Jung himself behaved as if his psychology was a religion.[80]

What makes an historical analysis of Jung's texts and utterances a true challenge to scholars is that his way of expressing his ideas was not exactly crystal-clear. Indeed, his fluency in the art of mystical exegesis is finely exemplified in his comments on the 'German revolution'. Instead of reality-oriented analysis of the developments in Germany, he offered hard-to-decipher interpretations that followed the tradition of esoteric hermeneutics of the likes of Böhme and Swedenborg. Quite effortlessly, he lifted the social and political phenomena from the mundane reality to the transhistorical level of archetypal symbolism, and interpreted National Socialism as an essentially religious phenomenon.

While the clarification and explanation of Jung's ideas is sometimes frustratingly difficult, what I believe is incontestable is that Jung was initially enthusiastic over the religious and depth-psychological aspects of the changes taking place in National Socialist Germany. His statements between the years 1933–7/8 indicate that his fundamental belief during this period was that, while the deepest level of the psyche was the matrix of collective psychic epidemics (such as Communism or National Socialism), it was *also* the matrix of psychoutopian renewal (the attainment of a new level of consciousness). Jung's view of National Socialism as a sort of 'evil lightbringer'[81] is manifest in his Visions seminar on 10 May

1933, when Jung referred to the persecution of the German Jews and the recent burning of Jewish literature by Nazi students. Jung, who would not have dared to give expression to his true sentiments in his publications, did not appear to be very upset about the Nazi book-burning when he was among his pupils: he said that he could not 'help smiling' when he learnt that among the books burned by the students were all the writings of the openly homosexual Jewish sexologist and psychoanalyst Magnus Hirschfeld, whose homosexuality Jung had probably already objected to in 1911, when Hirschfeld resigned from the Berlin Psychoanalytic Society[82] ('I happen to know something of that stuff of Hirschfeld's and I don't mind their burning it',[83] commented Jung on the Nazi book-burning). Later during this meeting he made the following observation on the 'very negative aspects of this actual German revolution':

> It is a regression and injustice, there is no doubt about that; but they [the Germans] cannot get together as a nation, they cannot celebrate their love feast, if strangers are in between. Of course you can say that Jews are scapegoats; of course they are scapegoats, but other people, individuals, do the same thing: in the process of individuation, for instance, they exclude many things, they may desert their relations, which is unjust, cruel, or foolish perhaps, but it serves that one purpose of individuation, of coming together.[84]

Here Jung explicitly compares the 'German revolution' with individuation process, whereby an individual becomes that which he or she truly is, attaining authenticity and wholeness. National individuation signifies an attainment of a new condition of collective consciousness, and during the process the Germans would have to 'exclude many things', Jews among them. While he saw the 'German revolution' as an individuation process writ large, Jung was also worried that 'the suppression of free speech' and expulsion of people who are

> enormously valuable to a nation ... may have a very bad influence on the further development of the German mind, because they are isolating themselves from the world ... Such things may mean the ultimate defeat of this movement, we don't know, but at all events for the time being we must suspend our judgment. The German revolution has positive and negative aspects.[85]

After 1936 and his essay on Wotan, where Hauer and his Faith Movement were interpreted as a positive symptom of German possession (*Ergriffenheit*), Jung became gradually convinced that the 'positive aspects' of the German revolution were outshone by the 'negative aspects'. He had to admit that, in the end, the brutal reality of the Third Reich refused to conform to his psychology, throwing archetypes overboard, as it were. Consequently, his attitude towards National Socialism became increasingly reserved and disillusioned, and the burning of synagogues in Germany during the *Kristallnacht* in November 1938 estranged

Jung even more from the *Weltanschauung* of the Third Reich. In December 1938, he wrote to his Jewish friend Erich Neumann, who had moved to Palestine:

> I ... foresaw bad things for Germany, actually very bad, but now that they have come to pass they seem unbelievable. Everyone here is profoundly shaken by what is happening in Germany.[86]

By 1938, Jung, whose popularity in the English-speaking world was steadily growing, had probably come to the conclusion that National Socialism was not, after all, an invigorating religious movement that would lead the German nation to the path of national individuation.

I shall now return to the question whether Jung was 'grateful to the Germans' because they seemed to be on the road to national individuation. My central argument is that, between 1933 and 1937/8, Jung believed that National Socialism was potentially a movement that would help bring about a spiritual and cultural regeneration of the German nation, and that such a national regeneration or individuation would exemplify, and give evidence for, his theory of individuation at the collective, national level. Although confused and misguided about the political goals of National Socialism, for a few years Jung assumed that, in an era of Western civilization characterized by deep cultural crisis, one great nation would experience psychospiritual and sociocultural renewal through a process that was violently initiated by National Socialism – or, rather, by the archetype of Wotan. I argue further that Jung regarded National Socialism as the necessary first step towards national regeneration: it was equivalent to an individual encounter with the Shadow, the dark, inferior and repressed side of one's personality. Jung saw National Socialism as an 'evil lightbringer' that would make the Germans give heed to the laws of inner nature, which demand an integration of all aspects – good and bad – of one's total personality. In short, the 'German revolution' meant *reculer pour mieux sauter*; in order to jump forwards (towards wholeness), you have to take a step backwards (and acknowledge your Shadow). Already in 1917, at a time when the idea of inner change was fomenting in his mind, Jung had written that 'a metamorphosis in the attitude of the individual is the only possible beginning of a transformation in the psychology of the nation'.[87]

Jung's burning ambition was not only to become a renowned psychological healer, but, above all, to be the creator of a new psychology and, even beyond that, to develop a new understanding of human nature. I would suggest that it was this ambition that made him evaluate political movements and phenomena in terms of his own theory. His approach to these issues is not that different from the way in which Freud interpreted cultural evolution as a massive neuroticizing process in *Civilization and its Discontents* (1930). Granted, Freud's pessimistic view of the neurosis-prone Western civilization can be placed in the critical Enlightenment tradition, while Jung's more esoteric and obscure references to national individuation are more difficult to contextualize. As Sonu Shamdasani's remark at the beginning of this chapter shows, the question of the proper context of Jung's ideas elicits widely diverging answers. In the following sections, I shall briefly discuss a mentality and a world-view which clarify the connection between Jung's beliefs (concerning the psychic functioning of people) and utopian intentions (with regard to politics and culture).

Antitemporalism

Notwithstanding Jung's increasing aversion to National Socialism at the end of the 1930s, there is one essential point of contact between Jung, a conservative Swiss depth-psychologist, and Hauer, a National Socialist German scholar of religion: their common preoccupation with the mythical, constant and transhistorical. Hauer examined the religious *Urphänomen*, the commonly-shared basic elements of religious experience (such as the eternal essence of man and how his ultimate destiny is determined by God), whereas Jung studied the psychic *Urphänomen* called archetypes, with which he approached purely historical phenomena and gave transhistorical interpretations of them. They both searched for some rational justification for their preoccupation with organic totality and wholeness, which could be attained through examining forms, structures and forces that were somehow beyond historical time and were often given the prefix 'ur' (*Urphänomen, Urkraft, Urform, Urtyp, Urgeschichte, Urgrund*, etc.).[88]

A culturally-shaped inclination to give far-reaching mythical *ur*-accounts of history was apparent, for example, in Thomas Mann's 'Jungian' tetralogy *Joseph und seine Brüder*, in the work of the German ethnologist (*Volkkundler*) Adolf Spamer, who searched for the mental-spiritual primordial forces in his studies of the Folk Soul (*Volksseele*), and in the whole scholarly work of Mircea Eliade, a prominent historian of religion. Eliade even operated with the term 'archetype', although for him it referred to the existence of Platonic-universal forms in the religious sphere rather than to psychic structures.[89] In the 1930s, many scholars who studied the 'elementary forces' in culture and human nature had either theoretical or overtly political connections to right-wing ideologies, which tended to glorify the mythical and the timeless and downplay the profane time of historical contingencies.[90]

I would suggest that Jung's preference for phenomena that he claimed were not subject to contingencies of historical time characterized his utopian yearning for a deeper and more meaningful world than the one he and his patients had to live in. In Jung's vision of *Ganzheit*, an individual encounters fascinating archetypes, which as mental invariables are essentially beyond time and place. As in all utopias, there is no history or diachrony in his psychological utopianism

– everything is privatized into the individual-yet-universal intrapsychic domain. The 'law of motion' that Jung discovered was not that of history and society, as in Marxist and other historically-determined utopias, but that of archetypal processes. What counted for Jung was the cycle of aeons or 'Platonic months', not the linear process of historical time, which he saw as stimulating pathological symptoms in its mechanical chronology and quantification of temporal processes.

As Jung saw it, historical time with its contingencies lacked sacred aura, mystery and imagination. The more modern individuals were cut off from the world of archetypal symbols, the more intense was their experience of cultural and psychological disenchantment (*Entzauberung*). One could say that Jung reacted against what he saw as the oppression of historical contingency and the seemingly limitless devaluation of timeless truths by devising psychoutopian ideas about the supratemporal structures of the Collective Unconscious which would function as a cure for the mythic-symbolic impoverishment of Western culture. He wanted to create a sense of experiencing Sacred Time by connecting his patients and readers with the inner universe, where the primordial era of myth continues its ur-existence in the form of transhistorical archetypal symbolism. Instituting the absolutism of archetypal images against the oppression of historical time, he represented this transportation to higher time as a healing and regeneration of the psyche. His psychological anti-temporalism signified a therapeutic move from the alleged pathogenicity of historical time to the timeless symbolic universe of (potentially) healing archetypes.[91]

Jung's remedy for the malaise of modernity was to impose an archetypal order on the haphazard or even chaotic flux of historical experience and to establish a transhistorical relationship between individuals and their psychological origins. This relationship could only be accounted for by mythical *ideograms*, not scientific concepts. The term 'ideogram' comes from the German theologian Rudolf Otto's book *Das Heilige* (1917), where he discusses the mysterious, numinous aspect of the 'holy', and argues that the different attributes of 'numinous' – especially *mysterium tremendum* and *fascinans* – do not function the way concepts in normal language do; they are rather 'near-equivalents' (*Begriffs-Ähnlichen*) to concepts. He calls them ideograms or 'pure interpretative signs', non-rational words that, while useless in conceptual operations which aim at defining things, refer to the sphere of the irrational which is inaccessible to conceptualization.[92] Jung adopted Otto's terms *numinous* and *fascinans* and used them in his descriptions of the religious function of the unconscious. But I would suggest that his own key term, the Collective Unconscious, was an ideogram denoting the deep, mysterious continuity between one's origins and one's current mental state, and impinging upon a form of mythical existence outside space and time. For the transcendentalist Jung, humans cannot be reduced to their historical conditions, for through myth they are in contact with the timeless sphere of the Collective

Unconscious, which in its archetypal representations changes through time and yet retains its basic identity. And in order to make sense of this archetypal sphere, he used terms that have the characteristics of Otto's ideograms.

Jung's anti-temporalism has its roots in the nineteenth-century German *Naturphilosophie*, which deliberated upon the essential holistic reality underlying the phenomenal world.[93] More often than not, this essential or ultimate reality was seen in spiritual and religious terms. Thus, it is not surprising that Jung, more than any other dynamic psychologist, struggled with religion all through his life and incorporated religious elements in his psychology. If, indeed, Christianity is 'one of the dominating influences in the development of utopianism',[94] then Jung's psychological utopia of individual (psychospiritual) and collective (cultural) wholeness can be seen as an example of modern utopianism that has not dismissed traditional religious ideas but only transformed (in Jung's case, psychologized) them so as to make them more acceptable for modern 'disenchanted' individuals.

For Jung, the Enlightenment tradition with its endless rationalizations expelled the various forms of mystery and imagination that he himself valued so much, and the great significance of the psychology of the unconscious is its successful avoidance of the depreciation of the psychic world that characterizes the 'enlightened' attitude. Therefore, dynamic psychology has a cultural mission: to revive the symbolic universe of Western culture, which has died or become obsolete in the external reality, but which is still vibrating in the deepest structures of the psyche in the form of archetypes. As early as 1910, Jung envisioned in his enthusiastic letter to Freud a culturally regenerative role for psychoanalysis:

> I think we must give it time to infiltrate into people from many centres to revivify among intellectuals a feeling for symbol and myth, ever so gently to transform Christ back into the soothsaying god of the vine, which he was, and in this way absorb those ecstatic instinctual forces of Christianity for the *one* purpose of making the cult and the sacred myth what they once were – a drunken feast of joy where man regained the ethos and holiness of an animal.[95]

Freud did not warm to Jung's enthusiasm, but Jung went on to create a psychology which would 'revivify among intellectuals a feeling for symbol and myth'. He became a great myth-maker who could not resist the temptation to interpret political phenomena in 'psychosymbolic' terms. Thus, while National Socialism was definitely a concrete historical phenomenon even to Jung, he simultaneously located its deeper meaning in the transhistorical sphere of the archetypes. For a few years after the birth of the Third Reich he saw something numinous in National Socialism, the essence of which could be captured with the ideograms *mysterium tremendum* and *fascinans*.

Holism

If anti-temporalism was a mentality that governed the way in which Jung treated psychological, sociocultural and political questions, German anti-positivist holism was a world-view that shaped the way in which many scientists, physicians and scholars, Jung among them, looked at reality. In the interwar years, a holistic attempt to overcome cultural and scientific fragmentation found favour with many Germans, who sought *Ganzheit* in life as well as in culture. As Mitchell G. Ash and Anne Harrington have demonstrated in their respective studies, organic, holistic ideas are in themselves neither fascist nor 'reactionary'.[96] The fact that Jung elaborated on the idea of psychic wholeness does not transmogrify him, any more than it does the liberal gestalt psychologist Kurt Goldstein, into a fascist. Quite the contrary, a number of respected German scientists and scholars (and not only muddle-headed *völkisch* obscurantists) were concerned with achieving wholeness in culture and society. Harrington argues that

> before 1933, various liberal, democratic, and Jewish scientists were attracted to both the intellectual and cultural promises of holism and managed to share concerns about the 'mechanization' of both science and society with their more reactionary, and, in some cases, anti-Semitic colleagues.[97]

Like Jung, these scientists and scholars tended to see modern technological culture as a mechanical 'Gorilla-Machine', devoid of life and meaning. What is more, some of them conceived ideas and theories that had striking resemblances to Jung's psychology.

Here I content myself with short references to two such representatives of holistic thinking, Constantin von Monakow and Felix Krueger. The renowned Swiss neurologist von Monakow was engaged in research on the way past and present experiences were coded in the brain, coining the term 'hormé' in 1918 to designate the 'primal mother of instinct'. In Harrington's words, von Monakow's hormé had its origins 'not in the world of visible, material biology, but in a domain that transcended biology and was inaccessible to direct empirical investigation'.[98] Just like Jung with his theory of archetypes, von Monakow drew inspiration from German *Naturphilosophie* and evolutionary vitalism, and, again like Jung, von Monakow was motivated to pursue his psychobiological vision by his existential observation that the 'meaninglessness of life tortures us. That is today the disease of our age.'[99] Yet, von Monakow was hardly a fascist or even a *völkisch* scholar just because he envisioned organic unity and wholeness, and fused the categories of biology and spirit to create an essentially moral tale of how to heal humanity and attain wisdom.

Another scholar who was searching for a unifying world-view was Felix Krueger, head of the Leipzig school of *Ganzheitspsychologie*, a conservative holistic psychology which in the Weimar era rivalled the liberal, Berlin-based *Gestaltpsychologie*. Krueger, who endorsed *völkisch* metaphors and the ultraconservative ideology behind them, introduced the term 'structure', which resembles Jung's archetype. 'Structure' is a mental operating system, an 'unconscious force' that is profoundly teleological and purposive as it is designed to meet a need for meaning and wholeness. Similarly, Jung's archetypes are 'structures' or 'categories' of imagination and fantasy, Jung attaching immense importance to our 'inherent tendency' to realize our psychic potentialities and achieve wholeness. Like Jung, most holistic theorists were conservative intellectuals and academics, who 'often employed holistic vocabulary in their efforts to counter the perceived threats of urbanization, industrialization, and democratization'.[100] In his later theory of synchronicity ('an acausal connecting principle'), Jung offered a distinctly holistic account of the interdependence of mind and matter, but it would be quite foolish to claim that this sort of holistic thinking, also exemplified in psychosomatic medicine, necessarily has reactionary political implications.

Holism represents a mode of thinking that cannot be easily categorized through its political ramifications. In their search for the unifying *Weltanschauung*, Jung and German holistic thinkers manifested thought patterns that seem to testify to the continuity of the questions that preoccupied nineteenth-century representatives of German Romanticism and *Naturphilosophie*. This is not to say that holism is an 'intellectual tradition' going back to the early nineteenth century (or even beyond); rather, it is a question of twentieth-century holistic thinkers tracing the lineage of their ideas to such paradigmatic authors as Goethe, who represented the *Urvater* of holism to such authors as Jung.

Jung, Germany and 'National Individuation'

Jung belonged to a relatively large group of (mainly Northern European) physicians and academics who were fascinated by National Socialism during the first years of Hitler's regime; who formulated ideas tallying with those propounded by people who were openly National Socialist or fascist; and who became over time disillusioned with National Socialism, which developed into a violent system of terror rather than into a popular movement that would pave the way for a better future for Germany. The political sentiments and opinions about Germany that Jung expressed in the 1930s were in the most part shared, for example, by Swedish conservative physicians, who felt great affinity with German culture and initially believed that National Socialism would function as a valuable counterforce against Communism, materialism and what they regarded as the moral degeneration of the West.[101] Like Jung, the majority of Swedish doctors were not, however, active supporters of National Socialism, and during the latter half of the 1930s their attitude towards the 'new' Germany cooled down considerably.

Still, there is more in Jung's attitude than his political naivety or his disregard of 'external reality', which made him (partially) blind to the terror that was National Socialism. Like his German contemporary, Martin Heidegger, Jung appeared to be unable to confront the issue of his thought system's relation to politics. Heidegger, who, remarkably enough, later considered *himself* to be a victim of National Socialism, explained away his utterances and manoeuvres in the 1930s by referring to his misjudgment about the true nature of National Socialism. As the political scientist Mark Lilla puts it in his account of Heidegger's involvement in politics,

> he [Heidegger] simply had been fooled into thinking that the Nazis' resolve to found a new nation was compatible with his private and loftier resolution to refound the entire tradition of Western thought, and thereby Western existence.[102]

That both Jung and Heidegger initially thought that the phenomenon of National Socialism would somehow be compatible with or a testimony to their own assumptions concerning the 'refounding of Western existence' (Heidegger) or 'national individuation' (Jung) suggests that their styles of reasoning were separated from reality. In the case of Jung, such separation was intrinsic to his psychology of archetypes, Jung interpreting contemporary problems through the prism of myths and symbols only dimly connected to them, and transforming politics into 'psychopolitics' that placed the locus of political ideas and acts in the unconscious.

My conclusion is that, with his archetypal interpretations of the alleged psychospiritual forces that were at play in Hitler's Germany, Jung made a serious error in substituting historical contingencies with the absolutism of archetypal images. This error was both epistemic and moral: Jung's theory of archetypes obfuscated rather than clarified the phenomenon of National Socialism, and in his lifting of historical reality to the supratemporal sphere of archetypal symbols, Jung belittled the concrete fact that the storm troopers, no matter which archetype was stirring in their Collective Unconscious, were killing and abusing German citizens. For Jung, the suffering and humiliation of the victims of Hitler's tyranny seemed to pale into insignificance compared with the spectacular unleashing of archetypal forces in the German unconscious. From the moral point of view, I find it disturbing that Jung either did not recognize or did not care about the fact that human dignity and the principles of justice were trampled underfoot in Germany. An unpublished interview of Jung's disciple Jolande Jacobi indicates that, during World War II, Jung was also personally intimidated by the sheer military power of the Third Reich, and that his conduct towards his Jewish pupil and assistant showed marked signs of cowardice. In 1941, Jung refused to attend a conference in Switzerland, which was devoted to Paracelsus's 400th anniversary, if Jacobi, who was also invited to the conference, would attend. The reason for Jung's negative reaction to Jacobi's attendance was that he was afraid lest the public appearance of a Jewish 'refugee', who was a friend of the former (pre-*Anschluss*) Chancellor of Austria (von Schuschnigg), would irritate Hitler. These and other incidents prompted Jacobi to call Jung a Petainist, a man who at all costs wanted to avoid getting into difficulties with (high-ranking and powerful) people.[103]

The Swiss author Axel von Muralt, who among Jung's contemporaries was perhaps the most trenchant critic of his 'Wotan', argued immediately after the war that Jung's greatest failure was

> his unwillingness to warn the world of Hitler's evil, and he [von Muralt] damned the entire essay as little more than 'a stab in the back from Switzerland' for those Germans who did try to resist.[104]

To me, von Muralt's criticism of Jung's political passivity if not acquiescence vis-à-vis Hitler's Germany is right on target, and an important reminder that all those who are prone to interpret sociocultural, political and religious phenomena with the help of archetypes or other 'timeless' categories run the risk of using many words to say nothing of cognitive value, but much that is morally questionable. Like many other scholars of his time, Jung created stories and developed theories about reality consonant with his *Weltanschauung*, and in so doing he may have been inclined to mitigate the destructive implications of ideologies and beliefs that appealed to his imagination, or that seemed to validate his theoretical framework for interpreting reality.

To sum up, in the 1930s Jung made statements about National Socialism that were grounded on beliefs I would characterize as illusory and irresponsible. After the war, Jung himself was painfully aware of his initial 'misjudgment' regarding Nazis, and he seemed to feel a little ashamed of his utterances about the Jews and National Socialism in the 1930s. In a rare mood of remorse he confessed to rabbi Leo Baeck that he 'slipped up' (*Jawohl, ich bin ausgerutscht*),[105] and a year later (in 1947) he gave a more self-critical comment on his past statements: he confessed to his pupil James Kirsch that he regretted having said all those questionable things about National Socialism in the 1930s – what he had written on this issue should have been used only as a toilet paper.[106]

Utopia, State and Swiss Republicanism

My account of Jung's initial enthusiasm over the psychological implications of the 'German Revolution' of 1933 may convey the view that Jung supported a strong authoritarian state and German right-wing nationalism. This was not the case at all: What clearly distinguished Jung from the majority of German conservatives of his time was that he did not give vent to the same authoritarian, intolerant spirit, and did not glorify a strong centralized state. On the contrary, he detested what he saw as the omnipresent terror of the state, which in its collectivist social engineering and demand for conformity represented the greatest threat to individual 'self-realization'.[107]

In order to portray a more authentic picture of Jung's political views, I argue in this section that Jung was a conservative Swiss republican rather than an authoritarian German nationalist.[108] He himself observed the conservative and cautious mentality of the Swiss with a mixed sense of reverence and mocking, and he appreciated the way his compatriots led their lives, distrusting novelties and preferring intimate connections with the 'old ways'. This can be easily seen in his review of Count Hermann Keyserling's book *Das Spektrum Europas* (1928).[109] In his review, Jung compares the aristocratic virtue that Keyserling himself represents with the virtues of the 'least aristocratic of nations', Switzerland. He admits that he admires

> that blunt Swiss who sits in his modest house and lets the world know that he has his own sense of values and can let the opinions of others roll off him.[110]

Jung explains his moderate admiration of the Swiss by the fact that Switzerland is a small, politically neutral and democratic nation where local traditions and practices are highly valued and where people are 'extremely materialistic' and bound to the earth and hence devoid of lofty ideals. The isolated geographical locations of many cantons and the land-locked position of Switzerland have furthered the national resentment towards outside influences, and he sees this resentment as a defensive reaction against political and spiritual interference. The fear of novelty that characterizes the Swiss makes Switzerland not only backward and conservative, but also a stable and self-reliant nation, and Jung envisages Switzerland's international role to be Europe's centre of gravity which occupies a neutral position amidst the rival aspirations and opinions of other European nations. This strict policy of neutrality has indeed characterized Switzerland all through the twentieth century.

In 1941, when there was nothing left of his earlier fascination with the 'German revolution' of 1933, Jung made another statement on his native land. This time he observes that, due to her national character and political insignificance, Switzerland is relatively safe from such political 'infections' as nationalism, and he refers to the 'positive fact' that community feeling (*Gemeinschaftssinn*) is sustained by the lack of tension between social classes in Switzerland. He also advises the people to maintain a cautious attitude towards artificial and manipulative promotions of 'community'.[111] It is remarkable how much his conceptions of community, nationality and citizenship reflect the age-old Swiss republican tradition, where political and social activity is centred around local government and the canton, and where centralization and nationalization are looked upon with deep mistrust. I believe we can understand Jung's social, political and even strictly psychological views more fully if we relate them to the context of the Swiss republican tradition, where the canton and not the confederation is the essential political unit, and where citizens of the commonwealth were bound to their respective cantons not only by constitutional ties but also by an emotional loyalty and sense of community and belonging.

My essential point is that Jung's political ideals reflect the peculiar republican spirit of the Swiss, which is discernible in the attitudes and convictions that characterize his personality and work. First of all, Jung preferred a particular form of self-governing community that has traditionally manifested itself in Swiss cantons and city republics, such as Basle and Zurich, where local autonomies, traditions and *Lokalitätsgeist* were guarded and sustained with unswerving fervour.[112] Second, Jung was a Swiss patriot, and patriotism in a republican tradition is related above all to the citizen's willingness to defend the common liberties of his country or town by force of arms. In Switzerland, every male citizen is obliged to have military training, and Jung himself was in military service each year (usually each period of training lasted two weeks) from 1895 to 1923.[113] Despite the fact that it interfered with his work, he obviously had a rather positive attitude towards military training and became a captain in the reserve. Third, Jung's rather sexist attitude towards women is in perfect concordance with republican virtues, which in their stress on common military action in the event of outside aggression were emphatically masculine. Politics in general was the realm of male citizens, and an unwillingness to grant full political rights to women can be seen not only in many Swiss cantons but also in other countries where the republican tradition has influenced politics and political thinking; in France, for instance, women were granted the right to vote only after World War II.[114]

The fourth aspect of Jung's republicanism concerns his insistence on the importance of the individual sovereignty and his affirmation of political pluralism (although he detested socialism). Jung's attitude has its cultural roots in the Swiss tradition of political and religious diversity, which has cultivated a specifically Swiss practice of tolerance in nationwide social and political issues, while the simplicity (and rigidity) of mores is a common feature of each canton. Unity in diversity was (and is) the political ideal in Switzerland, and this ideal is manifest in Jung's thinking. Fifth, Jung's historical erudition was a typical characteristic of the educated Swiss, whose sense of history was manifest in their appreciation of, for example, old chronicles, which have been a source of communal ('cantonal') and national pride and have therefore been diligently studied. Historical memories have been part and parcel of Swiss identity and chronicles and mythic-historical narratives (such as that of Wilhelm Tell) provided a means to sustain communal cohesion and national unity. For the more conservative Swiss, an interest in history revealed also a yearning for the idyllic, static patriarchal order of the past, which is apparent in Jung's anti-radical political outlook. This leads us to the sixth aspect of his republicanism, which manifested itself in his appreciation of an aristocratic or oligarchic political order, even if during and after World War II he paid lip service to the ideals of parliamentary democracy.[115] Jung was a true heir of the Burckhardtian type of Swiss republicanism, which displayed a suspicious attitude towards full democracy and the 'rule of the masses'. Moreover, like a backward-looking Swiss who longs for the glory days of cantonal self-government, he expressed lamentation for a world which has distinct resemblances with the stable social hierarchies of the pre-modern 'great chain of being' that was not yet threatened by 'rationalistic materialism'.[116] In his Nietzsche seminar in June 1936, he gave vent to his 'Burckhardtian' feelings by saying that democratic institutions will not work because intrinsic in them is a 'fundamental psychological error'.[117]

Also to be noted in the context of Jung's republicanism is his sympathy towards things German. This profound sympathy is easier to understand when we take into account not only the fact that his esteemed paternal grandfather was a German, but also the fact that 'originally the Swiss Confederation formed, by descent, language and feeling of belonging, a part of the German Reich. The Swiss called themselves "Alter grosser Bund in oberdeutschen Landen"'.[118] The members of the ruling class in the Confederation had traditionally felt themselves German, and it was only after the unification of the German nation under Prussian rule in the early 1870s that the German Swiss started to distance themselves more clearly from the Germans, who were now living under a centralized political order. However, in German-speaking Switzerland there was visible enthusiasm also for the new, unified Germany and for the ideology of Pan-Germanism, even to the extent that the antagonism between the German Swiss and the Latin-speaking Swiss increased at the turn of the century. World War I complicated the situation as there was now a split between the pro-German and pro-French or anti-German Swiss, the former believing in the greatness of German civilization and identifying themselves with Germany and German *Kultur*, while the latter, constituting an ethnic minority, disapproved of the whole notion of 'racial kinship' and in its stead emphasized the characteristically Swiss standpoint of unity in diversity. The widespread nationalistic fervour threatened if not the political order *per se* then at least the moral unity of Switzerland. However, the Swiss federalist democracy was strong enough to endure this national rift, and in the interwar years Switzerland was one of only a handful of European nations where fascism did not have political significance.[119]

I believe that Jung's personal attitudes and even his theoretical conceptions were related to the social and political practices of his native land and to the long tradition of Swiss republicanism, and that his analytic psychology has a Swiss flavour in its ideal of '(archetypal) unity in (psychic) diversity'. The fact that he favoured polis-type or cantonal-type communities with a strong stress on small-scale political units and local government follows quite naturally from his Swiss identity.[120] At the same time, Jung's preference of a republican 'polis' meant that beneath his affirmation of personal fulfilment and communal sense of relatedness there is a barely disguised Burckhardtian contempt for the 'masses', those undifferentiated human herds that populate the urban tenements in big cities and seem to represent everything that is 'unhealthy' or inferior in man: a lack of individuality, a lack of sense of traditions, a lack of rootedness, a lack of moral standards and a great suggestibility for 'mass psychoses'.[121]

Abhorring the 'mass-mindedness' and 'materialism' of modernity, Jung's own utopian ideal was an extraordinary amalgam of the pre-modern form of life with its stable social hierarchies and modern individualism that affords freedom for pursuing one's own interests. Remarkably, the question whether Switzerland itself is a utopian state has been taken up by Jean-Francois Thomas, who in his examination of utopian literature in Switzerland has suggested ironically that the reason there is so little Swiss utopian literature may be that there is very little need to write about utopia when one already lives in one! Thomas concludes his brief survey of Swiss utopias by stating that a society without tragedy would also be a society without utopian dreams.[122]

Individuation, Personal Myth and the Good Myth: Utopianism in Jung

When Jung began to develop his grand theory of the Collective Unconscious, he was no longer a behavioural scientist but rather a philosopher of nature who affirmed the unity between humanity and nature, and attempted to restore the harmony between the authentic self and consciousness or the social self. In his imaginative search for the 'psychoalchemical' philosopher's stone, he remade the unconscious in his own, more transcendental image, thereby abandoning empirical science. It seems as if Jung craved for an intimate connection with the higher spirit (not necessarily the Christian God) all through his life. He seemed to feel that at the deepest level of the Collective Unconscious there is a direct channel to God, and that with the help of a certain visionary technique – active imagination – one can momentarily glimpse the sphere of the transcendent.[123]

Jung was also a symbolizer par excellence. He saw everywhere archetypal symbols that were in need of psychodynamic deciphering. Characteristically, he removed even incest from the biological and familial sphere into the symbolic: while he acknowledged incest as a concrete phenomenon that is explicable in Freudian terms, he himself interpreted it as an archetype, as a symbol of union with one's own being and of the union of opposites (e.g., of consciousness and the unconscious).[124] Innate propensities and varieties of human behaviour interested him only to the extent they could be interpreted as having deep symbolic meaning. If his patient produced 'trivial', non-symbolic (i.e., non-archetypal) material out of his or her unconscious, Jung quickly got bored. At one time

> a long-standing patient arrived for his appointment to find that Jung had gone sailing on Lake Zurich. In a towering rage the patient hired a boat, set off in pursuit and, once he caught up with him, used a loud-hailer to upbraid him ... Jung then zigzaged away, with the patient in hot pursuit. When they again came within hailing distance, Jung cried out, 'Go away – you bore me!'[125]

Fortunately for Jung, he did not have to be content with the poor symbolic material of boring patients. In alchemy he found a rich storehouse of meaningful but hard-to-decipher symbols. He more or less dedicated the last three decades of his life to studying the obscure symbolic language of alchemy. He even symbolized coincidences and dubbed them 'synchronistic phenomena', by which he meant an 'acausal connecting principle' between two seemingly unrelated phenomena.[126]

As Sonu Shamdasani has observed, at one time an empirical test of Jung's doctrine of individuation was suggested to him. This happened in 1948 when Unesco was organizing a conference on methods of attitude change. P. W. Martin, the organizer of the conference, proposed such a testing in a letter to Jung. According to Shamdasani,

> Martin suggested getting together small groups of people with scientific training, such as biologists and social scientists, to do an experiment, which he thought could be taken on by Unesco. Each would be given instructions over a few months for carrying out dream analysis and active imagination, and kept in touch for a few years. Martin claimed that if between 20 and 30 per cent of them experienced something of the individuation process, then it would have been placed on a scientific basis.[127]

Unfortunately, Jung's reaction to Martin's empirical suggestion was not encouraging: he focused on the negative aspects of his own work (writing a 'shadow' of Martin's optimistic letter, as Jung put it), which Martin found completely unsuitable for his purposes. As far as I know, this is the one and only time when someone has made the proposal that the validity of the doctrine of individuation should be tested empirically. But, come to think of it, the very idea of testing a metaphysical and psychoutopian idea empirically seems a hopeless task: to ask test subjects after some years of using the very vaguely formulated techniques of active imagination and dream interpretation whether they had 'experienced something of the individuation process' would probably yield extremely unreliable results. I believe that, while it could be possible to relate one's experiences during the test period to a process in which one allegedly 'attains higher levels of consciousness', the insurmountable problem would be that the test itself is impossible to design without a tacit assumption that individuation is in principle a distinct possibility, and that one could explain *all* deeper feelings and moods (of elation, edification and inspiration, for example) in Jungian terms. Individuation is simply not something that could be grist for the mill of experimental psychology, even if it would be intriguing to study those people who believe that their contacts (via publications, Jungian analysis, work shops, etc.) with the Jungian cosmos have changed their values, attitudes and beliefs.

I would suggest that the relative popularity of Jungian psychology testifies to the fact that humans are storytelling animals who create 'good myths' by which to live.[128] Like Jung said, the archetypal 'inner man' has to be nourished with healing myths if he is not to become dangerous or disturbed.[129] Jung himself created a healing myth when he offered modern 'disenchanted' individuals a personal myth or a psychoutopian story of individuation which through the universal and archaic nature of archetypes connects them backwards with the ancient mythical world and forwards to the modern invidualistic search for authenticity.[130] Jungian individuation signifies something unattainable, something that, while glimmering on the psychic horizon, we can never really reach. It is a basic characteristic of utopianism that it empowers us to look for reality-transcending elements in the world while it eludes all attempts to actually establish utopia in the world. Individuation also entails the notion that it is much better to believe in untrue but positive fictions than to have a totally illusion-free conception of reality and of one's life. The reason for this is that if you believe in something that may not be true but that may have beneficial consequences to your life, it may save you from mental suffering, such as depression. As the social psychologist Shelley E. Taylor and her colleagues have argued, if you believe that you may have a chance to find deep satisfaction in the things that you do and in the way you live your life, this positive belief, even if it is illusory, can protect you from mental strain and suffering resulting from stressful events and adversities (I will discuss the idea of positive illusion in the Conclusion).[131]

Individuation seems to be a healing myth primarily because it has an element of self-fulfilling prophecy. The shortest definition of self-fulfilling prophecy is that if humans define situations as real, they *are* real in their consequences. Thus, in determining social reality, beliefs have consequences whether they are true or false. If we expect to be able to lead a good life and enjoy life even while we grow older and weaker, this hopeful expectation may become self-validating. And insofar as Jung succeeded in promoting his message that individuation is a real process, this message must have had a positive effect on people, regardless of the truth value of his doctrine. Hence, even though myths have no value as objective explanations of reality, they can function as self-fulfilling prophecies that have beneficial consequences to individuals who believe in these myths.

Myths are stories that are composed of a narrative sequence of events that are meaningful to the people among whom they originate, and if these mythical stories include utopian elements it means that they look far beyond the current state of reality to something that is beyond history, but that can be reached with the help of history, as it were. Jung's individuation is a mythical story about the (archetypal) origins of things, but it is simultaneously a utopian story about attaining wholeness. He maintained that intrinsic to human nature is the tendency to mythologize, because myths protect us from symbolic impoverishment, which can lead to neuroses or even worse tragedies, as the current 'cultural crisis' in the West shows. To illustrate Jung's thesis, he claimed that the German mystic Angelius Silesius went mad because the prevailing religious myth, Christianity, was in a state of crisis in the seventeenth century, and could not offer Angelius Silesius a symbolic shield against confusing and terrifying reality.[132]

Occasionally Jung made frank statements about the mythic character of his psychological work, implying that his own psychology was a healing myth. In one of his seminars he once called individuation 'our mythology', and his friend E. A. Bennett relates that when the ageing Jung was asked about his own personal myth, he would answer without hesitation: 'Well, the Collective Unconscious, of course'.[133] And in his memoirs he wrote:

> To the intellect, all my mythologising is futile speculation. To the emotions, however, it is a healing and valid activity; it gives existence a glamour [*Glanz*] which we would not like to do without. Nor is there any good reason why we should.[134]

Thus, to live in a world of facts is not enough, because we need healing untruths to give our existence a glamour and, thereby, to avoid sometimes unbearable mental suffering. I shall elaborate on the ideas of healing myth and positive illusion in the Conclusion, because these ideas say something essential about psychological utopianism as a whole, not only about Jung's utopianism.

I am not asserting that Jung deliberately constructed the notion of individuation as a false but therapeutic myth that was to function as an antidote against mental suffering. I do not believe he was as calculating as to intentionally create healing fictions. What I am quite convinced of, however, is that Jung perfectly well understood the therapeutic and moral implications of individuation, and his experiences in his consultation room must have strengthened his conviction of the importance of seeing our life as a mythical story that imposes some sort of order and coherence on the events and situations in which we find ourselves immersed.

In the last pages of his memoirs, Jung makes two things clear: first, his life testifies to the fact that he had a power to see what others did not see (the sphere of transcendence): 'The difference between most people and myself is that for me the "dividing walls" are transparent'.[135] Second, we can never totally solve the mystery concerning the Other (the unconscious, the Self, inner nature), and thus our lives remain in a very deep sense a quest, which does not necessarily deepen our self-knowledge. 'It seems to me', Jung writes, 'as if that alienation which so long separated me from the world has become transferred into my own inner world, and has revealed to me an unexpected unfamiliarity with myself'.[136]

Jung's final message in his memoirs appears to be that even the great man must acknowledge the mystery surrounding human life, although he is able to see what others cannot see. Perhaps it was his feeling that others could not follow him in his journey to the centre of the Self that prompted him to state in an interview with a Finnish journalist in February 1961, only a few months before his death, that 'the greatest disappointment in my life is that people do not understand what I have wanted to say. Maybe they are so simple-minded.'[137] As the interviewer noticed, however, Jung said these sombre words with an arch smile on his face, as if his underlying message was: I really don't care what people think about me, or if they will ever understand life. The secret remains, and far from being a loss, it is a gain, because life is 'whole' only when there are things and experiences that remain inexplicable and mysterious. This element of infinity and incomprehensibility is at the heart of Jung's utopianism, the essence of which is captured in the classic title of an Edgar Allan Poe book: *Tales of Mystery and Imagination*.

5 SEXUAL REVOLUTION AND THE POWER OF ORGONE ENERGY: UTOPIANISM IN WILHELM REICH

'I still dream of Orgonon'
Kate Bush, in 'Cloudbusting'

The Austrian psychiatrist, one-time psychoanalyst and 'orgone biophysicist' Wilhelm Reich (1897–1957) was a young medical student in Vienna when Otto Gross died in Berlin in early 1920. There is no evidence that Reich and Gross ever met in Vienna, where Gross lived occasionally during the last years of his life. Reich never referred to Gross in his writings, although his mode of thinking, especially in the 1920s and early 1930s, seemed to follow on the trail of Gross. Like Gross, Reich gained a reputation with his early psychoanalytic work, which the Viennese psychoanalysts, including Freud, recognized as innovative, even if his 'obsession' with sexuality caused some uneasiness among his professional peers. As in the case of Gross, however, Reich's growing interest in political and social issues, as well as his conceptualization of the 'sexual revolution', was perceived with growing suspicion in Vienna. His emphatically political psychology in the late 1920s and early 1930s turned him into a marginalized psychoanalyst who, like Gross, was branded as a radical extremist and mentally disordered by his professional peers. But unlike Gross in his later years, Reich did not abandon his work, for he remained fully committed to the kind of research that went far beyond psychoanalysis and medicine. Again unlike Gross, the later Reich distanced himself from Communism and developed ideas which fused psychology, physiology, physics, philosophy of nature and even cosmology. Still, in the end, Reich ended his life in circumstances that were no less tragic and sad than Gross's lonely collapse in front of a warehouse on a cold winter night in Berlin.

Reich's life and work have been the subject of a number of biographies, but his ideas have seldom been examined in a detailed fashion.[1] He is widely regarded as a radical Freudo-Marxist who 'preached an apotheosis of the body in all its parts and a worship of the orgasm',[2] under whose system 'each individual's biological urges are to be played out in complete freedom'.[3] In contrast to scholars who lay stress on the utopian elements of his Freudo-Marxism, I shall argue that utopianism became a more characteristic feature of Reich's work *after* his Freudo-Marxist period (*c.* 1927–37), during which he was committed to Marxism and psychoanalysis. After giving an overview of his life and work, I shall first examine Reich's ideas, beliefs and assumptions during his 'sexual-political' era in Austria, Germany and Norway (*c.* 1927–39), and then I shall turn to his American phase (1939–57) and to the utopian elements in his 'Orgonomic Functionalism'.

European Nomad I: 'The passion of youth'

Wilhelm Reich was born in 1897 in Bukovina in the eastern corner of the Austrian-Hungarian empire, which is now part of Ukraine.[4] Unlike the other authors discussed in this book, Reich belonged to the rural bourgeoisie, and he spent his childhood in the countryside. His parents, assimilated and well-to-do Jews, owned a farm estate, which Reich's father Léon Reich governed with stern discipline. His mother, Cecilie Roniger Reich, was only nineteen when Wilhelm was born, and the young Wilhelm apparently adored his mother. Scholars have noted that Wilhelm's relationship with his mother was 'deeply sexual',[5] but before we nod our heads and think that here we have another confirmation to the 'fact' that young boys develop Oedipal feelings towards their mothers, we should keep in mind that Reich, like Freud, spent much of his time *not* with his mother, but with his nanny or his maid. The Darwinian sociologist Edward Westermarck's theory about incest avoidance among people who live very closely together from early childhood explains why Reich or Freud adored or may have had sexual feelings towards their mothers: compared to nannies, these women did not spend enough time with their sons to allow aversion to incest to develop in the boys (or mothers).[6] Westermarck's theory – which is nowadays widely accepted among anthropologists, who refer to it as the 'Westermarck effect'[7] – thus explains why Freud could come up with the theory of the Oedipus complex, and why it was so easily accepted by so many middle-class Europeans in the early twentieth century: in childhood they spent most of their days with their nannies, not with their biological parents.

What is indisputable is that Wilhelm Reich had exceptionally strong sexual feelings towards women from his early life. In his recollections of his childhood and youth, Reich claims that he had his first sexual intercourse with the cook when he was only eleven-and-a-half. 'She was the first to teach me the thrusting motion necessary for ejaculation', writes Reich, who fully enjoyed the newly-found sphere of sexuality: 'From then on I had intercourse [with the servants] almost every day for years'.[8] When he became a little older, he began to frequent brothels, where he would also see his teachers, who were supposedly happily married. It seems that his observations of farm life, including mating animals, made him think about the mechanism of breeding, as it also made him appreciate nature and develop curiosity about natural phenomena. But even though Reich led a sexually active life in his teens, he seemed to be rather discontent. His feelings towards his tyrannical father appear to have been a mixture of resentment and respect.[9] Léon Reich used to beat the peasants on his estate, and also his children, and he regularly accused his wife, who was ten years younger than him, of infidelity. But, like Hans Gross, he also wanted to make sure that his sons (Wilhelm's brother Robert was three years younger than he) were properly educated. Wilhelm's relationship with his younger brother was not easy-going either, for the brothers' competition for paternal affection, which was not that easy to obtain, was at times fierce.

When Wilhelm was thirteen, a tragedy hit the Reich family: his mother committed suicide. What probably led to this tragedy was his mother's sexual relationship with a tutor, who was hired to prepare the two sons for the *Gymnasium*. When her husband discovered the infidelity, the desperate Cecilie poisoned herself. It was most probably Wilhelm who had told his father of the marital betrayal, of which he had been a witness a number of times. Apparently, there had been discord in the marriage from early on, but Léon Reich's rage at what had happened drove his wife to swallow one poison after another. Wilhelm Reich could never forget this tragedy, or the part he himself played in it. In 1944, he added a note to his autobiography in which he exclaimed:

> The situation has now become clear to me: what Mother did was perfectly allright! My betrayal, which cost her her life, was an act of revenge ... What a tragedy! I wish my mother were alive today so that I could make good for the crime I committed in those days, thirty-five years ago ... What a noble creature, this woman – my mother! May my life's work make good for my misdeed. In view of my father's brutality, she was perfectly right![10]

Léon Reich knew that his own brutal behaviour had triggered the tragedy, and it seems that he lost much of his will to go on living after Cecilie's suicide. But he wanted to make sure that his sons would not have to face financial difficulties if he died. He took out a life insurance policy for his sons and then, probably intentionally, caught a cold while fishing. His condition already weakened by the tragedy, he contracted tuberculosis, and although he travelled to the Alps for convalescence, the disease defeated him. He died in 1914, when Wilhelm was seventeen. Wilhelm and his brother Robert would also contract tuberculosis as adults in Vienna in the 1920s; Robert succumbed to the horrible disease in 1926, and Wilhelm had to spend several months in a sanatorium in Davos in 1927 (as all readers of Thomas Mann's *Der Zauberberg* know, mountain air was prescribed for tuberculosis sufferers). He survived, unlike his close relatives or many fellow Viennese: in 1927 alone, 3,815 people in Vienna died of tuberculosis.[11]

After their father's death, the orphaned brothers stayed on at the family estate, and Wilhelm continued his studies at a *Gymnasium* in Czernowitz. But then World War I broke out, and in the following winter the Russian soldiers arrived in his village and he was taken prisoner. Facing the frightening possibility of being taken to Russia to face an uncertain future, he managed to bribe his Russian guard via his farm hand and so escaped from the military column that was moving out of town. He could not remain on his estate, so he climbed into his sleigh, whipped up his horses and manage to escape behind the lines. The next spring he graduated from the *Gymnasium*, after which he joined the Austrian army. After a military training in officer's school in the summer of 1915, he was assigned to the front line on the Italian frontier. During the war years, he was promoted to the rank of lieutenant and company commander, but he was becoming increasingly disillusioned with the war and its atrocities, and totally fed up with the life on the frontier, where the troops could only think of survival, food and sex (Reich, who by that time had a rich experience of prostitutes, expressed moral indignation at the assembly-line ways in which sexual services were provided to the troops[12]). In the summer of 1918, he managed to become demobilized, and he travelled to Vienna with the idea of studying law at the university. But he soon dropped the idea and opted for medical studies instead. Only a few weeks later, World War I ended. The last phase of the magnificent Habsburg empire, called 'The Gay Apocalypse' (1848–1918) by the writer Hermann Broch, came to an end. Suddenly, Austria had become a small and politically rather insignificant European nation.

At the age of twenty-one, Reich was a war veteran and a student of medicine at the University of Vienna. He was a poor but very ambitious young man, who had seen much suffering, but who was now living in a new, democratic and much smaller Austria. Very soon after beginning his medical studies, he joined an unofficial seminar on sexology established by some of his student friends (most notably Otto Fenichel, who became a psychoanalyst) and became interested in psychoanalysis. He met Freud at his home in 1919, describing him later as 'different' from other authorities:

> He spoke with me like a completely ordinary person. He had bright, intelligent eyes, which did not seek to penetrate another person's eyes in some sort of mantic pose, but simply looked at the world in an honest and truthful way.[13]

The following year he became a member of the Vienna Psychoanalytic Society and, it seemed, a devoted disciple of Freud. The master himself was sufficiently impressed by the young medical student that he started to send him patients, which also helped Reich financially. However, as required by the rules of the

Society, he had to undergo analysis himself, and his first analysts (Isidor Sadger and Paul Federn) did not get on too well with the young and strong-willed analysand. Still, in psychoanalysis he had found a cause worth fighting for. As he put it later,

> the impact of psychoanalysis was enormous and far-reaching. It was a blow in the face to conventional thinking ... The Psychoanalytic Society was like a community of people who had to put up a united fight against a world of enemies. It was wonderful. Such scientists commanded respect.[14]

Soon after becoming a member of the Society, Reich suggested setting up a psychoanalytic seminar on technique for younger members. He assumed the chairmanship of the seminar in 1924, holding the chair until his move to Berlin six years later. In the mid-1920s, he was already widely respected as an innovator in the field of psychoanalytic technique. In 1922, when he received his degree from the medical school, he had treated patients with psychoanalytic methods for two years, and from 1922 to 1924 he also specialized in neuropsychiatry by working at the Neurological and Psychiatric University Clinic under the renowned professor Wagner-Jauregg. In 1922 he also married his former patient, Annie Pink, who became a psychoanalyst herself, and with whom he had two children (they separated in 1933). In his diary entry for 13 January 1921, he wrote about his future wife and compared her to another female patient, Lore Kahn, with whom he had also had a love affair, and who had died a year earlier in somewhat obscure circumstances.[15] He ended his diary entry with the observation that 'a young man in his twenties should not treat female patients'.[16]

In the mid-1920s, Reich was on his way to becoming a leading young psychoanalyst, being at the same time a clinically-oriented 'scientist of mind' and a vaguely left-wing intellectual, who wanted to bring psychoanalysis to the masses. It had become apparent to his psychoanalytic colleagues that Reich did not hide his light under a bushel: he was an extremely energetic and strong-willed young man, who wanted to make his own contribution to psychoanalysis. According to psychoanalyst Martin Grotjahn, who studied under Reich in the 1920s, Reich was the 'Prometheus of the younger generation', who 'brought light from the analytic Gods down to us'.[17] Another psychoanalyst, Charles Rycroft, notes that during the 1920s 'Reich contributed significantly to the developments in psychoanalysis'.[18] Freud, who had early recognized Reich's talent, was not altogether happy with the direction the young master of psychoanalytic technique was heading. He observed an extremist streak in Reich's own 'character structure', as can be seen in his letter to Lou Andreas-Salomé in May 1928:

> We have here a Dr Reich, a worthy but impetuous young man, passionately devoted to his hobby-horse, who now salutes in the genital orgasm the antidote to every

> neurosis. Perhaps he might learn from your analysis of K. to feel some respect for the complicated nature of the psyche.[19]

From the very beginning, Reich was attracted to Freud's libido theory, and his first psychoanalytic writings dealt with the libido and its significance as a source of energy.[20] Under the influence of the psychoanalyst Karl Abraham's concept of the 'genital character', he developed ideas of the 'character structure', concentrating on the significance of early 'genital disturbances' for the later psychological development. From the late 1920s onwards, Reich, whom his colleagues called the 'Character Smasher',[21] started to distinguish between the 'genital character' and the 'neurotic character' (his first book deals with the psychology of the 'impulsive character'[22]). His characterological work met with approval and enthusiasm among psychoanalysts, but the reception of his evolving views on 'orgastic potency' was much cooler. He was sometimes ridiculed as the 'prophet of better orgasm' and 'founder of a genital utopia', although he only gave a strong version of Freud's idea that disturbed sexuality causes neurosis: he began to argue that virtually *all* neuroses are caused by disturbances in the genital function.[23]

It is an interesting detail that, in his thick intellectual biography of Freud, the psychohistorian Peter Gay does not even mention Reich, as if Reich had not existed in the still relatively small psychoanalytic world in Vienna and Berlin.[24] I suspect that Reich's rapid fall from psychoanalytic grace, and especially the scheming manner in which he was ousted from the movement in 1934, has discouraged loyal servants of the Freudian cause for examining his psychoanalytic career, except perhaps for the purpose of joining the chorus of those who maintain that Reich was psychotic from the early 1930s onwards. This sort of silence vis-à-vis Reich is very similar to the disappearance of Otto Gross from the annals of psychoanalysis – of course, Peter Gay does not mention Gross either in his biography of Freud.

European Nomad II: From the Psychoanalytic Prometheus to a Marginalized Outsider

In the early 1920s, Reich, who by that time had many experiences of a violent *vaterrechtliche* society, became a member of the Social Democratic youth movement, which signified his first political involvement. In 1927, the politically-charged atmosphere in Vienna propelled Reich, until then a vaguely left-wing intellectual, into political activity. He became a Marxist, an active member of the Social Democratic party and, eventually, a leader of a small 'sex-political movement' (of which I shall speak later). His move to Berlin in autumn 1930 gave him ample opportunities to continue both his sex-political and psychoanalytic work with like-minded colleagues, such as Otto Fenichel (who was now living in Berlin), Edith Jacobsohn and the young Erich Fromm. Besides the deteriorating political situation in 'Red Vienna', the main reason for his move to Berlin was his conflict-ridden relationship with Freud and the members of his inner circle, who looked with growing apprehension at Reich's development towards a radical Marxist psychoanalyst. As the Reich scholar Myron Sharaf points out, 'Freud's objections to both sex-political work and [Reich's] ardent communism had grown in the intervening years'.[25]

In Berlin, Reich's political involvement also irritated the German Communist party functionaries, who by and large found Reich's insistence on the political significance of sexuality, as well as his psychoanalytic interpretations of social issues, both unacceptable and distasteful. In the spring of 1933, after Hitler's *Machtergreifung*, Reich, a Communist Jew, had to leave Germany in a hurry. He moved to Vienna but stayed there for only two months, after which he moved again, this time to Copenhagen, Denmark. Political opposition against Reich culminated in his expulsion from the Danish Communist Party, which he had in fact never joined, in November 1933. By that time, he was also perceived as a liability by some of his psychoanalytic colleagues, especially the older members of the Vienna Society. As a critic of socialism and all attempts at marrying psychoanalysis and politics, Freud had little sympathy for Reich's political activism. On Freud's suggestion, the publication of Reich's book *Charakter Analyse* was cancelled, and his and his inner circle's opposition to Reich culminated in August 1934 in the International Psychoanalytic Association's (IPA) conference in Lucerne. There, Reich learnt that he had been secretly expelled from the German Psychoanalytic Society in 1933, and that the IPA accepted the expulsion. Despite protests from his Scandinavian supporters, Reich was unable to regain his position.[26]

In 1934, Reich founded his own publishing house, *Verlag für Sexualpolitik*, not only because he encountered aggressive resistance in the KPD (German Communist Party) but also because he had suddenly found it difficult to get his papers published in psychoanalytic journals. He also founded his own journal (*Zeitschrift für politische Psychologie und Sexualökonomie*), which gave him an opportunity to publish his own material in a way he preferred. At the same time, it effectively separated him from a larger analytic and scientific community,[27] which in turn had effects on his increasingly idiosyncratic mode of scientific thinking. He would continue the practice of establishing his own journals in the United States in the 1950s.

Reich was originally at the centre of psychoanalytic terrain, and might have become a major force within psychoanalysis, had he not openly fused Marxism and psychoanalysis. He became a political activist, who did not shy away from making it clear to all concerned that he was not your usual academic armchair socialist, but rather a revolutionary attempting to pave the way for a radical political transformation at the grass-roots level. It was his political activism rather than his theoretical Marxism that was too much for Freud and his disciples, who manoeuvred the expulsion of Reich from the psychoanalytic movement in 1933–4. In their ardent desire to retain the precarious therapeutic position of psychoanalysis in Nazi Germany, Freud and his inner circle (especially Ernest Jones) were eager to convey the view that psychoanalysis was apolitical and had nothing to do with ideologies and world-views. In short, in order to secure their survival in the Third Reich, the leading psychoanalysts were willing to exclude openly Marxist psychoanalysts from their ranks. In this situation, Reich had become a liability, whose political psychology threatened to thwart Freud and the German psychoanalysts' plans for the professional survival of the Freudian movement in Nazi Germany.[28]

Reich's 'escape from persecution' did not end in Denmark. Danish psychiatrists and politicians launched a campaign against him, and at the end of 1933 he had to move to the Swedish town of Malmö, which was close to Copenhagen. Again, he was harassed by the local authorities, as a result of which he was forced to leave Sweden. First he returned illegally to Copenhagen, and from there he moved to Oslo, Norway, in the autumn of 1934, finding at last a relatively peaceful haven (of sorts). What is noteworthy in this historical context is that, on two different occasions, Freud refused to support the persecuted Reich: first in Copenhagen in 1933 and then in Sweden the following year.[29]

In Norway, Reich began to move away from both Marxist and psychoanalytic doctrines, and he was left in peace until his 'natural scientific' experiments in 'bions' started to win him notoriety in 1937. He presented bions as energy vesicles that build a bridge between living and non-living matter, and he was becoming convinced that bions could be found in all animate and inanimate nature, including in human beings. Even before his research on bions, he had become preoccupied with scientific investigations of the physiological – in contrast to the psychological – aspect of the sexual energy, and his conceptualization of 'character armour', as well as his new therapeutic technique, vegetotherapy, which focused on the relief of bodily tensions or 'muscular armour', moved him farther and farther away not only from psychoanalysis but from all forms of 'talking cure'.

Frustrated by his unsuccessful attempts to convince the Norwegian scientific community about the validity of his new 'bion' research, and alarmed by the tense political scene in Europe, he emigrated to the United States in August 1939. He was at first affiliated with the New School for Social Research in New York as a paid lecturer (this new institute could not offer a tenure-track position to Reich), and he also established a therapeutic practice in the 'capital of neurosis'. Less than a week after the Japanese wing had attacked Pearl Harbour in December 1941, he was arrested by the FBI and imprisoned on Ellis Island as a 'dangerous enemy alien'. The US authorities seemed to suspect that he might be a German spy who harboured un-American sentiments and, although he was freed in January 1942 after his well-connected friends had intervened on his behalf, the imprisonment had an effect on his subsequent interactions with the authorities (he wrote in his diary during his imprisonment that 'I want to get away from the U.S.A. I find the injustice and the meanness of my arrest intolerable'[30]).

With his little group of disciples, the most important of whom was Dr Theodore P. Wolfe (who translated his works into English), Reich carried on and expanded his biophysical work in the United States, financing his new Orgonomic activities by his psychotherapeutic work, in which he had less and less interest. In 1942, he bought 150 acres of land outside the town of Rangeley in Maine and named his estate Orgonon. By the end of the decade, Orgonon had become a research centre with a series of buildings (e.g. a laboratory and an observatory), and in 1950 he and his family (Ilse Ollendorff Reich and their son Peter, who was born in 1944) moved to Orgonon permanently. In December 1944, a young student by the name of Myron Sharaf met Reich in the latter's house in Forest Hills, and this is how he describes Reich in his intellectual biography of a man he calls 'fury on earth':

> There was an earthly, almost peasant look to his face. He was ruddy-looking – a redness I later learned was partly due to a skin condition he had long suffered from. His dark brown eyes were mobile and sparkling, reflecting interest and amusement, impatience and friendliness ... There was considerable physical strength in the oaklike frame, combined with a supple quality.

Reich appeared to Sharaf as an open and warm person, but he also noticed

> a certain quality of suffering in his face ... His face looked scarred, as though he had experienced considerable turmoil, and the shock of white hair combined with his expression gave the appearance of a man much older than forty-seven.[31]

It seems as if the long years in exile, together with his troubles with the psychoanalysts, Communists and the authorities both in Europe and in the United States, had left their marks on his physical outlook. It would not take long before he would again find himself in troubled waters.

After the relative success of two international Orgonomic conferences, held at his 'research centre' in Orgonon in Maine in 1948 and 1950, the modest attempt to institutionalize Reich's work was effectively blocked by a disastrous experiment with nuclear radiation in early 1951. This so-called Oranur experiment was an attempt to demonstrate that Cosmic Orgone Energy could counteract the effects of nuclear radiation. The Oranur experiment not only failed; it nearly cost lives and made further work in Orgonon impossible.[32] At this point, Reich's reputation reached its nadir and many of his students and assistants left him. In his isolation, his ideas became increasingly fantastic and both his physical and mental health seem to have begun to deteriorate. He had a severe heart attack in

October 1951 and, according to his second (official) wife Ilse Ollendorff Reich, during 1953–4 he 'often drank himself into an absolute stupor'.[33]

Reich's life was becoming more and more troubled in the early 1950s. The building of the Orgone Energy Accumulators and their interstate shipment prompted the Food and Drug Agency to investigate Reich's work in the late 1940s and early 1950s. The therapeutic idea behind the Orgone Accumulator box was that it absorbed atmospheric orgone energy, which had beneficial physical and biological effects on the human organism. It was the question of the curative power of Orgone Accumulators that made them look suspicious in the eyes of the medical and governmental officials. In 1954, a federal district court in Maine ordered an injunction preventing Reich and his followers from promoting the use of the Orgone Accumulator and, on the basis of misbranding and quackery, ordering the destruction of his books that dealt with Orgone Energy. Reich (or, rather, one of Reich's assistants, apparently unbeknownst to him) violated the injunction by shipping Orgone Accumulators across state lines, and he was sentenced to two years in a federal prison for the violation of the 1954 injunction. The court case against him caused his by now quite visible mental instability to increase even further.[34] In the mid-1950s, he became preoccupied with UFOs, built a device to make rain (a 'Cloudbuster') and wondered whether he was a spaceman who belonged to a new race on earth.[35] When he died of a massive heart attack in his prison cell in Lewisburg, Pennsylvania, in November 1957 at the age of sixty, he had only a handful of followers and he was commonly regarded as a crank, a charlatan and mentally disturbed. He had become an intellectual and scientific outsider in every sense of the term.

On Reich's Alleged Mental Illness

For practically all his adult life, Reich had been devoted to the psychoanalytic cause, and his later commitment to socialism was no less intense. Thus, it would not have been surprising if Reich had become mentally unbalanced after his expulsions from the Communist Party and the IPA. Indeed, by the mid-1930s rumours had begun to circulate in psychoanalytic circles that Reich was psychologically disturbed. The rumours were circulated by his first wife Annie, whom Reich divorced in 1933, and by his former friends and analysts, such as Paul Federn, Sandor Rado and Otto Fenichel. Fenichel's case is instructive, because he was a radical Freudian and Reich's comrade, whose relationship with Reich turned sour in the critical year 1934. Fenichel had not only not defended Reich on the occasion of his exclusion from the IPA, but he had also 'denied his links with Reich's work and attempted to undercut Reich's support'.[36]

When Reich moved to Oslo in October 1934, Fenichel was already living there, and Reich became his competitor for patients and students. Increasingly irritated by Reich's quick success in Oslo, Fenichel then purged Reich from his own clandestine organization of socialist psychoanalysts, the so-called *Rundbriefe* group, which represented the Marxist opposition within the IPA.[37] But it was Reich who won the battle for the loyalty of Norwegian therapists and students: in October 1935, Fenichel moved from Oslo to Prague and then to the United States, while Reich stayed in Norway for another four years. Fenichel and the remaining members of the *Rundbriefe* group began to spread rumours that Reich was mentally disturbed, while Reich claimed that Fenichel had suffered a nervous breakdown after leaving Norway![38]

Unlike Otto Gross, who was officially diagnosed as schizophrenic by Jung in 1908, the psychopathologization of Reich was built around rumours, anecdotes and the overall tendency of psychoanalysts to denounce their scientific and ideological opponents as neurotic or otherwise psychically disturbed. For example, Sandor Rado, who was Reich's analyst for a few months in Berlin, saw in Reich only a 'mild paranoid tendency' in 1931.[39] As Benjamin Harris and Adrian Brock have argued, 'considering that Reich was a famous Communist psychoanalyst from a Jewish family in a Germany undergoing Nazification in 1931, "mildly paranoid" suggests mental health rather than disease'.[40] The question of Reich's sanity was not a minor issue, for the pathologization of his mind perforce had negative effects on his therapeutic and scientific reputation.[41] According to Ernst Federn (son of Paul Federn), 'in the whole psychoanalytic movement, Wilhelm Reich is one of the most difficult figures to understand'.[42] For Federn, the reason for this difficulty lies in the 'fact' that Reich was suffering from an 'incipient schizophrenia', which meant that his behaviour was gradually becoming pathological. The French psychoanalysts Janine Chasseguet-Smirgel and Béla Grunberger in turn psychoanalysed all of Reich's life and work and concluded that Reich already exhibited symptoms of psychosis (not schizophrenia but paranoia) at the time of his break with Freud, and that he remained mentally disordered until the end of his life. From this psychopathological premise, they denounce Reich's thinking as 'illusory'.[43]

My own view as a rather well-informed layman who has studied the history of psychiatry is that Reich began to show signs of mental illness only in the early 1950s. True, he was an eccentric and volatile personality with rather grandiose ideas of his own importance, but notwithstanding these hypomanic traits, my conclusion is he was hardly mentally disordered in the clinical sense of the term until the increasing difficulties in his professional life started to undermine his mental health during the last decade of his life. What has struck me more than his alleged 'insanity' is the near-total lack of irony or humour in him. Like most utopians (and psychoanalysts?), Reich 'had little sense of humour and took himself and his work dead seriously'.[44] It was this fanatical streak in his personality, rather than his 'incipient psychosis', that added a disquieting element to his utopian search for truth and beauty.

Reich's Political Activism

Reich lived and worked in 'Red Vienna' between 1918 and 1930, and his political idea(l)s and sex-political work can be accounted for only if we relate them to the hectic intellectual life of Vienna in the 1920s.[45] At the end of World War I, after the collapse of the clay-footed dual empire, Austria became a small republic with a big city as its capital (almost one-third of Austria's entire population lived in Vienna). During the First Republic, Vienna was ruled by the Social Democrats (the SDAP), and the socialist members of the city council launched large-scale projects to improve the social conditions of the Viennese working class. As Eric Hobsbawm (himself a former Viennese) has noted, 'since most Viennese were tenants, this naturally made Vienna a Red city'.[46] The SDAP developed the structures of Red Vienna not only by new housing projects, social welfare services and educational reforms, but also through offering various forms of cultural activities to the working class. With their attempt to create a model of proletarian culture, the Socialist Party leaders blended culture and politics and endeavoured to produce a transformed working class and, by extension, a utopia of the new human being (*der neue Mensch*).[47] As the historian Helmut Gruber has observed, in their effort to develop practical socialism within a capitalist society, the Austro-Marxist leaders of Vienna were inspired by the idea of a 'revolution in the soul of man', and this implied a 'delving into the innermost reaches of life in the private sphere – an expansion of the notion of culture to encompass the workers' total life, from the political arena and workplace to the most personal and intimate settings'.[48]

Alongside Reich, who was the bright young star of the still rather small psychoanalytic universe, a number of other young analysts, such as Siegfried Bernfeld, Edith Jacobsohn and Otto Fenichel, were sincere left-leaning intellectuals. They sympathized with socialism and saw psychoanalysis as encouraging social criticism,[49] but they had no intention to become actively involved in the tainted world of politics. Reich himself wrote in his diary in 1920 that 'I profess to want a revolution but am not a revolutionary ... politics disgust me!'[50] But already in his first paper from 1919, he had referred to 'socialistic progress' approvingly, and had identified such a progress with 'phylogenetic maturation'.[51] In 1925, two years before his 'conversion' to Marxism, he envisaged a social role for psychoanalysis 'in the efforts toward liberation from neurotic misery'.[52] So the seeds for the growth of Reich's socialist sympathies were already sown in the early 1920s.

In the spirit of Red Vienna, Freud himself had suggested in 1918 that psychoanalysts should establish public clinics for the common people, and two years later a psychoanalytic polyclinic was set up in Berlin under Karl Abraham. In 1922, the Viennese analysts followed suit and opened the Vienna Psychoanalytic Polyclinic for destitute people.[53] Reich, who had first-hand experience of poverty, became one of the most active workers in the polyclinic, where he familiarized himself with the problems of the working class while standing aloof from party politics.[54]

What prompted Reich into political action was the workers' demonstration in Vienna in July 1927. Reich and his wife Annie joined the crowd out in the streets, where a police cordon started to move towards the demonstrators. They were outraged by the acquittal of right-wingers, who had killed some socialists in an affray. Then an officer gave his troops the fatal command to fire. After three hours of shooting, eighty-nine people were dead and over a thousand wounded. On that day, Reich, who was shocked and appalled at what he had witnessed, enrolled in a medical group affiliated with the Communist Party. He also became a member of the Social Democratic Party and began to read Marx, Engels and Lenin. Once he had become a man with a political and not only a psychoanalytic mission, Reich started to call himself and his close comrades 'militants in the revolutionary cause'.[55] The particular method of revolutionary work that Reich adopted differed considerably from that of the average socialist intellectual. His great ambition was to unite sexual enlightenment with radical politics, and he tested his new sex-political theories by founding the Socialist Society for Sexual Counselling and Sexual Research (*Sozialistische Gesellschaft für Sexualberatung und Sexualforschung*) in late 1928/early 1929.[56] As leader of a 'sex-political movement', he preferred not to propound abstract Marxist jargon during his public lectures and speeches. Instead, he propagated concrete improvements, such as better housing, legal abortion and women's right to divorce their husbands. Together with his wife and his close colleagues, he went out into various districts in and around Vienna with a van to give consultation to (mainly working-class) men, women and children. He later claimed that during these years he learned to understand the inner drives of the revolutionary movement of that day.[57]

That Vienna in those days was not full of waltzing joyousness is vividly described by the American psychoanalyst Esther Menaker, who in the early 1930s spent almost five years in Vienna studying psychoanalysis. Arriving from New York in August 1930, Menaker and her husband sat on a damp bench on the Ringstrasse (the main boulevard) and observed the Viennese:

> People seemed sad, embittered, preoccupied. The streets were full of beggars. The economic depression was reflected in the stolid faces of the citizenry ... The chilly sadness of the city turned our eager expectations into depressive doubts.[58]

In the coming years, Menaker and her husband familiarized themselves with a mentality and a mode of social behaviour that was quite arcane and unpleasant to young urban professionals from the United States. In her memoirs, she recalls the parades of Nazi youth, aggressive Nazi students – and student riots – at the university, and the prevalent abuse of power that was manifest at the university, in the rigid structure of social hierarchy and among the psychoanalysts. Of the latter, she made the observation that

> they regarded themselves as the masters of other people's 'true reality'. It is as if some understanding of the dynamic unconscious had infused their minds with a belief that they held the key to a complete understanding of the personalities of the others. Often this belief (which was frequently handed down with a sense of superiority and was called 'interpretation') translated itself into a pejorative judgment based on insufficient data and arbitrary norms.[59]

She summarizes her experiences of pre-war Austria by saying that 'for all its reputation for gaiety and *Gemütlichkeit*, it is an unkind culture'.[60]

Reich, of course, was a native Austrian who did not pay much attention to many of those things in Vienna that upset Menaker as an outsider. But what worried him probably more than it did Menaker was the growing popularity of National Socialism and the plight of the poor and downtrodden. It was characteristic of Reich's uncompromising attitude that he did not want to join the existing World League for Sexual Reform, because he thought it had an apolitical approach to sexuality. While renouncing all sexual reform associations which in his view depoliticized the sexual question away from the 'class struggle', Reich stressed the necessity of the politicization of the sexual, and, by extension, of the private sphere as a whole. He criticized the sexologist leader of the *World League*, Magnus Hirschfeld, not only for his apolitical outlook, but also for his relativistic stand with regard to various forms of sexual behaviour.[61] Reich refused to treat homosexual patients, and in addition to his strong dislike of homosexuality (Hirschfeld was openly homosexual[62]) and 'sexual perversions', he expressed explicit disdain for 'decadence' (including pornography). While attacking the 'life-negating' morality of 'bourgeois society', he was anything but a prophet of sexual debauchery à la the Marquis de Sade. Quite the contrary, there was an unmistakable streak of puritanism in him.[63]

Reich's emphasis on the interrelationship between sexuality and politics is succinctly expressed in his essay 'The Sexual Rights of Youth' ('*Der sexuelle Kampf der Jugend*', 1932), where he writes that

> the struggle to achieve a satisfactory sexual life can only be successful in conjunction with the fight against social inequalities and sexual reactionism. We must also establish sex-counseling centers for young people where they are not merely given contraceptive devices but are properly educated in social and sexual matters. This

> is necessary in order to increase their aggressiveness and their intellectual alertness, which are undermined by material want but even more so by sexual problems.[64]

For Reich, humans were sexual animals who in a sexually-repressive society did not want to acknowledge this basic fact, which led to all sorts of problems and complications.[65] While criticizing 'manipulative activity from above', Reich stated that

> the young must start now to shape their own lives in every sphere; they should put into practice and carry out whatever they consider right and whatever they please to bring about.[66]

Reich regarded the younger generation of the proletariat background as potentially capable of changing things for the better when their time comes. (No wonder Reich became popular in the 1968 student uprisings!)

Acting as the spokesman for the urban working-class youth, Reich constantly raised the concrete issue that caused problems to them: for example they lacked access to private spaces where they could make love in peace and quiet. This meant that the parents and especially the father could easily have full patriarchal control over the private life of their sexually mature offspring. This control of young people's private spaces in turn caused damage to their psychological health. Moreover, Reich emphatically embraced the idea that 'woman is not by nature inferior to man', stating that 'we want not only to eliminate the social and sexual enslavement of women but also to establish the complete emotional friendship of the sexes'.[67] As Benjamin Harris and Adrian Brock have noted, 'during its brief existence this "sex-pol" counseling and education was a popular alternative to the morally conservative public health services organized by churches and municipal bureaucracies'.[68] In 1930, Reich started to use the term 'sex-economy' to denote his original blend of political psychology and 'natural science', the former referring to his adherence to Marxist psychoanalysis, and the latter to his new ideas concerning the 'essence' of biopsychic energy.[69] His sex-economy was derived from his understanding of social mechanisms that regulate, promote or hinder gratification of sexual needs.[70]

Like many other leftist intellectuals, Reich saw the social reformations of marriage and sexual relations in post-revolutionary Russia as an exemplary model. He visited Moscow with his wife in 1929, when the days of revolutionary politics in the Soviet Union were all but gone, and psychoanalysis had been on the decline for many years (see Chapter 2). That Reich was invited to Moscow at all depended on the fact that he was known for his renunciation of the more 'idealistic' concepts of Freud, as well as on his ardent Communism. During his two-month visit, Reich gave several lectures at the Communist Academy, visited Vera Schmidt's psychoanalytic 'kindergarten' and had discussions with the remaining Russian psychoanalysts, as well as with psychiatrists who were still well disposed to Freudian theories. His message of the interrelationship between political and sexual revolution failed to convince the Academy, and it had no bearing on the declining psychoanalytic community in Moscow.

In an article written after the trip, Reich gave an inaccurate, far too optimistic portrait of the position of psychoanalysis in Soviet Russia. The Russian psychiatrist Moshe Wulff was among those who reacted to Reich's unrealistic article by writing a rejoinder in which he criticized Reich's views.[71] As for Freud, in his discussion with the American psychiatrist Joseph Wortis in 1934, he commented on Reich's trip to Moscow as follows: 'An analyst by the name of Wilhelm Reich went to Russia and lectured there, and talked so much about promiscuity that they finally invited him to leave'.[72] In time, a more truthful picture of the Soviet system modified Reich's attitude, and he became disillusioned with the development in Soviet-style Communism, which he had originally seen as an exemplary model of a reformed private sphere.[73] He wrote in his diary of 1936 that Stalin 'will undoubtedly become the Russian Hitler'.[74]

Sex-Politics and its Reception in Germany

In 1930, after two years of (sex-)political activism, Reich was expelled from the Austrian Social Democratic Party for his attacks on the party leadership and for his co-operation with Communists. He moved to Berlin in autumn 1930, joined the German Communist Party (KPD), and continued his own brand of sexual reformism in Germany. In Red Vienna, the powerful Catholic Church and the conservative parties fiercely opposed all forms of sexual counselling, and even the SDAP's sexual politics reflected the anti-sensual morality of the predominantly middle-class party leaders, who liked to emphasize the *ordentliche* family and the sublimation of sexuality.[75] Besides, the right wing was on the rise in Austria in the early 1930s. Therefore, it was only natural for a sexual radical such as Reich to move to Berlin, where the general atmosphere was much more congenial for a socialist who was looking for opportunities to continue both his sex-political and psychoanalytic work with unswerving fervour.

In Berlin, none of the younger generation of analysts (Otto Fenichel, Erich Fromm, Edith Jacobsohn, etc.) was as actively engaged in politics as Reich was: besides joining the KPD and giving numerous public talks in political meetings, he initiated sex-counselling clinics and tried to influence various organizations which worked in the field of sexual reform. As historian Kristine von Soden has noted, there was no lack of sexual counselling agencies in Weimar Germany: between 1919 and 1932, more than 400 agencies were founded in Germany, and 40 in Berlin alone.[76] In addition, there were about 100 ambulatory sexual counselling agencies in Weimar Germany. Thus Reich's work on sexual enlightenment was anything but unique, and von Soden does not even discuss Reich's contribution in her book. Her study shows that it was Magnus Hirschfeld and his Institute for Sexual Science (*Institut für Sexualwissenschaft*), founded in 1919 in Berlin, which played a significant role in the field of sexual enlightenment. There was an acute need for legal reforms and enlightenment in Weimar Germany, where abortion was prohibited by the German Civil Code: in the late 1920s, 40,000 German women died annually as a result of unhygienic and unprofessional abortions conducted by abortionists and quacks.[77]

Although Reich's views were supported by segments of young German socialists, they met with a cool reception among the Communist functionaries at the KPD, who were far less enthusiastic over Reich's sex-political activism. When Germany fell under National Socialist rule in 1933, Reich wrote *Mass Psychology of Fascism* (*Massenpsychologie des Faschismus*), one of the earliest (psycho)analyses of Hitler's Germany, which was published in Denmark in September 1933. In his book, he claimed correctly that fascism found favour among workers, and he explained this seemingly odd phenomenon, ignored by orthodox Marxists, by his theory of character structure: in patriarchal societies, conjectured Reich, the formation of the authoritarian character structure in sexually repressed people is conducive to violent and politically oppressive systems, such as fascism. He also stressed the fact that Nazi leaders were 'highly skilled in mass psychology', which made them a formidable adversary in the political fight over the minds of people.[78] He pointed out that if Marxist political psychology were to prove incapable of explaining what is truly going on in the mind of the average person, revolutionary socialism, and not the capitalist state, would wither away without so much as a whimper. In a review published in a clandestine Communist newspaper (*Deutsche Volkszeitung*), one of his Marxist critics dismissed the book as an expression of 'counter-revolutionary politics' and denounced Reich as an author who 'provides a sexual defence for the social fascist leaders'.[79] Another comrade, a Communist doctor, complained that 'Reich wants to turn our youth organizations into procuring agencies'.[80]

Reich in turn criticized Marxist politicians, who applied the term 'class consciousness' without being able to explain how it actually functioned in concrete situations. Moreover, these politicians managed to stifle the 'class feeling' of thousands of people by 'assuming the existence in the masses of interest in and the ability to appreciate economic analysis'.[81] Reich believed that instead of offering the common people abstract political jargon, politicians (and public intellectuals) should proceed from the actual needs and concerns of the common man and woman, and talk in a plain language that would find resonance in the hearts and minds of the workers. In his 'History of the German Sex-Pol Movement' (1934), Reich gives a list of the 'demands' of his movement. These include such practical items as the free distribution of contraception to those who cannot afford it, a complete abolition of anti-abortion legislation, an abolition of prostitution and all compulsory regulations concerning marriage, and the eradication of venereal diseases. In addition, he demands changes in education so as to prevent neuroses and sexual disturbances, and he calls for reforms in the training of doctors, pedagogues and nurses in matters relating to sexuality.[82]

In the early 1930s, Reich and his comrades published a number of writings that dealt with sex-political questions in an easily accessible style, devoid of heavy ideological baggage.[83] Their explicit aim was to reach the average working person, and it seems that some of their publications were rather widely read among working-class people.[84] In the end, however, Reich did not manage to convince the KPD of the importance of his work. Quite the contrary, he was vigorously opposed by established party comrades as a heretic of sorts, and the opposition culminated in his expulsion from the Danish Communist Party in 1933 (there was no longer a Communist party that could have expelled anyone in Germany, because the KPD was quickly dissolved when Nazis had taken over in Germany). That Reich was ostracized politically is partly explained by the overwhelming historical events (the rise of National Socialism), and partly by what was perceived by his fellow comrades as his sexual extremism, his refusal to compromise and his increasingly hazardous position as a Marxist psychoanalyst and sexologist.

In October 1933, when he was in exile, Reich wrote a letter to Trotsky (who had already been in exile for a number of years), describing to his 'fellow heretic' his work in the field of sexual politics in Germany and telling of his plan to mobilize international forces that would work together as a revolutionary organization for the purpose of the sexual revolution.[85] Such a revolution in the private sphere would in turn help bring about the political revolution. He also told Trotsky that, although he represented an opposition group in the KPD, he was still a party member. He explained that he had not been excluded from the Party because nobody had competence to criticize his sexual-political theories, and also because his influence was too strong (an exaggeration!).[86] He asked Trotsky whether he would like to become actively involved in a worldwide sexual-revolutionary movement. In his reply, Trotsky agreed that the question of sexuality is indeed significant in the education of working-class youth, but he politely declined Reich's offer by referring to his ignorance and lack of experience of this particular field of expertise. He also mentioned that he had received a copy of Reich's newly-published book, *Mass Psychology of Fascism*, which he had not yet read due to circumstances (in the 1930s, Trotsky himself wrote a number of articles and pamphlets on fascism and National Socialism, which were published in book form in 1971).[87] The short correspondence between Reich and Trotsky led to nothing of concrete value, but it revealed Reich's ambition to recruit the top leaders in the dissident communist movement for a fight against sexual and political oppression of the working class, as well as against the powerful Stalinist forces in the Communist organizations.

In Reich's explanatory framework during his sex-political years, the true causes of human misery arose from the interplay between sexuality, politics and psychology. As for the solution to human misery, it required a politicization of the private sphere and its patriarchal matrix, the family. His reasoning was based on the assumption that human neuroticism, sexual anxiety, alienation (etc.) and so-called

> 'destructive drives' are not biologically but socially determined, and that the most abhorrent form of misery, sexual repression, is of social origin. Sexual repression is an important ideological weapon, because it binds people to the Church and to the bourgeois social order, rendering them incapable of taking up critical attitudes.[88]

Hence, there is no such thing as 'death instinct' or the innate discontent of humans, as loyal Freudians claimed (after Freud had introduced the theory of death instinct in *Beyond the Pleasure Principle* in 1920). On the contrary, says Reich,

> social suppression is not part of the natural order of things. It developed as a part of patriarchy and, therefore, is capable of being eliminated, fundamentally speaking.[89]

Reich believed that his claim about patriarchy was empirically verified by the anthropologist Bronislaw Malinowski in his field studies in the Trobriand Islands.[90] For Reich, Malinowski, with whom he corresponded in the 1930s (and whom he also met in Oslo),[91] was able to show that due to the free flow of genital sexuality, perversions do not exist among the Trobriand Islanders. What this meant to Reich was that repression is sociologically and not biologically determined, as orthodox Freudians claimed. Moreover, Malinowski showed that sexual repression did not exist in matriarchy, in the *Urgesellschaft* that preceded the pathogenic patriarchal social order in the West and that still exists in some distant corners of the world.[92] Actually, the family in the Trobriand Islands was matrilineal, which meant that children took their mother's name and kinship status. Although such a custom refers to the relatively high status of women in a society, matriliny is not the same as matriarchy, which denotes the political and familial rule of women over men. In his belief in the myth of matriarchy, Reich's thinking converged with that of Otto Gross, who a generation earlier had made similar statements about the uninhibited sexual life in the allegedly matriarchal society. Unlike Gross, Reich only read Engels, not Bachofen, and Malinowski's anthropological studies, which were not available to Gross, seemed to give empirical evidence to the Marxist-matriarchal account of the history of the family.

The writing of *People in Trouble* (*Menschen im Staat*) in 1936 marks the watershed period between Reich's sex-political years and the ensuing 'non-political' period. In his book, he looks back to his political activities and evaluates his own position with regard to German Communists, from whom he was becoming more and more alienated. In his last sex-political article from 1937, which contains his bitter assault on (Marxist) intellectuals, he was still using terms associated with Marxism, such as 'dialectical materialism' and 'bourgeois society' (in the English translation, the article is entitled 'Dialectical Materialist Science Against Intellectual Dilettantism in the Socialist Movement'). But his conceptual framework was less and less political or overtly ideological, and in his bitterness he psychodiagnosed 'raging Marxists' as 'serious sexual neurotic cases' who 'act and write from bad motives'.[93] He ended his last explicitly political writing in a defiant mood by stating that

> we will under no circumstances allow ourselves to be disturbed in our work and in the revelation of what we know by anybody, no matter who. We will not give in to the narrowmindedness and abjection which at present rule the world, and we will dissociate ourselves from anyone too weak to resist.[94]

Although he never denied his debt to (the early) Freud in his post-Freudo-Marxist years, Reich wanted to minimize the degree of his previous commitment to Marxist doctrines. For example, in his 1942 preface to the third edition of *The Mass Psychology of Fascism*, Reich writes that in the early 1930s he was 'regularly forced to make use of the conventional Marxist sociologic concepts', and he claims with some bitterness that between 1934 and 1937 'it was always Communist party functionaries who warned fascist circles in Europe about the "hazard" of sex-economy'.[95] In a 1941 letter to his British friend A. S. Neill, Reich expressed disappointment in 'isms',[96] and in a 1952 interview with the psychoanalyst Kurt Eissler he said that by setting up his 'sex-economy' as a political movement he had made a 'great mistake', and that he never was a political Communist or Marxist.[97] After emigrating to the United States in 1939, he became increasingly anti-Marxist, denouncing Communists as 'Red Fascists' in his later writings.[98] As an explanation for his ultimate failure to establish a sex-political movement that would have had lasting value, Reich blames his extremist approach on social issues: he admits that he went too far, far enough to make far too many enemies. These included psychoanalysts, socialists, Communists, National Socialists and even the liberals. They were all against him.[99]

Mental Hygiene and the Psychology of Unmasking

Reich regarded it as self-evident that social factors play a major role in the aetiology of mental disturbances. Therefore, he considered it necessary to analyse social determinants and to promote appropriate social changes which would presumably alleviate neurosis and other forms of mental alienation. This mental-hygienic task was nothing short of formidable, for he estimated that as many as ninety per cent of all women and about seventy to eighty per cent of all men were sick![100] For the later Reich, virtually the whole of humanity was 'biologically sick', this sickness manifesting itself as the 'fear of freedom'. However, thanks to 'healers' such as Reich, 'thousands of years of human suppression were in the process of being eliminated', and the knowledge of life energy would bring about a 'new religion of life'.[101]

If psychomedical experts venture to make a diagnosis of the mental state of the 'masses', they have to be able to see through the 'character armour' or at least to pontificate on the 'essence' of inner nature. This is exactly what most psychoutopians did – they claimed to be able to see the 'hidden self'. The specific mentality behind this assertion can be traced back to Nietzsche's questioning of the authenticity of human ideals, which appeared in his writings in the form of *entlarvende Psychologie*, the psychology of unmasking. As a Nietzschean *entlarvende* psychologist, Reich was a true virtuoso. Besides being himself the subject of a psychoanalytic unmasking (which 'showed' that he was mentally unbalanced), he was far from reluctant to apply diagnostic labels to his foes and opponents, and – later in his life – to all the 'Little Men' who could only dream of such utopian qualities as 'full orgastic potency'.[102] Reich asserted that his 'depth psychology' was able to disclose 'biologic motives behind psychic phenomena', to demonstrate that 'most psychoanalysts were genitally disturbed', and to elucidate how the socialist radicalism of 'raging Marxists' was the 'outlet for a pathological rebellion against deep-seated attachments to the bourgeois family situation and bourgeois ideology'.[103] As for his claim that 'mechanistic' physicists were incapable of observing Orgone Energy, Reich explained that it was because their armoured character structure made them afraid of autonomic organ sensations.[104] As befits a man who saw through the masks of others and understood the true motivations of people, Reich suggested that he possessed knowledge that others (e.g., 'rigidly armored scientists') lacked. This can be seen in his self-assured claim that 'the broad mass of the earth's population must come to the gradual and unshakeable conviction that we are the only ones who understand them'.[105] His psychological X-ray revealed the darkest and most hidden corners of the human psyche, providing him with the necessary information he needed to heal the sick soul.

In the 'principles for our methods of work' from 1934, Reich states that

> the broad apolitical mass has a decisive effect upon the fate of the revolution, therefore politicise private life, fairs, dance-halls, cinemas, markets, bedrooms, hostels, betting shops! ... One must learn to politicise the personal.[106]

This was exactly what Reich was eagerly learning himself, for he wanted to investigate every nook and cranny of the private life of the 'masses' so as to make the human personality an object of a right kind of mental hygiene. He eradicated the boundaries between the private and public spheres and displayed an inclination to control humans at their most intimate level, to divine their private thoughts, and to reify one component of human life – sexuality – to the most real of all being. Besides declaring that the 'human structure' must be accommodated to the collective modes of existence, he proposed that all forms of literature which increase sexual anxiety (pornography, criminal fiction and children's horror stories) should be forbidden. He also suggested setting up exemplary educational institutions (*Mustererziehungsanstalten*) for the sex-economic supervision and regulation of people's sexual activities.[107] Moreover, as a dedicated Communist he demanded his wife Annie to choose between two options when they moved to Berlin: either to place their two daughters full-time in a Communist kindergarten or to divorce him. As Reich's second wife Ilse Ollendorff Reich writes in her biography of Reich,

> Annie consented to the children being sent to the home [kindergarten], although she feels today that this was a great mistake on her part. The children recall the home as a very unhappy experience.[108]

Like any mental hygienist, Reich wanted to control (sexual) behaviour and establish normative boundaries between 'good' and 'bad' (sexual) behaviour, and as a Communist he also wanted to abolish the 'bourgeois family' and collectivize the upbringing of children.

As sociologist Anna Bergmann has noted, Reich's programme of 'sexual revolution' was right in line with the technocratic and certainly patriarchal desire to control and dominate nature, including female sexuality. Moreover, Reich demolished the individual with his or her idiosyncrasies and instead focused on the masses, on the anonymous entity that must be educated according to the scientific principles of sexual and mental hygiene.[109] Psychologist and historian Kurt Danziger has pointed out that during the interwar years the mental-hygiene movement 'energetically pursued programs of intervention in the lives of individuals' and generated a whole ideology based on

> the twin beliefs that the causes of social and interpersonal problems were to be located in the maladjustment of individuals and that the origins of such maladjustment lay in the histories of individuals – that is, in childhood.[110]

The major difference between (American) mental hygienists and Reich was that whereas the former usually had no difficulty in finding funding for their activities, Reich had much more limited financial and political resources at his disposal. After his expulsion from the Communist party and the IPA, he became an increasingly isolated mental hygienist.[111]

Paradoxically, for all his exhortations to politicize and collectivize the most intimate spheres of life, Reich was an ardent defender of the rights of children, youths and women. It seems that whereas his Marxist political mindset prompted him to blur the boundaries between the private and the public spheres, his personal philosophy was rebellious and individualistic enough to make it exceedingly difficult for him to conform to any norms imposed from above, be they professional (psychoanalysis) or political (the Communist party). Even when he was zealously studying the social determinants of the private sphere, he thought he could instil revolutionary principles in the minds of humans so as to make them capable of governing their own lives. Notwithstanding his passing commitment to the idea of collectivizing the upbringing of children, his enthusiastic affirmation of the autonomy of youth and of their need to have their own dwelling, their own private space, appears to me as one of the most refreshing and enduring aspects of his life work. In some ways, Reich had an exceptionally enlightened attitude towards children and adolescents, and he surely swam against the tide of his time by propagating anti-authoritarian education (e.g., he deemed it necessary to organize an international propaganda movement against beating children[112]). In his fight against patriarchal upbringing and morality, he sided with the working-class women and youth, whom he saw quite plausibly as victims of the 'life-negating' social order and as potential agents of revolution. On the other hand, he also stigmatized the mother-child relationship, promoted the abolition of the family and reduced the erotic dimension of life to a tangible natural-scientific phenomenon of bioelectrical discharge of tension. It was love without tears, sexuality without mystery.

In conclusion, there is no doubt that Reich was a radical mental hygienist who had a definite view of how to heal the sick society, and who envisaged a fundamentally different mode of living and loving that might be realized after a transformation of the structures and institutions of society (especially the family). But what seemed to be uppermost in Reich's mind at this stage was to design means of creating a form of 'healthy' socialism which would allow humans not only to celebrate their sexuality, but also to seek expressive fulfilment in everyday life (including work and leisure) and, concurrently, to find the strength of their inner nature, exercise their critical faculties and work for the sexual and political emancipation of fellow humans. Reich was sharp and categorical in his condemnation of the 'bourgeois' social order, which he, like many other Marxist intellectuals, equated with fascism, but he gave full vent to his utopian inclinations only when he became immersed in the study of the essence of life in the late 1930s and the early 1940s.

Reich as the Orgone Biophysicist

By the end of the 1930s, Reich had replaced socialism by his own, apolitical concept of 'work-democracy', which he saw not as a political programme, but as a 'newly discovered bio-sociologic, natural, and basic function of society'.[113] He had simultaneously moved from psychodynamic conceptual categories to 'biodynamic' ones, which meant that he subsumed all psychic activity under the primal vegetative function. In 1939 and 1940, he continued his experiments with the microscopic vesicles called bions, unearthing the old idea of spontaneous generation.[114] In the course of his studies, he made the fundamental observation that bions emitted a particular kind of radiation. He concluded that these transitional forms between living and non-living matter are charged with a hitherto unknown form of energy.

In 1940, Reich made the even more startling observation that this unknown energy existed also in the atmosphere. This observation led him to conceptualize the new energy as a cosmic energy which is capable of charging organic matter, as well as measurable and demonstrable visually, thermically, electroscopically and by means of Geiger-Müller counters.[115] He coined this new form of energy 'Orgone', deriving the term from the words 'organism' and 'orgastic'.[116] He came to see Orgone Energy as universal primordial energy working behind all manifest biological energy and penetrating all existing matter. For the rest of his life he dedicated himself to the investigation of the nature of its functions, including the scientific, social, meteorological and medical (Orgone Accumulators) ramifications of this all-powerful life force. As he put it in *Ether, God and Devil* (1949),

> ORGONE ENERGY CAN BE DEMONSTRATED EVERYWHERE SINCE IT IS PRESENT EVERYWHERE. ACCORDINGLY, IT PENETRATES EVERYTHING, THOUGH AT VARYING RATES OF SPEED. [original in capital letters][117]

By 'discovering' Orgone Energy, Reich sincerely believed that he had stumbled upon the bioenergetic foundation of humankind, moreover a foundation that was an object not of metaphysical speculation but of natural scientific observation. 'The libido discovered by our teacher Freud is now both tangible and measurable as biologically efficacious Orgone Energy', wrote Reich in a 1942 letter to Dr Hitschmann. He went on to state: 'The existence of orgone can be objectively demonstrated'.[118] He could now see himself as a scientist who had revealed the 'secrets of the nature'.[119] In the late 1940s, he believed his research had expanded to universal proportions, for he was studying the putative origin of all matter and energy in living beings and in galactic systems. Reich called this universally existent, all-permeating primordial energy 'Cosmic Orgone Energy'.

Emphasizing the moving and pulsating nature of Orgone, he called his new science Orgonomic Functionalism.

As a self-proclaimed natural scientist, Reich was anxious to become a member of a scientific community and give up his boring therapeutic work for good.[120] Yet, by opposing research on genes and questioning some of the fundamental tenets of modern physics (such as the law of gravitation[121]), he could not find any support for his 'findings' among scientists. An insurmountable problem in his research was that he, as well as almost all his pupils and associates, were trained as physicians, clinical psychologists, sociologists or philosophers, not as physicists or biologists – in short, they were amateurs for whom conducting a scientific experiment in rigorous ways was too demanding. There was an additional problem which made research difficult for Reich: a chronic lack of financial resources, which required him to let his associates help him with money. And as most of the people who helped him were, or had been, in therapy with him, scientific and psychological issues became intertwined in ways that make his whole therapeutic business seem little suspicious. As Myron Sharaf puts it,

> with justification, Otto Fenichel has criticized Reich for abusing the transference situation – the patient's dependence upon and devotion to his therapist – by getting such people to help through working or giving money or both ... Often when for one reason or another they became disappointed in Reich, and when he was under attack from more scientifically trained professionals, they could regret their earlier enthusiasm. Sometimes they would ask for their money back which led to ugly scenes. Reich's reminder that he had expressly warned them before they gave money or other help seems somewhat self-serving in the face of the blinding power of transference.[122]

In short, Reich used his therapeutic practice as a recruiting office, enlisting patients and analysands in his scientific cause.

The great professional disappointment in Reich's life, even greater than his expulsion from the IPA, was the fact that he was unable to reach out to the wider world of science. What disappointed him most was his failure to convince Albert Einstein, whom he met two times at Princeton in January and February 1941. On his first visit, Einstein listened politely for more than four hours to what he had to say about Orgone Energy, and after the second visit, he let his assistant investigate the Orgone Accumulator box that Reich had brought with him to Einstein's laboratory. Orgone Accumulators were designed to concentrate the atmospheric Orgone Energy in the accumulator, which was a coffin-like box wherein one sat for a period of time. Reich believed that his accumulators had medical significance: an optimal exposure to Orgone Energy was to guarantee therapeutic effects on the whole organism. The investigation made by Einstein's assistant suggested that the difference between the temperature inside the accumulator and the surrounding air in the room, which Reich believed gave evidence of the existence of Orgone Energy, could be explained by the established theories of thermometry (convection currents between the air over the table – where the accumulator was placed– and the air of the room as a whole).[123] Apparently, at this point Einstein considered the case closed, but Reich kept on sending him long letters, to which Einstein no longer cared to reply. This was a heavy blow to Reich, who according to his wife had started to

> daydream of possibilities for working with Einstein at the Institute for Advanced Studies, where he would be in a community of scientists on a level where he, Reich, would not always be the giving one, with everybody else taking, as it was in his own Institute, but where he could find a give and take on his own level.[124]

Einstein's response to what he saw as irrefutable empirical evidence increased Reich's agony and frustration, which resulted in his decision to turn his back on the scientific community altogether.[125] Reich believed that if a genius such as Einstein was incapable of understanding him, there was no hope of getting the approval of lesser scientists. Nevertheless, he did send reports of Orgone Energy to the National Research Council, the Committee on Medical Research, American Academy of Sciences and the Atomic Energy Commission, but failed to arouse those agencies' interest in his research. Two years after his disappointing contact with Einstein, Reich wrote in his diary entry for 7 September 1943 that

> Doing orgone research could be compared to swimming the Pacific Ocean. You swim for days, weeks, months, put dozens, even hundreds of miles behind you! And still an infinite stretch always lies ahead. You cannot rest, enjoy your success – onward, onward, always farther, always more! It is like reaching for infinity! The orgone is the basic energy of the universe. How cruel![126]

Even though Reich's theory about Orgone is mythical rather than scientific, the fact that he became increasingly sensitive to manifestations of what he saw as Deadly Orgone Energy in the atmosphere means that, with his observations about air pollution, he was ahead of his time. Although his explanations of the causes of pollution were wrong, he made acute observations of changes in the atmosphere long before environmental issues became topical. He saw the atmosphere almost as if it was a higher being, something that can feel and act upon us.[127]

Reich's Vitalist Philosophy of Nature

Rather than going deeper into the story of how Reich attempted to make his Orgonomic Functionalism accepted as a new science of nature, I shall turn to Reich's Orgone-related assumptions and intentions. I would suggest that, with his conviction of the existence and power of a new form of universal energy, Reich was not so much a misguided natural scientist as a life philosopher whose observations were governed by his vitalist and holistic beliefs. More than anything, his ideas resemble early nineteenth-century German Romanticism (Novalis, Friedrich Schlegel and Friedrich Schelling) and especially *Naturphilosophie*, philosophy of nature, as inaugurated by Schelling with his seminal *Ideen zu einer Philosophie der Natur* (1797) and followed by such authors as Goethe, Lorenz Oken, C. G. Carus and Eduard von Hartmann. In the German cultural sphere, *Naturphilosophie* was an early representative of holism in its speculative search for organic unities lying behind the diversification of the phenomenal world. Behind the appearance of the mere physical facts of the universe there hid a grander purpose, the disclosing of which required not natural scientific but philosophical skills. Philosophy of nature has a long history, going back to Plato and Aristotle, and as a philosophical tradition it lived on through the nineteenth and twentieth centuries, assuming new forms.[128] As discussed in the previous chapter on Jung, historians Anne Harrington and Mitchell G. Ash have demonstrated in their respective studies that it was very typical of (German-speaking) researchers and thinkers of the interwar period to search for wholeness in life and science. German holism in turn was connected with *naturphilosophische* and early twentieth-century neo-vitalist issues.[129]

In his unyieldingly obstinate quest for an underlying unity, Reich represented a form of holistic thinking that wanted to transcend all the complexities, contradictions and uncertainties of the phenomenal world. As he asserted in 1949, 'since everything in nature is interconnected in one way or another, the subject of "orgonomic functionalism" is practically inexhaustible'.[130] This belief in the interconnectedness of 'everything in nature' is *naturphilosophische* through and through, because it emphasizes interdependencies and the functional unity of organisms. In his search for totality and wholeness, Reich discredited all but 'theories of all', as it were: if a theory gave an account of only a fragment of life, it was useless for Reich. With good reason, psychoanalyst Charles Rycroft calls the system of ideas that Reich developed in his later years as 'philosophy of life, a Weltanschauung, perhaps even a cosmology or theology'.[131] Rycroft has also noticed Reich's vitalism and his adherence to holistic thinking.

Although Reich tried hard to remove all philosophical speculations from his 'natural-scientific' investigations of living organisms, he inadvertently joined forces with early twentieth-century neo-vitalists, such as Hans Driesch and Henri Bergson, and became a natural philosopher with grandiose utopian ambitions. In his early career, Reich was influenced by Bergson's philosophical vitalism, and, as he later recounted, as early as 1922, when he had proposed a literal reading of Freud's conception of the 'sending out of libido', he fabricated a 'natural scientific fantasy' under the influence of Bergson and Richard Semon, an innovative researcher on the function of memory to whom I referred in my chapter on Jung.[132] Underlying Reich's work from the outset was an uneasy relationship with the speculative vitalist and *naturphilosophische* doctrines, which he first openly embraced as a young medical student and then, as a psychoanalyst and political psychologist, discarded as non-scientific. Yet, far from disappearing from the Reichian scene, vitalism and *Naturphilosophie* entered it from the back door and assumed major roles in the 1940s.

I argue that Reich's later utopianism had its philosophical roots in the metaphysical search for the governing principles of life in nature, which characterized nineteenth-century German *Naturphilosophie*. Reich himself saw the sixteenth-century Italian philosopher of nature Giordano Bruno as his true predecessor. Bruno, who was burned to death as a heretic by the Roman Inquisition, was a 'functionalist' who had anticipated 'some basic orgonomic thoughts'.[133] In Reich's vocabulary, what is 'functional' is close to 'natural', and a functionalist is therefore someone who is in immediate contact with both inner nature and external nature.[134] In his recent study of Reich, philosophical theologian Robert S. Corrington has noted Reich's vitalist and holistic assumptions about the universal *Lebenskraft*, even if he prefers to call Reich a 'radical naturalist' whose 'psychosemiotic' way of reading the signs of nature differed radically from that of 'mainstream' naturalists (e.g. physicists and evolutionary biologists). Corrington has also rightly noted the strong metaphysical, religious and ecstatic aspects of Reich's naturalism. But where he radically differs from the more sceptical scholars of Reich, including me, is in his belief in the truth value of some of Reich's research: Corrington has a 'growing sense that something like orgone exists and that Reich ... had it basically right'.[135]

What was characteristic of Reich's *Naturphilosophie* was its natural-scientific outlook: he insisted on the tangible, observable qualities of the vitalist life force or Orgone, the existence of which 'can be objectively demonstrated'.[136] In 1945, he wrote that, while Freudian *Id*, Aristotelian and Drieschian *entelechy*, Bergsonian *élan vital*, and his own Orgone describe the same thing (which in fact was not true), his concept fundamentally differed from these other concepts in that it was not merely an expression of 'human *intuitions* of the existence of such an energy', but '*a visible, measurable, and applicable energy of a cosmic nature*'.[137] Presenting his conjectures regarding the subjective emotional life and objective cosmic energy as scientific discoveries, he simultaneously elevated himself to the position of a genius who has revealed the 'secrets of the nature'[138] and alone disposed of the 'formula and the experiments which give mankind power over the raising of living substance from non-living substance'.[139] Consequently, Reichian Orgonomy, far from being just a branch of natural science, or a particular psychology or biology, was 'a body of knowledge which deals with the basic law of nature'.[140] In reality, his empirical investigations were dictated by a preconceived theoretical imperative, and hence the evidence that he found was always supportive of his theories. Reich's empirical observations, just like those of the other three authors discussed in this book, were extremely theory-laden.

This shortcoming, together with his lack of scientific 'truth community' and his inadequate knowledge of a scientific procedure helps to explain why he was not taken seriously as a scientist.

In the late 1940s, Reich, an assimilated Jew who had had a critical if not hostile attitude towards religion in his 'European' years, became increasingly preoccupied with religion. In *The Murder of Christ* (1953), his most explicit elaboration on this theme, he acknowledged that Orgonomy was 'basically not in disagreement with religious thought'.[141] He identified God with Cosmic Orgone Energy and himself with Christ, who in his embodiment of Orgonotic principles was a 'genital character' and as such symbolized an 'unarmored life'.[142] In his Orgonomic eschatology, he envisaged the Orgone Energy as the principal means of salvation, as something equivalent to the divine spark of the Gnostics or God's grace, which would bring about a 'majestic conquest of DOR[143] (Deadly Orgone Energy) by OR (Orgone Energy), as if what is dead should be declared dead and be eliminated from the process of living, seething life'.[144] True to his vitalism, he saw nature in terms of animate forces and regarded nuclear energy (NR) as a secondary, evil natural function. After his dangerous experiment with nuclear radiation in 1951 (the so-called Oranur experiment), he had the impression that he and his co-workers had 'somehow provoked the otherwise benign OR energy and turned it into a wild beast'.[145] It was as if they had provoked the wrath of God by trying to manipulate divine cosmic energy.

With his 'natural religion of orgonotic pulsation',[146] Reich was both transgressing the boundaries between the known and the unknown and dividing the world into black and white. He tried to put order in the world through a long list of binary categories: the principle of life versus emotional plague; primary drives versus secondary drives; orgastic potency versus orgastic impotence; functional versus mechanistic-mystical thinking; unarmoured versus armoured personality structure; bions versus T [Tod]-bacilli; true nature versus second nature; genital sex versus sexual repression; genital embrace versus sexual performance; matriarchy versus patriarchy; work-democracy versus politics; Orgone Energy versus Deadly Orgone Energy; laughter versus giggle. Reich subsumed all phenomena under binary categories, thereby disregarding the complexities and contingencies of any reality that refused to be categorized simplistically into good and bad. As psychiatrist Anthony Storr has succinctly put it, 'in an impossibly complex universe, we long for simplicity, for a world divided into black and white'.[147] In his adherence to the myth of polarity, Reich manifested a thought pattern that, as the medical historian Roy Porter has observed, 'run[s] deep in Western culture, encouraged by philosophical dualisms deriving from Platonic and Pauline sources and reinforced by Cartesian philosophy'.[148] This dualistic thought pattern can be seen in the fundamental opposition of body and soul, psyche and soma, heaven and hell, as well as in the medical concept of manic-depression and the cultural infatuation with Jekyll-and-Hyde doubles. The cosmic struggle of opposites in Reich's Orgonomic Functionalism can be situated in this traditional Western mythology of polarities.

'We are not utopians': Utopianism in Reich

In 1920, the young medical student Reich admitted that

> I have been imbued with much more idealism than is practicable. I strive for clearer vision and suffer the bitterest disappointments because of this.[149]

Later in his life, he was well aware that he had long been 'accused' of being a prophet of a better orgasm and an unrealistic utopian. In his sexual-political years, he criticized psychoanalysts who believed that

> psychoanalysis can reshape the world by a process of evolution and so replace social revolution. That is a utopian dream founded on total ignorance of economic and social reality.[150]

In a 1934 letter to his former wife Annie, Reich wrote that he and his little Norwegian group are not utopians ('*Wir sind keine Utopisten*'), because they proceed step by step, and from one detail to another, with the fundamental conviction that all details must be checked along the way.[151] And in his *Function of the Orgasm* (1942), he replied to the accusation that he was being a utopian, a prophet of pleasure, by pointing out that pleasure is only conceivable when it is concomitant with struggle; to be fully alive is to acknowledge and confront all situations in life, including by necessity unpleasant and painful ones.[152] What Reich wanted to convey with this claim was that he was not trying to achieve illusory goals, which he equated with utopianism.

In order to see Reich's negative statements about utopia in a proper context, two qualifications must be entered. First, his depreciatory statements reflected the predominantly negative attitude towards utopianism that was prevalent in European intellectual culture in the first half of the twentieth century.[153] Left-wing intellectuals, most of whom wanted to dissociate their ideas from utopian thought, were influenced by Marx's narrow understanding of utopianism:

> For (Marx), utopianism was not so much a scheme for a better society, which breaks radically with current social relations and ways of life, but rather a radical vision of a new, socialist society that overlooks socioeconomic trends and concomitant political forces, and thus contains 'unrealistic' suggestions for transforming it in actual existence.[154]

Second, during the 1940s and 1950s, when the utopian elements in his thinking were more pronounced than in the previous two decades, Reich did not even touch upon the issue of utopianism in his writings any more. Arguably, for Reich, utopianism was too close to the bone, as it were; he did not want to make explicit any possible links between utopianism and his Orgonomic Functionalism, because it would have further undermined his scientific credibility.

In the process of evaluating the quality of Reich's utopianism, we could start from his own understanding of the ultimate goal of his work. In his Orgonomic period, his fundamental aspiration was the same as it had been in his sex-political years: to save the great masses from misery. In a 1941 letter to A. S. Neill, he wrote that he had 'given birth to a very great knowledge', which could be of equally great benefit for humankind if only those who ran things would acknowledge his greatness.[155] In a similar vein, he stated in his interview with Kurt Eissler in the early 1950s, when he reminiscenced about the sex-political days, that 'I knew the people were sick, but I wanted freedom for them'.[156] In his article on psychoanalysis and utopia, psychoanalyst Emanuel Berman argues that the utopian visions of psychoanalysts have their psychological source in the unconscious rescue fantasy.[157] Such a psychodynamic perspective on utopianism, no matter how speculative and narrow, may shed some light on the Messianic ambition of Reich, who wanted nothing less than to save humanity. As his biographer Myron Sharaf has observed, Reich had a 'strong need to live a heroic life' and so he was inspired by a 'rescue fantasy, a desire to save the world, with a concomitant overestimation of the world's desire and capacity to be saved'.[158]

Almost from the start, Reich's life and work were guided by a strong vision of a good life that would come about if humans could be restructured so as to make their original unspoiled 'inner nature' free from the shackles of pathogenic culture. Instead of placing his ideal society in a future socialist society, as he had done in his sex-political years, he now tacitly assumed that only in a liberal-democratic society, such as the United States, could the human animal be brought into harmony again with his or her natural constitution and the surrounding social environment. He had strong faith in the possibility of inner transformation, for the whole raison d'être of his work was founded on the utopian belief that the discordance between the opposing forces of (inner) nature and culture could be reconciled and brought into harmony.

As a means to achieve such a harmony, Reich suggested a 'restructuring' of the human character and an ensuing personality transformation, which he regarded as the necessary prerequisite for the thorough transformation of society. In his utopian vision, a complete (genital) restructuring would lead to a 're-establishment of the unarmored, natural state ("paradise")', which would signify the freedom of the human organism from 'rigidity, dullness, immobility, and the rest of the biophysical straitjacket'.[159] As he wrote in *The Oranur Experiment* (1951), his belief in this particular 'dearmoring' or authentification of personality structure was based on the existence of 'forward-looking forces that are at work everywhere in the world'. Manifesting the utopian principles of hope, desire and renewal, he went on to proclaim:

> Only a very few responsible people are fully aware today that an old, tired, bound-up world is breaking down, and that a new, hopeful, young world is slowly and painfully being born. *The current biosexual revolution, which has been in progress for the past thirty years, constitutes its core.*[160]

According to Reichian 'natural law', to the extent we can fulfil our innate biological potentialities, we can lead an authentic life and become 'genital characters'. When Reich set this utopian ideal type against the 'neurotic' and 'armoured' personality structure, he gave a normative account of the difference between 'is' (fact) and 'ought' (value), and claimed to be in possession of 'objectively' true values. He conceptualized inner transformation in his sex-political years in political terms (as an emergence of the 'Revolutionary Personality') and then, from the late 1930s onwards, in biophysical terms (as an emergence of the 'Functional Personality'). His utopian exhortation of the unspoiled, spontaneous and harmonious inner nature had distinct Rousseauean and anthropological elements in it. He was inspired by the Rousseauean idea that social injustices and inequalities are the result of cultural evolution gone astray, and in a Rousseauean fashion he declared that if humans succeed in peeling off the layers of pathogenic culture within themselves (this is what he called 'dearmouring'), they will find the original source of good and thus initiate the building of a more just and humane society. His vision of unspoiled nature was stimulated by his friend Bronislaw Malinowski's anthropological fieldwork in the Trobriand Islands, as well as by the ideas of 'original matriarchy' put forward by Bachofen, Morgan and Engels (on the myth of matriarchy, see the chapter on Gross). According to Reich's 'Grossian' interpretation of matriarchy, there was no conflict between the individual and social regulation of sexuality in the primordial primitive society (*Urgesellschaft*). On the contrary, the imaginary 'primitives' lived in sexual harmony, which was shattered only after the rise of a pathological patriarchal social order in the distant past.[161]

In the mythical matriarchal society as conceived by Reich, humans lived in a paradise. This happy state of things came to an end with the emergence of a patriarchal 'mechano-mystical' civilization, which defeated the god-like human qualities and led to the structural armouring of personality. Consequently, when the free display of primary, naturally inborn drives gave way to the domination of secondary, perverted, evil drives, so-called civilized humanity experienced biological degeneration.[162] By means of the Reichian type of functional thinking and research, however,

> the blocking of natural contact with the self and the surrounding world will slowly … as the prevention of armoring in the newborn generations succeeds … completely vanish from the surface of this earth.[163]

Reich conjectured that the ultimate outcome of this beneficial process will be the re-establishment of the unity of culture and nature, and the simultaneous appearance of a 'new type of Man', which is concomitant with the passing of the age of 'Mechanism and Mysticism' to the functional 'Cosmic Age'.[164] Paradise lost and regained.

What probably most clearly distinguished Reich's later utopianism from his earlier work as a political psychologist was his antagonistic attitude towards historical time. As a Marxist psychoanalyst he had expressed faith in history, for the Russian Revolution of 1917 had apparently demonstrated that humans can invent themselves; that they can both make their history *and* be aware of the future implications of their acts. The hidden face of history was supposedly revealed in the Revolution, and this intensified the Marxist deification of history: it was history alone that could lead humanity to freedom.[165] By contrast, utopianism entails the idea that we cannot rely on history for salvation. Instead, we must envision a radical alternative to the prevailing order without pausing to think whether this alternative is grounded on any existing realities. History in the sense of change or rupture could actually cease to exist in a utopia, for in an ideal society historical change would only mean a change for the worse. This utopian transcendence of historical time is apparent in Reich's Orgonomic Functionalism, which revolves around the transhistorical and universal Orgone Energy that acts like the Aristotelian unmovable mover: it sets the world in motion without being itself affected by this motion (e.g. historical change). In Reich's polaristic view, not only human nature but the whole of the universe was radically divided against itself, and in his quest for a new social and cosmic order, he created a whole cosmological ontology, which culminated in the utopia of 'natural' living. His vision of the 'harmony of natural events'[166] looked beyond conflicts, compromises and frustrations that (in the modern view) constitute human history. For Reich, as for all psychoutopians, below the tumultuous surface of historical time there lies the solid rock of humanity that is resistant to change. It is this universal core of humanity that Reich, Gross, Jung and Fromm set against the contingency of history.

If Reich's understanding of historical time changed radically over the years, there was one thing that retained its principal role in his thinking from the early psychoanalytic days to the late bioenergetic system, where it functioned as the prime manifestation of the timeless Orgone Energy in history: genital sexuality. For Reich, sexuality was both *il primo motore*, the driving force in history, and *ens realissimum*, the most real of all being. When Reich observed post-World

War II American society, he noticed that a (bio)sexual revolution was going on around him. Such a revolution in the sexual sphere could, he believed, actualize utopian potentialities, because an individual's bio-energetic (i.e., natural) and sociocultural life would no longer oppose each other but would instead 'support, supplement, and enhance each other'.[167] In the next chapter we shall see how Erich Fromm, who was active in the United States in the 1950s and 1960s, made critical observations about the sexual emancipation of American youth – he argued in fact that Reich's theory about the reciprocal correspondence between sexual and political regeneration is patently false.

It would be quite foolish to claim that Reich was an apostle of uninhibited sexuality, for he was surprisingly puritan in sexual matters. Like most utopians, he was a moral crusader who made clear distinctions between good (healthy) and bad (perverse) sexuality, and who despised pornography and all instructions on 'sexual technique'. As I noted earlier in this chapter, he disliked homosexuality and other 'non-natural' forms of sexual behaviour, and considered the search for quick and easy sexual gratification detrimental to the human community.[168] In a tone of frustration, he lamented the fact that his sex-economy was regarded by some 'fools' as a doctrine of sexual orgy: 'I have no control over the many perverts and sadists who read my books and pass off their dirty fantasies as my doctrine'.[169] In Reich's utopia, sexual harmony did not mean sexual debauchery, and sexual emancipation was not an end in itself, but part of a deep-going biological revolution. Such an inner revolution would not only bring individuals closer to their genitals but, more importantly, closer to their inner truth. He also complained about psychoanalysts who had totally misunderstood his (and Freud's) message, and who, in their search for quick results, were advocates of a sexual short-circuit, preaching for 'instant gratification' (sexual intercourse, masturbation) without seeing that it was the inability to experience gratification which characterized neurosis in the first place.[170]

Reich's Utopian Mentality in the Face of Adversities

In the end, Reich expressed disappointment with his scientific achievements and especially with the muted or indifferent response from the scientific establishment to his research on Orgone Energy. As Reich lost his faith in history as salvation, there did not exist any ideological safety net for him on which he could have fallen back in those difficult moments when his utopian mentality could not guard him against doubt and self-doubt. In times of doubt, he could observe that widespread mental diseases would continue to have destructive effects on society and human life as long as the contradiction between nature and culture remained intact.[171] In times of self-doubt, he was ready to admit (in a letter to A. S. Neill in 1947) that his disciple's

> idea of saving the world with 500,000 (Reichian) vegeto-therapists is a completely illusionary one ... the presently living generation cannot be restructured. Only the misdeeds of the emotional pest can be limited and dammed in.[172]

What strikes the reader of Reich's recently published diaries and letters from 1934–47 is how often he expressed self-pity and lamented over his feeling of loneliness. His emigration to New York in 1939 and the accelerating world war intensified his melancholy mood. He wrote his former lover (an unofficial second wife) Elsa Lindenberg in 1940 that his 'old love for mankind has gone'[173] and, a year later, he noted in his diary:

> Who is supposed to save them [people] anyway? No one is capable of that! Whoever promises to save them will be their downfall. Either people will learn to be responsible adults or they will continue to be slaughtered like sheep by the millions – and rightly so.[174]

Thus, Reich's utopian mood occasionally gave way to anti-utopian sentiments that betrayed his disappointment with the way things had turned out.

Reich did not propagate doctrines of instant salvation, and he emphatically denied that orgone biophysics had anything to do with 'redemption'.[175] Yet, he also had dreams of the unity of all nations, of love becoming the only religion, and of Orgone Energy enabling us to 'visit distant stars and to contact other beings'.[176] Fully devoting himself to his work, he found consolation in his conviction that he was at the beginning of understanding life, and that he had achieved much more than his contemporaries.[177] In his diary entry for 12 July 1940 he wrote: 'Have I discovered the Basic Law of Nature? Or am I just a dreamer? No, I cannot deny the phenomena. They exist.'[178] In the end, his confidence in the crucial importance of his work was much stronger than his temporary feelings of uncertainty and self-doubt. Until the early 1950s, his enthusiasm was not defeated by a reality that was inimical to the timelessness of utopianism.

In 1951, things changed for the worse after the catastrophic Oranur experiment, from which Reich seemed never fully to recover. In October 1952, when psychoanalyst Kurt Eissler had told him that his former psychoanalytic colleagues and pupils from Europe, now living in New York, had only a peripheral interest in his work, Reich said in a mood of resignation: 'Nobody is interested. They can't be interested. The protoplasm doesn't sparkle any more.'[179] It was as if it had dawned on Reich that his utopia was destined to remain his own personal vision, shared by no one but a small core of loyal disciples who were not in a position to make his dream come true. For a man with so many original ideas, it must have been tragic to accept that, in the end, the protoplasm didn't sparkle any more. The utopian energies had been exhausted.

In the last decade of his life, when he was harassed by the Food and Drug Agency and the police, Reich turned his attention more and more away from biophysical aspects of human personality to universal Cosmic Orgone Energy and its counterpart, the Deadly Orgone Energy. At the centre of Reich's utopia there was no longer the human organism but the basic ur-energy of the whole physical universe, to which he related the 'human'-sized problems of unhappy people. In 1953, Reich saw the greatest peril in the 'bodily armoring', through which

> the human animal has separated himself from his biological origin, and thereby also from his cosmic origin, and has developed an instinctual structure that functions in an essentially irrational way. The result is the present chaos of our civilization, which man today can meet only with anxiety and horror.[180]

In this last phase of his utopianism, Reich became increasingly infatuated with religious terminology and saw the key to the 'tragedy of the human animal' in biological deterioration, which he conceived of as 'biological "original sin"'.[181] If Hegel's philosophy of the development of spirit found its fulfilment in the absolute, Reich's *naturphilosophische* utopia reached its culmination in the Cosmic Orgone Energy, which is the foundation of the 'Theory of Everything' and as such no less an absolute than the one we meet in Hegel.

Conclusion: Reality and Second Reality

When Reich was still a student, he wrote in his diary that 'my life, my actions, are dominated by one idea: reality is dirty'.[182] Indeed, in true utopian style, Reich was dissatisfied with the prevailing reality and, as he grew older, his urge to save humankind by envisaging the 'Second Reality' of expressive fulfilment and cosmic energy became more and more apparent. Like most psychoutopians, Reich was inclined to disregard historical reality in favour of a 'Second Reality', which he tacitly assumed to be closer to the truth, or even to represent the absolute truth itself. Reich's 'Second Reality' was a transcendental, higher reality, which was beyond history, but accessible to those who were unarmoured and thus rational enough to see the bioenergetic truth behind lesser truths. This allegedly non-mystic form of functional knowledge that Reich advocated was not so much an epistemological as a mystical category, for the proper method to achieve Reichian knowledge required something like an intuitive sensitivity to Orgonomic reality beyond mundane, profane reality. In his published writings, Reich never expressed doubts about the validity of his own theories nor reflected on the possibility that his belief system could in principle contain errors and inadequacies. This was contrary to a scientific attitude, which tolerates and even generates conflicting views. As physiologist and cancer researcher Theodore Hauschka put it, 'functional thinking à la Reich is wishful thinking so intense that one's experiments always corroborate one's intuitions'.[183]

After he was expelled both from the (Danish) Communist Party and the IPA, Reich gradually lost faith in Marxism and psychoanalysis, and began to develop his own *Wunschwelt*, the ultimate aim of which was to give natural scientific validity to his bioenergetic utopia. Until the mid-1930s, Reich was a politically radical psychoanalyst, who set forth not only a number of extremist and idiosyncratic ideas, but also rather reasonable, well-grounded suggestions, and his work had direct bearing upon the social reality of his contemporaries in Austria and Germany. Undoubtedly, he went further than other radical Freudians in pursuing his vision of a 'non-repressive' socialism, in which the sex-economic base and the ideological superstructure would stand in a harmonious relationship with one another. But when his Communist comrades and psychoanalytic colleagues disowned him, he began to construct his own bioenergetic reality. His Orgonomic utopia replaced the frustratingly indifferent or even hostile reality with the 'Second Reality', which manifested truth of a higher kind.

In order to articulate the newly-found Orgonomic law of motion, Reich created his own vocabulary. The key-terms 'Orgone Energy', the 'functional unity of life' and 'character armour' stand at the very limits of representation. Rather than concepts they are what the historian of religion Rudolf Otto called 'ideograms', non-rational linguistic frameworks for signifying the boundaries of the known and the unknown (on Otto and ideograms, see the chapter on Jung). Like Jung with his archetypes, Reich claimed to see what others did not see, and he created ideograms to account for his observations. In his insistence on the validity of those cosmic laws that he had 'discovered', he invented a new terminology, which became increasingly idiosyncratic and self-referential during the last decade of his life.

One of the reasons why Reich's vocabulary changed over time is that every time he made a new 'discovery' in nature he modified the conceptual framework of his anthropology accordingly. Thus, during his microscopic studies of the life of protozoa and amoeba in the mid-1930s, he asserted that in human organisms there is a wish to become spherical, and that this wish becomes acute in orgasm.[184] Twenty years later, after making observations of desert life (in conjunction with his attempt to make rain with his 'Cloudbuster'), he made comparisons between the desert and life in armoured people and characterized human life as if he was describing the life of the desert. As he himself noted in 1952, 'we are translating old, well-known psychological and bioenergetic terms into more fundamental physical terms'.[185] The point in Reich's physical reductionism was that, rather than subsuming biological and psychological terms under any known physicalistic language, he invented his own language, which was hard to reconcile with the scientific language of contemporary physics, chemistry and biology. Therefore, with his idiosyncratic vocabulary Reich himself made it exceedingly difficult for natural scientists to take him seriously – they just could not comprehend the conceptual universe Reich had created. And the cool or indifferent scientific reaction to 'Orgonomy' was probably the greatest disappointment he had to endure.

To fully understand the sad end of Reich's life, you could do no better than to read *Book of Dreams*, a lovely book authored by Reich's son Peter in the early 1970s. Peter Reich was thirteen when his father died in a federal prison in Lewisburg, and in *Book of Dreams* he gives a vivid, occasionally dreamlike portrait of his father, his home and the 'research centre' Orgonon in Maine, as well as of the problems his father encountered in the evening of his life. Peter Reich's book conveys the picture of a man who, while eccentric and moody at times, was a good father and a defender of the rights of children. He was also devastated by the court case against him, and even more so by the ensuing prison sentence.

In his book, Peter Reich describes an incident which provides a fitting final scene to my story of a 'fury on earth', who dreamt of saving humankind from sexual, social and psychological misery. One day in the mid-1950s, the local marshal received the order from the authorities to destroy the Orgone Accumulators that Reich kept in the premises of his estate. Peter Reich recalls that when the marshal and his assistants came down to Orgonon to execute the order, his father did not try to stop them. On the contrary, he remained calm and composed. According to Peter Reich, the marshal said to his father,

> 'Well, Doctor, the orders say that it is supposed to be done today, right here at Orgynon. I'm sorry, Doctor.'
>
> [Reich replied:] 'Well, don't be sorry. We must follow our orders, right?'
>
> The marshal tried to smile. 'Yup, that's right, Doctor.'[186]

When the marshal and his men had done their duty and were ready to leave, Reich asked them to burn his books too, like the police had done in New York. The marshal, who was feeling increasingly nervous and uneasy, politely declined and tried to get away from the embarrassing scene as quickly as possible:

> The marshal and one of the men walked around the far side of the black car and got in quickly. The other man, the driver, tried to walk around to the door but Daddy was in front of him. He stood in front of Daddy with his head lowered. Daddy just looked at him. After a long time, the driver raised his head and looked at Daddy and then he dropped his head again.
>
> 'Excuse me, Doctor. Please.'
>
> 'Yes, I'll excuse you. Of course.' He stepped aside and the man twisted past him and got into the car.
>
> Daddy walked around and looked at him in the window.
>
> The driver leaned out. His face was white.
>
> 'Doctor. I ... I'm sorry.'
>
> 'Yes. You're sorry. Of course. Aren't we all. Goodbye, gentlemen. Someday you will understand.'[187]

6 SOCIALIST HUMANISM AND THE SANE SOCIETY: UTOPIANISM IN ERICH FROMM

> Modern man is alienated from himself, from his fellow men, and from nature. He has been transformed into a commodity ... Modern man is actually close to the picture Huxley describes in his *Brave New World*: well fed, well clad, satisfied sexually, yet without self, without any except the most superficial contact with his fellow men
>
> Fromm, 1956[1]

The German-American psychoanalyst and social philosopher Erich Fromm (1900–80) proclaimed from the mid-1950s onwards that the life we live and the society we live in are sick, alienated and inadequate. The solution he offered for the sick society was 'Socialist Humanism', a fusion of Marxist, psychoanalytic and Messianic doctrines that would provide a viable political and existential alternative to state socialism and bureaucratic capitalism – the 'third way'.[2] In this chapter, I shall focus on the utopian aspects of Fromm's Socialist Humanism from the mid-1950s to the late 1960s. Most students of his life and work have analysed either his psychological theories or his relationship with the Frankfurt school; there are no detailed analyses of his Socialist Humanism and its utopian aspects.[3] My leading idea in this chapter is that a systematic inquiry into Fromm's social and political thought since the mid-1950s illustrates the intricate ways in which psychodynamic, religious and Marxist elements made up a particularly powerful form of utopian thought in the third quarter of the twentieth century.

Fromm is the youngest psychoutopian in this book; his last book was published in 1980, and his most utopian period began only with the publication of *The Sane Society* in 1955. By that time, Gross had been dead for thirty-five years; Reich was to die two years later; and the ageing Jung, who was immersed in alchemy and religion, had long ago ceased to develop ideas of 'national individuation'. Of these four authors, Fromm was the only one who did not have a medical degree; he became a 'lay analyst' who was early on interested in social psychology and especially in the various ways in which social structures have an impact on the human personality. Later in his life he became more of a social and moral philosopher who employed psychoanalytic and Marxist theories and concepts in his interpretations of psychological and sociocultural phenomena.

Like Reich, Fromm created his utopian ideas in the United States, where he found a relatively congenial environment for his therapeutic practice and psychoanalysis-inspired social cum moral philosophy. He was in fact one of the leading public intellectuals in the United States from the 1940s to the 1960s.[4] Starting with his study of the concept of freedom and the psychology of authoritarianism (*Escape from Freedom*, 1941), he wrote a number of widely-read books and became a 'modern guru to the middle classes in the postwar years'.[5] His works were often cited in sociological journals and his ideas were considered to be important for the social sciences.[6] But in the late 1960s his prestige waned, and his attempts to revive radical humanism did not find resonance among the younger generation of intellectuals, academics and political radicals. Today, Fromm is a 'forgotten intellectual', but as a 'revisionist' psychoanalyst he has a relatively secure status. There is an International Erich Fromm Society, based in Germany, and the bibliography of literature on Fromm comprises almost 4,000 titles.[7] There persists a lively scholarly interest in this 'forgotten intellectual's' ideas.

From Frankfurt to New York: Fromm's Life and Work

Erich Fromm was born in 1900 in Frankfurt as the only child of Naphtali Fromm, a wine trader, and Rose Fromm (née Krause).[8] The Fromm and the Krause families were well-established Orthodox Jewish families with strong religious traditions: there were a number of respected rabbis and Talmudic scholars in Erich's family line. Small wonder, then, that he was reared according to traditional Judaism, studied religious scriptures with Rabbi Nehemia Nobel, and, in his adolescent years, desired to study in a Talmudic university in Lithuania. The Hassidic teacher, Dr Salmon Baruch Rabinkow, a 'radical humanist', was especially important to the young Fromm.[9] Although he gave up his idea of becoming a religious scholar, he remained true to his family name (Fromm means 'pious' in German) until he rejected Orthodox Judaism at the age of twenty-six.

At the end of his life, when he reminiscenced about his youth, Fromm emphasized his early 'alienation' from modern life:

> For me, modern life was really not understandable, I didn't understand why people lived that way; I felt sorry for them. So my spiritual home was – one has to say – a medieval atmosphere, in which everything was directed to traditional learning, to the perfection of man, to spiritual values ... I was a stranger – very definitively so – and I indeed never regretted that.[10]

Considering the way the almost eighty-year-old Fromm looked back on his childhood, it seems he created a story of his life which highlighted the deep existential nature of his lifelong commitment to overcoming alienation, one symptom of which was the desire to make money – businessmen exemplified to the young, pious Fromm an altogether incomprehensible and intrinsically inferior world. That his own father was a merchant may have made Fromm's observations of the dichotomy between materialistic and spiritual values more acute.

After his graduation from the *Gymnasium* in Frankfurt, Fromm began to study law at the University of Frankfurt in 1918. The following year, he co-founded the Free Jewish Teaching Institute (Freie Jüdische Lehrhaus) in Frankfurt, and moved to the University of Heidelberg, where he studied national economy. His most important teacher at Heidelberg was Alfred Weber, Max Weber's brother, who supervised his dissertation, a study of the social function of Jewish law in three Diaspora communities.[11] At the same time, he continued Talmudic studies under Rabbi Rabinkow. After gaining his doctoral degree in sociology at Heidelberg in 1922, Fromm moved back to Frankfurt, where he was active at the Free Jewish Teaching Institute. There, he associated with such Jewish scholars as Franz Rosenzweig, Martin Buber and Gershom Scholem. He also befriended the psychoanalytic psychiatrist Frieda Reichmann, who – like Fromm – was at that time a strictly observant Jew.

Through Reichmann, who was eleven years older than he, Fromm discovered Freudian psychoanalysis, and he began personal analysis with her. The analysis was terminated when he started an affair with Reichmann, whom he married in 1926. By that time, he and Reichmann had opened a psychotherapeutic treatment facility in Heidelberg based on Orthodox Jewish principles. Leo Löwenthal, Fromm's friend, later recalled:

> The sanitarium was a kind of Jewish-psychoanalytic boarding school. An almost cultlike atmosphere prevailed there. Everyone, including me, was psychoanalyzed by Frieda.[12]

After further 'training analyses' with Wilhelm Wittenberg in Munich, Karl Landauer in Frankfurt and Hanns Sachs in Berlin, Fromm opened his own psychoanalytic practice in Berlin in 1930. A year before, he had co-founded the South-German Institute for Psychoanalysis together with his wife, Karl Landauer and Heinrich Meng, and in Berlin he befriended young Marxist psychoanalysts, most notably Reich, Siegfried Bernfeld and Otto Fenichel.

By the time he became a psychoanalyst in 1927, Fromm had abandoned Orthodox Judaism while becoming attracted to Marxism. Thus around the time of his renunciation of Orthodox Judaism, he found two other belief systems that would guide his intellectual life: psychoanalysis and Marxism. As was the case with many other intelligent Jewish middle-class scholars and physicians living in Germany in the aftermath of World War I, Fromm's road to Marxism was rather natural: he belonged to the Central European generation that had seen the disastrous effects of imperialism and nationalism, as well as the birth of the first socialist state in Russia in 1917, which showed that a radical transformation of society is a distinct possibility, and that the tyranny of money, commerce and exploitation of workers can be abolished. He did not, however, become a member of the German Communist Party; if anything, he was a Trotskyist, who assumed an increasingly critical attitude towards Stalin and Soviet-style Communism.[13] Later in his life, he corresponded for many years with Raya Dunayevskaja, the former secretary of Trotsky who developed Marxist humanism in the United States.

Navigating between Berlin and Frankfurt, Fromm led a busy life. In the late 1920s, he was introduced to Max Horkheimer, the Marxian director of the newly-founded Institute for Social Research (*Institut für Sozialforschung*) in Frankfurt. Horkheimer had a high regard for Fromm's ability to combine psychoanalytic and Marxist theories without succumbing to psychologism, and the two men worked rather closely together for a number of years.[14] At Horkheimer's Institute, Fromm took part in a methodologically primitive empirical study, based on questionnaires, on the values and political attitudes of mostly white-collar and skilled blue-collar workers in the Weimar Germany of the late 1920s and early 1930s (the study was first published in German in 1980). Fromm and his co-workers concluded that supporters of the workers' parties expressed 'a clearly authoritarian tendency'. Thus, the 'most important *result* is the small proportion of left-wingers who were in agreement in both thought and feeling with the Socialist line'.[15] In short, there was a discrepancy between manifest political outlook and underlying character structure among workers.

In 1931, Fromm separated from Frieda Reichmann, who later became a famous psychiatrist in the United States (they were officially divorced in the early 1940s).[16] In the same year, he fell ill with tuberculosis of the lungs, and in the following two years he had to spend much of his time in Davos, Switzerland, recovering from the disease. As the reader may recall, Reich had also been in a sanatorium in Davos because of tuberculosis (in 1927). Fromm, whose health was fragile during the 1930s, had to return to Davos in 1938 because of the second bout of the disease. In 1934, he emigrated from Nazi Germany, where life was becoming increasingly difficult for Jews. However, unlike Reich, who was a rather well-known Marxist political psychologist, Fromm was not in immediate danger when he left Germany. As a 'critical social psychologist', he had expressed his theoretical Marxist views in Horkheimer's *Zeitschrift für Sozialforschung* and in psychoanalytic journals, not in the streets of Berlin, like Reich had done. At the invitation of Karen Horney, also a refugee analyst from Europe, Fromm gave guest lectures in Chicago in 1933, and the following year he moved to New York, where he soon established his psychoanalytic practice. At first he analysed mainly sociologists and anthropologists who were keen on applying psychoanalytic theories within their fields. He became a guest professor at Columbia University and, for a period of time, continued his work at the relocated Frankfurt Institute, which had moved to New York and was linked to Columbia University.

Fromm had befriended the 'revisionist' psychoanalyst Karen Horney in Chicago, and in New York he began to co-operate with the psychoanalysts Clara Thompson and Harry Stack Sullivan, who was an influential psychodynamic psychiatrist and the founder of the journal *Psychiatry*. Sullivan also organized the Zodiac Club, an informal network of intellectuals, which was useful for Fromm in establishing his reputation. Together with Sullivan and a few other analysts, Fromm founded the William Alanson White Institute of Psychiatry, Psychoanalysis and Psychology in 1943. During this year, his intimate relationship with Karen Horney broke up, and the following year he married Henny Gurland, another refugee from Europe. By the early 1940s, he no longer had anything to do with the Frankfurt Institute: his relationship with Horkheimer and his associates, most notably Theodor Adorno, had turned sour, and his cultural revision of Freud's libido theory was denounced by his former colleagues at the Frankfurt Institute. In 1939, he parted with Horkheimer's Institute with mutual ill-feelings.[17]

Fromm's breakthrough to a large audience occurred with his 1941 book *Escape from Freedom*, which is perhaps his best-known work (with the possible exception of *The Sane Society*). Through his psychoanalytic work and his connections with such anthropologists as Margaret Mead and Ruth Benedict, he succeeded in building a reputation as an innovative theorist and analyst, who combined complex European psychopolitical thought patterns with uncomplicated but edifying reflections on the human condition, as well as with a clear and straightforward writing style. Due to his economic independence and the popularity of his books, he could disregard the increasingly antagonistic critique of the traditional psychoanalysts, who presented his revision of psychoanalysis as misleading and confusing. Reviews of his books in *Psychoanalytic Quarterly* reveal the extent to which mainstream psychoanalysts disliked Fromm's ideas. In 1942, Leon J. Saul wrote in his review of *Escape from Freedom* that Fromm gives 'a false impression of Freud and psychoanalysis which can only mislead and confuse the nonpsychoanalytic reader'.[18] Six years later, Rudolph M. Loewenstein wrote in his short review of *Man for Himself* that 'many will take issue with the rather questionable value of the ethical system he [Fromm] establishes [in the book]'.[19] In 1956, H. Robert Blank wrote in his review of *The Sane Society* that 'psychoanalysis is grossly misrepresented [in the book] ... Fromm's separating freudian [*sic*] psychoanalysis from Humanism is symptomatic of his incompatibility with psychoanalysis'.[20] He ends his rather negative review by stating that

> It is obviously easier to escape to the freedom of judging events of the past and blueprinting those of the future than to cope with real problems now. It is easier to talk

> about man over the centuries than to help enslaved and alienated men, women, and children.[21]

These three reviews are fairly representative of the 'official' US psychoanalytic criticism of Fromm's ideas.

In the early 1950s, Fromm, who did not have a medical degree, was excluded from the International Psychoanalytic Association (IPA),[22] which probably encouraged him to become more explicit in his critique of medicalized psychoanalytic doctrines and the psychoanalytic movement.[23] However, he never became an anti-Freudian, for he practised psychoanalysis as a 'lay analyst' and remained loyal to what he perceived as the true core of psychoanalysis (the study of unconscious processes). Despite his expulsion from the IPA, Fromm managed to remain a rather high-status analyst and a popular psychoanalytic thinker, whose 'marginalization' from official psychoanalysis and psychiatry did not have damaging effects on his life and work.[24]

In the 1940s, Fromm was a lecturer at the New School for Social Research in New York, as well as a professor at the Bennington College in Vermont. In 1950, he moved to Mexico with his wife, whose ailing health prompted the relocation to a more favourable climate. But in this regard the move did not have the hoped-for result, for his wife died in 1952. The following year, Fromm married his third wife, Annis Freeman. He became a professor extraordinary at the National Autonomous University of Mexico City, and was a pivotal figure in establishing the Mexican psychoanalytic society in 1956. At the Mexican institute, Fromm was an unchallenged master who 'personally analyzed the first generation of patients', many of whom were also his disciples,[25] a pattern not that uncommon in the rather hermetic or guild-like world of psychoanalysis. He stayed in Mexico for more than two decades, but continued to spend several months each year in the United States lecturing and conducting clinical seminars. In the late 1950s, he conducted a large-scale social-psychological field study on the social character in a Mexican village together with the young psychoanalyst Michael Maccoby and his Mexican assistants. A book based on the research was published in 1970 (*Social Character in a Mexican Village*, co-authored by Maccoby).

This is how the psychotherapist Robert Akeret, who as a young man was in training analysis with Fromm, describes Fromm's external appearance when he was in his mid-fifties:

> Physically Fromm was hardly an imposing figure. Rather short and somewhat plump, he was modestly dressed in open shirt, tweed jacket, and dark trousers. His thick graying hair was combed straight back from his squarish face, and he wore rimless bifocals that seemed to emphasize the bushiness of his eyebrows. But the man's famed intensity – his highly focused energy – was instantly palpable. I felt it in the powerful intelligence that shone through his eyes, yet it also seemed to radiate from his entire face; for lack of a better term, I would say that Erich Fromm had a robust aura.[26]

By the mid-1950s, the man with a robust aura had become a public intellectual and an oft-cited social critic, who articulated his views and opinions in a way that found resonance with a large audience in the United States and Europe (e.g. in the Nordic countries). He reached the peak of his popularity with his 1956 book *The Art of Loving*, which has been translated into thirty-five languages and has sold more than twenty-five million copies. He became a political and social activist in the latter half of the 1950s, and for more than a decade he was involved in various movements that opposed nuclear arms, the arms race and what he saw as the conformist aspects of American Cold War liberalism. He was the co-founder of an American peace movement, the Committee for a Sane Nuclear Policy (SANE, 1957), and, together with Harvard sociologist David Riesman, he founded the Committee for Correspondence, which published a newsletter arguing for arms control and the need for a dialogue with the Soviet Union.[27] In 1959, he joined the American Socialist Party, which was the most explicit manifestation of his new political activism. But he was not idle on the psychomedical front either: in 1962 he was one of the founders of International Federation of Psychoanalytic Societies, an umbrella organization of 'non-orthodox' psychoanalytic societies.[28] He also published several books and articles between the mid-1950s and his death in 1980. During these years, and especially between 1955 and 1968, he was an extremely productive author, who seemed to be driven by a burning ambition to realize his childhood dream of resolving the dilemma of alienation.

Fromm vigorously contested the authoritarian and accommodating inclinations of Cold War liberalism, which made him popular among students and the educated middle classes. In May 1966, for example, he had a total audience of 60,000 during a three-week lecture tour in California. His social activities prompted the FBI to monitor his work, and over the years the FBI officials accumulated a thick file on him.[29] However, unlike Gross and Reich, he was never actually harassed by the authorities either in Europe or in the United States. Although intellectual radicals in the American elite universities regarded the Marxist philosopher and Fromm's rival (and one-time friend) Herbert Marcuse rather than Fromm as their main source of inspiration, Fromm was not a 'forgotten intellectual' in the 1960s. After the failed presidential campaign of the Democratic senator Eugene McCarthy in 1968, Fromm became increasingly disillusioned with politics. In 1966, a heart attack had led to his retreat from active duties in Mexico, and after Nixon's victory in the 1968 elections he withdrew from political activism. He returned home to Mexico, and from there he moved back to Europe, settling in Locarno, Switzerland, in 1974. His last major work, *To Have or To Be?*, was published in 1976. He died as a result of heart attack (his fourth) in Locarno four years later, at the age of eighty.

The Character Juggler: Fromm's Gallery of Characters

The idea of 'character' played a pivotal role in Fromm's thinking from the time he introduced the psychoanalytic 'characterological' approach to social and political issues to a large English-speaking audience in *Escape from Freedom* (1941). He had first formulated such an approach in the early 1930s, and in 1947 he emphasized the crucial importance of the 'character system' for the study of man: 'The character system can be considered the human substitute for the instinctive apparatus of the animal'.[30] Because humans lack 'instinctual apparatus', human behaviour is largely governed by the specific ways in which 'psychic energy' is canalized. This means that there is a marked tendency in humans to think and act in accordance with their character, which is not innate but the result of upbringing and socialization.

Fromm's idea of the social character grew from his earlier Freudian interest in the social unconscious, which he examined as an 'analytic social psychologist' in the 1930s. Discounting Freud's theory of sexual instinct as inadequate, he developed a sociocultural explanation of human psychology, which owed much to the cultural-anthropological studies of Margaret Mead and Ruth Benedict. In his social-psychological contribution to the Frankfurt School's 1936 study on 'Authority and Family', he introduced the concept of the authoritarian character to explain the rise of fascism and National Socialism. In *Escape from Freedom*, which he first intended to call 'The Individual in the Authoritarian State', he was concerned with the various ways in which socialization moulds 'psychic energy' in order to make the collective character structure of a people (class, nation, etc.) useful for the smooth functioning of that society.[31] In particular, the concept of 'social character' elicited a positive response from social scientists who were well disposed to psychology, and Fromm regarded the concept – and the theory around it – as his most important contribution to social psychology.[32] His definition of the concept underwent changes, and it is perhaps most adequately expressed in his 1962 work on Marx and Freud, in which he defined the social character as an intermediary between the economic basis and the ideological superstructure. As an intermediary, the social character works both ways: it is influenced by the basis and by the superstructure, but it also creates ideas that in turn influence these two structures.[33] Thus the social character is perhaps as much a Weberian as a Marxist concept. As we shall see, it was Fromm's insistence on the importance of the social aspects of the mind that constituted an essential theoretical framework for his later utopianism.

In *Escape from Freedom*, and in many other writings, Fromm singled out the 'petty bourgeoisie' as the social group most eager to embrace authoritarian rule because of their social and political insignificance and their sense of being threatened by the working class, which led them to seek salvation in totalitarian dictatorships and in the law-and-order mentality. With his disdainful attitude towards the lower-middle class, which was supposedly responsible for much that was wrong in the modern world, Fromm represented a rather typical Central European intellectual. It was of course among the petty bourgeoisie that one could find the strongest support for authoritarian ideologies and an overall inclination to conform, but an additional problem with them was that they had no taste: by and large, they were crass materialists and gadget-oriented consumerists to whom Fromm spared his most disagreeable character structures: the anal character and the authoritarian character. His scornful attitude towards the vulgar desires of the lower-middle class was shared by, *inter alia*, his former colleagues Horkheimer and Adorno, who in their *Dialectic of Enlightenment* (1947) used much ammunition attacking the petty bourgeoisie and their tasteless 'consumerism'.[34]

In *Man for Himself*, his 1947 follow-up to *Escape from Freedom*, Fromm introduced the important concept of the marketing orientation. It referred to a new kind of character that was driven by the culturally-constructed need to sell oneself on the 'personality market', to possess the kind of personality that makes oneself attractive to employers and those in power, and to present oneself as a 'protean self' that is easily accommodated to different situations, especially those created by new demands in working life. As Fromm aptly put it,

> like the handbag, one has to be in fashion on the personality market, and in order to be in fashion one has to know what kind of personality is most in demand.[35]

Undoubtedly, with his concept of the marketing orientation (or 'the marketing character', as he called it in 1976), Fromm made an acute observation of a trend that has now, in the early twenty-first century, become increasingly dominant. What nowadays counts as an essential asset in working life is a personality that is geared up for constant changes, competition and flexibility in the workplace, and which reflects the image of infinite adaptability, sociability and busy activity.[36]

As a counterforce to the marketing orientation, Fromm introduced in *Man for Himself* the 'productive character', describing it as a 'mode of relatedness in all realms of human existence'. More specifically, the productive character denotes the human ability to realize all the potentialities within people, to make productive use of all of their powers: with the power of reason people can 'penetrate the surface of phenomena and understand their essence', with the power of love they can 'break through the wall which separates one person from another', and with the power of imagination they can 'visualize things not yet existing'.[37] Fromm's conceptualization of the productive character has elements of Jungian individuation (self-realization), the psychoanalytic technique of unmasking the unconscious psyche, Grossian emphasis on relatedness (*Wille zur Beziehung*) and the broad utopian propensity to 'visualize things not yet existing'. As if to make the significance of the productive character absolutely clear to the reader, he declares that 'the productive orientation is the basis for freedom, virtue and happiness'.[38]

The productive character signified the first of Fromm's 'utopian characters'. In 1961, Fromm reintroduced the 'revolutionary character', to which he had originally referred in 1936, and which has remarkable resemblances with the productive character.[39] The distinct trait in the revolutionary character is that he is independent and free, and identifies himself with humanity (it was always 'he' that represented humanity in Fromm's texts). The revolutionary character uses his freedom to criticize society from the rational and humanistic perspective, and he also has a deep love and reverence for life (just like the productive character has). As if the productive and revolutionary characters were not utopian enough, Fromm introduced in 1964 the grandest of his characters, the 'biophilous character'. Since the biophilous character compresses into two words the most essential aspects of Fromm's utopianism, I shall return to it (him?) later in this chapter. What I would like to suggest here is that the productive character, the revolutionary character and the biophilous character represent Fromm's utopian desire to create a 'New Man'. By contrast, the 'authoritarian character', the 'anal character' (originally devised by Freud and his pupil Karl Abraham) and their extensions, the 'hoarding orientation' (1947), the 'narcissistic character' (1964), the 'necrophilous character' (1964) and the 'marketing' or 'alienated character' (1976), represent Fromm's rogues' gallery. In addition, there are various personality types in Fromm's arsenal, including organization man, the automaton man, *homo consumens*, *homo mechanicus* and *homo esperans*. Late in his life, he created yet another 'type', the 'monocerebral orientation', which is characterized by an exceedingly intellectualistic and narcissistic approach to oneself and to the whole world.[40]

In real life, as Fromm readily admitted, one cannot find 'pure' characters, but rather a combination of various orientations.[41] But a watering down of the colourful descriptions of different characters and orientations by referring to them as 'ideal types' does not diminish the suggestive force of the productive character and the marketing orientation, which capture something essential about the different aspects of the human personality. A more sceptically-minded reader might say that classifications based on the interpretations of character traits can multiply infinitely to no avail if they are not related to a sound theory founded on systematic empirical observations. I would suggest that Fromm's typologies are occasionally very perceptive and insightful (I am especially convinced of the heuristic significance of the marketing orientation), but they are also rather arbitrary and value-laden constructions. They may indeed tell us something relevant about modern man, but they reveal more pronouncedly Fromm's own likes and dislikes. Moreover, the fact that Fromm was so enamoured of 'characters' suggests that he may have been more in debt to Reich's 'characterology' than he would have been ready to admit. It is a distinct possibility that Fromm was inspired by Reich's formulations when he first began to develop the idea of the 'authoritarian character', which he first coined the 'sadomasochistic character'.[42] If Reich was called the 'Character Smasher' (in his early career), Fromm could have been called the 'Character Juggler'. And if Fromm had created a 'categorizing character structure', he should have included himself in the list of people who represent such an orientation.

Homo normalis, or the Pathology of Normalcy

The development of welfare societies, massive economic growth and a rise in the standard of living created a large, affluent middle class in the West during the second half of the twentieth century. These developments also changed the lives of the workers, who were no longer dependent to the same extent on economic conjectures and the sometimes arbitrary rule of employers. In Western societies, all this created a mentality of ontological security, a mentality derived from a deep sense of continuity and order in events, which showed to the workers and other traditionally underprivileged groups that history has its benevolent face. The radicalization of the intellectual and political culture in the 1960s seemed to signify the last goodbye to the vestiges of pre-war authoritarianism, rigid social hierarchies and the whole law-and-order mentality of the inegalitarian past. Erich Fromm lived to see these remarkable changes in the West, and I shall now analyse his stand on these issues.

From the mid-1950s to the late 1960s, Fromm wrote and edited twelve books and a number of articles and essays. In these books and papers he emerged as an author who aspired to transcend the role of a social critic and provide frameworks for the 'good life' for 'alienated' westerners. His great ambition was to offer tools for restructuring society along the lines laid out by what he presented as the great tradition of Socialist Humanism. Although he had been committed to the Freudo-Marxist social critique since the late 1920s, as well as to humanist ethics since the mid-1940s,[43] his aspiration to provide a cure for the malaise of modernity first became apparent in the mid-1950s, when he published his utopian classic *The Sane Society* (1955). In his foreword to the book, Fromm writes that the volume is a continuation of *Escape from Freedom* in that *The Sane Society* 'proceeds from the purely critical analysis presented in *Escape from Freedom*, to concrete suggestions for the functioning of a Sane Society'.[44] Thus Fromm has assumed the role of a doctor treating disorder, diagnosing pathologies of modern society and providing a cure for these pathologies. Equipped with his interpretations of humanism, socialism and psychoanalysis, he attempts to 'save the Western world from an increasing insanity'.[45] Fromm had no modest ambition.

Fromm's thesis in *The Sane Society* is that it is not only individuals who can be sick (neurotic, schizoid or in a 'false consciousness'), but that the whole society can be pathogenic. He calls this collective sickness the 'pathology of normalcy' and diagnoses its main symptom as 'alienation'. With this thesis he attacks the then prevailing conception of mental health, which saw socialization or a patient's restoration to citizenship as the defining characteristics of mental health.[46] This definition of mental health was originally put forward in the interwar years by Adolf Meyer, one of the founding fathers of American psychiatry who saw mental disorder not as a disease but as a functional deficit that he interpreted in terms of maladaptation, or maladjustment. A person who suffers from a mental disorder is a social failure, and the main task of physicians is to help patients adapt to their environment. The Meyerian equation of mental health with good citizenship fitted in with the desperate attempts of American psychiatrists to find ways to decrease the patient population in overcrowded state hospitals. The Meyerian model conceptualized psychiatrists' task in terms of resocialization, and it also gave them a new social role as counsellors of right living.[47]

Fromm turned this 'conformist' conception of mental health on its head by asserting that it is the society that should be adjusted to the true needs of its citizens and that so-called 'normalcy' is in fact a symptom of social pathology.[48] He claimed that people who cannot stand the humdrum boredom of normal life may develop neurotic symptoms in order to make their lives more meaningful. Indeed, a main characteristic of 'normalcy' is boredom, which Fromm regarded as 'one of the greatest tortures'.[49] Since conformity to social demands can sometimes lead to mental illness,[50] it is necessary to restructure the society so that it no longer produces mental disturbances that go by the name of 'normalcy':

> From the standpoint of normative humanism we must arrive at a different concept of mental health; the very person who is considered healthy in the categories of an alienated world, from the humanistic standpoint appears as the sickest one – although not in terms of individual sickness, but of the socially patterned defect.[51]

Fromm had introduced the idea of a 'socially patterned defect' in *Escape from Freedom* to illustrate his social-psychological thesis that our statistically normal character traits, which enhance our adaptation to society, can also diminish our capacity to think critically and to feel solidarity towards people who are not members of our group. In the social context, 'normality' is thus potentially dangerous, because it breeds conformism, which in its turn breeds submissiveness to the authorities. As the social scientist Stephen Berger pointed out in an e-mail message to the author on 23 April 2003, normalcy in the 1950s probably had several facets. One was the relief policy makers felt when the expected economic decline after World War II had not happened. The second facet was the opening up of suburbia, fuelled by funding the national highway system as a defence effort, and the third was McCarthyism – it became dangerous to stand out. Remarkably, the famous 'dissident thinker' Fromm was not affected by McCarthy's anti-Communist witch-hunt, and, unlike some other European-born intellectuals (such as his friend Leo Löwenthal), he did not raise his voice to attack McCarthyism in public.[52]

In *The Sane Society*, Fromm focused his critical attention not on 'pathological' forms of political machinery (such as McCarthyism) but on other behaviour scientists who in his view propagated a psychology of adjustment. As a lay analyst and a critic of the 'medicalization' of mental health, Fromm accused psychiatry and psychology of accepting the prevailing conceptions of normalcy and thus encouraging citizens to become conformists. Far from trying to expose and criticize socially patterned defects, behaviour experts were using their skills to manipulate individuals by 'helping' them to adjust to the dystopian reality of the Brave New World.[53] He directed his harsh words not only to behaviourists but also to comformist psychoanalysts. In fact, he retained a critical attitude towards the psychoanalytic movement to the very end of his life. In his last book (on Freud), published in 1980, he makes a sweeping observation that psychoanalysis has been transformed 'from a radical into a liberal theory of adjustment', while psychoanalysts 'adopted the philosophy of their [bourgeois] class and for all practical purposes became supporters of consumerism'.[54] Psychoanalysis became part of the consumer society that Fromm detested so much, and as early as 1947 he had castigated psychoanalysis for not increasing 'our knowledge of how man ought to live and what he ought to do'.[55] As a psychoutopian, he did not want to discard psychoanalysis but rather to turn psychoanalysis into a normative guide to a better life.

Alienation

In *The Sane Society*, Fromm proclaims that when mental health is defined in the 'humanistic sense', it is characterized not by 'adjustment' but by the ability to love and to create and to become 'authentic' in one's relations to oneself and to others. In light of this definition, modern individuals are not so much mentally disordered in the medical sense of the term as depressed and bored, which in Fromm's terminology are almost synonymous words. Thus, most people are able to function socially while they sense their boredom and depression and try to find ways to avoid these feelings. However, in doing so they revert to cheap amusement and fail to fulfil their human potential. They have become self-alienated, schizoid robots who will 'destroy their world and themselves because they cannot stand any longer the boredom of a meaningless life'.[56] Fromm interpreted mental disorders as a psychological and existential response to a sick world and equated a 'neurotic' person with an 'alienated' person.

'Alienation' is Fromm's key term, not only in *The Sane Society*, but also in his later works.[57] As a psychoanalyst, he believed that alienation is a pathological state of mind that 'must be studied empirically by dynamic psychology'.[58] When he sketches the genealogy of this concept, he goes as far back as the Old Testament prophets, who referred to the polytheistic worship of idols as 'idolatry'. In the early modern world, 'alienation' was used to denote mental disorder, and, says Fromm, Hegel and Marx used the term to illustrate 'self-estrangement'.[59] Fromm had picked the term from the young Marx, who used it to criticize the inability of bourgeois society to satisfy the needs of its citizens, especially but not exclusively the needs of the proletariat.[60] Alienation is, however, a necessary stage in the process of self-realization, which Marx – in contrast to the German idealist philosophers – saw in materialist terms as an outcome of 'man's own labour'. Alienation, which for Marx is always 'self-alienation', prevents humans from developing their inherent morality and hence from adapting their lives to their true nature. In the mature Marx, the term plays only a minor role, but Fromm was mainly inspired by the young Marx's so-called Paris Manuscripts (*Economic and Philosophical Manuscripts of 1844*), which were published only in 1932 in Moscow, and which, when they started to circulate among left-wing intellectuals in Central Europe, inspired Fromm probably more than anything else he ever read, including all of Freud's writings.

In its vagueness, 'alienation' is an exemplary representative of German idealism, but it has suggestive force not unlike the Freudian term 'the unconscious' or the Foucauldian term 'power'; they all function like magic words that ostensibly reveal an essential but hard-to-pin-down component of human psychology and social order. In the 1950s and the 1960s, the notion of alienation appealed to such diverse thinkers as existentialists, psychologists, literary critics, non-Communist Marxists (such as Fromm) and Christian and Jewish theologians. As David Coute observes in his analysis of 'two types of alienation', alienation fulfils 'in modern ideology the same function as the Fall in Christian mythology'.[61] It seems it was an important term for the intellectuals, who prided themselves on the alleged fact that they had privileged insight into sociocultural processes and/or the functioning of the unconscious, and that their acute awareness of the inadequate and corrupt state of society alienated them from the established (false) value system. As the social scientist Paul Hollander has noted in his study of the Western intellectuals' fascination with totalitarian societies and Communism, 'alienation' did not have the same (positive) association when it was applied to alienated workers, who, in contrast to 'alienated intellectuals', tended to exhibit less favourable character traits, such as apathy, conformism, inclination to cheap thrills, etc.[62] Fromm exemplified such an understanding of the alienation of the 'masses', whose way of life was largely inimical to the higher values he himself embraced and promoted.

In *The Sane Society*, Fromm gives a sweeping historical overview of the conditions that have made people alienated. As a true Marxian (but unlike Marx himself), he puts the blame on capitalism as it evolved from the seventeenth to the twentieth century and sees the United States as the capitalist model towards which other Western countries are developing. Through the economic processes of 'quantification' and 'abstractification', the United States has produced a new type of human being, a person whose main duty is to spend and to consume (and not to hoard), to be flexible (and not commit oneself to objective moral principles), and to co-operate smoothly in large groups as a cog in the machine (instead of being self-employed or working in a close personal contact with fellow humans). The capitalist system of mass production requires a social character driven by self-interest, opportunism and conformism. As a result, the contemporary social character in the West tends to be devoid of altruistic impulses, solidarity and an understanding of itself as an active agent. The modern individual in a capitalist society, driven by marketing orientation, has become a thing, a mere commodity. The potential end result of total alienation, exemplified in the extreme form of marketing orientation, is the fall of civilization and the end of the human race. Thus, there is much at stake in the phenomenon of alienation.[63]

While accusing capitalism of producing alienation on a mass scale, Fromm did not think that Communism represented de-alienation and the triumph of altruism. He readily admitted that

> life in the Western world has been, and is even now sometimes as rich and joyous as it has ever been anywhere in human history; life in the Soviet system can never be joyous, as indeed it can never be where the executioner watches behind the door.[64]

Therefore, while the West 'develops rapidly in the direction of Huxley's *Brave New World*, the East *is* today Orwell's "1984"'.[65]

Although a champion of 'democratic socialism', Fromm occasionally made statements that relativized his critique of Soviet-style Communism. In *May Man Prevail?* (1961), he compared the Stalinist terror system to those of Batista in Cuba and General Trujillo in the Dominican Republic, claiming that Stalin's terror was no more inhuman, cruel or revolting than the systems in these 'free' countries.[66] He even applauded Stalin's achievements in modernizing the Soviet Union:

> He transformed, within less than thirty years, the economically most backward of the great European nations into an industrial system that soon would become the economically most advanced and prosperous, second only to the United States.[67]

These positive statements about the speed and efficiency of the Soviet Union's industrialization clash with Fromm's pronouncedly negative views on the technological imperative of industrial world, but they should be seen in the context of Fromm's attempt to contribute to the dialogue between the Communist bloc and the 'free world' in the midst of the Cold War. He probably wanted to 'de-demonize' the Soviet Union by highlighting its economic achievements and its structural similarities to the industrialized Western nations, particularly the United States. He was no friend of the Soviet Union, but neither was he an admirer of Western consumer societies. His Socialist Humanism aspired to offer a viable Third Way between Communism and capitalism.

The Oppressive Family and the Utopian Matriarchy

When Fromm looks for the principal agent of (false) socialization, he turns to the family. This is not surprising, for psychoanalysts have traditionally looked with suspicion at the affectionate ties between family members ('I had very neurotic parents', said Fromm in an interview in the 1960s[68]). So-called 'guilty mothers' have fared especially badly in the hands of psychoanalysts, who have blamed them for every problem or difference in their children.[69] Far from seeing the family as a natural form of bonding, the family is, for Fromm, the psychic agency of society, the 'institution which has the function of transmitting the requirements of society to the growing child'.[70] This socialization process is twofold: first, the character of the parents has a direct influence on the character formation of the growing child, and, second, the culturally sanctioned methods of training and education mould the child's character in a 'proper' direction. The former process is more important, because the methods of socialization depend on the social character of the parents. The family relations tend to be pathological, because the social structures that determine them are pathogenic, illness-inducing. Here Fromm presents a strict culturalist perspective on what primatologist Frans de Waal has called the 'oldest mammalian union' (the mother-child bond).[71]

Fromm, who did not have children of his own, had a negative and skewed view of the family dynamics. In *The Sane Society* and elsewhere he typically asserted that small children do not love their parents and that parental love, even the mother's love for her child, is rare ('While conventionally, parents are supposed to love their children as a matter of course, this is rather the exception than the rule'[72]). He elaborated on his assertion about maternal love by making the astonishing claim that the links of attachment between the mother and her child are potentially damaging: 'The boy's or girl's pre-Oedipus attachment to mother ... is one of the main causes of neurosis and psychosis'.[73] This is so because a small child's 'pathological mother fixation' prevents him or her from developing towards psychological independence. It is therefore of utmost importance that in their late teens, if not earlier, young people cut their ties with their mother. Fromm also made an even more astonishing claim that the child's helplessness and weakness tends to elicit the parents' contempt for the child and strengthen their impulse to humiliate him or her. Moreover, the father's love for the child (the son) is not unconditioned, but is motivated by the father's need to have an heir to his property and worldly functions.[74]

In a seminar given for students in Locarno in 1974, Fromm said that parental love is

> one of the greatest fictions that have ever been invented. Usually parental love masks – as [R. D.] Laing has said quite correctly – the power the parent wants to have over the child ... the main interest of most parents is control of the children, and that what their love is I would call a kind of sadistic level: 'I mean your best, and I love you inasmuch as you don't try to rebel against my control.'[75]

In the same seminar, Fromm made no bones about his professional attitude towards the parents: 'I think the analyst should be the accuser of the parents'.[76] The psychoanalysts did indeed fulfil that role rather well: Fromm and other analysts conjectured, without solid evidence, that the mother is often responsible for the child's autism and schizophrenia and, in the last analysis, for any 'pathological' personality trait (such as 'anal character') or deviant behaviour.[77] For the parents of autistic or schizophrenic children, Fromm's 'humanist psychoanalysis' may have appeared rather inhuman.

While having a dim view on the modern family, Fromm, like Gross and Reich, embraced the myth of matriarchy. He contended that if the suppressive, 'patriarchal-authoritarian' family were abolished, it would be a major step towards human emancipation.[78] In 1934, when he was still a rather orthodox Marxist psychoanalyst, he wrote an article on Bachofen's, Engels's and Morgan's studies on matriarchy and the history of the family, and assessed the relevance of their work for social psychology. He also wrote a positive review of the English anthropologist, historian and novelist Robert Briffault's study on mothers (*Mothers. A Study of the Origins of Sentiments and Institutions*, 1927), where Briffault argued that there is a tendency for marriage to revert from patriarchal to so-called matriarchal forms (that is, to a very loose and unstable association).[79]

There was nothing particularly original in Fromm's approach to the question of matriarchy. His contribution to the discussion was limited to his psychologization of patriarchy and matriarchy: he conjured up the notions of 'patricentric and matricentric complexes'. That he preferred the 'matricentric complex' becomes very clear to the reader:

> Summing up, we can say that the patricentric individual – and society – is characterised by a complex of traits in which the following are predominant: a strict superego, guilt feelings, docile love for paternal authority, desire and pleasure at dominating

> weaker people, acceptance of suffering as a punishment for one's own guilt, and a damaged capacity for happiness. The matricentric complex, by contrast, is characterized by a feeling of optimistic trust in mother's unconditional love, far fewer guilt feelings, a far weaker superego, and a greater capacity for pleasure and happiness. Along with these traits there also develops the ideal of motherly compassion and love for the weak and others in need of help.[80]

Fromm believed that in modern Europe the matricentric type exists in Catholic countries in Southern Europe, while the patricentric type plays a cultural role in the Protestant countries in Northern Europe.[81] Today, one could argue against Fromm's typology that even if Protestantism 'expurgated' the matricentric traits of Christianity, it is in the Protestant part of Europe – and in North America – that women have enjoyed the degree of political and social autonomy unattained by women in any other part of the world, including Southern Europe. One reason for Fromm's negative identification of the 'patricentric complex' with 'Protestantism' is that in a Weberian fashion he saw the spirit of capitalism reflecting the Protestant mentality.[82] And as a lifelong enemy of capitalism, he looked at Protestantism – the Weberian religo-ideological matrix of capitalism – with suspicious eyes, to say the least.

In 1934, the Marxist Fromm claimed that the working class has represented matricentric tendencies in Western societies, and that 'the psychic basis of the Marxist social program was predominantly the matricentric complex'.[83] He believed that the connection between socialism and matricentric ideas explained why so many socialist authors had sympathized with the theory of matriarchy. But later in his life he also gave sarcastic comments on leftist intellectuals whom he regarded as misguided advocates of neo-matriarchy. One such advocate was none other than his favourite enemy Herbert Marcuse, whose

> appeal to the young seems to rest largely on the fact that he is the spokesman for infantile regression to matriarchalism and that he makes this principle more attractive by using revolutionary rhetoric.[84]

To be a champion of matriarchy was not automatically a good thing for Fromm, especially if matriarchal ideas were propounded by a rival intellectual whose ideas appealed to the more radical youth of the 1960s. Fromm, as we shall see later in this chapter, had no sympathy for the 'culture of the Beatles', which certainly did not make his ideas more attractive to students, who in Fromm's view showed clear signs of matriarchal tendencies. The problem with such tendencies, which were in principle laudable, was that a 'regressive neo-matriarchalism' did not harmonize at all with Fromm's Messianic understanding of the good life. It is the frameworks of the good life à la Fromm that I shall examine next.

Sane Society

In the last main chapter of *The Sane Society*, Fromm gives an outline of a society that would be 'sane' – a society in which humanist principles of the young Marx and other 'prophets' would provide the social, psychological and spiritual foundation for the good life. Fromm's 'Sane Society' is one in which 1) full self-realization is possible; 2) altruistic virtues flourish; and 3) communitarian ideals of direct political, social and cultural participation in the local community are employed. What are needed to achieve these goals are thoroughgoing transformations in economic, political and cultural spheres. Fromm asserts that the Sane Society is attainable because humans are not innately selfish, but have altruistic inclinations. Since we are altruistic socialists rather than greedy capitalists by nature, the striving for 'sanity' is innate. However, in the course of history, human actions have had unintended consequences, which have resulted in 'perverted' social structures that have become dominant both in the West and the East. Thus Fromm could explain why the innate altruistic virtues of true socialism are not exactly flourishing in present societies. In his adherence to the notions of innate altruism, co-operation and the political significance of voluntary relationships, Fromm's mode of thinking has distinct resemblances with the ideas of classical anarchism, which I have examined in the chapter on Gross.[85]

Fromm offers not only abstract principles of the good life but also a number of practical solutions.[86] First of all, he discusses the social aspect of the work situation and envisages the transformation of workplaces from anonymous, large-scale bureaucratic-industrial organizations to small, decentralized work communities. He is enthusiastic about existing work communities in Europe and takes a closer look at one such community, a watch factory Boimondeau in France. The workers' participation in decision-making and the very idea of boosting solidarity among them impressed Fromm and incited him to see such a work community as an ideal workplace. (Years later, Fromm's assistant and friend Michael Maccoby tried to find out what happened to Boimondeau. He learned that the factory did not survive in the competitive marketplace. Like many other promising and short-lived co-operative enterprises, Boimondeau depended on an exceptional leader who left.[87]) Another manifestation of decentralization would be the organization of the whole population into groups of about five hundred people, who would meet regularly to discuss both local and national political issues and make political decisions.

As the social scientist Uri Zilbersheid has observed, in his reconceptualization of work Fromm built on Marx's idea of the abolition of labour (*Aufhebung der Arbeit*), by which Marx meant (in his early career) an abolition of instrumental technological production that is characterized by alienation, the system of exploitative and stultifying relations in human society. Zilbersheid notes that

Fromm modified Marx's historical conception, which holds that exploitation is not caused by capitalism, but by instrumental production that has existed since the beginning of human history. Fromm saw in the rise of capitalism the beginning of the unfortunate process which turned production into instrumental activity and, thereby, into alienated labour. The alienated work of an industrial labourer has lost all aspects of self-activity, and Fromm's debt to Marx lies in his attempt to create a form of socialism in which alienated labour could be transformed into creative self-activity, into productive labour. On a concrete level, Fromm suggested increased participation of workers in the management of production, and he argued for deepening the workers' understanding of both technical and economic aspects of the process of production.[88] A Sane Society encourages 'non-utilitarian' or 'creative' kinds of work by letting people become actively involved in the social structuring of labour. As Fromm knew very well, such an 'abolition of alienated labour' had not happened in the socialist countries, where industrial workers had become exactly like those anonymous cogs in the machine that had traditionally toiled in the factories and work-shops in the capitalist West.

Fromm's second suggestion is the idea of subsidy or a guaranteed free income to all citizens for a limited time, regardless of their specific situations (e.g., unemployment or sickness). Such a guaranteed minimum income would abolish the threat of economic poverty while making it impossible for employers to force people to work under conditions that they find hard to accept (as Fromm notes, Bertrand Russell had made the same suggestion earlier). It would minimize the exploitation of workers and make the relationship between employers and employees more equitable and free.[89] Third, Fromm outlines an educational system in which theory and practice would function in unison, and adult education would be encouraged. When an educational system emphasizes this unity, the spirit of knowledge-based civic activity is promoted. Like Goethe and Marx, he insists on the necessity of uniting *theoria* and *praxis*, *vita contemplativa* and *vita activa*. Fourth, he advocates active participation in 'collective art' and ritual, which fulfils the need of a common artistic expression and a shared experience. A 'productive' orientation to life requires that people give an expression of the 'wholeness' of their being by singing together, walking together, dancing together and admiring together. Fifth, and last, he delineates a new humanistic religion, which would be universalistic, non-theistic and syncretistic in its embracing of the humanistic teachings of all 'great religions' of the East and West. Such a humanistic religion (which the zoologist Julian Huxley had discussed some years earlier) would not only provide people with a spiritual and altruistic orientation to life but would also satisfy a human need for myth and ritual.

It is not so much these concrete suggestions that prompt one to discern utopian aspects in Fromm's thought. In fact, the idea of a guaranteed income has resurfaced in recent years in political discussions in Europe (e.g. in the Nordic countries); the accomplished reforms in adult education in Western societies are compatible with Fromm's proposal; and the strictly hierarchical, inflexible workplace that Fromm criticized is increasingly a relic in today's information society, which requires rather the sort of competitive flexibility he attributed to the marketing orientation. Moreover, the whole Aristotelian-communitarian ideal that Fromm promoted has re-emerged in Anglo-American philosophy in recent decades (see, e.g., the works of Michael Sandel, Charles Taylor and Alasdair MacIntyre). Fromm's utopianism is not founded on these rather sound practical suggestions, but on his vision of the restructuring of the human personality and the concomitant restructuring of society. Fromm's Sane Society would definitively not be a social-democratic welfare state bent on piecemeal reforms and a universal social policy. What was in Fromm's mind was not the Swedish model of the Third Way, but a world in which the very foundations of human existence would accord with the visions of the great 'humanist prophets', such as Marx. After *The Sane Society*, Fromm dedicated himself to showing the way to a society in which we would all be 'fully human' – self-liberated, self-directed citizens who know their true selves and their true values.[90]

Socialist Humanism

With the exception of Fromm's arch-enemies, the 'orthodox psychoanalysts', *The Sane Society* was received rather favourably and it boosted his reputation as a public intellectual (it reached number five on the *New York Times* best-seller list). After his best-selling book on the 'art of loving' (1956) and his harsh criticism of the psychoanalytic movement (*Sigmund Freud's Mission: An Analysis of his Personality and Influence*, 1959), he published a number of books and papers in which he returned to the themes that he had discussed in *The Sane Society*. He became a trenchant critic of the prevailing conservative tide in American political and intellectual life, but he was also dissatisfied with the current state of socialism.[91]

Fromm explains in *Beyond the Chains of Illusion* (1962) that he became politically active during the Cold War era, because he felt it to be his duty 'not to remain passive in a world which seems to be moving towards a self-chosen catastrophe'.[92] In the political spectrum, Fromm represented democratic socialism, rejecting Stalinism while challenging the rather conservative American Cold War liberalism, which the political scientist Glenn Perusek defines

> by its low toleration of deviation from a narrow definition of citizenship. Intolerance was used as a tool, first of all, against the unions, then to sanitize much of American society against principled dissent.[93]

In the 1950s, liberalism was constantly – and very effectively – attacked by Republicans, and it was probably only in the 1960s that the academic left began to see liberalism as the dominant American ideology. Thus American liberalism was still on the defensive in the late 1950s when Fromm began to 'challenge' it by promoting the idea of Socialist Humanism.

In 1960, Fromm tried in vain to provide the Socialist Party with a new programme when he published *Let Man Prevail: A Socialist Manifesto and Program*. There, he reformulates his idea of the Third Way, criticizing this time not so much capitalism as socialism: he proclaims that, in the early twentieth century, the humanistic aims of socialism were forgotten and that its deepest roots – 'the prophetic-messianic faith in man, justice, and the brotherhood of man' – were lost when socialism was absorbed by capitalism.[94] Socialism became exclusively concerned with the economic improvement of the working class, and ceased to be a radical movement rooted in prophetic Messianism. In World War I, the failure of socialism became complete when its leaders abandoned internationalism and pacifism and succumbed to nationalistic sentiments. After 1914, then, most of the authentic spirit of socialism disappeared, but Fromm observes that the questions asked by the young Marx have now re-emerged, particularly among scholars in Yugoslavia, Czechoslovakia and Poland. He presented his 'humanist psychoanalysis' as expressing 'authentic' (i.e. humanist) Marxism by supplementing and revising Marx's and Engels's analyses.

In the early 1960s, Fromm wrote two books in which he examined and promoted Marx's ideas, which by that time had become more precious to him than ever before.[95] In one of these books, *Marx's Concept of Man* (1961), he published an English translation of Marx's *Economic and Philosophical Manuscripts* with an extensive introductory chapter (the translator was Tom Bottomore). By this time, Marx had become the single most important authority for Fromm: Marx's aim was the 'spiritual emancipation of man'; his philosophy represents a 'protest against man's alienation'; it is imbued with faith in humans; and it is a 'new and radical step forward in the tradition of prophetic Messianism'. Fromm looked back on 'authentic Marxism' as 'perhaps the strongest spiritual movement of a broad, non-theistic nature in nineteenth-century Europe'.[96] In a letter to the famous economist and public intellectual Karl Polanyi, he notes,

> I never ceased to be a socialist, but I am more strongly convinced than ever that the spiritual content which has to be found in socialism, and especially in the ideas which Marx expressed in the Paris manuscripts to which you refer, are still as vital as they were a hundred years ago.[97]

Fromm's excitement over the young Marx was probably the single most important incentive to his advocacy of Socialist Humanism in the 1960s. The young Marx seemed to embody most if not all of the elements that were so precious to

Fromm's way of thinking: Marx was a humanist, a Messianic prophet, a trenchant social critic and a predecessor of Freud in his relentless unmasking of bourgeois morality. Fromm regarded it as his mission to fulfil the 'humanist-prophetic' legacy of the young Marx, who 'visualized the *pathology of normalcy*'.[98] To Fromm, (the young) Marx was the most important source of inspiration, and Marxism the most important *religious* movement of the nineteenth century.[99]

Fromm wanted to develop the 'humanist' project of (the young) Marx and update it with the help of psychoanalysis, although he declared in 1962, 'I consider Marx, the thinker, as being of much greater depth and scope than Freud'.[100] For the renaissance of Western humanism, Marx was much more important than Freud, who was not a 'prophet', even if psychoanalysis was the 'most scientific form of psychology'.[101] Psychoanalysis was indispensable for illuminating the phenomenon of alienation, which for Fromm was a psychological experience and as such had to be examined in the context of 'narcissism, depression, fanaticism, and idolatry'.[102] His Socialist Humanism aspired to synthesize humanistically-oriented psychoanalysis (i.e. Fromm's psychoanalysis) and 'genuine' (i.e. humanist) Marxist theory. 'The main motive and aim of my work', writes Fromm to historian Martin Jay in 1971, 'has been a synthesis of psychoanalytic and Marxian thought'.[103]

Fromm did not interpret history in terms of Marxist dialectics, which would have provided him with a neat conceptual scheme with the help of which he could have seen the renaissance of humanism as the 'dialectical negation' of the anti-humanist socialist tradition of the twentieth century. He did not seem to have any interest in the finer nuances of dialectical materialism or in the mature Marx's economical analyses of capitalism. Unlike many European intellectuals, Fromm preferred clarity of thinking and lucidity of writing style to opaque theorizing, and he did not respect the often abstruse jargon that characterizes Continental philosophy. He took the Marx he needed and left the 'other' Marx to such philosophers as Louis Althusser, whose esoteric 'structuralist' approach to Marx was diametrically opposed to Fromm's.[104]

Fromm found kindred spirits not only in the Messianic-humanist tradition but also among his contemporaries. He sought contact especially with the new humanist interpreters of Marx and Marxism in Eastern Europe, such as the Yugoslavian Praxis group[105] and the Polish philosopher Adam Schaff, who was another expert in alienation, and to whose book *Marxism and the Human Individual* (1970) Fromm wrote the introduction. He also had a high regard for Bertrand Russell, Albert Einstein, Albert Camus, Ernst Bloch, Albert Schweitzer and even Pope John XXIII. He tried to establish a dialogue with the politically engaged representatives of the Catholic Church, and in 1966 he made a futile attempt to persuade Pope Paul VI to initiate an international conference on the future of humanity.[106] Fromm was an inspiring figure to many socialist thinkers, especially to dissident democratic socialists in Eastern Europe.[107] The British socialist and London School of Economics professor Tom Bottomore, whose translation of Marx's *Economic and Philosophical Manuscripts* was published in Fromm's book *Marx's Concept of Man*, wrote to Brian Betz in 1972: 'Erich Fromm's influence in this field [socialism] was considerable; it helped to crystallize for me an alternative kind of socialist movement, after the disillusioning experiences of the 1950s'.[108]

The Revolution of Hope

Manifesting the utopian impulse in his Socialist Humanism, Fromm declared in 1962 that the 'principle of hope' has governed Western history for two thousand years.[109] Six years later he devoted a whole book, *The Revolution of Hope* (1968), to the illustration of this principle. In his book, he did not bring anything essentially new to the social critique he had presented in *The Sane Society*. Neither was his discussion of the 'principle of hope' particularly original, for he built on the ideas put forward by Ernst Bloch, the 'spiritual father of Marxist utopianism',[110] in his three-volume work *The Principle of Hope* (written in the United States in 1938–47 and published in German in 1959 as *Das Prinzip Hoffnung*). As a young Marxist scholar, Bloch had written a book on 'Messianic Marxism' (*Geist der Utopie*, 1918) in which he had argued that Marxism must become theological. He later abandoned the theological view, but he continued to believe that religion contains utopian goals that have to be realized. There is in Bloch's view a continuum between the sacred and the profane, and the atheism of Marxism realizes the 'dialectical secularization' of Messianism. Like Fromm, he represented an imaginative, spiritual trend in twentieth-century Marxism.[111] He mixed in his writings Judeo-Christian Messianism and Marxism, and, together with Fromm, he was most responsible for revivifying the spirit of utopianism in Marxist thought.

In *The Revolution of Hope*, Fromm acknowledged (in a footnote) the importance of Bloch in expressing most forcefully the prophetic principle of hope in Marxist thought.[112] To Fromm, Bloch represented authentic Socialist Humanism and, in the collection of essays he edited in the mid-1960s (*Socialist Humanism*), he included a previously-published essay by Bloch ('Man and Citizen According to Marx'). Following Bloch, Fromm saw hope as an essential condition of being human, and thus humans could be defined as *homo esperans*, 'Hoping Man'.[113] The modern age, however, was characterized not by hope, but by hopelessness: the period in the West after 1914 has been a dystopian era, representing a counter-image to a world run according to the principles of Socialist Humanism. Despite the existential tones in his dark depiction of the present human condition, Fromm had no sympathy for existentialists, such as

Heidegger or Sartre, whom he saw as expressing the 'despair of Western man' and 'an extreme bourgeois egotism and solipsism'. He singled out Sartre and his followers and attacked their 'ungrounded' claim that 'there are no objective values valid for all men'.[114] He described Sartre's psychology as 'superficial', and Sartre's attempt to combine existentialism and Marxism as 'futile'.[115] In a letter to Raya Dunayevskaja (an exponent of Marxist humanism), he compares Sartre's extreme form of 'egocentric individualism' with Max Stirner's anarchist views, and juxtaposes Sartre's 'profound hopelessness and despair about man' with Marx's humanist *Menschenbild*.[116]

In another letter to Dunayevskaja, Fromm complains that in his visit to Czechoslovakia in the spring of 1966, he noticed to his dismay that existentialism has more influence there than in Poland or Yugoslavia.[117] He clearly thought that the central tenets of existentialism, which was a strong philosophical movement in post-war Continental Europe, collided violently with the principle of hope that was intrinsic to his Socialist Humanism. He may also have been a little jealous of the popularity of a rival theory of the human condition in the intellectual marketplace. Betraying his own increasing alienation from the 'radical' youth of the 1960s, he condemned the pop music of the Beatles and fretted about the 'fact' that the young people who find solace in mass culture lead empty lives characterized by a lack of (true) stimulation, interest and hope.[118]

When he turned from social criticism to the delineation of his updated version of the Sane Society, Fromm proclaimed in *The Revolution of Hope* that active citizenship is the core virtue of the 'Good Society'. All citizens should actively participate 'in the affairs of the country as a whole and of states and communities as well of large communities'. This requires such activity on the grass-roots level as the formation of face-to-face groups 'within which the process of information exchange, debate, and decision making would be conducted'.[119] In addition to these small groups, he envisaged a modern equivalent of town meetings, in which larger groups of town meeting size would acquire all relevant information on the political issue in question, debate it and make decisions that would be part of the decision-making on the national and (he refers to the United States) state level. In such meetings, modern technology (e.g., telecommunications) would be put to a 'human' use. In the spirit of socialism, he also discussed the benefits of free commodities (such as bread) and services (such as transportation) and free higher education. He admitted that such a vision is utopian but insisted that it is also rational.[120] At the end of his book, in a chapter entitled 'Can We Do It?', he gave a sketch of a new social movement that would 'educate its members for the new kind of society in the process of striving for it'.[121]

In 1968, the same year that *The Revolution of Hope* was published, Fromm was for the last time politically engaged, when he took an active part in the presidential campaign of the Democrat Eugene McCarthy. He travelled widely around the United States, giving speeches and attending election events. McCarthy was not elected, and Fromm, who had problems with his ailing health, returned to Mexico. After a full decade of involvement in it, he disappeared from the active political scene, resigned from the Socialist Party, and all but gave up his utopian aspirations. He continued to write books on such diverse topics as the 'social character in the Mexican village' (co-authored with Michael Maccoby), aggression, (religious) ethics and Freud, but he ceased to actively advance Socialist Humanism.

Although he was no longer a social activist in the 1970s, Fromm's ideas inspired new activist movements in Germany and Italy.[122] As a result of the publication of *To Have or To Be?* in 1976, he became a well-known intellectual and something of a sage in Europe, and the leftist European media was interested in his critical views on capitalism, socialism and alienation, as well as in his support of dissident socialist thinkers in the Eastern bloc. But there was a limit to his expressed sympathy for dissident groups who lived out the virtue of disobedience: when he was invited to appear in court as a witness for the defence in the Bader-Meinhoff terrorist trial in Germany in 1976, he declined.[123]

Utopianism in Fromm I: The Renaissance of Humanism

Fromm made only a few explicit references, most of them positive, to utopianism in his writings.[124] In *Man for Himself* (1947), he anticipated his later utopian propensities when he wrote in a footnote that

> Utopias are visions of ends before the realization of means, yet they are not meaningless; on the contrary, some have contributed greatly to the progress of thought, not to speak of what they have meant to uphold faith in the future of man.[125]

In this book, Fromm also noted that twentieth-century intellectual culture is devoid of visions of a better humanity; the emphasis has been on critical studies of man and society. While readily conceding that such a critical attitude is very important for the development of society, he pointed out that the absence of utopian visions 'has had the effect of paralyzing man's faith in himself and his future'.[126] In the 1940s, utopianism was germinating in Fromm's mind, and in the following decade it would spring up in full force with the publication of *The Sane Society*.

Fromm's most extensive discussion of utopian thought can be found in his foreword to Edward Bellamy's utopian-socialist novel *Looking Backward* (1888), as well as in his afterword to George Orwell's *Nineteen Eighty-Four* (1949).[127] In the former piece, Fromm describes socialism as the realistic and scientific expression of the goals of utopia and laments the fact that 'in our materialistic world' utopia mostly means 'idle dreaming'. Not surprisingly, he sees the source of utopian visions in the Messianic ideas of the Old Testament prophets, and, when discussing Thomas More, he notes how in the Renaissance utopias, prophetic visions were fused with the classic Greek faith in reason and science. After describing nineteenth-century utopian socialism in general and Bellamy's book in particular, he goes on to condemn twentieth-century 'consumerism', which has abandoned the Messianic vision of society with its message of solidarity and love. The goals of Bellamy and Socialist Humanism are essentially the same: human emancipation and the overcoming of alienation.[128]

In his afterword to *Nineteen Eighty-Four*, Fromm reiterates what he said in his foreword to Bellamy a year earlier. Again, he proceeds from the idea that the Messianic visions of the Old Testament prophets have been the main source of Western utopianism. And again he laments that World War I ended a two-thousand-year tradition of hope and started a new era of hopelessness in the West. Fromm presents Orwell's book as an expression of a new hopelessness still barely recognized. He notes that Zamyatin and Huxley are the two other authors who have expressed the dystopian atmosphere of hopelessness. Whereas Orwell's and Zamyatin's dystopias bear distinct resemblances to the dictatorships of Stalin and Hitler, Huxley's book portrays the potentially bleak future of the Western industrial world. To Fromm, the dystopian works of Orwell, Huxley and Zamyatin are wake-up calls. He sees the nuclear strategist Herman Kahn's Dr Strangelove-type approach to nuclear war as exemplifying Orwellian 'doublethink' in today's world (Kahn formulated nuclear war in terms of cost/benefit analysis and proclaimed that both war *and* peace are 'horrible'!). In Fromm's view, if we do not fight the prevailing trend towards the passivity of the human spirit and do not support the active self-liberation of human beings, we will be closer to the Orwellian world than we dare to think.[129]

Fromm saw two alternative roads for humanity: the destruction of the human race or the dawn of a new era, which would be ushered in by the vanguard of new Socialist Humanism. He insinuated that a failure to adopt the principles of Socialist Humanism could mean the end of the world, no less. Thus there was much at stake in his proposal for a new kind of socialism. In the preface to *Socialist Humanism* (1965), he defines humanism as the 'belief in the unity of the human race and man's potential to perfect himself by his own efforts' and adds that 'all Humanists have shared a belief in the possibility of man's perfectibility'.[130] Fromm's idea of the perfectibility of the human species is at the root of Western utopianism, and his Socialist Humanism is an exemplary representative of 'social dreaming', for he was inspired by the utopian desire to transform 'alienated' people into 'living' people. Building a new society on the principles of Socialist Humanism would mean the 'end of "humanoid" history, the phase in which man has not yet become fully human'.[131]

Fromm envisioned the emergence of the naturally benevolent 'One Man', someone who 'transcends the narrow limits of his nation and who experiences every human being as a neighbour, rather than as a barbarian; a man who feels at home in the world'.[132] Fromm put great emphasis on the psychoutopian idea of inner transformation, for he believed that the 'Age of Man', the renaissance of humanism, can come into being 'only if a New Man comes into being'.[133] An inner transformation is therefore a prerequisite for the transformation of society. Here Fromm revised the utopian aspect of Marxism by downplaying Marx's deterministic account of consciousness, suggesting that a change of consciousness precedes a change of society.

Like utopian authors, and unlike Marxist historical materialists, Fromm did *not* put his faith in history, which would lead humanity into freedom and bring about the natural goodness of human beings. Rather than being a socioeconomic determinist, he nurtured the Messianic-utopian hope that the inner transformation of humans would usher in a new era, and he contended that the precondition for the improvement of the human condition is not that there occur changes in the socioeconomic sphere but that people become aware of their true needs and true values. Only after the breakthrough of such awareness will it be possible to make drastic changes in social arrangements (such as the abolishment of an intrinsically authoritarian patriarchal society).

Utopianism in Fromm II: The Biophilous Character

In the early 1960s, Fromm created new personality structures to match his descriptions of Humanist Socialism. One of them was the 'revolutionary character', to which I have already referred. Buddha, the Old Testament prophets and Jesus were revolutionary characters, as also were Meister Eckhardt, Giordano Bruno, Galileo, and Marx and Engels. Modern representatives of such a character are Einstein, Schweitzer, Lukacs, Bertrand Russell, Ernst Bloch – and, although he does not say it aloud, Fromm himself. He also described a character structure that was diametrically opposite to the 'revolutionary character': a 'type of personality which is attracted to death, destruction, and decay, rather than life ... This type of character can be called necrophilous.'[134] Quite surprisingly, Fromm sees not only such vicious Nazis as Hitler and Eichmann but also his colleague Jung as representing the 'necrophilous character' (Jung's 'sympathies for Hitler and his racial theories are another expression of his affinity with death-loving people').[135] Jung had died three years before the publication of Fromm's book, so he could not reply to Fromm's character assassination.

In 1964, Fromm introduced yet another personality structure, the biophilous character, to which he attributed the utopian qualities of 'New Man' that would embody the principles of Socialist Humanism.[136] The essence of the biophilous character is 'love of life', while the essence of the necrophilous character is 'love of death'. Fromm did not claim that one could find such characters in real life; what he asserted rather was that in the character structures of people one can detect both biophilous and necrophilous tendencies, and that the crux of the matter is the respective intensity of these two fundamental orientations.[137]

The biophilous character, the Frommian Socialist Humanist *par excellence*, is not the product of a restructured society but its precondition. This means that the mature Fromm was anything but a strict environmental determinist claiming that humans are merely the product of their social environment. Although he believed that, due to the lack of 'instinctual equipment', people are relatively malleable to outside influences, he also believed that there is a hard core in human nature which is resistant to the pressures of the social environment.[138] He argued against the proponents of environmentalism that if humans ('Man') were infinitely malleable,

> Man would be only the puppet of social arrangements and not – as he has proved to be in history – an agent whose intrinsic properties react strenuously against the powerful pressure of unfavorable social and cultural patterns.[139]

He explicitly denied that the human mind is a blank slate on which culture writes its texts.[140] He also rejected the culturalist thesis that there are no intrinsic psychological differences between men and women, and late in his life he criticized the psychoanalytic 'dogma' of infant determinism.[141] Fromm, then, had moral as well as scientific reasons for promoting the idea that universal human nature is manifest in cross-cultural behaviour patterns, such as a yearning for love and solidarity and a tendency for all people to defend their personal freedom. As the Fromm scholar Daniel Burston has pointed out, Fromm acknowledged the importance of innate disposition or 'temperament', which he differentiated from acquired traits ('character') and formulated in terms of authenticity.[142]

While discarding the 'non-humanist' idea of the universal 'animal nature' of human beings (the 'survival of the fittest' doctrine and the notion of blind instinctuality), Fromm embraced the idea put forward by Aristotle, David Hume, Adam Smith and Edward Westermarck, namely that morality is grounded in human nature. In *Man for Himself*, he refers approvingly to Lord Shaftesbury's notion of the moral sense, as well as to Adam Smith's moral psychological understanding of conscience.[143] These philosophers argued that humans, like higher mammals, are essentially moral animals, but their conception of human nature differed from Fromm's Rousseauean notion of the purity of the inner nature of humans. Westermarck, for example, did not think that innate moral emotions make us innately good or noble, because, for him, jealousy, anger, envy and inclination to nepotism were also moral emotions, or human universals. I certainly do not claim that Fromm was a Pollyanna whose Sane Society would be populated by shiny happy people who do not suffer or feel miserable – as a Central European intellectual born in the early century, he had a very developed sense of the tragic side of the human condition, it was only that his own 'character structure' was tuned in a way that made him emphasize not only the dystopian elements in existing societies, but also the utopian possibilities of a different kind of society.

Fromm's moral ideas tally remarkably well with those of classical anarchists, especially Kropotkin, who emphasized the innate tendency to mutual aid. One could even say that Fromm, Gross and Reich were Kropotkin's 'spiritual sons', since they all believed that we have an innate inclination to reciprocal altruism, solidarity and co-operation – in short, that we are basically moral animals whose empirical self (ego, consciousness, the social character) is corrupted by the pathological structures of Western societies. But insofar as we succeed in getting in touch with the original unspoiled source of good within ourselves, we are empowered to defy the prevailing social and moral order and fight for the good life as we conceive it. Fromm was aware of Kropotkin's ideas on reciprocal altruism, writing in a footnote in 1976 that 'one of the most important sources for understanding the natural human impulse to give and share is P. A. Kropotkin's classic, *Mutual Aid*'.[144]

Fromm's 'biophilous character' invites comparisons with Gross's '*mutterrechtliche* Communist', Jung's 'individuated individual' and Reich's 'genital character'; they were all embodiments of their respective modes of utopian thought. Fromm's understanding of 'biophily' is much closer to Jung's conception of individuation than to either Reich's or Gross's utopian ideas. Neither Jung nor Fromm regarded a free and healthy sexuality or Eros as the key to complete happiness, and Fromm made it clear on many occasions that Reich was wrong in assuming that sexual freedom would make people more humane or politically radical.[145] In his last book (*Greatness and Limitations of Freud's Thought*, 1980), Fromm gave his final verdict on Reich's work: Reich did not understand the relationship between society and the character structure, and he understood Marx even less, especially the young, humanist Marx, who appeared to Fromm as a major representative of Messianism.[146] As Fromm's commitment to Messianism is the most distinct and original component in his utopianism, I shall take a closer look at his understanding of the Messianic tradition.

Utopianism in Fromm III: Messianism

Fromm regarded Messianism rather broadly as a fundamental mode of thinking about the world. But in traditional rabbinical thought, the Messiah is the 'king who will redeem and rule Israel at the climax of human history and the instrument by which the kingdom of God will be established'.[147] The Messiah was expected to reconcile the people of Israel with God and 'introduce a period of spiritual and physical bliss'.[148] The Messianic idea lived on through the Middle Ages and into the modern age as a major component of Jewish ideology, and an eschatological literature developed around the idea of the end of the world and the beginning of a new one. In the Messianic tradition, Judaism had a universal mission to become the religion for all people and to perfect the world, although only a relatively small number of Jews has tried to act this out on a social stage. In the twentieth century, the extremely violent historical events (especially the Holocaust) and the birth of the state of Israel seemed to exhaust the universalistic Messianic idea of its power (Fromm, like many other Jewish intellectuals, was an anti-Zionist[149]). However, among modern Jewish thinkers there were some who invoked the idea of Messianism as a way of transforming the 'soul' of humanity. The Jewish scholar Mordecai Kaplan wrote in 1956 that the 'idea of the Messiah can still figure symbolically to express the valid belief in the coming of a higher type of man than this world has yet known'.[150]

It was this Messianic notion of a 'higher type of Man' that was so appealing to Fromm. As a young observant Jew in Frankfurt, he socialized with a number of renowned Jewish scholars (Scholem, Nobel, Buber, etc.) whose teachings had a lasting influence on his thinking. As the Fromm scholar Micha Brumlik has pointed out, Messianic ideas influenced not only Fromm but also the thought patterns of his Jewish colleagues at the Institute for Social Research (the Frankfurt School). Among other things, Fromm, Adorno, Horkheimer and Benjamin adopted anti-capitalist attitudes and despised commerce and other 'vulgar' dealings with money, even though, or perhaps just *because*, their fathers, and those of many other Jewish socialists, including Fromm, were often entrepreneurs and businessmen.[151] Fromm complained all through his life that people have lost their moral convictions and are instead driven by an individualistic self-interest and the 'cash-nexus', a situation in which money becomes a substitute for personal relations.[152] In his reference to the 'cash nexus', Fromm repeated the claims of Marx and Engels, who had picked the term from the work of another nineteenth-century social critic, Thomas Carlyle (who wrote in 1839 that 'Cash Payment has become the sole nexus of man to man!').[153]

Fromm was a well-off man who could afford things that most people in his time could only dream about, and it seems to me that he did not understand the importance of purely material goods for the 'ontological security' of people.[154] That his humanist devaluation of materialism did not always come across favourably among his audience is evident in his letter to Raya Dunayevskaja, to whom he described his visit to Czechoslovakia in 1966. In presentations that he gave there, he expressed his disapproval of the purely material incentives to increase production in Czechoslovakia, and he complained about the increasing consumption and the materialistic interest in money that he identified as a general trend in all socialist countries. The Czech audience reacted to Fromm's tirade against materialism and consumerism not with applause, but with a 'stony silence', which to Fromm meant that they hardly had any understanding of this problem.[155] Like John Lennon, a millionaire who dreamt of a world without possession, Fromm appeared to take his own affluence for granted, and did not consider the less affluent people's interest in material goods from the perspective of deprivation and concern for the material security of their near and dear ones.

With his degradation of material values (as exemplified in the 'simple, often sentimental and meaningless' music of the Beatles), Fromm's tone began to resemble the age-old Christian idealization of poverty, which since feudalism has been effectively used by the secular rulers in Europe to justify hierarchies and deprivation. On a more mundane level, I find it quite astonishing that, as a Marxist, he did not seem to pay any attention to the economic situation of people in socialist 'peoples' democracies'. Perhaps he thought that the relative equalization of income, as well as the 'collective' ownership of the means of production, guarantees that there is no true poverty in socialist countries. Paul Hollander, who has studied Western intellectuals' dualistic approach to poverty in capitalist and socialist societies, gives a plausible explanation of Fromm's seeming idealization of poverty:

> Intellectuals are capable of regarding poverty as a wholesome condition when it is associated with purity, egalitarianism, and the subordination of material needs to higher, spiritual purpose.[156]

It seems to me that Fromm was much more worried about the relative affluence of ordinary people in the West than about the relative poverty of ordinary people in socialist societies (and in the Third World). To Fromm, it was better to be poor and authentic than to be affluent and alienated.

What I believe is indubitable is that Fromm did not subscribe to the 'capitalist' view on self-interest as articulated by Adam Smith:

> It is not from the benevolence of the butcher, the brewer, or the baker that we expect our dinner, but from their regard to their own interest. We address ourselves, not to their humanity but to their self-love.[157]

In contrast to Smith, Fromm addressed himself to the humanity of people, and he appeared to be genuinely disappointed when he observed that human selfishness provides a mighty opponent to the realization of a humanist society where, in the words of Steven Pinker, 'the butcher, the brewer, and the baker will provide us with dinner out of benevolence or self-actualization'.[158] To Fromm, humans are inclined to selfishness not because it is intrinsic to human nature, but because people have adopted false values in a society that puts a premium on material wellbeing, competition and consumption.

During the last fifteen years of his life, Messianic and religious themes became more pronounced in Fromm's writings. In *You Shall Be as Gods*, his 1966 interpretation of the prophetic writings of the Old Testament, Fromm writes that he has studied the Old Testament and Talmud since childhood. His book is therefore a result of a long period of reflection on the topic and expresses his lifelong commitment to radical humanism.[159] In a letter to Brian Betz, he expresses his approval of Betz's characterization of his style as 'prophetic':

> The prophetic writings are to me unique in their spirit but also in their language and style, and there is almost nothing in literature which moves me as much as the writings of some of the prophets (including Marx).[160]

While he tended to downplay the fact that many prophets were not in fact Messianic, Fromm saw continuity in the Messianic tradition from the Old Testament prophets, Buddhism and Taoism to Renaissance utopianism, Enlightenment progressivism and – as the culmination – to Marx's socialism. As he wrote to Adam Schaff in 1965,

> I believe that Marxist socialism is, indeed, the secular expression of a tradition which is to be found among the Jews, although there is, at the same time, a reactionary, nationalistic and clerical one.[161]

Obviously, Fromm saw his Socialist Humanism as being part of this tradition. In addition to his moral commitment to Judeo-Christian Messianism and its modern Western offspring, he was interested in the mystical traditions of Islam and Buddhism (especially Sufism and Zen Buddhism). He even wrote a book together with the famous Japanese Zen Buddhist Daisetz Suzuki.[162]

Although Fromm repudiated organized religion and claimed not to believe in God, in his 'ultimate concern with the spiritual reality' he was deeply religious.[163] In his later years, religious figures became more emphatically a source of inspiration for him, and in his last major work, *To Have or to Be* (1976), he devoted a whole chapter to the Bible and to the German mystic and theologian Meister Eckhardt, whose spiritual teachings fascinated the mature Fromm. Like Jung, who also had a high regard for Eckhardt, Fromm maintained that true faith is an expression of authenticity, and that losing religious faith – in Fromm's loose sense of the term – may have detrimental psychological consequences to the individual as well as to the society. 'True' religiosity is therefore good for one's health, but it is also an important ingredient in Fromm's utopianism: '"Religious" impulses contribute the energy necessary to move men and women to accomplish drastic social change'.[164]

It seems, however, that Fromm did not consider Protestantism a manifestation, but rather a degradation, of true religiosity. For the most part, he saw Protestantism as a religion of greedy capitalism, and in the early 1950s he conjectured that life in the small and prosperous Protestant countries in (Northern) Europe must be quite miserable and boring indeed, because people in these countries suffer in 'explosive' numbers from mental illnesses.[165] His antipathy towards both Protestantism and capitalism probably had its roots in his commitment to Messianism. Even if he seemed to think that Communism was anything but a 'progressive' force in history, he also had faith in its ideological commitment to extreme altruism. Communism was the 'lesser evil' in comparison with capitalism, an ideology of egoistic self-interest that has its ideological roots in Protestantism.

In the mid-1960s, the Protestant theologian Stanley Glen objected to what he regarded as Fromm's distorted presentation of Protestantism in his writings, and he also raised an issue about Fromm's religiosity that had wider implications, at least for practising Christians:

> The open atheism of Marx, who rejects all religion, is less dangerous that that of Fromm, which assumes a religious form combined with an optimistic view of man. The former can be recognized for what it is, but the latter is more concealed. For this reason Fromm's esoteric atheism is more competitive of the Christian faith than open atheism. It comes forward with its own form of gospel. It proclaims the new man – the man-God as the hope of the world.[166]

Notwithstanding the religious tone in his voice, Glen was right in his interpretation of Fromm's 'esoteric atheism' as a competitor to traditional Christianity. Fromm, like Jung, probably appealed to many 'secular' Christians and Jews whose religious traditions did not find resonance in them anymore, but who, through acquainting themselves with Frommian or Jungian conceptual cosmos, were able to interpret Christianity and Judaism from a standpoint that was modern and 'scientific' and yet affirmed the significance of religion and spirituality.[167]

At the age of seventy-five, when he had lost much of his earlier utopian zest, Fromm estimated that if Humanist Christians succeeded in awakening in at least 10 per cent of the Western population the awareness of the need to make the crucial choice between idolatry (*Götzendienst*) and authentic, humanist religiosity, the catastrophe looming ahead could be avoided.[168] In his 1974 study of Marx and Meister Eckhardt, he delineated humanism as a 'secular Messianism' that would redeem humanity without any reference to a (religious) redeemer. He discussed the etymological origins of the English word 'salvation' with the intention of tearing down its theistic connotations. He emphasized that different religions have provided different answers to the question that had haunted the young Marx: how to redeem the alienated people. Marx was concerned with the same dilemma that great religions had struggled with for centuries.

At the end of his life, Fromm found inspiration in the idea that humanism as he conceived it is part of the spiritual tradition which, rather than seeking salvation in the other-worldly sphere of divinity, has its highest goal in the perfectibility (*Vollendung*) of humans.[169] He pointed out that natural sciences have contributed to the realization of *technical* utopias; now it is time to realize the human utopia of the 'Messianic Time':

> A united new humankind living in solidarity and peace ... can be achieved, provided we spend the same energy, intelligence, and enthusiasm on the realization of the human Utopia as we have spent on the realization of our technical Utopias.[170]

In his last book, where his subject was the 'greatness and limitations' of Freud's thought, Fromm referred to the historically conditioned nature of the truth before making a statement that betrayed his lasting commitment to Messianism: 'To use a politico-religious expression, only in the Messianic Time can the truth be recognized insofar as it is recognizable'.[171]

Fromm frequently found exemplary representatives of the 'biophilous character' in the history of religion, and he saw religiosity as intrinsic to human nature. But in the last analysis he was a 'humanist prophet' who was concerned with the essence of humanity rather than with the Kingdom of Heaven. Deeply religious people could very well be biophilous characters, but in order to be classified as a biophilous character you did not have to be religious. As he put it in 1976, 'social life itself ... will be the expression of the "religious" spirit, and no separate religion will be necessary'.[172] There may have been strong religious impulses in Fromm, but they were held in check by his deep commitment to secular humanism that saw the perfectibility of human beings in historical time – the 'human Utopia' – as its highest goal.

Despite his disillusionment with politics and social activity, Fromm's utopian energies were not totally exhausted in the 1970s. He envisioned the synthesis of the late medieval vision of the City of God and the modern vision of the Earthly City of Progress, which, however, degenerated to the vision of the Tower of Babel in the twentieth century. Fromm called his vision of the new synthesis of medieval spiritualism and modern scientific rationalism the 'City of Being'.[173]

Positive and Negative Freedom

As a critical depth psychologist, Fromm thought he possessed the necessary tools for unlocking the secrets of the unconscious and diagnosing 'false consciousness'. Like Marx and Freud, his two heroes, he claimed that people are often aware of their 'false' needs and 'unconscious' of their real ones. Due to the cunning of the unconscious, our mental functioning is characterized by constant self-deception. Therefore, the 'task of the analyst of society is precisely to awaken man so that he can become aware of the illusory *false* needs and of the reality of his *true* needs' [italics added].[174] Fromm relied on to the cognitive theory of values, according to which it is possible to have objective knowledge about values. Thus the sphere of values is a legitimate object of epistemic inquiry and, as such, accessible to all who are capable of acquiring knowledge about objectively valid values. If you believe in the objectivity of values, it does not necessarily mean that you also believe that you *know* what these objective values are. But Fromm both believed in the objectivity of values and claimed to know what these values were.[175] Thus the version he adhered to was the strong version of value cognitivism, which all our psychoutopians, as well as the classical anarchists, especially Godwin and Kropotkin, supported.

Proceeding from the strong cognitive theory of values, Fromm challenged the value-relativistic liberalism of his day by stating that 'values are rooted in the very conditions of human existence'.[176] The way he saw it, the Western world is plagued by the exclusion of values from the public sphere: 'We have no principles; we have no sense of values nor any standards of values'.[177] He admitted that objective morality 'tends to produce authoritarianism',[178] but he also criticized liberal pluralistic thinking for its insistence that state and society should not attempt to give positive content to 'freedom' (freedom *to*), but must restrict themselves with a negative conception of freedom (freedom *from*). Fromm's positive conception of freedom revolves around the idea that humans are free to make self-realization, the unfolding and development of all their innate potentialities, the very aim of their lives.[179] From this standpoint, a good society is one which does not only 'repress the evil drives in people', but, above all, helps the human possibilities to flourish.[180]

In the late 1960s, the political philosopher and historian Isaiah Berlin referred to Fromm when he discussed the 'positive' and 'negative' conceptions of liberty. Berlin, a champion of value-pluralism, admitted that the 'modern horror of uniformity, conformism and mechanization of life is not groundless',[181] but he disagreed with Fromm's positive conception of freedom and contested Fromm's Marx-inspired ideal of *vita activa* as the essence of freedom. In fact, while Fromm idealized Marx and portrayed him as a humanistic prophet, Berlin saw Marx rather as a menace to humanism and liberty.[182] Berlin challenged some of the basic tenets of modern liberalism,[183] but he represented the broad Lockean liberal tradition, which stresses tolerance of political difference, individualism, a limited state and the ideal of negative freedom.[184] The notion of negative freedom means that 'you lack political liberty of freedom only if you are prevented from attaining a goal by human beings'.[185]

According to Berlin's 'agonistic liberalism', which emphasizes the value of choice and the (sometimes tragic) incommensurability of constitutive goods, freedom is 'opportunity for action, rather than action itself'.[186] To illustrate, if I am a passive, apolitical citizen, and could not care less about civic activism or about dancing with my fellow man in a Frommian 'life-enhancing' ritual, would it be incompatible with Fromm's notion of freedom? Berlin thinks it probably would be. As if he were responding to Fromm's activist vision of the Sane Society, he writes:

> A man may leave a vigorous and genuinely 'participatory' democratic state in which the social or political pressures are too suffocating for him, for a climate where there may be less dynamic and all-embracing communal life, less gregariousness but also less surveillance. This may appear undesirable to those who look on distaste for public life or society as a symptom of *malaise*, of a deep alienation.[187]

Indeed, Fromm endorsed Marx's notion that in their most individual mode of being humans would at the same time be thoroughly socialized beings in the ideal society, and, like Hannah Arendt (and the classical republican tradition), he maintained that political activity is the supreme end of human life.

Berlin argues that a fundamental problem with positive liberty is that there are ultimate values that may be incompatible with each other (such as democracy and individual freedom, or mercy and justice, or spontaneity and efficiency). Where such values are irreconcilable, there are no clear-cut political solutions to be found:

> If, as I believe, the ends of men are many, and not all of them are in principle compatible with each other, then the possibility of conflict – and of tragedy – can never wholly be eliminated from human life, either personal or social. The necessity of choosing between absolute claims is then an inescapable characteristic of the human condition.[188]

In Berlin's darker version of value-pluralism, there is no rational standard by which you can solve the competition among rivalries and conflictual goods. Consequently, he is wary of 'philosophical monists', whose demands for final solutions and harmony at any price may have disastrous consequences in practice. He points out that the rhetoric of positive liberty has played its historical role 'as a cloak for despotism in the name of wider freedom'.[189]

In his study of classical anarchism, George Crowder analyses the concepts of negative and positive freedom, defending what he regards as the anarchists' commitment to positive freedom. He connects their idea of freedom with their anthropological conception of the 'authentic self' (which I referred to in Chapter 1):

> The anarchists are most concerned to promote freedom to act in accordance not with the empirical self but with the authentic self, with that part of my personality which identifies me most fundamentally.[190]

Crowder argues that the anarchist assumption about positive freedom is founded on the belief that rationality and morality are intrinsic to human nature (the authentic self), and that it is the anarchists' subscription to the tradition of 'natural law' that prompts them to favour a kind of society where people naturally obey this law. In their social philosophy, the nature or the essence of human beings is fully realized only in a society without government, and freedom means freedom to bring one's moral nature to perfection.

I believe Fromm subscribed to the anarchist conception about freedom as a freedom to develop morally, even if he did not believe in a society without government. Fromm was committed to the idea of positive freedom, because, like anarchists, he believed in the idea that we can only realize our authentic selves in a society where our innate biophilous tendencies are allowed to actualize themselves only as an intrinsic part of the character structure that is moulded by socialization. In an ideal society, biophilous tendencies are given opportunities to develop as fully and freely as possible, as a result of which the biophilous character and the social character would become identical. In other words, Fromm's understanding of positive freedom is based on the perfectionist tradition which argues for the realization of that which is most valuable in humans. As he wrote in *To Have or To Be?*, freedom 'means obedience to the laws that govern optimal human development'.[191]

So far so good. From the standpoint of his Socialist Humanism, Fromm had valid reasons for advocating positive freedom. But when one takes a closer look at Fromm's assumptions about a society that would provide an ideal matrix for the perfectibility of humanity, the intrinsic problems in his thought system become more apparent. Above all, even if he was not arguing for a conflict-free society, he never bothered to explicate the potential limitations of his Sane Society, nor give any reasons why anyone should disagree with his version of the good life. He believed that a harmonious state of affairs can be attained if one accepts the premise that systems are desirable which

> produce the maximum of vitality and intrinsic harmony ... An examination of the system Man can show that the biophilous norms are more conducive to the growth and strength of the system while the necrophilous norms are conducive to dysfunction and pathology.[192]

As anyone who has read Fromm's works can confirm, his growth-oriented language mostly avoids the pitfalls of simplistic psychobabble that characterize the language of modern therapeutic culture.[193] But it is difficult to see how these Frommian goods can be defined in a way that pre-empts the dispute about what actually constitutes 'growth' and 'vitality'. Due to the vagueness of the concepts, and the multiplicity of the criteria involved, there is a fatal ambiguity in Fromm's key-words, such as 'freedom', 'wellbeing' and 'authenticity'. Thus it is exceedingly hard to clarify what Fromm actually means when he refers to the Sane Society.

Political philosopher John Schaar, one of the earliest non-psychoanalytic critics of Fromm, argued in his 1961 book on Fromm that he is above all a moralist and a utopian who does not shed light on his own basic assumptions:

> Beneath the clear and placid surface of Fromm's formulations lie restless and murky premises and implications, which he nowhere examines and which the reader must therefore identify for himself.[194]

Indeed. While Fromm was eager to unmask the hidden secrets of the unconscious and of 'socially patterned defects', his method was not to discuss the potential dangers involved in trying to formulate the programme for a different and better modernity. I find his assertions that he 'knows' what the true values of people are both discomforting and rather arrogant.[195] His posture as an anatomist of human nature and of the social character may be thought-provoking and stimulating, but it is also scientifically unconvincing, because he offers sweeping psychoanalytic and Marxist assertions that are invulnerable to empirical criticism. It was Fromm's inclination to value-ladenness of observation which prompted the psychologist Hans Eysenck to write in his review of one of Fromm's later books that 'like all psychoanalysts, the very notion of proof is too much for Fromm, he is content to argue, to comment, and to illustrate'.[196]

In Isaiah Berlin's spirit, we could ask: what is to guarantee that the Sane Society will not educate its recalcitrant citizens to right living by coercion and make them obedient to the directives of an elite of Platonic guardians? Is there a place in Fromm's ideal world for those who do not pursue self-knowledge and civic activism? And how can Fromm justify his assertion that he knows what people truly need better than they do themselves? To declare that as a psychoanalyst he has privileged access to the mental processes is to avoid the question. Far from being value-pluralists, psychoanalysts both in Europe and the United States have tended to ascribe psychological disorders to those whose opinions have differed from their own. Fromm wishes all of us to find authenticity by embracing the form of life that he has invented for us, and he never doubts the adequacy of his formulations. He implies that because the Sane Society would realize the higher principles of Socialist Humanism, anyone who *opposes* such a society represents an alienated state of mind by definition.

There is a disquieting element of authoritarianism in Fromm's commitment to human emancipation that is more in line with religious doctrines than with the kind of 'agonistic' value-pluralism that Isaiah Berlin was concerned with. As Berlin writes in his essay on liberty, 'The sage knows you better than you know yourself, for you are the victim of your passions, slave living a heteronomous life, purblind, unable to understand your true goals'.[197] Undoubtedly, Fromm was such a sage. In his essay on 'Prophets and Priests' (dedicated to Bertrand Russell), he notes:

> It is the function of the prophet to show reality, to show alternatives and to protest; it is his function to call loudly, to awake man from his customary half-slumber. It is the historical situation which makes prophets, not the wish of some men to be prophets.[198]

Apparently, the 'dystopian hopelessness' of the Cold War era was the particular historical situation that made Fromm a prophet. When he became active in the Socialist Party and in the peace movement, he was inspired by the idea that he could help revive the Messianic-humanist tradition and contribute to producing a new edition of humans. His ambition was to create a 'New Man', who carries within himself all of humanity.[199]

Conclusion: Fromm's World of Biophilous Characters

The fundamental virtue in Fromm's political thought is that of *sharing*: sharing work, sharing profits, sharing information and sharing experience. 'The experience of sharing', writes Fromm in 1976, 'makes and keeps the relation between two individuals alive; it is the basis of all great religious, political, and philosophical movements'.[200] Fromm's is the vision of the self-realization of innate reciprocal altruism, a vision of a world in which we are capable of realizing all our innate altruistic potentialities and thus becoming 'fully human'.[201] It is a world in which mutual aid, a sense of solidarity and common purpose are the guiding principles. With his Socialist Humanism, he aspired to offer the Third Way, a social arrangement that would avoid the intrinsic problems of both corporate capitalism and state socialism. Fromm assumed that in a society based on the principles of Socialist Humanism, human beings would find fulfilment through co-operative labour, voluntary associations and other forms of solidarity. His vision depended on his commitment to the altruistic ideal that if humans are truly liberated, they treat each other as equals, as brothers. This emphasis on natural brotherhood is the key to understanding Fromm's utopianism. 'All men', wrote Fromm in 1947, 'are in need of help and depend on one another. Human solidarity is the necessary condition for the unfolding of any one individual.'[202]

Fromm wanted to change the basic attitudes of people and transform them into Socialist Humanists. To dream of a utopian world populated by Frommian biophilous characters who perform virtuous actions because they have natural motives to do so can be a morally edifying experience: if you believe that you can improve your life and contribute to human flourishing, this belief may function as a self-fulfilling prophecy. In the 1960s, Fromm was an inspiring figure to socialist thinkers who related Marxism to humanistic tradition, and he found kindred spirits among revisionist democratic socialists in Eastern European countries.

It is easy to write him off as a prophet of authenticity who deduced a 'value' from a 'fact' only by a conceptual sleight of hand, but occasionally Fromm made observations that can be considered sound and even thought-provoking. To me, his ideas on the need for dissent and disobedience, the innate morality of humans and the marketing orientation are indeed thought-provoking. There are valid points in Fromm ideas, but it is an intellectual challenge to relate them to a sound theoretical framework that could help us to understand the relevant issues in our current social and political order.

I have maintained throughout this chapter that Fromm's image of the Sane Society shares more features with utopian thought than with reality-oriented political theories. This apparently negative assessment does not mean that Fromm's utopian ideas are perforce inferior to more analytic and less normative forms of political thought. One could plausibly contend that it is exactly *because* of his utopian inclinations that Fromm's political thought is worth discussing: rather than merely analysing what already exists, he puts an admirable effort to showing what *could* be.[203] Late in his life, he returned to the idea that had inspired and motivated him for decades: 'The "utopian" goal is more realistic than the "realism" of today's leaders'.[204] Unlike the sceptic Isaiah Berlin, Fromm had faith in the ideal that one could make a straight thing out of the crooked timber of humanity.

CONCLUSION: UTOPIA, ILLUSION AND SECOND REALITY

> A map of the world that does not include Utopia is not worth even glancing at.
>
> Oscar Wilde, in 'The Soul of Man under Socialism', 1891

In *Darwin's Dangerous Idea*, the philosopher Daniel Dennett makes a useful distinction between two metaphors for two different forms of scientific thinking. There is a form of thinking which uses 'skyhooks' and another form of thinking which uses 'cranes'. A skyhook is an imaginary contrivance in the sky, something which lifts you aloft without any help from below. A crane, by contrast, is something which lifts things up from the ground. In Dennett's words,

> cranes can do the lifting work our imaginary skyhooks might do, and they do it in an honest, non-question-begging fashion. They are expensive, however. They have to be designed and built, from everyday parts already on hand, and they have to be located on a firm base of existing ground. Skyhooks are miraculous lifters, unsupported and insupportable. Cranes are no less excellent as lifters, and they have the decided advantage of being real.[1]

For Dennett, Darwinian natural selection is very much a crane mechanism, while Lamarckian theory of inherited acquired characteristics and Teilhard de Chardin's evolutionary utopianism exemplify thinking which uses skyhooks.

I would suggest that, in the field of social and political theory, utopianism bears the characteristics of Dennett's 'skyhook' theory, and that this is true of psychological utopianism as well. Jung's and Reich's biology-oriented theories bear more resemblances to the nineteenth-century vitalist *Naturphilosophie* than with the naturalism of Darwinian biology, while Gross's Communist matriarchy was equally far removed from contingencies of empirical reality. Fromm's Socialist Humanism was somewhat closer to the existing ground, but it still did not exemplify thinking which uses cranes: there was so much Messianism, Marxism and psychoanalytic speculation in his thinking that it is another prime example of a skyhook theory. There is in fact a revelationary element in all psychoutopian thinking, one of the primary functions of which seems to be that it allows us to think that we know something when we know nothing at all. Methods of our psychoutopian authors are long on interpretation and assertion, and short on empirical evidence, and this is what gives their ideas a distinct skyhook feeling.

Positive Illusion, Self-Deception and Utopianism

I believe that the cultural significance of psychological utopianism lies not in its explanatory power but in its function as a good myth. I shall illustrate the mythical character of psychological utopianism by discussing its possible connection with positive illusions. In their studies on the psychological function of illusory beliefs, social psychologist Shelley E. Taylor and her associates (Jonathan D. Brown, David A. Armor and others) have argued that positive illusions may be beneficial for mental health and wellbeing.[2] Taylor has challenged the well-established thesis (propounded by Fromm, for example) that contact with reality is the crucial component of mental health by suggesting that mild positive illusions about the self, personal control and the future are true for normal people, and that these illusions, as long as they indeed remain mild, contribute to mental health:

> The mentally healthy person appears to have the enviable capacity to distort reality in a direction that enhances self-esteem, maintains a belief in personal efficacy, and promotes an optimistic view of the future. These three illusions ... appear to foster traditional criteria of mental health.[3]

By contrast, individuals who are moderately depressed or low in self-esteem seem to have a more accurate view of themselves and of the future. For Taylor, empirical evidence indicates that specific positive illusions promote mental health, because they can create self-fulfilling prophecies, whereas the relative absence of such illusions is what characterizes mild depression and low self-esteem.[4] She has also replied to her critics by distinguishing between 'illusion-proneness' in two different mindsets:

> When individuals are in a deliberative mindset, attempting to make a decision, their positive illusions are quite modest; but when they are in an implemental mindset, attempting to put a decision into effect, illusions increase dramatically.[5]

In Taylor's theory, positive illusions are 'health-inducing' only insofar as people who hold these illusions make use of the feedback from their social environment.

Taylor's and her associates' theory of the mental health promoting aspects of positive illusions is controversial, but its assumption about the role of self-deception is supported by the pioneer studies of the evolutionary biologist Robert Trivers, who has been interested in this phenomenon for decades. In his *Natural Selection and Social Theory* (2002), he writes:

> Self-deception appears to be a universal human trait which touches our lives at all levels – from our innermost thoughts to the chance that we will be annihilated together

> in warfare. It affects the relative development of intellectual disciplines (the more social the content, the less developed the discipline: contrast physics and sociology) as well as the relative degree of consciousness of individuals (generally, more self-deceived, less conscious). An evolutionary analysis suggests that the root cause is social, including selection to deceive others, selection on others to manipulate and deceive oneself, and selection on competing sections of one's own genotype.[6]

Trivers's evolutionary theory of self-deception supports Taylor's suggestion that misconceptions may be adaptive to mental health and wellbeing. The mechanism that produces self-serving illusions may therefore be an essential part of an inherent mental configuration, which implies that to be 'healthy' may not be the same as to have a 'realistic' view of the world. As the psychologist Steven Pinker, inspired by Trivers's work, notes in his discussion of the theory of self-deception:

> Self-deception is among the deepest roots of human strife and folly. It implies that the faculties that ought to allow us to settle our differences – seeking the truth and discussing it rationally – are miscalibrated so that all parties assess themselves to be wiser, abler, and nobler than they really are.[7]

Hence an active, positive misrepresentation of reality to the conscious mind may, as Robert Trivers argues, 'serve to orient the organism favorably toward the future'.[8]

There is of course an important cultural factor in individuals' self-evaluations that should be in kept in mind when concepts such as 'self-esteem' and 'optimism' are analysed. Taylor and her associates are North American psychologists doing research in the United States, and deeply-embedded values that are emphasized in their own culture may play only a minor role in some other culture. The 'feel good about oneself' ideology is very prominent in the United States, where self-confidence, self-esteem and the celebration of the individual's uniqueness and his or her capacities are systematically boosted in pre-schools, schools and other institutions of socialization. As a result of the so-called false uniqueness bias (the tendency to see oneself as better than most others), there may be among North Americans only a weak correlation between one's level of self-confidence and one's abilities.[9] As psychologist Steven J. Heine and his collaborators have argued, in another culture, in their case in Japan, people may not hold such over-optimistic and unrealistic conceptions of their capabilities as Americans/westerners do. Their studies indicate that Americans have a much stronger need for positive self-regard than the Japanese, who are more self-critical and much less individual-centred.[10] Heine and his collaborators' comparative cultural perspective relativizes the universality of Taylor's theory of positive illusions, but it does not refute her empirical argument that mild positive illusions seem to have a beneficial effect on the life of (American or Western) people, especially when they have to adjust to stressful events. Besides, as the Finnish sociologist Janne

Kivivuori has noted, there have been many thinkers in modern and pre-modern Europe who have claimed that unverifiable beliefs (e.g. concerning the existence of God) or good myths protect people from the blows of fate (these thinkers include Plato, Cicero, Machiavelli, More, Francis Bacon, Montaigne, Rousseau and Kant).[11]

If some illusions are beneficial to mental health, and if the subtle mechanism of self-deception is a product of natural selection, then the dreams of psychological utopianism can be seen as a specific way of articulating misconceptions and self-deception – and to avoid 'depressive realism'. Psychological utopianism, like all forms of utopian thought, promotes the principle of hope, and thus it can function as an antidote to a more realistic view of self, which by definition is less optimistic and hopeful. I believe psychological utopianism supports and justifies the positive illusion that better days are ahead and that we can realize our authentic (virtuous, rational, co-operative, altruistic, etc.) selves and become what we think we truly are. If the value of a particular belief is contingent not on its cognitive status, but on whether it has positive consequences to self and society, then one can distinguish between a harmful and a useful illusion. In its promotion of mental wellbeing, reciprocal altruism, solidarity, individual and social harmony, expressive fulfilment, and other forms of human flourishing, psychological utopianism seems to testify to the relative power of mild positive illusions and the concomitant need to avoid depressive realism.

To use an analogy, depressed people who suffer from a sense of hopelessness may feel like elderly people who are placed in homes for the aged. It seems to be the case that most people view entry into homes for the aged as the end of the line. These are places where one goes to die, where hope ends and one – quite literally – has nothing to look forward to. And it would appear that in comparison to elderly people who can remain in their own homes, mortality rates are higher among those admitted to homes for the aged (compared to other age groups, depression is more common among elderly people). Depressed people are people who metaphorically find themselves in homes for the aged. No hope, nothing to look forward to. It is probably not a coincidence that elderly people seem to find Jung's psychology more appealing than other versions of dynamic psychology: Jung emphasized the importance of the second half of life (starting from the age of thirty-six to thirty-eight) in general, and the developmental process of individuation in particular. Jungian individuation denotes a psychospiritual growth that really begins in mid-life and lasts until the end of life. Especially for religiously- or 'innerworldly'-oriented people, Jungian psychoutopia may sometimes function as a good myth that wards off depression in old age.

Did the psychoutopians believe, then, that it is possible to create a world where people do not suffer, grieve, feel alienated and lonely, and plague others? Did they believe that the world could be healed psychically? I believe the answer to these questions is 'No'. Despite their search of authenticity, and their implicit wish that all people could attain a new state of consciousness (like they themselves had), they did not try to downplay the tragic dimension of the human condition. They were not like contemporary pop-psychologists, who in their publications, seminars, workshops (etc.) promise psychospiritual bliss and happiness to all people. On the contrary, they all held the rather commonplace belief among European intellectuals of the early twentieth century that human existence is a rather sad if not a meaningless undertaking. To varying degrees all four authors in this book depicted the modern '*Gesellschaft*' society negatively, as the producer of procedural rationalism, technological and bureaucratic hubris, materialism, consumerism, moral relativism, a restrictive and charmless lower-middle-class value system and lifestyle, tasteless mass culture and the 'naive' belief that average people themselves know what is good for them.

The point of the psychoutopian emphasis on the darker aspects of life was not, however, to fan the spirit of despair, but rather to highlight the dramatic elements in their utopianism. Life is indeed hard, and only a few people can sail through it without damage, but it is precisely the sorry state of modern man and modern culture that fuelled the psychoutopian visions of a better life with so much hope. The desire for a good life becomes more intense and dramatic in a society where most of us feel alienated, mentally crippled and neurotic. To paint a picture of the human condition in dark colours gives a dramatic effect to the portrayal of a different kind of reality, where alienation can be overcome, human capacities can freely develop and mental health or wholeness is not the prerogative of the psychodynamic elite. Contrasting their vision of a state of authenticity with a world gone wrong, they conveyed the message that, in principle, all of us carry within ourselves the seeds of a better future. It was only that people needed (psycho)spiritual and moral leaders who could revitalize forgotten wisdom, teach that wisdom to people and restore the original unity of humankind.

In sum, psychological utopianism may express the need of its creators to believe in and promote good myths or positive illusions, and the suggestions of psychoutopian authors may function as an antidote to depressive realism. To read about Jung's individuation or Fromm's biophilous character may make some people feel better about themselves and their future prospects. At the same time, one can argue that in their aspiration to see beyond the confinements of the human condition, psychoutopians created a 'Second Reality' that could be almost hermetically shut off from the empirical realities of everyday life. In their conceptualization of the good life, they presented radical alternatives to the prevailing social order without seriously considering whether these alternatives are grounded on any existing realities. For the more realistically-minded readers, this is the intrinsic problem with psychological utopianism, and a critical assessment of the basic scientific, ideological and moral assumptions of psychoutopian authors may lead a sceptic to conclude that their utopianism is based on illusory views on the human condition.

Utopianism, Ideology and the Second Reality

By abandoning or revising psychoanalytic theory, Gross, Jung, Reich and Fromm replaced (psycho)ideological elements with (psycho)utopian elements. What I mean by this shift is the following: ideologies are concerned with explaining the purported 'laws' of history and nature, laws that reveal the course of historical and natural processes.[12] By giving an account of these processes, ideologists pretend to be capable of seeing the determinants of human experience. Dismissing the notion of contingency, according to which that which exists is neither necessary nor impossible, advocates of ideologies offer absolutes, ultimate explanations of the total structure of reality. The psychological power of ideologies is aptly expressed in the social psychologist Stanley Milgram's famous study on 'obedience to authority', where he states:

> Control the manner in which a man interprets his world, and you have gone a long way toward controlling his behavior. That is why ideology, an attempt to interpret the condition of man, is always a prominent feature of revolutions, wars, and other circumstances in which individuals are called upon to perform extraordinary action ... There is propensity for people to accept definitions of action provided by legitimate authority.[13]

Milgram's interest in the control of the ways in which we interpret reality was related to his experimental study of obedience (which showed that we are prone to follow orders if we regard the authority as legitimate), whereas our concern is the ideological nature of psychodynamic interpretations of reality. Since these interpretations come from intellectual rather than political authorities, their legitimation is tied up with the plausibility and suggestibility of the theory that provides the framework for their interpretations. If such expert interpretations of reality are accepted and affirmed as true (i.e., legitimate), they can attain a position whereby they control to some extent the manner in which we look at our world.

In his famous work *Utopia and Ideology* (1936), the sociologist of knowledge Karl Mannheim criticized ideologies for three different reasons: first, their function is to 'conceal the actual meaning of conduct rather than to reveal it'; second, they resort to the 'device of escape from themselves and the world ... thereby conjuring up false interpretations of experience'; and, third, they fail to 'take account of the new realities applying to a situation' and instead attempt to conceal these realities by 'thinking of them in categories which are inappropriate'.[14] The political philosopher Hannah Arendt was even more severe in her critique of ideologies, arguing that totalitarian elements are intrinsic in all ideologies, and that, while claiming to give a total explanation, ideological thinking

> becomes independent of all experience from which it cannot learn anything new ... Hence ideological thinking becomes emancipated from the reality that we perceive with our five senses, and insists on 'truer' reality concealed behind all perceptible things.[15]

In Arendt's view, there are two basic elements in ideological argumentation: the element of movement and of emancipation from reality and experience. Arendt's conception of the totalitarian nature of ideologies is applicable to utopianism as well, for neither utopian nor ideological thinking tolerates dissent.

What is remarkable about ideologies is that they appear to us to be perfectly logical and consistent, provided that we only accept their premise. In the case of psychoanalysis, one unverifiable premise is the claim that unconscious mental life is made accessible by psychoanalytic methods. Because of the logic inherent in their ideas, political ideologies such as Marxism or liberalism and psychological ideologies such as psychoanalysis claim to know the determinants of the historical process. The main difference between these two forms of ideology is that while psychoanalysis has little to say about the laws of history, it is very confident in its ability to explain the objective psychic laws of the individual life history. As the social anthropologist Ernest Gellner has noted, both Marxism and psychoanalysis are an 'account of the central human predicament, a recipe for its remedy (partial or total), and hence, by implication, a morality'.[16] Using the term 'belief system' instead of 'ideology', Gellner manages to analyse those components in psychoanalysis that might equally be called 'ideological'. I would suggest that when Gross, Jung, Reich and Fromm broke with (or were expelled from) the psychoanalytic movement, they also broke with a powerful ideology, which has enjoyed a 'privileged access to the psychological processes of human functioning'.[17]

The philosopher of history Eric Voegelin has applied the term 'Second Reality' to describe the attempts of ideologies to destroy language 'inasmuch as the ideological thinker has lost contact with reality and develops symbols for expressing not reality but his state of alienation from it'.[18] Both Voegelin and Arendt see ideologies as systems of ideas in which the standards of thought are corrupted and the reality of experience is replaced by 'truer', higher reality. In his discussion of Second Reality, Voegelin was influenced by the Austrian writer Robert Musil, to whom Second Reality was a key theme when he wrote *The Man Without Qualities* (*Der Mann ohne Eigenschaften*, 1930–43), one of the landmarks of twentieth-century literature. In 1937, Musil gave two lectures on 'stupidity', in which he differentiated between an 'honourable' and 'simple' stupidity (*eine ehrliche und schlichte Dummheit*) and a 'higher' stupidity (*eine höhere Dummheit*).

Honourable stupidity denotes a weakness in intellectual capacities, whereas higher stupidity is a much more dangerous form of stupidity because of its hubris, its lack of modesty and proportion. The former is human, quite harmless and an almost charming phenomenon, whereas the latter is a true disease of culture, working not so much against reason as against spirit (*Geist*) and feeling (*Gemüt*). In Musil's own words, higher stupidity

> reaches into the highest intellectual sphere ... Years ago I wrote about this form of stupidity that 'there is absolutely no significant idea that stupidity would not know how to apply; stupidity is active in every direction, and can dress up in all the clothes of truth. Truth, on the other hand, has for every occasion only one dress and one path, and is always at a disadvantage.' The stupidity this addresses is no mental illness yet it is most lethal; a dangerous disease of the mind that endangers life itself.[19]

The question of stupidity was not a minor issue for Musil, for, as the Musil scholar David S. Luft has pointed out, he considered 'On Stupidity' to be 'one of his most important works'.[20] And although he had some respect for Freud's ideas concerning the unconscious, Musil regarded Jung and Freud as 'pseudo-poets', representatives of *psychologia phantastica*, who deny poetry the support of psychology. As Musil saw it, thinkers such as Jung, Freud, Heidegger and Stefan George were spiritual dictators, whose popularity was due to the human need for (intellectual) submission and leadership. Their movements resembled National Socialism in that the members of all these sects were able to explain the world with a mere handful of concepts.[21]

Eric Voegelin elaborates on Musil's categories of higher stupidity and Second Reality in his own, rather anti-modernist interpretation of Western culture and modern 'gnostic movements', including Marxism, psychoanalysis and National Socialism. Voegelin holds that Musil's higher stupidity amounts to the loss of reality, where

> words acquire their own existence; language becomes an independent reality in itself ... If one amuses oneself with second reality, then language too becomes part of second reality, and then these problems arise, which indeed are only semantic and are resolved as soon as one starts thinking.[22]

Voegelin calls the 'transformers' of one reality into the other, 'magicians'. Magicians manipulate words and their meanings so that, by employing their perverted vocabulary, people can create for themselves a false idea of reality and live according to it.[23] Despite the moralistic tone of Voegelin's writings, I believe his ideas are applicable to much of modern intellectual culture, including psychological utopianism, which 'transforms one reality into the other' by a mere conceptual sleight of hand, without any need for a reality check.

In its all-encompassing vision and its self-referential character, psychological utopianism can be seen as representing a Second Reality, a closed system which can stimulate and inspire, but which can also make more dogmatic claims, and opt for a more intolerant and monistic ideology than the society to which it aspires to supply an alternative. However, while both utopias and ideologies include monistic elements and replace reality with a Second Reality, they are fundamentally different in that, unlike ideologies, utopias are not oriented towards history and to the question of how something comes to pass. Utopias are concerned not with movement and the historical process but with the ultimate result of the (historical) process. The utopian Second Reality is a transhistorical reality, which rejects the contingencies and complexities of historical time and seeks instead the timeless sphere of truth and beauty beyond that which is merely historical. Gross's Communist Matriarchy, Jung's Archetypal Cosmos, Reich's Orgone Energy and even Fromm's Socialist Humanism all insist on a supraindividual ground of existence. Fromm expressed this understanding of time in his late work on 'having' and 'being', where he pointed out that 'being is not necessarily outside of time, but time is not the dimension that governs being'.[24]

One could say that the psychoutopian authors belong to the school of transcendentalism, the framework of which is built on the mythical and the timeless, and on the dismissal of the chronological time of historical contingencies. This 'school' had emerged on the eve of World War I, when the younger generation in Europe revolted against what they perceived to be the soulless materialism of their fathers' generation. Around 1910, this revolt manifested itself, for example in a journal published by Stefan George and his circle (*Jahrbuch der geistigen Bewegung*), in the bohemian counterculture of Ascona, and in expressionist art.

Like their literary colleagues Thomas Mann and James Joyce, psychoutopians reasoned that as people are the same in (their archetypal or Orgonomic) essence, they will act essentially in the same way throughout time. Consequently, if human nature is universal and invariable, the contingencies and chance occurrences of history are not the true constituents of human life. Psychoutopians imposed a transhistorical order on the haphazard or even chaotic flux of man's historical experience, and established a transcendental relationship between individuals and their psychological origins. The aesthetic, psychological and spiritual transcendentalists were in search of new stimulants to the imagination, an authentic self, and an experience of infinity. For the modern transcendentalists, the traditional substantial goods (God, nature and reason) no longer gave meaning to the world, at least not until they were radically transformed. This was what happened with nature, which could be perceived by the transcendentalist advocates of inner nature (such as Jung) as a creative fusion of biology and spirit. But there were also political transcendentalists, whose faith in Marxism was motivated by their utopian conviction that Communism transcends both individual and collective selfishness once and for all, and gives birth to a classless society, where the beautiful ideal of the brotherhood of man would become a reality.

The school of transcendentalism had its deep roots in the Platonic theory of the 'Two Worlds', but this does not necessarily mean that this school was nothing but an anti-modernist remnant of Platonic metaphysics, manifesting a faint-hearted escapist attempt to avoid the anxieties generated by a 'civilization in crisis', or a Communist daydream about a society where not only class and private property but the state itself would wither away. What the transcendentalists pursued was not a rejection of reality per se, but rather an articulation of a reality that was rooted not in 'things in time', but in the transcendence of the given social reality and in the affirmation of timelessness in time. As Fromm put it, 'in the mode of being, we respect time, but we do not submit to it'.[25] The non-Marxist transcendentalists repudiated the idea of a tabula rasa, the main tenet of social constructivists, which stresses the all-important role of volition, the break with the past and the almost infinite malleability of human nature. In its adherence to the ideas of the longevity and durability of basic human concerns, the transcendentalist school replaces the sociocultural determinism of the doctrine of the tabula rasa with the more indeterminate notion of the timeless dimension of a higher reality.

The Nature of the Utopian Second Reality

My own attitude towards psychological utopianism is that, at their best, the ideas of psychological utopians are exciting and inspiring thought experiments that provide us with new vistas onto the human condition; and, at their worst, are either monotonous or absurd prescriptions for a perfect world, failing to contribute anything of permanent value to the storehouse of human thought. Therefore, I would say that, while psychoutopian authors are certainly worth reading, they are not necessarily worth believing. But even if we disagree with them – and it seems we sceptics often do – we may be provoked to examine the thought processes that make us perhaps not happier, but at least more sensitive to the various manifestations of hope, desire and renewal. Because of their utopian propensities, many people continue to find inspiration in the writings of Gross, Jung, Reich and Fromm regardless of their scientific reputation. There are undoubtedly also many people who find their ideas nonsensical, or even irritating, because their observations are so value-laden and seemingly removed from existing realities. When it comes to accepting or rejecting the ideas that psychoutopian authors advocated in the name of science, very much depends on whether or not the values that they promoted find resonance in us.

With its aspiration to create a world where the authentic needs and desires of all people would be amply fulfilled, psychological utopianism is easy to write off as naive, unrealistic daydreaming that failed to adequately address the burning social issues of the time. But while there is good reason to be sceptical about the utopian negation of reality manifest in the writings of the psychoutopian authors, I would also like to refer to Karl Mannheim's way of looking at utopias. With all his well-grounded reservations about the utopian negation of reality, he nevertheless contended that the 'complete elimination of reality-transcending elements from our world would lead us to a "matter-of-factness" which ultimately would mean the decay of the human will'.[26] Following Mannheim, I believe that attempts to put into practice the principles of a utopian Second Reality could result in a society more oppressive than the one to which it purports to offer an alternative. But there is another side to the coin: utopian visions also nourish our imagination, and may prompt us to reflect on the historical fact that our society and its prevailing ideology are not a destiny that we just have to accept as they are. Thus one can plausibly argue for the necessity of utopianism, if the whole of intellectual culture is not to decline into narrow expertise, sterile risk-avoidance or market-oriented entrepreneurship.

Hence, there is more to psychological utopianism than a desire for a total explanation, a fulfilment of (healthy) sexual needs or a Messianic urge to rescue humanity. Gross, Jung, Reich and Fromm may have been moral crusaders rather than scientific psychologists, and they may have failed in their ambition to see beyond the limits of human understanding. But even if their utopianism fails to carry conviction, it can command some respect. This is because the very idea of offering alternative perspectives on reality can have suggestive force, and it would seem that even today there are educated people in the world who prefer original insights into human nature and imaginary visions of the good life to cool objectivity and systematic coherence. My guess is that the current interest in the ideas of Gross, for example, has much to do with his utopian ideas, which may find resonance in people who refuse to believe *either* that we live in the best of possible worlds, *or* that nothing can be done to change the social order and its prevailing value system. Utopia may not offer viable tools for analysing society, but what it can do is to inspire us to think otherwise. And to think otherwise is – put simply – to think.

Attaining the Unattainable

It seems to me that, late in their lives, Gross, Jung, Reich and Fromm came to realize that their attempts to contribute to the inner transformation of man had amounted to very little. What may have worked in the clinical face-to-face situation, or among like-minded associates, friends and pupils, had little influence on the collective cultural level. For the most part, our authors made observations suggesting that 'western Man' had remained the same, or deteriorated further, and that the world was not getting any better – if anything, it was getting worse. True, for a German émigré psychoanalyst who mixed psychodynamic, moral and sociopolitical categories, Fromm was an exceptionally popular author in the 1940s and the 1950s, and Jung became one of the best-known twentieth-century psychologists and psychological healers. But in their old age even these two 'winners' in the psychomedical marketplace appeared to become acutely aware that no one is capable of changing the mental structures of people, no matter how many books they sell, or how many hopeful people want to visit them and venerate them as 'Wise Old Men' or 'Prophets of the Unconscious'. The ageing Jung escaped from unbearable modernity into the 'timeless' realm of alchemy, myth and religion, while the equally unmodern Fromm sought consolation in the Messianic and prophetic writings of mystics and humanists. Gross and Reich, the two 'losers' among our quartet, succumbed under the pressure of adverse external conditions, as well as of their own inner demons: Gross died prematurely as a penniless, stigmatized drug addict, while Reich perished in a federal prison following a period of increasing intellectual and social isolation and mental confusion.

With regard to their visions for a better world, I sense resignation if not disillusionment in the late writings of all these authors, even in those of Gross, who waved the utopian flag to the very end. History, that nasty destroyer of hopes and illusions, left them in the lurch, as it does all of us who venture to create, and have faith in, alternative realities of utopian proportions. As Max Beerbohm so aptly put it:

> So this is Utopia,
> Is it? Well –
> I beg your pardon;
> I thought it was Hell.[27]

NOTES

Introduction

1. As I use the terms 'dynamic psychology' and 'psychodynamic' constantly throughout this book, a short clarification of these key terms is in order. By dynamic psychology I mean a broad psychological tradition including Freudian psychoanalysis, Jungian analytical psychology, Adlerian individual psychology and Pierre Janet's psychology of the 'subconscious', all of which are based on the premise that psychopathologies and, by extension, all 'unconscious' mental activities cannot be localized and explained mechanically, because they are by their very nature intrapsychic *processes*. As such, they can be accounted for only through an examination of the *genealogy* of these processes. Only by shedding light on their origins, and on the way an individual deals (through 'abreactions', reflections, neurotic symptoms, etc.) with these processes here and now, can we explain human psychological functioning. There are marked differences between the psychologies of these four figures, but together they are the founding fathers of a psychology that is characteristically *dynamic*.
2. F. E. Manuel and F. P. Manuel, *Utopian Thought in the Western World* (Cambridge, MA: Belknap Press of Harvard University Press, 1979).
3. J. G. Morawski, 'Assessing Psychology's Moral Heritage through our Neglected Utopias'. *American Psychologist*, 37:10 (1982), pp. 1082–95.
4. E. Berman, 'Psychoanalysis, Rescue and Utopia', *Utopian Studies*, 4:2 (1993), pp. 44–56; and E. Berman, 'The Utopian Fantasy of a New Person and the Danger of a False Analytic Self', *Psychoanalytic Psychology*, 17 (2000), pp. 38–60.
5. M. W. Barclay, 'Utopia and Psychological Theory', *Theory and Psychology*, 3:2 (1993), pp. 173–90.
6. A. Etkind, *Eros of the Impossible: The History of Psychoanalysis in Russia* (1993), trans. N. and M. Rubins (Boulder, CO: Westview Press, 1997).
7. R. Noll, *The Jung Cult: Origins of a Charismatic Movement* (Princeton, NJ: Princeton University Press, 1994); and R. Noll, *The Aryan Christ: The Secret Life of Carl Jung* (New York: Random House, 1997).
8. G. Heuer, 'The Influence of the Life and Ideas of Otto Gross on the Life and Ideas of C. G. Jung' (unpublished PhD thesis, University of Essex, 2004).
9. P. A. Robinson, *The Freudian Left: Wilhelm Reich, Geza Roheim, Herbert Marcuse* (New York: Harper & Row, 1969).
10. On such a psychoanalytic approach to utopianism, see J. Whitebook, *Perversion and Utopia: A Study in Psychoanalysis and Critical Theory* (Cambridge, MA: MIT Press, 1996).

11. R. G. Collingwood, *The Idea of History*, rev. edn, intro. J. van der Dussen (Oxford: Oxford University Press, 1994); R. G. Collingwood, *An Essay on Metaphysics*, rev. edn, ed. R. Martin (Oxford: Oxford University Press, 1998); and R. G. Collingwood, *An Autobiography* (1939; Oxford: Clarendon Press, 2002); Q. Skinner, *Visions of Politics*, 3 vols (Cambridge: Cambridge University Press, 2002).
12. 'The history of thought, and therefore all history, is the re-enactment of past thought in the historian's own mind', Collingwood, *The Idea of History*, p. 215.
13. Skinner, *Visions of Politics*, vol. 1: 'Regarding Method'; J. Tully (ed.), *Meaning and Context: Quentin Skinner and his Critics* (Cambridge: Cambridge University Press, 1988).
14. Skinner, *Visions of Politics*, vol. 1, pp. 101–2.
15. L. Wittgenstein, *Philosophical Investigations*, trans. G. E. M. Anscombe (Oxford: Blackwell, 1953).

1 The Nature of Psychological Utopianism

1. T. More, *Utopia* (1516), trans. P. Turner (London: Penguin Books, 1965), Preface: 'Lines on the Island of Utopia by the Poet Laureate, Mr Windbag Nonsenso's sister's son'.
2. There are several studies on More's novel. For bibliographical guides, see A. J. Geritz, *Thomas More: An Annotated Bibliography of Criticism, 1935–1997* (Westport, CT: Greenwood Press, 1998).
3. For historical studies of utopian thought, see Manuel and Manuel, *Utopian Thought*; K. Kumar, *Utopia and Anti-Utopia in Modern Times* (Oxford: Basil Blackwell, 1987); K. Kumar, *Utopianism* (Minneapolis, MN: University of Minnesota Press, 1991).
4. K. Marx, *Capital, Vol. 1* (1867; London: Lawrence and Wishart, 1983), p. 26.
5. E. Hobsbawm, *The Age of Extremes: A History of the World, 1914–1991* (New York: Vintage Books, 1996).
6. U. Segerstråle, *Defenders of the Truth* (Oxford: Oxford University Press, 2001), pp. 95–132.
7. For those interested in the scholarly studies on utopias and utopian thought, there is an international Society for Utopian Studies, which publishes its own journal, *Utopian Studies*. See http://www.utoronto.ca/utopia/.
8. Skinner, *Visions of Politics*, vol. 1, p. 88.
9. For a recent discussion of various theoretical aspects of utopianism, see B. Goodwin (ed.), *The Philosophy of Utopia* (London: Frank Cass, 2001).
10. For an analysis of the utopian elements in Marxism, see V. Geoghegan, *Utopianism and Marxism* (London: Methuen, 1987).
11. See L. T. Sargent, 'The Three Faces of Utopianism Revisited', *Utopian Studies* 5:1 (1994), pp. 1–37.
12. For example, in the late nineteenth and early twentieth centuries, the famous sociologist Edward Westermarck built his observations and theories on Darwinism, and won acclaim for his evolutionary approach to the origins of the family and to the evolution of moral ideas. But by the mid-twentieth century, his legacy was in disrepute and, in the human sciences, Darwinism and biology became associated with Auschwitz, racism and reactionary ideologies. It is only in recent years that Darwinism has made a comeback of sorts in the human sciences, largely because of evolutionary psychology, a new neo-Darwinian paradigm that seeks to explain the function of the human mind (emotions, beliefs, moral commitments) from the evolutionary perspective. For an informative overview on recent evolutionary theories about human behaviour, see K. N. Laland and G.

R. Brown, *Sense and Nonsense: Evolutionary Perspectives on Human Behaviour* (Oxford: Oxford University Press, 2003).

13. C. N. Degler, *In Search of Human Nature* (Oxford: Oxford University Press, 1991).
14. For a study of the American tradition of psychology-inspired human engineering, see R. Lemov, *World as Laboratory: Experiments with Mice, Mazes and Men* (New York: Hill and Wang, 2005).
15. C. Quarta, 'Homo Utopicus: On the Need for Utopia', *Utopian Studies*, 7:2 (1996), pp. 153–66, on pp. 163–4.
16. G. W. F. Hegel, *Reason in History: A General Introduction to the Philosophy of History*, trans. R. S. Hartman (Indianapolis, IN: Bobbs-Merrill, 1953), § 27.
17. S. Freud, *Civilization and its Discontents* (1930), trans. J. Strachey, in *Civilization, Society and Religion*, The Penguin Freud Library, Vol. 12 (London: Penguin Books, 1991), p. 264.
18. Quoted in D. J. Fisher, *Cultural Theory and Psychoanalytic Tradition* (New Brunswick, NJ: Transaction Publishers, 1991), p. 124.
19. W. Reich, *Reich Speaks of Freud*, ed. M. Higgins and C. M. Raphael, trans. T. Pol (New York: Farrar, Straus and Giroux, 1974), p. 44; W. Reich, *Function of the Orgasm: Sex-Economic Problems of Biological Energy* (1942), trans. V. R. Carfagno (London: Souvenir Press, 1973), pp. 207–8.
20. S. Freud, *The Future of an Illusion* (1927), trans. J. Strachey, in *Civilization, Society and Religion*, p. 232. Sociologist Yiannis Gabriel suggests that, in *The Future of an Illusion*, 'we can in fact discern a utopian paradigm, which although seriously qualified, has a lot of the attributes of pre-Marxist utopias', Y. Gabriel, *Freud and Society* (London: Routledge & Kegan Paul, 1983), pp. 139–40. He calls Freud's implicit utopia a 'Utopia of Logos'.
21. Ibid., p. 131.
22. On this issue, see R. Sennett, *The Fall of Public Man* (New York: Vintage Books, 1978); M. L. Gross, *The Psychological Society* (New York: Random House, 1978); E. Gellner, *The Psychoanalytic Movement: The Cunning of Unreason* (1985; London: Fontana Press, 1993); and F. Furedi, *Therapy Culture: Cultivating Vulnerability in an Uncertain Age* (London: Routledge, 2003).
23. J. Chasseguet-Smirgel and B. Grunberger, *Freud or Reich? Psychoanalysis and Illusion*, trans. C. Pajaczkowska (New Haven, CT: Yale University Press, 1986), p. 30.
24. F. Nietzsche, *The Birth of Tragedy* (1872; Garden City, NY: Doubleday Anchor Books, 1956), p. 92.
25. P. Ricoeur, *Freud and Philosophy: An Essay on Interpretation* (1965), trans. D. Savage (New Haven, CT: Yale University Press, 1970), pp. 32–6.
26. About the term 'eupsychia', see A. H. Maslow, *The Farther Reaches of Human Nature* (Harmondsworth: Penguin Books, 1973).
27. F. E. Manuel (ed.), *Utopias and Utopian Thought* (1966; London: Souvenir Press, 1973), pp. 86–95.
28. Manuel and Manuel, *Utopian Thought*, ch. 34.
29. Kumar, *Utopianism*, p. 40.
30. In *Utopian Studies*, the psychoanalyst Emanuel Berman has published an article in which he examines the relationship between utopian visions in psychoanalysis and 'rescue fantasy'. See Berman, 'Psychoanalysis, Rescue and Utopia'.
31. R. Levitas, *The Concept of Utopia* (New York: Philip Allan, 1990), p. 192.

32. On Marxism and psychoanalysis, see H.-P. Gente (ed.), *Marxismus, Psychoanalyse, Sexpol*, 2 vols (Frankfurt am Main: Fischer Bücherei, 1970); S. Kätzel, *Marxismus und Psychoanalyse: Eine ideologiegeschichtliche Studie zur Diskussion in Deutschland und der UdSSR 1919–1933* (Berlin: Deutscher Verlag der Wissenschaften, 1987); and H. Dahmer, *Libido und Gesellschaft: Studien über Freud und die Freudsche Linke* (Frankfurt: Suhrkamp, 1973).
33. On behaviourist human or social engineering in the United States, see Lemov, *World as Laboratory*.
34. Morawski, 'Assessing Psychology's Moral Heritage', pp. 1083, 1090.
35. G. C. Claeys and L. T. Sargent, 'Introduction', in G. C. Claeys and L. T. Sargent (eds), *The Utopia Reader* (New York: New York University Press, 1999), pp. 1–5, on p. 1.
36. Manuel and Manuel, *Utopian Thought*, p. 792.
37. Barclay, 'Utopia and Psychological Theory'.
38. Berman, 'Psychoanalysis, Rescue and Utopia', p. 45.
39. More, *Utopia*, p. 76.
40. E. Fromm, *Humanismus als reale Utopie*, ed. R. Funk (Weinheim and Basel: Beltz Verlag, 1992), p. 90.
41. On Jung's reception of Nietzsche, see P. Bishop, *The Dionysian Self: C. G. Jung's Reception of Friedrich Nietzsche* (Berlin, Walter de Gruyter, 1995).
42. T. Adorno et al., *The Authoritarian Personality* (New York: Harper & Row, 1950); N. Elias, *The Germans: Power Struggles and the Development of Habitus in the Nineteenth and Twentieth Centuries*, ed. M. Schroter (Cambridge: Polity Press, 1996).
43. J. J. Bachofen, *Myth, Religion, and Mother Right: Selected Writings of J. J. Bachofen*, trans. R. Manheim (Princeton, NJ: Princeton University Press, 1967).
44. Kumar, *Utopia and Anti-Utopia*, p. 421.
45. Sargent, 'The Three Faces of Utopianism', p. 21.
46. For a comparative study of the therapeutic ideas of Jung and Reich, see J. P. Conger, *Jung and Reich: The Body as Shadow* (Berkeley, CA: North Atlantic Books, 1988).
47. S. Pinker, *The Blank Slate: The Modern Denial of Human Nature* (New York: Viking, 2002), p. 150.
48. Ibid., p. 162.
49. See P. Pietikainen, 'National Typologies, Races, and Mentalities in C. G. Jung's Psychology', *History of European Ideas*, 24:6 (1998), pp. 359–73.
50. About racism in psychology, see D. Howitt and J. Owusu-Bempah, *The Racism of Psychology* (New York: Harvester Wheatsheaf, 1994).
51. P. Rieff, *The Triumph of the Therapeutic* (New York: Harper & Row, 1968).
52. For a comprehensive historical and philosophical account of the self, see C. Taylor, *Sources of the Self* (Cambridge: Cambridge University Press, 1992); and R. Martin and J. Barresi, *The Rise and Fall of Soul and Self* (New York: Columbia University Press, 2006).
53. See, for example, Taylor, *Sources of the Self*; A. MacIntyre, *After Virtue* (Notre Dame: University of Notre Dame Press, 1984); A. Giddens, *Modernity and Self-Identity: Self and Society in the Late Modern Age* (Stanford, CA: Stanford University Press, 1991).
54. B. F. Skinner, *Beyond Freedom and Dignity* (Toronto, Bantam Books, 1972), p. 205.
55. Taylor, *Sources of the Self*, p. 93.
56. G. Crowder, *Classical Anarchism: The Political Thought of Godwin, Proudhon, Bakunin, and Kropotkin* (Oxford: Clarendon Press, 1991), p. 10.

2 The New Soviet Man

1. E. Hobsbawm, *Interesting Times* (London: Allen Lane, 2002), p. 13.
2. Ibid., p. 97.
3. On the communist deification of history, see F. Furet, *The Passing of an Illusion: The Idea of Communism in the Twentieth Century*, trans. D. Furet (Chicago, IL: University of Chicago Press, 1999).
4. One author who became disillusioned with communism was the Hungarian-born writer Arthur Koestler. In 1949, he described his conversion to Marxism as follows: 'The whole universe falls into pattern like the stray pieces of a jigsaw puzzle assembled by magic at one stroke. There is now an answer to every question, doubts and conflicts are a matter of a tortured past – a past already remote, when one had lived in dismal ignorance in the tasteless, colorless world of those who don't know', A. Koestler, in R. Crossman (ed.), *The God that Failed* (New York: Harper & Brothers, 1949), pp. 15–75, on p. 23.
5. M. A. Miller, *Freud and the Bolsheviks* (New Haven, CT: Yale University Press, 1998), p. 24. On Freud's familial ties to Russia, see J. L. Rice, *Freud's Russia: National Identity in the Evolution of Psychoanalysis* (New Brunswick, NJ: Transaction Publishers, 1993).
6. Miller, *Freud and the Bolsheviks*, pp. 24–35; Etkind, *Eros of the Impossible*, pp. 112–18.
7. Ibid., p. 190; Miller, *Freud and the Bolsheviks*, pp. 56, 169. Miller has published a small collection of previously unpublished letters, written by Freud to Osipov after the latter's emigration to Prague. See ibid., pp. 169–73.
8. Etkind, *Eros of the Impossible*, pp. 188–90; Miller, *Freud and the Bolsheviks*, pp. 55–6.
9. Etkind, *Eros of the Impossible*, pp. 216–17; Miller, *Freud and the Bolsheviks*, pp. 32, 88.
10. Etkind *Eros of the Impossible*, pp. 203–4.
11. Miller, *Freud and the Bolsheviks*, p. 67.
12. Etkind, *Eros of the Impossible*, p. 251.
13. Miller, *Freud and the Bolsheviks*, pp. 68, 70.
14. B. N. Tugaybayeva, 'Comments on the History of Psychoanalysis in Russia', in V. A. Koltsova et al. (eds), *Post-Soviet Perspectives on Russian Psychology* (Wesport, CT: Greenwood Press, 1996), pp. 253–66, on p. 258.
15. Ibid., p. 261.
16. For the life and work of Trotsky, see I. Deutscher's three-volume biography: *The Prophet Armed: Trotsky 1879–1921* (1954); *The Prophet Unarmed: Trotsky 1921–1929* (1959); and *The Prophet Outcast: Trotsky 1929–1940* (1963) (Oxford: Oxford University Press, 1987). See also D. Volkogonov, *Trotsky: The Eternal Revolutionary*, trans. and ed. H. Shukman (London: HarperCollins, 1997).
17. Quoted in Miller *Freud and the Bolsheviks*, p. 87.
18. Deutscher, *The Prophet Armed*, p. 193. Trotsky mentions in his private papers that the revolution 'healed Joffe better than psychoanalysis of all his complexes', quoted in ibid.
19. Quoted in Etkind, *Eros of the Impossible*, p. 236.
20. Quoted in ibid., p. 237. See also L. Trotsky, *Problems of Everyday Life and Other Writings on Culture and Science* (New York: Monad Press, 1973).
21. On the New Economic Policy, see R. Service, *A History of Twentieth-Century Russia* (Cambridge, MA: Harvard University Press, 1998), pp. 123–49.
22. Etkind, *Eros of the Impossible*, p. 243.
23. D. Joravsky, *Russian Psychology* (Oxford: Basil Blackwell, 1989), pp. 384–9.
24. V. N. Voloshinov, *Freudianism: A Marxist Critique* (1927), ed. N. H. Bruss, trans. I. R. Titunik (New York: Academic Press, 1976).

25. Etkind, *Eros of the Impossible*, p. 241.
26. Quoted in Tugaybayeva, 'Comments on the History of Psychoanalysis', p. 263.
27. A. Etkind, 'The Fate of Psychoanalysis in the Soviet Utopia', unpublished presentation at the Conference on Psychological Utopias, Avesta, Sweden, 18 June 2000. Zinaida Volkova's analysis was done in Russian and was paid for by Trotsky. The name of the analyst is not known (ibid.).
28. Volkogonov, *Trotsky*, p. 79.
29. Tugaybayeva, 'Comments on the History of Psychoanalysis', p. 264.
30. On the 'Lysenko affair', see D. Joravsky, *The Lysenko Affair* (Chicago, IL: University of Chicago Press, 1986); and N. Roll-Hansen, *The Lysenko Effect: The Politics of Science* (Amherst, NY: Humanity Books, 2005).
31. J. McLeish, *Soviet Psychology: History, Theory, Content* (London: Methuen & Co., 1975), p. 130.
32. A. Kozulin, *Psychology in Utopia: Toward a Social History of Soviet Psychology* (Cambridge, MA: MIT Press, 1984), p. 89.
33. On Zalkind's life and work, see Etkind, *Eros of the Impossible*, pp. 272–7; Miller, *Freud and the Bolsheviks*, pp. 76–7, 102–5; J. Valsiner, 'Social Utopias and Knowledge Construction in Psychology', in Koltsova et al., *Post-Soviet Perspectives*, pp. 70–84, on pp. 76–9.
34. Like psychoanalysts, Zalkind was interested in sexuality, but, unlike most Freudians, his approach to the sexual domain of life was ideological through and through. In his notorious 'Twelve Commandments of Sexuality', he stated that 'a class has the right to interfere in the sex life of its members for the sake of revolutionary expediency', quoted in Etkind, *Eros of the Impossible*, p. 186. On sexual health policy in revolutionary Russia, see F. Bernstein, 'Visions of Sexual Health and Illness in Revolutionary Russia', in R. Davidson, and L. A. Hall (eds), *Sex, Sin and Suffering: Venereal Disease and European Society since 1870* (London: Routledge, 2001), pp. 93–117.
35. Quoted in Etkind, *Eros of the Impossible*, p. 261.
36. Quoted in A. Etkind, 'There Are No Naked Thoughts: Psychoanalysis, Psychotherapy and Medical Psychology in Russia', in E. L. Grigorenko, P. Ruzgis and R. J. Sternberg (eds), *Psychology of Russia: Past, Present, Future* (Commack, NY: Nova Science, 1997), pp. 59–77, on p. 62.
37. Ibid., p. 62.
38. Quoted in Valsiner 'Social Utopias and Knowledge Construction', p. 77.
39. Quoted in ibid., p. 78.
40. Ibid.
41. Voloshinov, *Freudianism*, p. 24.
42. Quoted in Joravsky, *Russian Psychology*, p. 340.
43. Ibid., p. 341.
44. According to the writer K. Zelinskii, who was present at this meeting at Gorky's house, Stalin uttered these words to the writers: 'The man is being remade by life. But you also help to remake his soul. This is an important manufacture – human souls. You are engineers of human souls', quoted in D. Joravsky, 'The Construction of the Stalinist Psyche', in S. Fitzpatrick (ed.), *Cultural Revolution in Russia, 1928–1931* (Bloomington, IN: Indiana University Press, 1978), pp. 105–28, on p. 127. See also Joravsky, *Russian Psychology*, p. 329.
45. McLeish, *Soviet Psychology*, pp. 164–6.

46. Quoted in Etkind, *Eros of the Impossible*, pp. 264–5. V. N. Voloshinov gives expression to the same environmental determinism in his 1927 book on 'Freudianism': 'This content of our consciousness and of our psyche in its entirety ... [is] in every respect determined by socioeconomic factors', Voloshinov, *Freudianism*, p. 86.
47. Quoted in Joravsky, 'The Construction of the Stalinist Psyche', p. 125.
48. G. Orwell, *Nineteen Eighty-Four* (1949; Harmondsworth: Penguin Books, 1983), p. 232.
49. Etkind, *Eros of the Impossible*, p. 277.
50. V. Ovcharenko, 'Love, Psychoanalysis and Destruction', *Journal of Analytical Psychology*, 44:3 (1999), pp. 355–74, on pp. 367, 372. Sabina Spielrein and her two daughters were killed by the Nazis in Rostov in 1942.
51. Joravsky, 'The Construction of the Stalinist Psyche', p. 118.
52. Ibid., p. 121.
53. G. Hosking, *The First Socialist Society: A History of the Soviet Union from Within*, 2nd edn (Cambridge, MA: Harvard University Press, 1996), p. 220.
54. For an outstanding analysis of the technique of political myths in Nazi Germany, see E. Cassirer, *The Myth of the State* (New Haven, CT: Yale University Press, 1946).
55. On the formation of Soviet Man, see M. Heller [Geller], *Cogs in the Soviet Wheel: The Formation of Soviet Man*, trans. D. Floyd (London: Collins Harvill, 1988); G. Smirnov, *The Soviet Man: The Making of a Socialist Type of Personality*, trans. R. Daglish (Moscow: Progress Publishers, 1973).
56. See also M. Heller [Geller] and A. Nekrich, *Utopia in Power: The History of the Soviet Union from 1917 to the Present* (New York: Summit Books, 1986).
57. An apocryphal story goes that when Freud and Jung arrived together in the United States in 1909, Freud turned to Jung and said: 'We are bringing the pest to America'.

3 Anarchy, Eros and the Mother Right

1. E. Jones, *Free Associations* (London: Hogarth Press, 1959), p. 173.
2. M. Green *The von Richthofen Sisters: The Triumphant and the Tragic Modes of Love* (New York: Basic Books, 1974).
3. The web address of the Otto Gross Society is http://www.ottogross.org.
4. See, for example, Noll, *The Jung Cult*; Noll, *The Aryan Christ*; and D. Bair, *Jung: A Biography* (Boston, MA: Little, Brown and Company, 2003).
5. O. Gross, *Collected Works 1901–1907: The Graz Years*, ed. and trans. L. Madison (Hamilton, NY: Mindpiece, 2000).
6. Bair, *Jung*, pp. 135–44.
7. For biographical details, I mainly rely on J. Michaels, *Anarchy and Eros: Otto Gross' Impact on German Expressionist Writers* (New York: Peter Lang, 1983); M. Green, *Otto Gross: Freudian Psychoanalyst, 1877–1920* (Lewiston, NY: Edwin Mellen Press, 1999); and Heuer, 'The Influence of Gross on Jung'.
8. Michaels, *Anarchy and Eros*, p. 12; E. Hurwitz, *Otto Gross: 'Paradies'-Sucher zwischen Freud und Jung* (Zürich: Suhrkamp Verlag, 1979).
9. H. Gross, 'Degeneration und Deportation', *Politisch-Anthropologische Revue*, 6:5 (1905), also published in H. Gross, *Gesammelte Kriminalistische Aufsätze*, 2 vols (Leipzig: Vogel, 1902–8), vol. 2, pp. 70–7.
10. Hurwitz, *Otto Gross*, p. 217.

11. K. Goldstein, 'Carl Wernicke', in W. Haymaker (ed.), *The Founders of Neurology* (Springfield, IL: Charles C. Thomas, 1953), pp. 406–9.
12. This is evident in Gross's early writings, which have been translated into English and published by Lois Madison. See Gross, *Collected Works*.
13. In 1907, Gross writes that 'psycho-physiological identity – the monistic viewpoint – is the basis for all scientific psychiatry', O. Gross, 'Freud's Idiogenetic Element and its Significance in Kraepelin's Manic-Depressiviness' (1907), in Gross, *Collected Works*, pp. 162–92, on p. 162.
14. For an introduction to Gross's early psychiatric work, see L. Madison, 'Introduction', in Gross, *Collected Works*, pp. 1–58.
15. O. Gross, 'On the Question of Socially Repressive Images' (1901), in Gross, *Collected Works*, pp. 59–64.
16. Ibid., p. 63.
17. O. Gross, 'The Cerebral Second Function' (1902), in Gross, *Collected Works*, pp. 73–92, on p. 87.
18. Gross refers to Darwin when he discusses 'cultural perspectives on mind typology', see ibid., p. 91.
19. See, for example, O. Gross, 'On the Phylogenetic Origin of Ethics' (1902), in Gross, *Collected Works*, pp. 65–7.
20. See, for example, Gross, 'Freud's Idiogenetic Element', p. 181.
21. On the history of Ascona, see M. Green, *Mountain of Truth: The Counterculture Begins – Ascona, 1900–1920* (Hanover, NH: University Press of New England, 1986).
22. J. Turner with C. Rumpf-Worthen and R. Jenkins (eds and trans.), 'The Otto Gross – Frieda Weekley Correspondence', *D. H. Lawrence Review*, 22:2 (1990), pp. 137–227; S. Whimster with G. Heuer, 'Otto Gross and Else Jaffé and Max Weber', *Theory, Culture and Society*, 15:3–4 (1998), pp. 129–60.
23. Quoted in Green, *Otto Gross*, p. 245. See also Hurwitz, *Otto Gross*, pp. 288–9.
24. Quoted in ibid., p. 280.
25. E. Jones, *Sigmund Freud, Life and Work*, 2 vols (London: Hogarth Press, 1955), vol. 2: 'Years of Maturity 1901–1919', p. 33.
26. Jones, *Free Associations*, pp. 173–4.
27. Freud, S., and C. G. Jung, *The Freud/Jung Letters: The Correspondence between Sigmund Freud and C. G. Jung*, ed. W. McGuire, trans. R. Manheim and R. F. C. Hull (Princeton, NJ: Princeton University Press, 1974), p. 67 (28 June 1907).
28. Ibid., p. 69 (1 July 1907).
29. Ibid., p. 85 (11 September 1907).
30. On Gross's 1902 patient record at the Burghölzli, see Hurwitz, *Otto Gross*, pp. 136–8.
31. On the doctrine of degeneration, see R. A. Nye, *Crime, Madness and Politics in Modern France: The Medical Concept of National Decline* (Princeton, NJ: Princeton University Press, 1984); D. Pick, *Face of Degeneration: A European Disorder, c. 1848–c. 1918* (Cambridge: Cambridge University Press, 1989); I. Dowbiggin, *Inheriting Madness: Professionalization and Psychiatric Knowledge in Nineteenth-Century France* (Berkeley, CA: University of California Press, 1991).
32. *The Freud/Jung Letters*, p. 90 (25 September 1907).
33. Ibid., p. 126 (25 February 1908).
34. O. Rank, 'Bericht über die I. Private Psychoanalytische Vereinigung in Salzburg am 27. April 1908', *Zentralblatt für Psychoanalyse*, 1:1 (1911–12), pp. 125–9; Jones, *Sigmund Freud*, vol. 2, p. 45.

35. W. Stekel, *The Autobiography of Wilhelm Stekel: The Life Story of a Pioneer Psychoanalyst*, ed. E. A. Gutheil (New York: Liveright, 1950), p. 122.
36. O. Gross, 'Ludwig Rubiner's "Psychoanalyse"', *Die Aktion*, 3:20 (1913), pp. 506–7.
37. *The Freud/Jung Letters*, p. 141 (19 April 1908).
38. Ibid., p. 142 (24 April 1908).
39. On Bleuler's life and work, see D. Hell, C. Scharfetter and A. Möller, *Eugen Bleuler, Leben und Werk* (Bern: Huber, 2001).
40. Hurwitz, *Otto Gross*, pp. 139–47.
41. *The Freud/Jung Letters*, p. 153 (25 May 1908).
42. Ibid., p. 153 (25 May 1908).
43. Jones, *Free Associations*, p. 174. In his biography of Freud, Jones writes that one analytic session between Jung and Gross 'continued for twenty-four hours until both their heads were nodding like china mandarins', Jones, *Sigmund Freud*, vol. 2, p. 33.
44. *The Freud/Jung Letters*, p. 153 (25 May 1908).
45. Ibid., p. 154 (29 May 1908).
46. Ibid., p. 156 (19 June 1908).
47. S. Freud and E. Jones, *The Complete Correspondence of Sigmund Freud and Ernest Jones 1908–1939*, ed. R. A. Paskauskas (Cambridge, MA: Belknap Press of Harvard University Press, 1993), p. 3 (27 June 1908).
48. Ibid., pp. 3–4 (27 June 1908).
49. *The Freud/Jung Letters*, p. 156 (19 June 1908).
50. Ibid., p. 158 (21 June 1908).
51. Ibid., pp. 160–1 (26 June 1908).
52. Ibid., p. 162 (30 June 1908).
53. Quoted in J. Read, L. R. Mosher and R. P. Bentall, *Models of Madness: Psychological, Social and Biological Approaches to Schizophrenia* (Hove: Brunner-Routledge, 2004), p. 26.
54. O. Gross, 'Über Bewusstseinszerfall', *Monatsschrift für Psychiatrie und Neurologie*, 15 (1904), pp. 45–51.
55. Ibid.; O. Gross, 'Zur Nomenklatur "Dementia sejunctiva"', *Neurologisches Centralblatt*, 23:24 (1904), pp. 1144–6. See also O. Gross, 'Zur Differentialdiagnostik negativistischer Phänomene', *Psychiatrisch-Neurologische Wochenschrift*, 37 (1904), pp. 345–53, and 38 (1904), pp. 357–63.
56. Freud's letter to Jung, *The Freud/Jung Letters*, p. 414 (7 April 1911).
57. For example, Freud described Gross's book *Über psychopathische Minderwertigkeiten* ('On Psychopathic Inferiorities', 1909) as 'another outstanding work, full of bold syntheses and overflowing with ideas', *The Freud/Jung Letters*, p. 227 (3 June 1909).
58. Heuer, 'The Influence of Gross on Jung', p. 152.
59. On the relationship between Jung and Sabina Spielrein, see A. Caruteneto, *A Secret Symmetry: Sabina Spielrein between Jung and Freud*, trans. A. Pomerans, J. Shepley and K. Winston (London: Routledge & Kegan Paul, 1982); J. Kerr, *A Most Dangerous Method: The Story of Jung, Freud and Sabina Spielrein* (New York: Vintage Books, 1993); and Z. Lothane, 'Tender Love and Transference: Unpublished Letters of C. G. Jung and Sabina Spielrein', *International Journal of Psychoanalysis*, 80:6 (1999), 1189–204. See also *The Journal of Analytical Psychology*, 46:1 (2001), which is devoted to Sabina Spielrein.
60. Caruteneto, *A Secret Symmetry*, p. 107.
61. *The Freud/Jung Letters*, p. 414 (7 April 1911).

62. C. G. Jung, 'The Significance of the Father in the Destiny of the Individual' (1909), in *Collected Papers on Analytical Psychology*, ed. and trans. C. E. Long (London: Baillière, Tindall and Cox, 1917), pp. 156–75, on p. 157.
63. C. G. Jung, 'The Significance of the Father in the Destiny of the Individual' (1949), in C. G. Jung, *Collected Works of C. G. Jung*, trans. R. F. C. Hull (except vol. 2), 18 vols (London: Routledge & Kegan Paul, 1953–81), vol. 4, pp. 301–23.
64. *The Freud/Jung Letters*, p. 416 (19 April 1911).
65. E. Hurwitz, 'Hans und Otto Gross', in A. G. von Olenhusen and G. Heuer (eds), *Die Gesetze des Vaters: 4. Internationaler Otto Gross Kongress* (Marburg an der Lahn: Literatur Wissenschaft.de, 2005), pp. 33–44; Hurwitz, *Otto Gross*, pp. 183–98.
66. B. A. Laska, 'Otto Gross zwischen Max Stirner und Wilhelm Reich', in R. Dehmlow and G. Heuer (eds), *Bohème, Psychoanalyse und Revolution: 3. Internationaler Otto Gross Kongress* (Marburg an der Lahn: Literatur Wissenschaft.de, 2003), pp. 125–62, on p. 139.
67. C. G. Jung, *The Psychology of Dementia Praecox* (1907), in Jung, *Collected Works*, vol. 3, pp. 1–151.
68. Jones, *Sigmund Freud*, vol. 2, p. 33; Jones, *Free Associations*, p. 174.
69. *The Freud/Jung Letters*, p. 171 (9 September 1908).
70. Ibid., p. 229 (4 June 1909).
71. This suggestion is also made by Gottfried Heuer; see G. Heuer, 'Jung's Twin Brother: Otto Gross and Carl Gustav Jung', *Journal of Analytical Psychology*, 46:4 (2001), pp. 655–88.
72. See C. G. Jung, *Memories, Dreams, Reflections*, recorded and ed. A. Jaffé, trans. R. and C. Winston (1963; London: Fontana Paperbacks, 1983), pp. 194–225.
73. An unpublished letter from Jung to Ernest Jones, 25 February 1909, quoted in Heuer, 'The Influence of Gross on Jung', p. 83; and Jones, *Sigmund Freud*, vol. 2, pp. 157–8. I have slightly modified Heuer's translation of the original German passage, which is given in Hauer's text, and which goes as follows: 'Ich glaube, dass man mit der offenen Verkündigung gewisser Dinge den Ast absägt, auf dem die Cultur sitzt ... jedenfalls ist das Extrem, das Gross verkündet, ganz entschieden falsch and derganzen [*sic*] Richtung gefährlich – Gross sterilisiert sich, daher wird sich seine Gefährlichkeit vermindern', Heuer, 'The Influence of Gross on Jung', p. 83n.
74. Freud and Jones, *The Complete Correspondence*, p. 1 (13 May 1908).
75. Jung's letter to Franz Wittels, 4 January 1935, Sigmund Freud Collection, Library of Congress Manuscript Division, Washington, DC, United States. The letter is translated into English (with the permission of the C. G. Jung Estate) in Heuer, 'Jung's Twin Brother', pp. 670, 681–2.
76. On the early history of Ascona, see Green, *Mountain of Truth*; and C. Riess, *Ascona: Geschichte des seltsamsten Dorfes der Welt* (Zürich: Europa Verlag, 1964). For the history of 'anti-bourgeois' movements in Germany, see C. Conti, *Abschied vom Bürgertum: Alternative Bewegungen in Deutschland von 1890 bis heute* (Reinbek bei Hamburg: Rowohlt, 1984).
77. On Gross's influence on German expressionist writers, see Michaels, *Anarchy and Eros*. See also R. F. Allen, *Literary Life in German Expressionism and the Berlin Circles* (Ann Arbor, MU: UMI Research Press, 1983.)
78. O. Gross, *Über psychopathische Minderwertigkeiten* (Wien: Wilhelm Braumüller, 1909), p. 47.

79. N. McLaughlin, 'Optimal Marginality: Innovation and Orthodoxy in Fromm's Revision of Psychoanalysis', *Sociological Quarterly*, 42:2 (2001), pp. 271–88; and J. Bos, D. Park and P. Pietikainen, 'Strategic Self-Marginalization: The Case of Psychoanalysis', *Journal of the History of the Behavioral Sciences*, 41:3 (2005), pp. 207–24, on pp. 214–17.
80. Ibid., pp. 221–3.
81. E. Goffman, *Stigma: Notes on the Management of Spoiled Identity* (1963; New York: Simon & Schuster, 1986), p. 3.
82. G. Neundörfer, 'Otto Gross und die Königliche Psychiatrische Klinik in München', in Dehmlow and Heuer (eds), *Bohème, Psychoanalyse und Revolution*, pp. 47–52, on p. 50.
83. Quoted in E. Bertschinger-Joos, 'Frieda Gross – Briefe aus Graz 1882–1906', in von Olenhusen and Heuer (eds), *Die Gesetze des Vaters*, pp. 310–19, on p. 314.
84. O. Gross, 'Offener Brief an Maximilian Harden' (1914), in *Von geschlechtlicher Not zur sozialen Katastrophe*, ed. K. Kreiler (Frankfurt am Main: Robinson Verlag, 1980), p. 26.
85. Ibid.
86. On the question of 'making' and 'unmaking' of a psychoanalyst, see Jaap Bos's analysis of the relationship between Freud and Wilhelm Stekel: J. Bos, 'A Silent Antipode: The Making and Breaking of Psychoanalyst Wilhelm Stekel', *History of Psychology*, 6:4 (2003), pp. 331–61.
87. On the relationship between Gross's and Reich's ideas, see B. Nitzschke, 'Verinnerlichung äusserer Konflikte – Entäusserung innerer Konflikte: Über einige Gemeinsamkeiten und Differenzen zwischen Otto Gross, Wilhelm Reich und Sigmund Freud', in R. Dehmlow and G. Heuer (eds), *1. Internationaler Otto Gross Kongress* (Marburg an der Lahn: LiteraturWissenschaft.de; Hannover: Laurentius, 2000), pp. 39–54; G. Heuer, 'Die Wiederkehr des Verdrängten: Revolution und Konterrevolution in der Psychoanalyse', in G. Heuer (ed.), *2. Internationaler Otto Gross Kongress* (Marburg an der Lahn: LiteraturWissenschaft.de, 2002), pp. 77–104, on pp. 90–1; and Laska, 'Otto Gross zwischen Max Stirner und Wilhelm Reich', pp. 156–8.
88. O. Gross, 'Themen der revolutionären Psychologie', in von Olenhusen and Heuer (eds), *Die Gesetze des Vaters*, pp. 421–3.
89. Heuer, 'Die Wiederkehr des Verdrängten', p. 91.
90. On the ways in which Gross was depicted in novels written by authors who knew him, see Michaels, *Anarchy and Eros*.
91. See, for example, J. Michaels, 'Otto Gross und das Konzept des Matriarchats', in Heuer (ed.), *2. Internationaler Otto Gross Kongress*, pp. 105–15; S. Wolf, '"[...] ich werde noch einmal unter euch fahren, dass euch Hören und Sehen vergeht": – Gustav Landauer, Otto Gross und die Psychoanalyse', in von Olenhusen and Heuer (eds), *Die Gesetze des Vaters*, pp. 240–85, on p. 250.
92. Green, *Otto Gross*; and M. Green, 'The Recurrence of New Age Mythology', in Heuer (ed.), *2. Internationaler Otto Gross Kongress*, pp. 331–6.
93. Jones, *Free Associations*, p. 173.
94. Quoted in Allen, *Literary Life in German Expressionism*, p. 25.
95. Riess, *Ascona*, pp. 49–52.
96. Michaels, *Anarchy and Eros*, p. 25.
97. Hans Gross in his last will, as quoted in Green, *Otto Gross*, p. 231.
98. Hurwitz, 'Hans und Otto Gross', p. 44.
99. Heuer, 'The Influence of Gross on Jung', p. 121.
100. H. van den Berg, *Avantgarde und Anarchismus: Dada in Zürich und Berlin* (Heidelberg: Universitätsverlag C. Winter, 1999), pp. 90–102. On Franz Jung and his friendship with

Gross, see Green, *Otto Gross*, pp. 255–9; A. Hansen, 'Eine "Art von innerlich revolutionärer Vorarbeit": Koordinaten bei der Begegnung zwischen Franz Jung und Otto Gross', in Dehmlow and Heuer (eds), *1. Internationaler Otto Gross Kongress*, pp. 74–87; A. G. von Olenhusen, 'Wahnsinn in den Zeiten des Krieges: Otto Gross, Franz Jung und das Kriegsrecht', in von Olenhusen and Heuer (eds), *Die Gesetze des Vaters*, pp. 82–128.

101. On this incident and the ensuing press campaign initiated by Gross's friends, see C. Jung and T. Anz (eds), *Der Fall Otto Gross: Eine Pressekampagne deutscher Intellektueller im Winter 1913/14* (Marburg an der Lahn: Literatur Wissenschaft.de, 2002).
102. J. Berze and D. K. Stelzer, 'Befund und Gutachten über den Geisteszustand des am 15. Dezember 1913 über Auftrag des k.k. Bezirkgerichtes Tulln untersuchten Dr. Otto Gross', ed. A. Hansen, *Gegner*, 3 (1999/2000), pp. 24–36, on p. 24.
103. On the history of classical anarchism, see G. Woodcock (ed.), *The Anarchist Reader* (Hassocks, Harvester Press/Humanities Press, 1977); D. Goodway (ed.), *For Anarchism: History, Theory, and Practice* (London: Routledge, 1989); Crowder, *Classical Anarchism*; P. Marshall, *Demanding the Impossible: A History of Anarchism* (London: HarperCollins, 1992).
104. G. Woodcock, 'Anarchism: A Historical Introduction', in Woodcock (ed.), *The Anarchist Reader*, pp. 11–56, on p. 18; and Crowder, *Classical Anarchism*, pp. 136–46.
105. R. Graham, 'The Role of Contract in Anarchist Ideology', in Goodway (ed.), *For Anarchism*, pp. 150–75.
106. Crowder, *Classical Anarchism*, p. 11.
107. Ibid., pp. 160–6; P. Marshall, 'Human Nature and Anarchism', in Goodway (ed.) *For Anarchism*, pp. 127–49, on pp. 134–7; and Woodcock, 'Anarchism', pp. 18–19.
108. Ibid., pp. 48–9.
109. On Gross's understanding of anarchism and his relationship with anarchists, see A. Mitzman, 'Anarchism, Expressionism and Psychoanalysis', *New German Critique*, 10 (1977), pp. 77–109; Green, *Mountain of Truth*, pp.163–5; H. Müller, 'Der Mauersprung von Zürich. Otto Gross, C. G. Jung und die Anarchisten von Zürich-Ascona', in Heuer (ed.), *2. Internationaler Otto Gross Kongress*, pp. 27–48; C. Hirte et al., 'Anarchismus und Psychoanalyse zu Beginn des 20. Jahrhunderts', special issue of *Schriften der Erich-Mühsam-Gesellschaft*, 19 (2002); R. Bochsler, 'Der Überfall auf die Zürcher Polizeikaserne 1907, Oder: Welche Rolle spielte Hans Gross im Anarchistenprozess 1912?', in Dehmlow and Heuer (eds), *Bohème, Psychoanalyse und Revolution*, pp. 105–24; and G. Heuer, '"Ganz Wien in die Luft sprengen? ... Das wäre ja wunderbar!" Otto Gross und der Anarchismus', in von Olenhusen and Heuer (eds), *Die Gesetze des Vaters*, pp. 223–39.
110. Crowder, *Classical Anarchism*, p. 151.
111. Ibid., pp. 153–5.
112. Ibid., p. 168.
113. For the anthropologist Donald E. Brown's list of human universals, see D. E. Brown, *Human Universals* (New York: McGraw-Gill, 1991).
114. O. Gross, 'On the Biology of Language Apparatus' (1904), in Gross, *Collected Works*, pp. 139–61, especially p. 160.
115. O. Gross, 'Protest and Morality in the Unconscious' (1919), *New German Critique*, 10 (1977), pp. 105–9, on p. 106; O. Gross, 'Zum Solidaritätsproblem im Klassenkampf', in von Olenhusen and Heuer (eds), *Die Gesetze des Vaters*, pp. 415–21, on p. 417.
116. D. A. Stack, 'The First Darwinian Left: Radical and Socialist Responses to Darwin, 1859–1914', *History of Political Thought*, 21:4 (2000), pp. 682–710; P. Kropotkin, *Mutual Aid: A Factor of Evolution* (Mineola, NY: Dover Publications, 2006). On reci-

procal altruism, see R. Trivers, 'Reciprocal Altruism' (1971), in *Natural Selection and Social Theory: Selected Papers of Robert Trivers* (Oxford: Oxford University Press, 2002), pp. 3–55.
117. Heuer, 'Die Wiederkehr des Verdrängten', p. 94.
118. Crowder, *Classical Anarchism*, p. 166.
119. For a contemporary version of this thesis by the primatologist and 'cultural philosopher' Frans de Waal, see F. de Waal, *The Ape and the Sushi Master* (New York: Basic Books, 2001).
120. Quoted in Crowder, *Classical Anarchism*, p. 162.
121. Marshall, 'Human Nature and Anarchism', p. 135.
122. Stack, 'The First Darwinian Left', p. 699.
123. Gross, 'On the Phylogenetic Origin of Ethics', p. 67.
124. Hurwitz, *Otto Gross*, p. 303.
125. Green, *Otto Gross*, p. 234.
126. Michaels, *Anarchy and Eros*, p. 167. On the political engagement of Zurich Dadaists (especially Hugo Ball), see van den Berg, *Avantgarde und Anarchismus*, pp. 399–407.
127. Ibid.
128. O. Gross, 'Zur Überwindung der kulturellen Krise' (1913), in *Von geschlechtlicher Not*, pp. 13–16, on p. 13.
129. O. Gross, 'Zur neuerlichen Vorarbeit: vom Unterricht' (1919), in *Von geschlechtlicher Not*, pp. 35–41.
130. Gross, 'Zum Solidaritätsproblem', p. 417.
131. Gross, 'Themen der revolutionären Psychologie', p. 421.
132. O. Gross, 'Über Destruktionssymbolik', *Zentralblatt für Psychoanalyse und Psychotherapie*, 4 (1914), pp. 524–34, on p. 531; O. Gross, 'Vom Konflikt des Eigenen und Fremden' (1916), in *Von geschlechtlicher Not*, pp. 27–31, on p. 28; O. Gross, 'Über Konflikt und Beziehung', in *Drei Aufsätze über den inneren Konflikte* (Bonn: A. Marcus & E. Webers Verlag, 1920), pp. 3–20, on pp. 4, 14.
133. Gross, 'Themen der revolutionären Psychologie', p. 422.
134. Gross, 'Über Destruktionssymbolik', p. 529.
135. Gross, 'Vom Konflikt des Eigenen und Fremden'. On Gross's reflections on *das Eigene und das Fremde*, see also Gross, 'Über Destruktionssymbolik'; and Gross, *Drei Aufsätze über den inneren Konflikt*.
136. For Gross's views on what he called 'the loneliness of children', see especially O. Gross, 'Über Einsamkeit', in *Drei Aufsätze über den inneren Konflikt*.
137. Gross, 'Vom Konflikt des Eigenen und Fremden'; Gross, 'Zur Überwindung der kulturellen Krise', p. 14.
138. Van den Berg, *Avantgarde und Anarchismus*, pp. 139–40.
139. Gross, 'Vom Konflikt des Eigenen und Fremden', p. 27.
140. Bachofen, *Myth, Religion, and Mother Right*, pp. 92–5.
141. T. R Trautman, *Lewis Henry Morgan and the Invention of Kinship* (Berkeley, CA: University of California Press, 1987).
142. C. Eller, *The Myth of Matriarchal Prehistory* (Boston, MA: Beacon Press, 2000), p. 31.
143. Erich Neumann used Jung's archetypal psychology in his interpretation of the ancient myths and symbols depicting motherhood. I shall not discuss his ideas in this book, but those who are interested in this issue should consult his book *The Great Mother: An Analysis of the Archetype*, trans. R. Manheim (London: Routledge & Kegan Paul, 1955).

144. F. Engels, *The Origin of the Family, Private Property, and the State* (1884; Moscow: Progress Publishers, 1968).
145. Eller, *The Myth of Matriarchal Prehistory*, p. 32.
146. On the Cosmic Circle, see Green, *The von Richthofen Sisters*, pp. 73–85; and H.-J. Linke, *Das Kultische in der Dichtung Stefan Georges und seiner Schule* (München: Helmut Küpper vormals George Bondi, 1960).
147. Bachofen, *Myth, Religion, and Mother Right*, p. 94.
148. 'The myth of matriarchal prehistory has found adherents among socialists, anthropologists, communists, fascists, psychoanalysts, sexologists, folklorists, religionists, and a whole host of other notable characters. It has been used to justify patriarchy and to overthrow it, to hustle women back to hearth and home and to place them at the helm of the ship carrying us into the future', Eller, *The Myth of Matriarchal Prehistory*, p. 31.
149. Bachofen, *Myth, Religion, and Mother Right*, p. 102.
150. Ibid., p. 190.
151. Gross, 'Vom Konflikt des Eigenen und Fremden', p. 30.
152. Eller, *The Myth of Matriarchal Prehistory*, p. 41.
153. Engels, *The Origin of the Family*, pp. 12–15. In his book, Engels refers to MacLennan's *Studies in Ancient History* (1886).
154. E. Westermarck, *The History of Human Marriage* (London: Macmillan, 1891).
155. Gross, 'Vom Konflikt des Eigenen und Fremden', pp. 30–1.
156. Gross, 'Zur Überwindung der kulturellen Krise', p. 16.
157. Gross, 'Zum Solidaritätsproblem' and Gross, 'Themen der revolutionären Psychologie'.
158. Gross, 'Zum Solidaritätsproblem', p. 415.
159. O. Gross, 'Orienterung der Geistigen' (1919), in *Von geschlechtlicher Not*, pp. 32–5, on p. 34; and O. Gross, 'Zum Problem: Parlamentarismus' (1919), in *Von geschlechtlicher Not*, pp. 60–3.
160. Gross, 'Zum Solidaritätsproblem', p. 417.
161. Ibid., p. 418.
162. Ibid.
163. A.-S. Ohlander, *Kvinnor, barn och arbete i Sverige 1850–1993*, Statens Offentliga Utredningar 38 (Stockholm: Fritzes, 1994).
164. Gross, 'Zum Solidaritätsproblem', p. 419.
165. 'Mitteilungen', in *Sowjet*, 8/9 (8 May 1920), as quoted in Hurwitz, *Otto Gross*, pp. 278–9.
166. C. Kanz, 'Mütterlichkeitskonzepte und Geschlechterdebatten Anfang des 20. Jahrhunderts. Otto Gross – ein Vorreiter der "Gender Studies"?', in Heuer (ed.), *2. Internationaler Otto Gross Kongress*, pp. 279–89, on p. 284.
167. F. Jung, 'Von geschlechtlicher Not zur sozialen Katastrophe (Introduction)', in Michaels, *Anarchy and Eros*, pp. 183–219, on p. 197.
168. O. Gross, 'Die kommunistische Grundidee in der Paradiessymbolik' (1919), in *Von geschlechtlicher Not*, pp. 41–54.
169. See Gross, 'Zur Überwindung der kulturellen Krise' and *Drei Aufsätze über den inneren Konflikt*.
170. D. Roochnik, *Beautiful City: The Dialectical Character of Plato's Republic* (Ithaca, NY: Cornell University Press, 2003).
171. Heuer, 'Die Wiederkehr des Verdrängten', p. 83.
172. For a discussion of Gross's understanding of *das Mutterrecht*, see Michaels, *Anarchy and Eros*, pp. 71–8; and Michaels, 'Otto Gross und das Konzept des Matriarchats'.

173. O. Gross, 'Zur funktionellen Geistesbildung des Revolutionärs' (1919), in *Von geschlechtlicher Not*, pp. 64–70, on p. 68.
174. O. Gross, 'Affective Rejection' (1902), in Gross, *Collected Works*, pp. 93–101, on p. 94.
175. O. Gross, 'Disintegration of Consciousness' (1902), in Gross, *Collected Works*, pp. 107–11.
176. F. Jung, 'Von geschlechtlicher Not', p. 215.
177. Webster's Online Dictionary, http://www.websters-online-dictionary.org/definition/orgy (accessed 10 January 2007).
178. Ibid.
179. F. Jung, 'Von geschlechtlicher Not', p. 216.
180. See P. Wild, *Sointula: Island Utopia* (Madeira Park: Harbour, 1995).
181. A. G. von Olenhusen, '"Il poeta bello" oder der Mann, der immer dabei war: Der Anarchist, Literat und Psychologe Johannes Nohl (1882–1963) und Erich Mühsam, Otto Gross und Hermann Hesse', in Dehmlow and Heuer (eds), *1. Internationaler Otto Gross Kongress*, pp. 101–10, on p. 105; G. Heuer, '"Der Skorpion im Messkelch" und "der Teufel unter der Couch": Oskar Panizza und Otto Gross – eine Seelenverwandtschaft', in Dehmlow and Heuer (eds), *Bohème, Psychoanalyse und Revolution*, pp. 163–95, on pp. 181–2; E. W. White, 'Otto Gross: The Taos Connection', in von Olenhusen and Heuer (eds), *Die Gesetze des Vaters*, pp. 375–402, on p. 380.
182. E. Goffman, *The Representation of Self in Everyday Life* (New York: Doubleday, 1959); R. Trivers, 'Self-Deception in Service of Deceit' (2002), in *Natural Selection and Social Theory*, pp. 255–93; and Sennett, *The Fall of Public Man*.
183. Gross, *Über psychopathische Minderwertigkeiten*, p. 119.
184. Gross, 'Zum Solidaritätsproblem', p. 419.
185. Engels, *The Origin of the Family*.
186. Westermarck, *The History of Human Marriage*; E. Westermarck, *A Short History of Marriage* (London: Macmillan, 1926); and E. Westermarck, *The Future of Marriage in Western Civilisation* (London: MacMillan, 1936).
187. R. Elboim-Dror, *Yesterday's Tomorrow*, 2 vols (Jerusalem: Yad Izhak Ben-Zvi, 1993), vol. 1: 'The Zionist Utopia' [in Hebrew]; and R. Elboim-Dror, *Clean Death in Tel Aviv* (Lincoln, NE: iUniverse, 2003).
188. See A. Balaban, *Mourning a Father Lost: A Kibbutz Childhood Remembered*, trans. Y. Lotan (Lanham, MD: Rowman & Littlefield, 2004).
189. O. Gross, 'Elterngewalt' (1908), in *Von geschlechtlicher Not*, pp. 9–13.
190. Heuer, 'The Influence of Gross on Jung', pp. 145–8.
191. Gross, 'Zur funktionellen Geistesbildung', pp. 66–7.
192. Gross, 'Über Konflikt und Beziehung', p. 7.
193. Gross, 'Über Einsamkeit', pp. 21–2, 25.
194. Gross, 'Zur funktionellen Geistesbildung', p. 68; and Gross, 'Zum Solidaritätsproblem', pp. 419–20.
195. Gross, 'Zur funktionellen Geistesbildung', p. 67.
196. A. S. Neill, *Summerhill: A Radical Approach to Child Rearing* (New York: Hart, 1960).
197. Heuer, 'The Influence of Gross on Jung', p. 130.
198. Gross, 'Themen der revolutionären Psychologie', p. 423.
199. Quoted in Heuer, '"Der Skorpion im Messkelch"', p. 176.
200. A. Stärcke, 'Geisteskrankheit und Gesellschaft', in A. J. Storfer (ed.), *Almanach für das Jahr 1926* (Wien: Internationaler Psychoanalytischer Verlag, 1926), pp. 93–112.
201. On the 'tyranny of intimacy', see Sennett, *The Fall of Public Man*.

202. MacIntyre, *After Virtue*, pp. 213–15.
203. On deception and self-deception as part of human psychological configuration, see Trivers, 'Self-Deception in Service of Deceit'; and Pinker, *The Blank Slate*, pp. 259–66.
204. L. Eilittä, *Approaches to Personal Identity in Kafka's Short Fiction* (Helsinki: Finnish Academy of Science and Letters, 1999), p. 96; Michaels, *Anarchy and Eros*, pp. 164–5. As Jennifer Michaels notes, in his criticism of his (authoritarian) father, Kafka focused on paternal tyranny rather than on Freudian complexes. Michaels plausibly surmises that 'it may be that Gross had an impact on the way Kafka understood his father problem. More likely it seems that Kafka and Gross came independently to their conclusions', Michaels, *Anarchy and Eros*, p. 165.
205. Ibid., p. 161.
206. M. Brod, *Das grosse Wagnis* (Leipzig: Kurt Wolff, 1918), p. 252.
207. Gross, 'Themen der revolutionären Psychologie', p. 423.

4 Individuation and 'National Individuation'

1. C. G. Jung, 'Psychology of the Unconscious Processes' (1916), in *Collected Papers on Analytical Psychology*, ed. and trans. C. E. Long (London: Baillière, Tindall and Cox, 1917), pp. 354–444, on p. 444.
2. S. Shamdasani, *Jung and the Making of Modern Psychology* (Cambridge: Cambridge University Press, 2003), p. 1.
3. G. Cocks, *Psychotherapy in the Third Reich: The Göring Institute*, 2nd rev. edn (New Brunswick, NJ: Transaction Publishers, 1997), p. 40.
4. H. Gess, *Vom Faschismus zum Neuen Denken – C. G. Jungs Theorie im Wandeln der Zeit* (Luneburg: Zu Klampen, 1994).
5. Noll, *The Jung Cult*; Noll, *The Aryan Christ*; P. Pietikainen, 'Dynamic Psychology, Utopia, and Escape from History: The Case of C. G. Jung', *Utopian Studies*, 12:1 (2001), pp. 41–55.
6. In my account of Jung's life, I rely on B. Hannah, *Jung – His Life and Work: A Biographical Memoir* (New York: G. P. Putnam's Sons, 1976); G. Wehr, *Jung: A Biography*, trans. D. M. Weeks (Boston, MA: Shambhala, 1987); F. McLynn, *Carl Gustav Jung* (New York: St Martin's Griffin, 1997); and Bair, *Jung*. For a critical survey of Jung biographies, see S. Shamdasani, *Jung Stripped Bare, by his Biographers, Even* (London: Karnac Books, 2005).
7. These materials are kept at the C. G. Jung Biographical Archive, Francis A. Countway Library of Medicine, Harvard Medical School, Boston, MA, United States.
8. 'In the first draft of *Memories*, with its penciled and penned additions and deletions, Jung indicated some of the circumstances surrounding his mother's hospitalization in Basle. He explained that she was hysterical from disappointment with her husband, whose life took a turn for the worse after his final examinations at the University. In the original version of his autobiography, Jung had included even more details of his mother's mental aberrations, but other family members, fearing these would tarnish the family image, insisted that they be removed', R. C. Smith, *The Wounded Jung* (Evanston, IL: Northwestern University Press, 1996), pp. 17–18. Cf. C. G. Jung, *Dream Analysis: Notes of the Seminar Given in 1928–1930 by C. G. Jung*, ed. W. McGuire (London: Routledge & Kegan Paul, 1984), p. 87 (23 January 1929), where Jung states that 'my mother had a split mind'.
9. P. Burckhardt, *Geschichte der Stadt Basel* (Basel: Helbing & Lichtenhahn, 1942), pp. 151–9, 184, 216.

10. Noll, *The Aryan Christ*, p. 22.
11. 'Women came from all over the world to see him [Jung], starting from before the First World War. They came from Austria, Germany, Israel, but most often, England and America. Their journey took on a mythical quality, almost like a religious pilgrimage. They came to be healed, and often something happened that made them stay and become healers in their turn', M. Anthony, *The Valkyries: The Women Around Jung* (Longmead: Element Books, 1990), p. xii.
12. Jung, *Memories*, pp. 129–30. Cf. C. G. Jung, *Analytical Psychology: Notes of the Seminar Given in 1925 by C. G. Jung*, ed. W. McGuire (London: Routledge, 1989), p. 7 (23 March 1925).
13. C. G. Jung, *On the Psychology and Pathology of So-Called Occult Phenomena* (1902), in Jung, *Collected Works*, vol. 1, pp. 3–88.
14. About Jung's polygamous tendencies, see Noll, *The Aryan Christ*; and Smith, *The Wounded Jung*.
15. Jung claims in his memoirs that they talked non-stop for thirteen hours, Jung, *Memories*, p. 172.
16. F. Alexander and S. T. Selesnick, 'Freud-Bleuler Correspondence', *Archives of General Psychiatry*, 12 (1965), pp. 1–9, on p. 5.
17. For a comprehensive historical study of this period, see Kerr, *A Most Dangerous Method*. See also R. S. Steele, *Freud and Jung: Conflicts of Interpretation* (London: Routledge & Kegan Paul, 1982); and P. Vandermeersch, *Unresolved Questions in the Freud/Jung Debate* (Leuven, Leuven University Press, 1991).
18. Jung, *Memories*, pp. 194–225.
19. For a detailed account of the relationship between Jung and the Rockefeller family, see Noll, *The Aryan Christ*.
20. C. G. Jung, *Psychological Types* (1921), in Jung, *Collected Works*, vol. 6, pp. 273–88.
21. On the history of the Jungians and Jung's analytical psychology as a movement, see T. B. Kirsch, *The Jungians: A Comparative and Historical Perspective* (London: Routledge, 2000).
22. On the intellectual context of Jung's archetypal theory, see P. Pietikainen, *C. G. Jung and the Psychology of Symbolic Forms* (Helsinki: Finnish Academy of Science and Letters, 1999).
23. See Jung, *Collected Works*, vol. 9.
24. R. Semon, *Mnemic Psychology* (1904; New York: Macmillan, 1923).
25. D. L. Schachter, *Searching for Memory* (New York: Basic Books, 1996), p. 57.
26. Ibid.
27. L. Otis, 'Organic Memory and Psychoanalysis', *History of Psychiatry*, 4 (1993), pp. 349–72. In his old age, Bleuler wrote books in which he set forth his 'Semonian' ideas on memory. See, for example, E. Bleuler, *Die Psychoide als Prinzip der organischen Entwicklung* (Berlin: J. Springer, 1925).
28. Jung, *Psychological Types*, pp. 376, 443; and C. G. Jung, 'On the Psychology of the Unconscious' (1917/43), in Jung, *Collected Works*, vol. 7, pp. 3–119, on p. 98.
29. On Jung's evolutionary assumptions, see P. Pietikainen, 'Soul Man Meets the Blind Watchmaker: C. G. Jung and Neo-Darwinism', *Psychoanalysis and History*, 5:2 (2003), pp. 195–212.
30. C. G. Jung, *Experimental Researches*, Jung, *Collected Works*, vol. 2.
31. S. J. Gould, *The Mismeasure of Man* (Norton: New York, 1981), p. 114.

32. C. G. Jung, 'Child Development and Education' (1928), in Jung, *Collected Works*, vol. 17, pp. 47–62, on p. 53; S. J. Gould, *Ontogeny and Phylogeny* (Cambridge, MA: Belknap Press of Harvard University Press, 1977); F. Sulloway, *Freud, Biologist of the Mind* (1979; Cambridge, MA: Harvard University Press, 1992).
33. C. G. Jung, *Psychology of the Unconscious: A Study of the Transformations and Symbolisms of the Libido* (1916; New York: Dodd, Mead and Company, 1925), pp. 27–8.
34. E. Mayr, *The Growth of Biological Thought* (Cambridge, MA: Belknap Press of Harvard University Press, 1982), pp. 698–701.
35. This can be seen very clearly in Freud's theory of the Oedipus complex, according to which every son has an instinctual urge to patricide, which reflects an actual event in the remote past when a group of young men killed the leader of the 'primal horde', S. Freud, *Totem and Taboo* (1912–13), trans. J. Strachey, in *The Standard Edition of the Complete Psychological Works of Sigmund Freud*, Vol. 13 (London: Hogarth Press, 1981), pp. 1–162.
36. C. G. Jung, *Aion* (1951), in Jung, *Collected Works*, vol. 9/ii, p. 180.
37. Jung, *Analytical Psychology*, pp. 133–4 (6 July 1925).
38. Pietikainen, 'National Typologies, Races, and Mentalities'; P. Pietikainen, 'The *Volk* and its Unconscious: Jung, Hauer, and the "German Revolution"', *Journal of Contemporary History*, 35:4 (2000), pp. 523–39; and Noll, *The Aryan Christ*.
39. Jung, *Memories*, pp. 210–14; and Jung, *Analytical Psychology*, passim.
40. Jung, *Memories*, pp. 224–5.
41. On the importance of French and French-Swiss psychological thinking on Jung's theories, see S. Shamdasani, 'From Geneva to Zürich: Jung and French Switzerland', *Journal of Analytical Psychology*, 43 (1998), pp. 115–26; and J. R. Haule, 'From Somnambulism to the Archetypes: The French Roots of Jung's Split with Freud', in P. Bishop (ed.), *Jung in Contexts* (London: Routledge, 1999), pp. 242–64.
42. C. G. Jung, 'Instinct and the Unconscious' (1919), in Jung, *Collected Works*, vol. 8, pp. 129–38.
43. On the 'Ghost in the Machine', see Pinker, *The Blank Slate*.
44. C. G. Jung, 'On Psychic Energy' (1928), in Jung, *Collected Works*, vol. 8, pp. 3–66, on p. 58.
45. See H. Driesch, *The Science and Philosophy of the Organism* (London: A. and C. Black, 1908); and H. Driesch, *The History and Theory of Vitalism* (London: Macmillan, 1914).
46. M. O. Beckner, 'Vitalism', in P. Edwards (ed.), *The Encyclopedia of Philosophy*, 8 vols (New York: Macmillan Company & Free Press, 1967), vol. 8, pp. 253–6, on p. 254.
47. Mayr, *The Growth of Biological Thought*, p. 131.
48. Beckner, 'Vitalism', p. 254.
49. P. A. Y. Gunter, 'Bergson and Jung', in Bishop (ed.), *Jung in Contexts*, pp. 265–82.
50. T. Lindner, 'Review of C. G. Jung, *Seelenprobleme der Gegenwart*', *Nordisk Medicinsk Tidskrift*, 5 (1933), pp. 1013–14. On contemporary Jung studies where Jung's neo-vitalism is discussed, see M. Nagy, *Philosophical Issues in the Psychology of C. G. Jung* (Albany, NY: State University of New York Press, 1991); Noll, *The Jung Cult*; and Shamdasani, *Jung and the Making of Modern Psychology*.
51. Jung, 'On the Psychology of the Unconscious', pp. 69–70.
52. C. G. Jung, *Visions: Notes of the Seminar Given in 1930–1934 by C. G. Jung*, ed. C. Douglas (London: Routledge, 1998), p. 977 (10 May 1933).
53. C. G. Jung, 'Picasso', (1932) in Jung, *Collected Works*, vol. 15, pp. 135–41, on p. 140.
54. Pietikainen, *C. G. Jung*, pp. 172–80.
55. Jung, *Visions*, p. 496 (22 May 1935).

56. W. Hanegraaff, *New Age Religion and Western Culture* (Leiden: E. J. Brill, 1996), p. 513.
57. C. G. Jung, 'The Structure of the Unconscious' (1916), in Jung, *Collected Works*, vol. 7, pp. 269–304. On the development of Jung's notion of individuation, see C. D. Smith, *Jung's Quest for Wholeness: A Religious and Historical Perspective* (Albany, NY: State University of New York Press, 1990).
58. For Jung's most detailed discussion of the Self, see Jung, *Aion*.
59. C. G. Jung, 'The Fight with the Shadow' (1946), in Jung, *Collected Works*, vol. 10, pp. 218–26, on p. 221.
60. C. G. Jung, 'Circular Letter' (1934), in Jung, *Collected Works*, vol. 10, pp. 545–6.
61. Bair, *Jung*, pp. 444–8.
62. On Jung's relationship to the Third Reich and his racial psychology, see A. Maidenbaum and S. A. Martin (eds), *Lingering Shadows: Jungians, Freudians, and Anti-Semitism* (Boston, MA: Shambhala, 1991); Cocks, *Psychotherapy in the Third Reich*; Pietikainen, 'National Typologies, Races, and Mentalities'; S. Grossman, 'C. G. Jung and National Socialism', in Bishop (ed.), *Jung in Contexts*, pp. 92–121; Pietikainen, 'The *Volk* and its Unconscious'; A. Samuels, *The Political Psyche* (London: Routledge, 1993).
63. Jung, *Visions*, pp. 976–7 (10 May 1933).
64. On the relationship between Jung and Hauer, see Pietikainen, 'The *Volk* and its Unconscious'.
65. For the history of the German Faith Movement, see U. Nanko, *Die Deutsche Glaubensbewegung: Eine historische und soziologische Untersuchung* (Marburg: Diagonal Verlag, 1993).
66. Jung, 'Wotan' (1936), in Jung, *Collected Works*, vol. 10, pp. 179–93, on pp. 191–2.
67. C. G. Jung, *Nietzsche's Zarathustra: Notes of the Seminar Given in 1934–1939 by C. G. Jung*, ed. J. L. Jarrett, 2 vols (Princeton, NJ: Princeton University Press, 1988), vol. 2, p. 813 (5 February 1936).
68. Jung, *Visions*, p. 975 (10 May 1933).
69. Jung, *Nietzsche's Zarathustra*, vol. 1, p. 374 (13 February 1935).
70. Ibid., vol. 1, p. 376 (13 February 1935).
71. Ibid., vol. 1, p. 377 (13 February 1935).
72. Ibid., vol. 1, p. 378 (13 February 1935).
73. Ibid. The individual in question was Mrs Martha Sigg, who used the saying as a comment on Jung's idea that it is difficult to judge Germany, because '[F]rom one aspect things are positive, and from another, quite negative'.
74. Ibid.
75. Jung, 'Wotan', p. 192.
76. The last lines of the quotation are as follows: 'O'er the sea from the north there sails a ship, With the people of Hel, at the helm stands Loki; After the wolf do wild men follow, And with them the brother of Byleist goes', Jung, 'Wotan', p. 193.
77. Grossman, 'C. G. Jung and National Socialism', pp. 113–14. See also R. Ellwood, *The Politics of Myth: A Study of C. G. Jung, Mircea Eliade, and Joseph Campbell* (Albany, NY: State University of New York Press, 1999).
78. Jung, *Nietzsche's Zarathustra*, vol. 2, pp. 813–14 (5 February 1936).
79. Jung regarded religions as psychotherapeutic systems, as becomes clear in the following statement he made in 1929: 'Both Christianity and Islam are psychological methods of treating diseases of the human soul', Jung, *Dream Analysis*, p. 419 (4 December 1929).

80. Gene Namachi's interview of Jolande Jacobi, December 1969 and January 1970, C. G. Jung Biographical Archive, H MS c 29 Box 3.
81. According to Jolande Jacobi in ibid., Jung wrote her a letter in which he compared Nazis to the evil that is the bringer of light.
82. Abraham's letter to Freud, in S. Freud and K. Abraham, *The Complete Correspondence of S. Freud and K. Abraham, 1907–1925*, ed. E. Falzeder, trans. C. Schwarzacher (London: Karnac 2002), pp. 139–41 (29 October 1911).
83. Jung, *Visions*, p. 971 (10 May 1933).
84. Ibid., p. 976 (10 May 1933).
85. Ibid., pp. 976–7 (10 May 1933).
86. C. G. Jung, *Letters*, ed. G. Adler, with A. Jaffé, trans. R. F. C. Hull, 2 vols (London: Routledge & Kegan Paul, 1973), vol. 1, p. 251 (19 December 1938).
87. Jung, 'Psychology of the Unconscious Processes', p. 353.
88. On antitemporalism in European intellectual culture from the early to mid-twentieth century, see D. K. Wood, *Men Against Time: Nicolas Berdyaev, T .S. Eliot, Aldous Huxley and C. G. Jung* (Lawrence, KS: University Press of Kansas, 1982).
89. See M. Eliade, *The Myth of the Eternal Return* (1949), trans. W. R. Trask (Princeton, NJ: Princeton University Press, 1971).
90. G. Mosse, *The Crisis of German Ideology: Intellectual Origins of the Third Reich* (London: Weidenfeld and Nicholson, 1964); G. Mosse, *Masses and Man: Nationalist and Fascist Perceptions of Reality* (New York: Howard Fertig, 1980); and R. Griffin, *The Nature of Fascism* (London: Pinter Publishers, 1991).
91. For a more detailed discussion of Jung's antitemporalism, see Pietikainen, *C. G. Jung*.
92. R. Otto, *The Idea of the Holy* (1917), trans. J. W. Harvey (Oxford: Oxford University Press, 1990), pp. 21–2, 28–31, 39–40, 75.
93. On *Naturphilosophie*, see A. Faivre, *Philosophie de la nature: physique sacrée et théosophie XVIIIe–XIXe siècle* (Paris, A. Michel, 1997).
94. Claeys and Sargent (eds), *The Utopia Reader*, p. 6.
95. *The Freud/Jung Letters*, p. 294 (11 February 1910).
96. M. G. Ash, *Gestalt Psychology in German Culture, 1890–1967: Holism and the Quest for Objectivity* (Cambridge: Cambridge University Press, 1995); A. Harrington, *Reenchanted Science: Holism in German Culture from Wilhelm II to Hitler* (Princeton, NJ: Princeton University Press, 1996).
97. Ibid., p. xxi.
98. Ibid, p. 90.
99. Quoted in ibid., p. 87.
100. Ash, *Gestalt Psychology in German Culture*, p. 12.
101. M. Eklöf, *Läkarens ethos: Studier i den svenska läkarkårens identiteter, intressen och ideal 1890–1960* (Linköping: Linköpings Universitet, 2000).
102. M. Lilla, *The Reckless Mind: Intellectuals in Politics* (New York: New York Review of Books, 2001), p. 29.
103. Gene F. Nameche's interview of Jolande Jacobi, C. G. Jung Biographical Archive.
104. Bair, *Jung*, p. 455.
105. See Gershom Scholem's 1963 letter to Jung's former secretary, Aniela Jaffé, where Scholem describes the meeting that took place between Jung and Baeck in Zurich in 1946, A. Jaffé, *From the Life and Work of C. G. Jung*, trans. R. F. C. Hull (New York: Harper & Row, 1971), p. 98.

106. Gene Namache's interview of Dr James Kirsch, December 1968, C. G. Jung Biographical Archive, H MS c 29 Box 3.
107. For Jung's negative views on the state, see Jung, *Nietzsche's Zarathustra*, vol. 2, pp. 1025, 1354, 1517; C. G. Jung, *The Undiscovered Self* (1957), in Jung, *Collected Works*, vol. 10, pp. 245–305.
108. On Swiss nationalism and its relation to National Socialism in the 1930s, see O. Zimmer, '"A Unique Fusion of the Natural and the Man-Made": The Trajectory of Swiss Nationalism', *Journal of Contemporary History*, 39:1 (2004), pp. 5–24.
109. About Keyserling and his School of Wisdom, see W. Struve, *Elites Against Democracy: Leadership Ideals in Bourgeoisie Political Thought in Germany, 1890–1933* (Princeton, NJ: Princeton University Press, 1973), pp. 274–352.
110. C. G. Jung, 'The Swiss Line in the European Spectrum' (1928), in Jung, *Collected Works*, vol. 10, pp. 479–88, on p. 483.
111. C. G. Jung, 'Return to Simple Life' (1941), in Jung, *Collected Works*, vol. 18, pp. 582–8.
112. See H. Carol, 'Man and His Environment' (1950), in *C. G. Jung Speaking: Interviews and Encounters*, ed. R. F. C Hull and W. McGuire (Princeton, NJ: Princeton University Press, 1977), pp. 201–4.
113. Bair, *Jung*, pp. 69, 674n.
114. As the Swiss scholar J.-R. de Salis points out, a peculiarity of the Swiss republic is the fact that it has traditionally been a men's republic. J.-R. de Salis, *Switzerland and Europe: Essays and Reflections* (Alabama: University of Alabama Press, 1971), p. 36.
115. Jung, *Nietzsche's Zarathustra*, vol. 2, p. 1003 (17 June 1936).
116. Jung, *Aion*, p. 181.
117. Jung, *Nietzsche's Zarathustra*, vol. 2, p. 1003 (17 June 1936).
118. H. Kohn, *Nationalism and Liberty: The Swiss Example* (New York: G. Allen & Unwin, 1956), p. 16.
119. W. Wolf, *Faschismus in der Schweiz* (Zürich: Flamberg, 1969). However, as Robert Ellwood has pointed out, there were Nazi groups as well as overall pro-German sympathies during the war in Switzerland, see Ellwood, *The Politics of Myth*, pp. 72–4.
120. Carol, 'Man and His Environment', p. 203.
121. For Jung's negative views on 'mass society', see, for example, Jung, *Nietzsche's Zarathustra*, vol. 2, pp. 1003, 1022, 1026; Jung, *The Undiscovered Self*, passim.
122. J.-F. Thomas, 'Le Suisse Est-Il Utopiste?', in G. Slusser, P. Alkon, R. Gaillard and D. Chatelain (eds), *Transformations of Utopia* (New York: AMS Press, 1999), pp. 89–97.
123. On active imagination, see especially C. G. Jung, 'The Transcendent Function' ([1916]/1957), in Jung, *Collected Works*, vol. 8, pp. 67–91.
124. C. G. Jung, 'The Psychology of the Transference' (1946), in Jung, *Collected Works*, vol. 16, pp. 163–323.
125. McLynn, *Carl Gustav Jung*, pp. 292–3.
126. C. G. Jung, *Synchronicity: An Acausal Connecting Principle* (1952), in Jung, *Collected Works*, vol. 8, pp. 417–519. See also P. Bishop, *Synchronicity and Intellectual Intuition in Kant, Swedenborg, and Jung* (Lewiston, ME: Edwin Mellen Press, 2000).
127. Shamdasani, *Jung and the Making of Modern Psychology*, p. 345.
128. On 'good myths', see F. Miele, 'The Imperial Animals 25 Years Later: An Interview with Lionel Tiger and Robin Fox', *Skeptic*, 4:1 (1996), pp. 78–85; and J. Kivivuori, *Paha Tieto* [*Evil Knowledge*] (Helsinki: Nemo, 2003).
129. G. Gerster, 'Jung and the Christmas Tree' (1957), in *C. G. Jung Speaking*, pp. 353–8, on p. 358.

130. P. Pietikainen, 'Jung's Psychology in the Light of his "Personal Myth"', *Psychoanalysis and History*, 1:2 (1999), pp. 237–51.
131. S. E. Taylor and J. D. Brown, 'Illusion and Well-Being: A Social Psychological Perspective on Mental Health', *Psychological Bulletin*, 103 (1988), pp. 193–210; S. E. Taylor and J. D. Brown, 'Positive Illusions and Well-Being Revisited: Separating Fact from Fiction', *Psychological Bulletin*, 116:1 (1994), pp. 21–7; and S. E. Taylor and D. A. Armor, 'Positive Illusions and Coping with Adversity', *Journal of Personality*, 64:4 (1996), pp. 873–97.
132. C. G. Jung, 'Brother Klaus' (1933), in Jung, *Collected Works*, vol. 11, pp. 316–23.
133. Jung, *Nietzsche's Zarathustra*, vol. 1, p. 208 (31 October 1934); E. A. Bennet, *What Jung Really Said* (London: Mcdonald & Co, 1966), chapter on 'Archetypes and Instincts'.
134. Jung, *Memories*, p. 331.
135. Ibid., p. 388.
136. Ibid., p. 392.
137. K. Nordenstreng, 'Kompleksien profeetta' ('The Prophet of Complexes'), *Suomen Kuvalehti*, 25 (26 July 1961), p. 26.

5 Sexual Revolution and the Power of Orgone Energy

1. R. S. Corrington, *Wilhelm Reich: Psychoanalyst and Radical Naturalist* (New York: Farrar, Straus and Giroux, 2003); M. Sharaf, *Fury on Earth: A Biography of Wilhelm Reich* (New York: Da Capo Press, 1983); D. Boadella, *Wilhelm Reich: The Evolution of his Work* (1973; London: Arena, 1985); E. W. Mann and E. Hoffman, *Wilhelm Reich: The Man who Dreamed of Tomorrow* (Wellingborough: Crucible, 1980). See also the memoirs of his son Peter Reich and his second wife Ilse Ollendorff Reich: P. Reich, *Book of Dreams* (New York: Harper & Row, 1973); and I. Ollendorff Reich, *Wilhelm Reich: A Personal Biography* (New York: St Martin's Press, 1969). On Reich's life and work in Vienna and Berlin, see K. Fallend, *Wilhelm Reich in Wien* (Wien: Geyer-Edition, 1988); K. Fallend and B. Nitzschke (eds), *Der 'Fall' Wilhelm Reich: Beiträge zum Verhältnis von Psychoanalyse und Politik* (Frankfurt am Main: Suhrkamp, 1997); and B. A. Laska, *Wilhelm Reich* (Hamburg: Rowohlt, 1981).
2. Manuel and Manuel, *Utopian Thought*, p. 793.
3. S. Frosh, *The Politics of Psychoanalysis* (Houndsmill: Maxmillan, 1987), p. 149.
4. In the biographical section, I shall mainly rely on the studies listed in note 1. But Reich's own reminiscences of his life, as well as his published letters and diaries, are also extremely important. See W. Reich, *Menschen im Staat* (Frankfurt am Main: Stroemfeld, 1995); W. Reich, *Passion of Youth: An Autobiography, 1897–1922*, ed. M. B. Higgins and C. M. Raphael, trans. P. Schmitz and J. Tompkins (New York: Farrar, Straus and Giroux, 1988); Reich, *Reich Speaks of Freud*; W. Reich and A. S. Neill, *Record of a Friendship: The Correspondence between Wilhelm Reich and A. S. Neill 1936–1957*, ed. B. R. Placzek (London: Victor Gollanz, 1982); W. Reich, *Jenseits der Psychologie: Briefe und Tagebücher 1934–1939*, ed. M. B. Higgins (Köln: Kiepenheuer & Witsch, 1997); W. Reich, *American Odyssey: Letters and Journals 1940–1947*, ed. M. B. Higgins (New York: Farrar, Straus and Giroux, 1999).
5. See, for example, Corrington, *Wilhelm Reich*, p. 3.
6. 'There is a remarkable absence of erotic feelings between persons living very closely together from childhood. Nay more, in this, as in many other cases, sexual indifference is combined with the positive feeling of aversion when the act is thought out. This I take to

be the fundamental cause of the exogamous prohibitions. Persons who have been living closely together from childhood are as a rule near relatives. Hence their aversion to sexual relations with one another displays itself in custom and law as a prohibition of intercourse between near kin', Westermarck, *A Short History of Marriage*, p. 80. For Westermarck's critique of psychoanalysts (such as Freud) who claimed, contrary to Westermarck, that the earliest sexual inclinations of children are regularly of an incestuous nature, see E. Westermarck, *Three Essays on Sex and Marriage* (London: Macmillan, 1934).

7. Westermarck's theory has been confirmed not only by anthropological studies of marriage customs and the development of incest aversion in the Israeli kibbutz children who lived very closely together from early childhood. Modern genetics also confirms Westermarck's theory: aversion to breeding with close relatives results in fewer congenital diseases. See A. Dixon, *Primate Sexuality* (Oxford: Oxford University Press, 1998); and D. Lieberman, J. Tooby and L. Cosmides, 'Does Morality have a Biological Basis? An Empirical Test of the Factors Governing Moral Sentiments Relating to Incest', *Proceedings of the Royal Society of London: Series B, Biological Sciences*, 270 (2003), pp. 819–26.
8. Reich, *Passion of Youth*, p. 25.
9. 'I was about eight years old. I both hated and feared my father. But the submissive attitude of the peasant [whom his father had beaten] must have left a deep impression on me, an impression of my father's power. His power over the servants and peasants was in fact enormous. Whoever spoke to him had to take off his hat. If anyone forgot, his hat was sure to fly off with a blow', ibid., p. 10.
10. Ibid., p. 32n.
11. Fallend, *Wilhelm Reich in Wien*, p. 73.
12. Reich, *Passion of Youth*, p. 63.
13. Reich, *Function of the Orgasm*, p. 35.
14. Ibid., pp. 38, 46.
15. Lore Kahn's mother, who committed suicide in December 1920, claimed that Reich had made Lore pregnant and then forced her to have an illegal abortion, and that her daughter had died because of complications following the abortion. See Sharaf, *Fury on Earth*, p. 60.
16. Reich, *Passion of Youth*, p. 153.
17. M. Grotjahn, *My Favorite Patient: The Memoirs of a Psychoanalyst* (Frankfurt am Main: Peter Lang, 1987), pp. 32, 148.
18. C. Rycroft, *Reich* (London: Fontana/Collins, 1971), p. 9.
19. S. Freud and L. Andreas-Salomé, *Letters*, ed. E. Pfeifer (New York: W. W. Norton, 1985), p. 174 (9 May 1928).
20. See W. Reich, *Early Writings*, trans. P. Schmitz (New York: Farrar, Straus and Giroux, 1975).
21. Grotjahn, *My Favorite Patient*, p. 148.
22. Reich, *Early Writings*, pp. 237–332.
23. Sharaf, *Fury on Earth*, p. 86. On Reich's understanding of the aetiology of neurosis, see Reich, *Early Writings*, p. 203.
24. P. Gay, *Freud: A Life for our Time* (New York: Norton, 1988).
25. Sharaf, *Fury on Earth*, p. 171.
26. See Reich, *Reich Speaks of Freud*, pp. 255–61; and B. Harris and A. Brock, 'Freudian Psychopolitics: The Rivalry of Wilhelm Reich and Otto Fenichel', *Bulletin of the History of Medicine*, 66 (1992), pp. 578–612, on pp. 600–3.

27. For the 'manifesto' of the *Zeitschrift*, see W. Reich, *Selected Sex-Pol Writings: 1934–37: Articles from the 'Zeitschrift für Politische Psychologie und Sexualökonomie'* (London: Socialist Reproduction, 1973), p. 35.
28. I thus agree with Bernd Nitzschke, who has advanced this argument in his writings. See B. Nitzschke, '"Ich muss mich dagegen wehren, still kaltgestellt zu werden". Voraussetzungen, Umstände und Konsequenzen des Ausschlusses Wilhelm Reich's aus der DPG/IPV in den Jahren 1933/34', in Fallend and Nitzschke (eds), *Der 'Fall' Wilhelm Reich*, pp. 68–130; and Nitzschke, 'Verinnerlichung äusserer Konflikte – Entäusserung innerer Konflikte'.
29. About Freud's reluctance to help Reich, see Erich Carsten's letter to Freud, in Reich, *Reich Speaks of Freud*, pp. 173–6.
30. Reich, *American Odyssey*, p. 129 (diary entry for 19 December 1941).
31. Sharaf, *Fury on Earth*, p. 16.
32. See W. Reich, 'The Oranur Experiment' (1951), in W. Reich, *Selected Writings: An Introduction to Orgonomy* (London: Vision Press, 1973), where Reich gives an extensive account of the experiment and its results. Due to the radiation, his wife Ilse became seriously ill and had to be operated upon. For her account of the events, see Ollendorff Reich, *Wilhelm Reich*, pp. 104–10.
33. Ibid., p. 120.
34. On Reich's problems with the United States authorities, see J. Martin, *Wilhelm Reich and the Cold War* (Fort Bragg, CA: Flatland Books, 2000); and J. Greenfield, *Wilhelm Reich versus the U.S.A.* (New York: Norton, 1974). Before his imprisonment, Reich was evaluated psychiatrically. According to the psychiatric report, Reich manifested paranoid schizophrenia (without concrete evidence of Reich being mentally incompetent). See Martin, *Wilhelm Reich and the Cold War*, p. 419.
35. W. Reich, *Contact with Space, ORANUR Second Report: OROP Desert Ea 1954–55* (New York: Core Pilot Press, 1957), p. 1. Reich identified himself with the spaceman in a 1951 Hollywood movie, the minor science-fiction classic *The Day the Earth Stood Still* (dir. Robert Wise), which he thought depicted his own life, ibid., pp. 1–2.
36. Harris and Brock, 'Freudian Psychopolitics', p. 602.
37. O. Fenichel, *119 Rundbriefe* (1934–45), ed. E. Mühlleitner and J. Reichmayr, 2 vols (Frankfurt am Main: Stroemfeld-Verlag, 1998).
38. Harris and Brock, 'Freudian Psychopolitics', p, 607. Fenichel died in the United States in 1946, and Reich got the last word when he ridiculed Fenichel in his *Listen, Little Man!* in 1948. Without mentioning Fenichel by name, he wrote about a 'little psychiatrist with a past in the youth movement', who became Reich's enemy when he thought that Reich was finished as a psychoanalytic and political authority, W. Reich, *Listen, Little Man!* (1948; Harmondsworth: Penguin Books, 1975), p. 102.
39. In the early 1960s, Rado claimed in an interview that even in the early 1930s Reich was not mildly paranoid but 'schizophrenic in the most serious way', P. Roazen and B. Swerdloff, *Heresy: Sandor Rado and the Psychoanalytic Movement* (Northvale, NJ: Jason Aronson, 1995), p. 84. Paul Federn also claimed to detect an 'incipient schizophrenia' in Reich in the early 1930s; see P. Federn, *Witnessing Psychoanalysis* (London: Karnac Books, 1990), p. 252.
40. Harris and Brock, 'Freudian Psychopolitics', p. 608n.
41. For Reich's own comments on his 'insanity', see Reich, *Reich Speaks of Freud*, p.112; W. Reich, *Character Analysis* (1933), trans. V. R. Carfagno (London: Vision Press, 1973), pp. 526–7.

42. Federn, *Witnessing Psychoanalysis*, p. 252.
43. 'We will consider Reich's work, and its impact, as these are indicative of the phenomenon of paranoia', Chasseguet-Smirgel and Grunberger, *Freud or Reich?*, p. 124.
44. Rycroft, *Reich*, p. 96.
45. For a comprehensive study of intellectual culture in the Austrian-Hungarian Empire and Austria between the years 1848–1938, see W. M. Johnston, *The Austrian Mind: An Intellectual and Social History* (Berkeley, CA: University of California Press, 1983).
46. Hobsbawm, *Interesting Times*, p. 12.
47. H. Gruber, *Red Vienna: Experiment in Working-Class Culture 1919–1934* (Oxford: Oxford University Press, 1991), pp. 146, 179; and J. Lewis, *Fascism and the Working Class in Austria, 1918–1934: The Failure of Labour in the First Republic* (New York: Berg, 1991), pp. 78–80.
48. Gruber, *Red Vienna*, p. 6.
49. As historian Russell Jacoby has pointed out, 'many early psychoanalysts identified themselves as socialists and Marxists', R. Jacoby, *The Repression of Psychoanalysis: Otto Fenichel and the Political Freudians* (New York: Basic Books, 1983), p. 12. In a similar vein, sociologist Edith Kurzweil has noted that the early psychoanalysts 'supported the leftist ideals of their fellow intellectuals and expected psychoanalysis to advance them', E. Kurzweil, *The Freudians* (New Haven, CT: Yale University Press, 1989), p. 36.
50. Reich, *Passion of Youth*, p. 116.
51. Reich, *Early Writings*, p. 58.
52. Ibid., p. 332.
53. E. A. Danto, *Freud's Free Clinics: Psychoanalysis and Social Justice, 1918–1938* (New York: Columbia University Press, 2005).
54. Fallend, *Wilhelm Reich in Wien*, pp. 46–7.
55. Reich, *Selected Sex-Pol Writings*, p. 104. For a detailed account of Reich's Freudo-Marxist years and his relationship to another radical Freudian, Otto Fenichel, see Fallend and Nitzschke (eds), *Der 'Fall' Wilhelm Reich*. For Reich's own story of his life as a political psychologist, see Reich, *Menschen im Staat*.
56. Ibid., pp. 119–28; Fallend, *Wilhelm Reich in Wien*, pp. 115–40; and Gente (ed.), *Marxismus, Psychoanalyse, Sexpol*.
57. Reich, *Menschen im Staat*, p. 83.
58. E. Menaker, *Appointment in Vienna* (New York: St Martin's Press, 1989), p. 10.
59. Ibid., p. 191.
60. Ibid., p. 67.
61. Reich, *Selected Sex-Pol Writings*, pp. 124–5; and Sharaf, *Fury on Earth*, p. 162.
62. Readers may recall from Chapter 4 that Jung disliked Hirschfeld's homosexuality and did not mind if the Nazi students burned his book in a bonfire in 1933.
63. See, for example, Reich's negative views on masturbation: Reich, *Early Writings*, p. 131; on homosexuality: W. Reich, *Children of the Future*, ed. M. Higgins and C. M. Raphael, trans. D. and I. Jordan and B. Placzek (New York: Farrar, Straus and Giroux, 1984), p. 202; W. Reich, *What is Class Consciousness?* (1934; London: Socialist Reproduction, 1973) [originally published in as a series of articles under the pseudonym Ernst Parell], p. 28; W. Reich, *Die sexuelle Revolution: Zur charakterlichen Selbststeuerung des Menschen* (1936; Frankfurt am Main: Europäische Verlagsanstalt, 1971) [originally titled *Die Sexualität im Kulturkampf*], pp. 258–9; and on 'sexual short-circuit': Reich, *What is Class Consciousness?*, pp. 18–19.
64. Reich, *Children of the Future*, p. 183.

65. W. Reich, *Mass Psychology of Fascism* (1933), trans. V. R. Carfagno (London: Souvenir Press, 1972), p. 339.
66. Reich, *What is Class Consciousness?*, p. 68.
67. Reich, *Children of the Future*, p. 206.
68. Harris and Brock, 'Freudian Psychopolitics', p. 590.
69. For Reich's description of the 'laws' of sex-economy, see W. Reich, *Der Einbruch der sexuellen Zwangsmoral* (1932; Köln: Kiepenheuer & Witsch, 1972), pp. 161–3.
70. For Reich's account of the essence and development of sex-economy, see Reich, *Function of the Orgasm*, passim; and Reich, *Menschen im Staat*, pp. 19, 132.
71. On Reich's trip to Moscow, see Etkind, *Eros of the Impossible*, pp. 242–4; Miller, *Freud and the Bolsheviks*, pp. 90–2; and Boadella, *Wilhelm Reich*, pp. 72–5. For Reich's own account of his trip, see Reich, *Selected Sex-Pol Writings*, p. 133; Reich, *Der Einbruch*, p. 20; and Reich, *Die sexuelle Revolution*, p. 229.
72. J. Wortis, *My Analysis with Freud* (Northvale, NJ: Jason Aronson, 1994), p. 106.
73. W. Reich, *Dialectical Materialism and Psychoanalysis* (1929; London: Socialist Reproduction, 1972), p. 64; Reich, *Selected Sex-Pol Writings*, p. 103.
74. 'Stalin wird zweifellos der russische Hitler', Reich, *Jenseits der Psychologie*, p. 125 (diary entry for 8 September 1936).
75. See Gruber, *Red Vienna* for an analysis of the SDAP's population politics.
76. K. von Soden, *Die Sexualberatungsstellen der Weimarer Republik 1919–1933* (Berlin: Edition Hentrich, 1988), p. 9.
77. Ibid., p. 144.
78. Reich, *What is Class Consciousness?*, p. 34.
79. Reich, *Selected Sex-Pol Writings*, pp. 38–9.
80. Ibid., p. 54.
81. Reich, *What is Class Consciousness?*, p. 21.
82. Reich, *Selected Sex-Pol Writings*, pp. 48–9.
83. See Reich, *Children of the Future*; and Reich, *Selected Sex-Pol Writings*.
84. Fallend, *Wilhelm Reich in Wien*, pp. 127–31.
85. Trotsky Archive, Houghton Library, Harvard University, Cambridge, MA, United States.
86. Reich to Trotsky, October 1933, Trotsky Archive.
87. Trotsky to Reich, 7 November 1933, Trotsky Archive. On Trotsky's interpretations of National Socialism, see L. Trotsky, *The Struggle Against Fascism in Germany* (New York: Pathfinder Press, 1971).
88. Reich, *Selected Sex-Pol Writings*, p. 62.
89. Reich, *Mass Psychology of Facism*, p. 218.
90. B. Malinowski, *The Sexual Life of Savages in North-Western Melanesia* (London: Routledge, 1932).
91. Reich, *Jenseits der Psychologie*, pp. 77, 125, 262–3, 266–8.
92. See Reich, *Function of the Orgasm*; pp. 229 ff; Reich, *Der Einbruch*, pp. 64–5, 93–8.
93. Reich, *Selected Sex-Pol Writings*, p. 126.
94. Ibid., p. 132.
95. Reich, *Mass Psychology of Facism*, pp. xix–xx.
96. Reich and Neill, *Record of a Friendship*, p. 55 (2 April 1941).
97. Reich, *Reich Speaks of Freud*, pp. 80, 114.
98. See, for example, Reich, *Menschen im Staat*, pp. 213ff; Reich, *Reich Speaks of Freud*, pp. 33, 114; Reich and Neill, *Record of a Friendship*, pp. 42, 75–6; Reich, *American Odyssey*,

p. 411; and W. Reich, *The Murder of Christ: Vol. 1 of The Emotional Plague of Mankind* (1953; New York: The Noonday Press/ Farrar, Straus and Giroux, 1974), p. 66.

99. Reich, *Reich Speaks of Freud*, p. 82.
100. Ibid., p. 77.
101. Reich, *Mass Psychology of Facism*, p. 322; Reich, *American Odyssey*, p. 360 (diary entry for 1 December 1946).
102. Reich, *Listen, Little Man!*
103. Reich, *Selected Sex-Pol Writings*, p. 126; Reich, *Mass Psychology of Facism*, p. 373; Reich, *Reich Speaks of Freud*, p. 17.
104. W. Reich, *Ether, God and Devil* (1949), in *Ether, God and Devil / Cosmic Superimposition* (New York: Farrar, Straus and Giroux, 1973), pp. 85–6.
105. Reich, *What is Class Consciousness?*, p. 56.
106. Ibid., pp. 73, 75.
107. Reich, *Die sexuelle Revolution*, pp. 287, 322–3.
108. Ollendorff Reich, *Wilhelm Reich*, p. 23.
109. A. Bergmann, 'Sexualhygiene, Rassenhygiene und der rationalisierte Tod. Wilhelm Reichs "sexuelle Massenhygiene" und seine Vision einer "freien" Sexualität', in Fallend and Nitzschke (eds), *Der 'Fall' Wilhelm Reich*, pp. 270–96, on pp. 284–94.
110. K. Danziger, *Constructing the Subject: Historical Origins of Psychological Research* (Cambridge: Cambridge University Press, 1990), p. 164.
111. For Reich's own account of his expulsion from the German Psychoanalytic Association and IPA, see Reich, *Menschen im Staat*, pp. 233–61. For a perceptive historical analysis of these events, see Nitzschke, '"Ich muss mich dagegen wehren"'.
112. Reich, *What is Class Consciousness?*, p. 42.
113. Reich, *Mass Psychology of Facism*, p. 315.
114. Reich apparently failed to understand what every student of bacteriology learns: air contains microbes that can contaminate cultures. Instead of accepting this commonplace fact, he stubbornly clung to the absurd idea that life can be generated from inanimate organic matter. See W. Reich, *The Bion Experiments on the Origin of Life* (1938; New York: Octagon Books, 1979) for a book-length study of bions.
115. On Reich's discovery of Orgone Energy, see W. Reich, *Cancer Biopathy: Vol. 2 of The Discovery of the Orgone* (1948), trans. A. White with M. Higgins and C. M. Raphael (New York: Farrar, Straus and Giroux, 1973), p. 14; Reich, *Function of the Orgasm*, pp. 383–6; Reich, *Selected Writings*, pp. 193–4; Sharaf, *Fury on Earth*, pp. 276–8.
116. Reich, *Cancer Biopathy*, p. 30.
117. Reich, *Ether, God and Devil*, p. 142.
118. Reich, *Reich Speaks of Freud*, p. 227.
119. Ibid.
120. Reich, *American Odyssey*, p. 106 (diary entry for 11 June 1941).
121. 'There is no gravitation – i.e. no falling – in space, but only oscillations in the orgone ocean, in the rotating orgone ocean', ibid., p. 368 (diary entry for 30 December 1946). 'The motion of celestial bodies is determined by the waves of the cosmic orgone ocean. There is no attraction between sun and planets', ibid., p. 385 (diary entry for 2 March 1947).
122. Sharaf, *Fury on Earth*, pp. 224–5.
123. See Reich's letters to Einstein, as well his diary entries during this episode, in Reich, *American Odyssey*.
124. Ollendorff Reich, *Wilhelm Reich*, p. 58.

125. For example, in his letters to his friend A. S. Neill, Reich repeatedly asked Neill not to propagate his ideas among British scientists. See Reich and Neill, *Record of a Friendship*.
126. Reich, *American Odyssey*, pp. 202–3.
127. Reich, *The Murder of Christ*, p. 168. On Reich's observations of air pollution, see Mann and Hoffman, *Wilhelm Reich*, pp. 220–4.
128. A. N. Whitehead, Hans Reichenbach, Nicolai Hartmann and C. F. von Weizsäcker represent twentieth-century philosophy of nature. They were inspired by modern science (quantum physics especially) and philosophy (phenomenology, logical empiricism), and developed philosophy of nature in new directions. Reichenbach, for example, transformed *Naturphilosophie* into a philosophy of science based on logic and empiricism. Philosophy of nature is a multifarious tradition, and German idealistic *Naturphilosophie* represents just one, albeit historically important, offshoot of this tradition. See R. Breil (ed.), *Naturphilosophie* (München: Verlag Karl Alber Freiburg, 2000).
129. According to the philosopher M. O. Beckner, vitalism 'holds, first, that in every living organism there is an entity that is not exhaustively composed of inanimate parts and, second, that the activities characteristic of living organisms are due in some sense to the activities of this entity'. In other words, vitalists suggested that there is an inherent developmental disposition in the regulatory processes of the organism, which can only function through a complex of 'self-activities'. Beckner, 'Vitalism', p. 254.
130. Reich, *Ether, God and Devil*, p. 8.
131. Rycroft, *Reich*, p. 79. See also Mann and Hoffman, *Wilhelm Reich*, pp. 181–204.
132. Reich, *Function of the Orgasm*, p. 262.
133. Reich, *The Murder of Christ*, pp. 103–9.
134. Reich, *Ether, God and Devil*, pp. 11–12.
135. Corrington, *Wilhelm Reich*, p. xii.
136. Reich, *Function of the Orgasm*, p. 386.
137. Reich, *Mass Psychology of Facism*, p. 297n.
138. Reich, *Function of the Orgasm*, p. 386.
139. Reich's letter to Neill, in Reich and Neill, *Record of a Friendship*, p. 55 (2 April 1941).
140. Reich, *Selected Writings*, p. 426.
141. Reich, *The Murder of Christ*, p. 200.
142. His second wife, Ilse Ollendorff Reich, writes in her biography of Reich: 'In his later years, he undoubtedly began to identify more and more with Christ whose true message, he thought, was distorted by his disciples, and he feared that the same would happen to his work', Ollendorff Reich, *Wilhelm Reich*, p. xxi. By 'armour', Reich referred to the 'total defense apparatus of the organism, consisting of the rigidities of the character and the chronic spasms of the musculature, which functions essentially as a defense against the breakthrough of the emotions – primarily anxiety, rage, and sexual excitation', Reich, *Selected Writings*, p. xix. 'Dearmouring' would thus mean breaking down this more or less pathological defence mechanism or 'social self'.
143. DOR denoted an 'immobilized, or stagnant, atmospheric life energy ... When an organism dies and ceases to function as an integrated unit, it begins to decay, i.e. it loses its energy level. The energetic system disintegrates into smaller functional units, rot bacteria and ultimately to T-bacilli [Tod-bacilli, meaning Death-bacilli]', Reich, *Selected Writings*, pp. 450–1. He connected DOR to air pollution, desertification and the biopsychological character armour.
144. Ibid., p. 466.
145. Ibid., p. 427.

146. Corrington, *Wilhelm Reich*, p. 217.
147. A. Storr, *Human Destructiveness* (New York: Ballantine Books, 1992), p. 137.
148. R. Porter, 'Mood Disorders – Social Section', in G. E. Berrios and R. Porter (eds), *A History of Clinical Psychiatry: The Origin and History of Psychiatric Disorders* (London: Athlone, 1995), pp. 409–20, on p. 415.
149. Reich, *Passion of Youth*, p. 84.
150. Reich, *Dialectical Materialism*, p. 53.
151. Reich, *Jenseits der Psychologie*, p. 45 (17 November 1934).
152. Reich, *Function of the Orgasm*, p. 201.
153. For a discussion of the widespread negative attitude towards utopias in the first decades of the twentieth century, see Kumar, *Utopia and Anti-Utopia*.
154. U. Zilbersheid, 'The Idea of Abolition of Labor in Socialist Utopian Thought', *Utopian Studies*, 13:1 (2002), pp. 21–42, on p. 21.
155. Reich's letter to Neill, in Reich and Neill, *Record of a Friendship*, pp. 52, 55 (2 April 1941).
156. Reich, *Reich Speaks of Freud*, p. 46.
157. Berman, 'Psychoanalysis, Rescue and Utopia', p. 45.
158. Sharaf, *Fury on Earth*, pp. 51, 240.
159. Reich, *Children of the Future*, p. 18.
160. Reich, *Selected Writings*, p. 428.
161. Reich, *Der Einbruch*.
162. Reich, *The Murder of Christ*, p. 97.
163. Reich, *Cosmic Superimposition* (1951), in *Ether, God and Devil / Cosmic Superimposition*, p. 298.
164. W. Reich, 'New Goals on the Horizon', *Orgone Energy Bulletin* 3:2 (1951), p. 116.
165. For an analysis of the Communist cult of history in the twentieth century, see Furet, *The Passing of an Illusion*.
166. W. Reich, 'The Developmental History of Orgonomic Functionalism', *Orgonomic Functionalism: A Journal Devoted to the Work of Wilhelm Reich*, 1 (1990), pp. 1–29, on p. 1.
167. Reich, *The Murder of Christ*, p. 8.
168. Ibid., p. 188.
169. Reich, *Ether, God and Devil*, p. 73. In a letter to Nic Hoel, Reich remarked: 'The sex-hungry people around me tend, in a mystical way, to expect me to create a paradise on earth', Reich, *American Odyssey*, p. 292 (28 June 1945).
170. Reich, *Function of the Orgasm*, pp. 152–3.
171. Reich, *American Odyssey*, p. 61 (no date).
172. Reich's letter to Neill, in Reich and Neill, *Record of a Friendship*, p. 186 (26 February 1947).
173. Reich, *American Odyssey*, p. 39 (8 November 1940).
174. Ibid., p. 81 (21 February 1941).
175. Ibid., pp. 343–4 (diary entry for 23 July 1946).
176. Ibid., p. 167 (diary entry for 20 December 1942).
177. Ibid., pp. 99, 122 (diary entries for 22 May and 18 October 1941).
178. Ibid., p. 30.
179. Reich, *Reich Speaks of Freud*, p. 119.
180. Reich, *Selected Writings*, p. xxiv.
181. Ibid.
182. Reich, *Passion of Youth*, p. 119.

183. T. Hauschka, 'The Cancer Biopathy of Wilhelm Reich', MS (1949–50), The Wilhelm Reich Microfiche Collection, Reel 5, No. 228E, Helsinki University Library, p. 4.
184. W. Reich, *The Bioelectrical Investigation of Sexuality and Anxiety* (1934–7), ed. M. Higgins and C. M. Raphael, trans. M. Faber with D. and I. Jordan (New York: Farrar, Straus and Giroux, 1982), pp. 40–1.
185. Reich, *Selected Writings*, p. 462.
186. P. Reich, *Book of Dreams*, pp. 52–3.
187. Ibid., p. 58.

6 Socialist Humanism and the Sane Society

1. E. Fromm, *The Art of Loving* (1956; London: George Allen & Unwin, 1975), p. 86.
2. Throughout this chapter, 'Socialist Humanism' is capitalized in order to differentiate Fromm's version of it from other authors who have used the same term. Fromm himself did not capitalize 'Socialist Humanism'.
3. On the utopian aspects of Fromm's thought, see J. H. Schaar, *Escape from Authority: The Perspectives of Erich Fromm* (New York: Basic Books, 1961), p. 23; Manuel and Manuel, *Utopian Thought*, pp. 792–4; D. Burston, *The Legacy of Erich Fromm* (Cambridge, MA: Harvard University Press, 1991), p. 172; N. McLaughlin, 'How to Become a Forgotten Intellectual: Intellectual Movements and the Rise and Fall of Erich Fromm', *Sociological Forum*, 13 (1998), pp. 215–46, on p. 215; H. J. Eysenck, 'Utopia in Dreamland', review of E. Fromm, *The Anatomy of Human Destructiveness*, *The Spectator* 26 October 1974; B. Goodwin and K. Taylor, *The Politics of Utopia* (London: Hutchinson, 1982), p. 34; and R. Funk, *Erich Fromm: His Life and Ideas* (New York: Continuum, 2000), p. 142. For a denial of the suggestion that Fromm was a utopian author, see S. E. Bronner, *Of Critical Theory and its Theorists* (Oxford: Blackwell, 1994), p. 225; and S. E. Bronner, 'Fromm in America', in M. Kessler and R. Funk (eds), *Erich Fromm und die Frankfurter Schule* (Tübingen: Francke Verlag, 1992), pp. 41–60, on p. 54.
4. On Fromm as a public intellectual in the United States, see McLaughlin, 'How to Become a Forgotten Intellectual'; and Bos et al., 'Strategic Self-Marginalization'.
5. L. A. Coser, *Refugee Scholars in America* (New Haven, CT: Yale University Press, 1984), p. 74.
6. Bronner, *Of Critical Theory*, p. 209; P. Roazen, *Political Theory and the Psychology of the Unconscious* (London: Open Gate Press, 2000), p. 100.
7. R. Funk, 'Erich Fromm's Life and Work', in K. Anderson and R. Quinney (eds), *Erich Fromm and Critical Criminology* (Urbana and Chicago, IL: University of Illinois Press, 2000), pp. 3–19, on p. 14. The web address of the International Erich Fromm Society is http://www.erich-fromm.de/e/index.htm.
8. In my account of Fromm's life, I rely mainly on Funk, *Erich Fromm*; Burston, *The Legacy of Erich Fromm*; and M. Cortina and M. Maccoby (eds), *A Prophetic Analyst: Erich Fromm's Contribution to Psychoanalysis* (Northvale, NJ: Jason Aronson, 1996).
9. E. Fromm, 'Reminiscences of Shlomo Barukh Rabinkow', in L. Jung (ed.), *Sages and Saints* (Hoboken: Ktav Publishing House, 1987), pp. 99–105.
10. Fromm in an interview in 1978 and 1979; quoted in Funk, *Erich Fromm*, p. 6.
11. E. Fromm, 'Das Jüdische Gesetz' (1922), in E. Fromm, *Gesamtausgabe*, 12 vols, ed. R. Funk (Stuttgart: Deutsche Verlags-Anstalt, 1999), pp. 19–126.
12. Quoted in G. A. Hornstein, *To Redeem One Person is to Redeem the World* (New York: Free Press, 2000), p. 65.

13. On Fromm's Trotskyism, see Burston, *The Legacy of Erich Fromm*, p. 13; K. Anderson, 'Erich Fromm and the Frankfurt School Critique of Criminal Justice', in Anderson and Quinney (eds), *Erich Fromm and Critical Criminology*, pp. 83–119, on p. 92; and F. Erös, 'Fromm's Theory and the Problems of "Real Existing" Socialism', *Wissenschaft vom Menschen / Science of Man: Yearbook of the International Erich Fromm Society*, 2 (1991), pp. 315–23, on p. 318.
14. E. Klein-Landskron, 'Max Horkheimer und Erich Fromm', in Kessler and Funk (eds), *Erich Fromm und die Frankfurter Schule*, pp. 161–80.
15. E. Fromm, *The Working Class in Weimar Germany: A Psychological and Sociological Study*, ed. W. Bonss, trans. B. Weinberger (London: Berg Publishers, 1984), p. 228. For a critical assessment of both this study and the later (1950) attempt by Theodor Adorno and his co-workers at an empirical social-psychological study of the 'authoritarian character', see F. Samelson, 'The Authoritarian Character from Berlin to Berkeley and Beyond: The Odyssey of a Problem', in W. F. Stone, G. Lederer and R. Christie (eds), *Strength and Weakness: The Authoritarian Personality Today* (New York: Springer Verlag, 1993), pp. 22–43.
16. On Frieda Reichmann's life and work, see Hornstein, *To Redeem One Person*.
17. The reasons for the break-up are complex, for personal, intellectual and professional ties between Horkheimer and Fromm were tightly intertwined. See Kessler and Funk (eds), *Erich Fromm und die Frankfurter Schule*. For Fromm's own views on the Institute, see his letter to Martin Jay ('Erich Fromm an Martin Jay'), 14 May 1971, in ibid., pp. 249–56.
18. L. J. Saul, 'Review of Erich Fromm, *Escape from Freedom*', *Psychoanalytic Quarterly*, 11:2 (1943), pp. 245–8, on p. 247.
19. R. M. Loewenstein, 'Review of Erich Fromm, *Man for Himself*', *Psychoanalytic Quarterly*, 17 (1948), pp. 534–5, on p. 534.
20. H. R. Blank, 'Review of Erich Fromm, *The Sane Society*', *Psychoanalytic Quarterly*, 25 (1956), pp. 270–2, on pp. 270–1.
21. Ibid., p. 272.
22. P. Roazen. 'The Exclusion of Erich Fromm from the IPA', *Contemporary Psychoanalysis*, 37:1 (2001), pp. 5–42.
23. E. Fromm, *Sigmund Freud's Mission: An Analysis of his Personality and Influence* (New York: Harper, 1959).
24. On Fromm's 'optimal marginality', see McLaughlin, 'Optimal Marginality'; on his 'self-marginalization', see Bos et al., 'Strategic Self-Marginalization', pp. 214–17.
25. M. Maccoby, 'The Two Voices of Erich Fromm: The Prophetic and the Analytic', in Cortina and Maccoby (eds), *A Prophetic Analyst*, pp. 61–92, on p. 74.
26. R. U. Akeret, *Tales from a Traveling Couch* (New York: W. W. Norton & Co., 1996), p. 113.
27. For a short account of SANE, see P. Buhle, 'Peace Movements', in M. J. Buhle, P. Buhle and D. Georgakas (eds), *Encyclopedia of the American Left* (New York and Oxford: Oxford University Press, 1998), pp. 592–8.
28. The International Federation of Psychoanalytic Societies originally included the German Psychoanalytic Society, Fromm's Mexican group, the Austrian group, and the William Alanson White Institute in New York. Today more than twenty associations belong to the Federation. See Funk, *Erich Fromm*, p. 135.
29. Ibid., p. 145.
30. E. Fromm, *Man for Himself: An Inquiry into the Psychology of Ethics* (1947; London: Routledge & Kegan Paul, 1967), p. 67.

31. E. Fromm, *Escape from Freedom* (1941; New York: Holt, Rinehart and Winston, 1961).
32. E. Fromm's letter to Martin Jay, 14 May 1971, in Kessler and Funk (eds), *Erich Fromm und die Frankfurter Schule*, p. 252. See also E. Fromm, *Beyond the Chains of Illusion* (1962; London: Abacus, 1980), p. 75n.
33. Ibid., p. 83.
34. On the relation between utopianism and the cultural elites' contempt for mass society in general and the lower-middle class in particular, see C. Brinton, 'Utopia and Democracy', in Manuel (ed.), *Utopias*, pp. 50–68.
35. Fromm, *Man for Himself*, p. 71.
36. For Fromm's later discussion of the marketing orientation ('the marketing character'), see E. Fromm, *To Have or To Be?* (1976; London: Cape, 1979), pp. 147–54.
37. Fromm, *Man for Himself*, pp. 87–8.
38. Ibid., p. 229.
39. E. Fromm, 'Psychoanalysis – Science or Party Line?' (1958), in E. Fromm, *The Dogma of Christ and Other Essays on Religion, Psychology and Culture* (New York: Holt, Rinehart, and Winston, 1963), pp. 131–46.
40. E. Fromm, *The Anatomy of Human Destructiveness* (1973; Harmondsworth: Penguin Books, 1987), pp. 467–8.
41. Fromm, *Man for Himself*, p. 112.
42. Fromm scholar Daniel Burston suggests that, in his early inclination to characterization, Fromm was influenced by Reich's formulations, as well as by Freud. Burston, *The Legacy of Erich Fromm*, pp. 37, 64.
43. Fromm, *Man for Himself*.
44. E. Fromm, *The Sane Society* (1955; New York: Holt, Rinehart and Winston, 1969), p. viii.
45. Ibid., p. 103.
46. N. Pressman, *Last Resort: Psychosurgery and the Limits of Medicine* (Cambridge: Cambridge University Press, 1998), p. 20.
47. Ibid., pp. 11, 428, 363.
48. Fromm, *The Sane Society*, pp. 72, 193.
49. E. Fromm, 'Medicine and the Ethical Problem of Modern Man' (1957), in Fromm, *The Dogma of Christ*, pp. 169–90, on p. 181.
50. E. Fromm, *Gesellschaft und Seele: Beiträge zur Sozialpsychologie und zur psychoanalytischen Praxis*, ed. R. Funk (Weinheim and Basel: Beltz Verlag, 1992), p. 109.
51. Ibid., p. 203.
52. Burston, *The Legacy of Erich Fromm*, pp. 26–7.
53. Fromm, *The Sane Society*, pp. 168–9.
54. E. Fromm, *Greatness and Limitations of Freud's Thought* (London: Abacus, 1982), pp. 137–8.
55. Fromm, *Man for Himself*, p. 6.
56. Fromm, *The Sane Society*, p. 360.
57. See E. Fromm, *Marx's Concept of Man* (1961; New York: Frederick Ungar Publishing, 1983), pp. 43–57; E. Fromm, 'The Present Human Condition' (1955–6), in Fromm, *The Dogma of Christ*, pp. 95–106.
58. R. I. Evans, *Dialogue with Erich Fromm* (1966; New York: Praeger, 1981), p. 89.
59. Fromm, *The Sane Society*, p. 121.
60. See N. Lobkowics, 'Alienation', in C. D. Kernig (ed.), *Marxism, Communism and Western Society*, 8 vols (New York: Herder and Herder, 1972–3), vol. 1, pp. 88–109.

61. D. Coute, *The Illusion: An Essay on Politics, Theatre and the Novel* (London: Deutsch, 1971), p. 172.
62. P. Hollander, *Political Pilgrims: Travels of Western Intellectuals to the Soviet Union, China, and Cuba* (New York: Harper & Row, 1983), p. 405.
63. For a critique of the way modern Western intellectuals, including Fromm, have conceptualized alienation, see ibid.
64. Fromm, *The Sane Society*, p. 358.
65. Ibid., p. 359.
66. E. Fromm, *May Man Prevail? An Inquiry into the Facts and Fictions of Foreign Policy* (New York: Doubleday & Co., 1961), p. 22.
67. Ibid., p. 46.
68. See Evans, *Dialogue with Erich Fromm*, p. 56.
69. See E. Dolnick, *Madness on the Couch: Blaming the Victim in the Heyday of Psychoanalysis* (New York: Simon & Schuster, 1998).
70. Fromm, *The Sane Society*, p. 82. It was typical of Fromm to characterize the family as the 'psychic agency of society' in his writings. This definition fits in well with his theory of social character.
71. De Waal, *The Ape and the Sushi Master*, p. 291.
72. E. Fromm, *Love, Sexuality, and Matriarchy: About Gender*, ed. R. Funk (New York: Fromm International Publishing Corporation, 1997), p. 188.
73. E. Fromm, *The Heart of Man* (1964; New York: Harper & Row, 1968), p. 97.
74. E. Fromm, *Die Gesellschaft als Gegenstand der Psychoanalyse*, ed. R. Funk (Frankfurt am Main: Suhrkamp, 1993), p. 153; Fromm, *The Sane Society*, p. 46. See also Fromm, *The Heart of Man*, pp. 54–5; and Fromm, *The Anatomy of Human Destructiveness*, pp. 483–4, where Fromm argues for the probable causal relationship between the child's autism and the mother's 'emotional coldness'.
75. E. Fromm, *The Art of Listening* (New York: Continuum, 1994), p. 53.
76. Ibid., p. 55.
77. Fromm, *The Anatomy of Human Destructiveness*, pp. 483–4; Fromm, *The Heart of Man*, p. 54.
78. See E. Fromm, 'The Significance of the Theory of Mother Right for Today' (1970) and 'The Theory of Mother Right and its Relevance for Social Psychology' (1934), both in E. Fromm, *The Crisis of Psychoanalysis* (New York: Holt, Rinehart and Winston, 1970), pp. 79–83 and 84–109. See also Fromm, *Love, Sexuality, and Matriarchy*.
79. Ibid., pp. 76–84.
80. Fromm, 'The Theory of Mother Right', p. 104.
81. In his late work on 'having' and 'being', Fromm wrote that 'Luther established a purely patriarchal form of Christianity in Northern Europe that was based on the urban middle class and the secular princes', Fromm, *To Have or To Be?*, p. 146.
82. Fromm, 'The Theory of Mother Right', pp. 105–9.
83. Ibid., p. 108.
84. Fromm, 'The Significance of the Theory of Mother Right', p. 82.
85. As the scholar of anarchism George Woodcock has noted, Fromm's ideas – especially in *Escape from Freedom* – appealed to anarchists in the 1940s. Woodcock, 'Anarchism', p. 48.
86. Fromm, *The Sane Society*, pp. 270–352.
87. Maccoby, 'The Two Voices of Erich Fromm', p. 70.

88. Zilbersheid, 'The Idea of Abolition of Labour'. See also U. Zilbersheid, *Jenseits der Arbeit. Der vergessene sozialistische Traum von Marx, Fromm und Marcuse* (Frankfurt am Main: Peter Lang, 1999).
89. For his later discussion of the guaranteed income, see E. Fromm, *The Revolution of Hope* (New York: Harper & Row, 1968), pp. 126–8; E. Fromm, 'The Psychological Aspects of the Guaranteed Income' (1966), in E. Fromm, *On Disobedience and Other Essays* (New York: Seabury Press, 1981), pp. 91–101; and Fromm, *To Have or To Be?*, pp. 190–1.
90. For Fromm's later discussion of a 'sane' and a 'sick' society, see Fromm, *Beyond the Chains of Illusion*, pp. 41–59.
91. For a critique of liberalism from the right wing of the political spectrum, see J. Burnham, *Suicide of the West* (New York: John Day Co., 1965). Burnham's basic thesis in his book is that liberalism is the 'ideology of Western suicide'. For a history of socialism in western Europe, see D. Sassoon, *One Hundred Years of Socialism: The West European Left in the Twentieth Century* (London: I. B. Tauris, 1996).
92. Fromm, *Beyond the Chains of Illusion*, p. 10. On Fromm's activism in the peace movement, see H. A. Jack, 'Die Friedensbewegung und Erich Fromm', in L. von Werder (ed.), *Der unbekannte Fromm: Biographische Studien* (Frankfurt: Haag und Herchen Verlag, 1987), pp. 61–70.
93. G. Perusek, 'Shifting Terrain: Styles of Liberalism, Periodization, and Levels of Analysis', *International Journal of Politics, Culture and Society*, 15:3 (2002), pp. 405–26, on p. 417. For an overall account of American liberalism in the early Cold War era, see R. Pells, *The Liberal Mind in a Conservative Age: American Intellectuals in the 1940s and the 1950s* (New York: Harper & Row, 1985). See also P. Buhle, *Marxism in the United States* (London: Verso, 1987).
94. E. Fromm, 'Let Man Prevail', in Fromm, *On Disobedience*, pp. 58–74, on p. 71.
95. Fromm, *Marx's Concept of Man*; and Fromm, *Beyond the Chains of Illusion*.
96. E. Fromm, 'Introduction' (1965), in E. Fromm (ed.), *Socialist Humanism: An International Symposium* (New York: Anchor Books, 1966), pp. vii–xii, on p. x.
97. E. Fromm to K. Polanyi, 14 April 1960, The Erich Fromm Archives, c/o Rainer Funk, Ursrainer Ring 24, D-72076 Tübingen, Germany. Quotation with permission of the Literary Estate of Erich Fromm.
98. E. Fromm, 'Marx's Contribution to the Knowledge of Man' (1968), in Fromm, *The Crisis of Psychoanalysis*, pp. 46–58, on p. 68.
99. E. Fromm, 'Foreword', in H. Brandt, *The Search For a Third Way* (New York: Doubleday & Co., 1970), pp. xi–xvii, on p. xv.
100. Fromm, *Beyond the Chains of Illusion*, p. 11. He later regretted that he had made this evaluative comparison. See his letter to Martin Jay, 14 May 1971, in Kessler and Funk (eds), *Erich Fromm und die Frankfurter Schule*, p. 252.
101. Evans, *Dialogue with Erich Fromm*, p. 74.
102. E. Fromm, 'The Application of Humanist Psychoanalysis to Marx's Theory' (1965), in Fromm (ed.), *Socialist Humanism*, pp. 228–45, on p. 244.
103. Fromm to Martin Jay, 14 May 1971, in Kessler and Funk (eds), *Erich Fromm und die Frankfurter Schule*, p. 251. See also Fromm, 'The Application of Humanist Psychoanalysis'.
104. Fromm rejected Althusser's contribution to the collection of essays on Socialist Humanism that he was editing. See Fromm's letter to Althusser, 8 January 1964, and Althusser's letter to Adam Schaff, 1 February 1964, both in the Erich Fromm Archives.

105. The Praxis group denotes a group of Marxist philosophers and sociologists who focused on Marx's idea of praxis, or self-creative activity. In 1964, they founded the journal *Praxis*, which published a translation of one of Fromm's essays on Marx. From the 1960s onwards, many of Fromm's articles and books were translated into Serbo-Croatian, Czech, Polish and, in the 1990s, into Russian.
106. Funk, *Erich Fromm*, p. 148.
107. T. Bottomore, 'Fromm, Erich', in T. Bottomore (ed.), *A Dictionary of Marxist Thought* (Oxford: Blackwell, 1991), p. 213. 'His (Fromm's) ideas and even more his gift for popularization made him an important figure for the early New Left', H. Paget, 'Erich Fromm', in Buhle et al. (eds), *Encyclopedia of the American Left*, pp. 248–9, on p. 248.
108. T. Bottomore to B. Betz, 17 July 1972, in B. Betz, 'An Analysis of the Prophetic Character of the Dialectical Rhetoric of Erich Fromm' (unpublished PhD thesis, Northwestern University, 1974), p. 334.
109. Fromm, *Beyond the Chains of Illusion*, p. 154.
110. Goodwin and Taylor, *The Politics of Utopia*, p. 81.
111. W. Goldstein, 'Messianism and Marxism: Walter Benjamin and Ernst Bloch's Dialectical Theories of Secularisation', *Critical Sociology*, 27 (2002), pp. 246–81.
112. Fromm, *The Revolution of Hope*, p. 19n. In *To Have or To Be?* (again in a footnote), Fromm writes that 'nobody has dealt with the theme of atheistic religious experience more profoundly and more boldly than has Ernst Bloch', Fromm, *To Have or To Be?*, p. 139n.
113. Fromm, *The Revolution of Hope*, p. 58.
114. Fromm, *The Heart of Man*, p. 13n. On existentialist themes in Fromm's own thought, see Burston, *The Legacy of Erich Fromm*, pp. 84–97.
115. Evans, *Dialogue with Erich Fromm*, p. 99.
116. Fromm's letter to Raya Dunayevskaja, 13 September 1965, The Erich Fromm Archives. For Fromm's rather positive comments on Stirner's philosophy, see Fromm, *Man for Himself*, pp. 123–4. See also Fromm, *To Have or To Be?*, p. 71.
117. Fromm's letter to Raya Dunayevskaja, 29 October 1966, The Erich Fromm Archives.
118. E. Fromm, *Ethik und Politik: Antworten auf aktuelle politische Fragen*, ed. R. Funk (Weinhem and Basel: Beltz, 1990), p. 38.
119. Fromm, *The Revolution of Hope*, p. 107.
120. Karl Popper called utopian rationalism 'pseudo-rationalism' and 'self-defeating rationalism' in his famous critique of utopianism. See K. Popper, *Conjectures and Refutations* (London: Routledge & Kegan Paul, 1963), pp. 358–76.
121. Fromm, *The Revolution of Hope*, p. 151.
122. As Fromm's biographer points out, 'After the publication of *To Have or To Be?* (in 1976), Fromm became almost as well known in Europe as he had been during the 'sixties in America', Funk, *Erich Fromm*, p. 162.
123. Ibid. Fromm did not condemn terrorism outright. However, in a 1976 interview he said that a greater danger to the freedom of Germany lay in the methods used by the authorities against terrorists than in the terrorist activities themselves. Fromm, *Ethik und Politik*, pp. 212–15.
124. See the index of Fromm's *Gesamtausgabe*, vols 10 and 11 ('Utopie', 'Utopismus').
125. Fromm, *Man for Himself*, p. 30n.
126. Ibid., p. 83.
127. But see also E. Fromm, 'Meister Eckhart und Karl Marx: Die reale Utopie der Orientierung am Sein' (1974), in Fromm, *Gesamtausgabe*, vol. 12, pp. 485–526.

128. E. Fromm, 'Vorwort zu Edward Bellamy "Looking Backward"' (1960), in Fromm, *Gesamtausgabe*, vol. 5, pp. 273–84.
129. E. Fromm, 'Nachwort zu George Orwell "1984"' (1961), in Fromm, *Gesamtausgabe*, vol. 5, pp. 285–93.
130. Fromm, 'Introduction', p. ix.
131. Fromm, 'The Present Human Condition', p. 103.
132. Fromm, *Beyond the Chains of Illusion*, p. 162.
133. Fromm, *The Revolution of Hope*, p. 169.
134. E. Fromm, 'The Revolutionary Character' (1963), in Fromm, *The Dogma of Christ*, pp. 147–68, on p. 158.
135. Fromm, *The Heart of Man*, p. 44.
136. Ibid.
137. Ibid., p. 48.
138. See Fromm, *The Revolution of Hope*, pp. 60–2.
139. Fromm, *Man for Himself*, p. 21.
140. Ibid., p. 23.
141. Fromm, *Love, Sexuality, and Matriarchy*, p. 121; Fromm, *To Have or To Be?*, p. 106.
142. Burston, *The Legacy of Erich Fromm*, p. 171.
143. Fromm, *Man for Himself*, p. 143.
144. Fromm, *To Have or To Be?*, p. 103n.
145. Fromm, *The Art of Listening*, p. 92; Fromm, *Ethik und Politik*, pp. 38–9; E. Fromm, *The Revision of Psychoanalysis*, ed. R. Funk (Boulder, CO: Westview Press 1992), p. 35.
146. Fromm, *Greatness and Limitations*, p. 137.
147. *Encyclopaedia Judaica*, 16 vols (Jerusalem: Keter Publishing House, 1971–2), vol. 11, p. 1410.
148. Ibid., p. 1411.
149. M. Friedman, *Martin Buber's Life and Work: The Later Years, 1945–1965* (New York: E. P. Dutton, 1983), p. 236.
150. Quoted in *Encyclopaedia Judaica*, vol. 11, p. 1416.
151. M. Brumlik, 'Messianic Thinking in the Jewish Intelligentsia of the Twenties', in *Wissenschaft vom Menschen / Science of Man, Yearbook of the International Erich Fromm Society*, 2 (1991), pp. 20–32. See also Z. Tarr and J. Marcus, 'Erich Fromm und das Judentum', in Kessler and Funk (eds), *Erich Fromm und die Frankfurter Schule*, pp. 211–20.
152. Fromm, *The Anatomy of Human Destructiveness*, p. 154.
153. On the 'Cash Nexus' and the 'breakdown of connections' as discussed in nineteenth-century sociology, see B. Mazlish, *A New Science* (Oxford: Oxford University Press, 1989).
154. In Finland, historian Juha Siltala from the University of Helsinki has emphasized the positive aspect of people's 'materialism': ordinary people pursue material goods, especially owner-occupied houses and flats, in order to attain a space of their own where they can be autonomous and independent with regard to society. To buy a house or a flat is therefore a material investment that in Siltala's view is motivated by people's need for ontological security. He discusses this idea in his study on the 'deterioration of the working life' in contemporary Finland. J. Siltala, *Työelämän huonontumisen lyhyt historia* (Helsinki: Kustannusosakeyhtiö Otava, 2004).
155. Fromm's letter to Raya Dunayevskaja, 29 October 1966, The Erich Fromm Archives.
156. Hollander, *Political Pilgrims*, p. 87.
157. Adam Smith, as quoted in Pinker, *The Blank Slate*, p. 161.
158. Ibid.

159. E. Fromm, *You Shall Be as Gods* (New York: Holt, Rinehart and Winston, 1966), pp. 12–13.
160. Fromm to Betz, 14 October 1972, in Betz, 'An Analysis of the Prophetic Character', p. 331.
161. Fromm to A. Schaff, 13 January 1965, The Erich Fromm Archives. Quotation with permission of the Literary Estate of Erich Fromm.
162. See D. T. Suzuki and E. Fromm, *Zen Buddhism and Psychoanalysis* (New York: Harper & Row, 1960).
163. Fromm, *The Art of Loving*, p. 72. In a letter to historian Martin Jay (who was the first to write a book on the history of the Frankfurt School), Fromm wrote that 'I gave up all theistic belief, but retained an attitude which I would describe as religious, if one does not imply by this belief in God', Fromm to Martin Jay, 14 May 1971, in Kessler and Funk (eds), *Erich Fromm und die Frankfurter Schule*, p. 250.
164. Fromm, *To Have or To Be?*, p. 133. See also E. Fromm, *Die Pathologie der Normalität: Zur Wissenschaft vom Menschen*, ed. R. Funk (Weinheim and Basel: Beltz Verlag, 1991), pp. 32–6.
165. Ibid., p. 30. See also Fromm, *Escape from Freedom*, pp. 101–2.
166. J. S. Glen, *Erich Fromm: A Protestant Critique* (Philadelphia, PA: Westminster Press, 1966), p. 196.
167. For a discussion of the fact that there have been – and still are – many Jewish people among Jungian psychologists, see Kirsch, *The Jungians*, pp. 238–40.
168. Fromm, *Humanismus als reale Utopie*, p. 112.
169. Ibid., pp. 158–9, 195.
170. Fromm, *To Have or To Be?*, pp. 174–5.
171. Fromm, *Greatness and Limitations*, p. 4. Fromm discusses the concept of 'Messianic Time' in Fromm, *You Shall Be as Gods*.
172. Fromm, *To Have or To Be?*, p. 202.
173. Ibid.
174. Fromm, *Marx's Concept of Man*, p. 63.
175. Fromm, 'Values, Psychology, and Human Existence' (1959), in Fromm, *On Disobedience*, pp. 1–15; Fromm, *The Sane Society*, p. 20; Fromm, *Die Pathologie der Normalität*, pp. 19, 138; Fromm, *The Revolution of Hope*, pp. 89–91; Fromm, *Gesellschaft und Seele*, p. 108.
176. E. Fromm, 'Values, Psychology, and Human Existence', p. 1.
177. Fromm, 'Medicine', p. 176.
178. Fromm, *Marx's Concept of Man*, p. 67.
179. Fromm, 'The Application of Humanist Psychoanalysis', p. 243.
180. Fromm, *Gesellschaft und Seele*, p. 109.
181. I. Berlin, *Four Essays on Liberty* (Oxford: Oxford University Press, 1969), p. lii.
182. See I. Berlin, *Karl Marx: His Life and Environment* (London: T. Butterworth, 1939), in which Berlin critically examines Marx's historical theodicy.
183. See J. Gray, *Isaiah Berlin* (Princeton, NJ: Princeton University Press, 1996) for a discussion of Berlin's challenge to the liberal tradition.
184. Perusek, 'Shifting Terrain'.
185. Berlin, *Four Essays on Liberty*, p. 122.
186. Ibid., p. xlii. The term 'agonistic liberalism' was coined by the philosopher John Gray to illustrate Berlin's political outlook. See Gray, *Isaiah Berlin*.
187. Ibid., p. lvii.
188. Ibid., p. 169.

189. Ibid., p. xlvii.
190. Crowder, *Classical Anarchism*, p. 10.
191. Fromm, *To Have or To Be?*, p. 80.
192. Fromm, *The Revolution of Hope*, p. 91.
193. For a critique of therapeutic culture, see Rieff, *The Triumph of the Therapeutic*; M. L. Gross, *The Psychological Society*; Furedi, *Therapy Culture*; P. Pietikainen (ed.), *Modernity and its Discontents: Sceptical Essays on the Psychomedical Management of Malaise* (Stockholm: Ax:son Johnson Foundation, 2005).
194. Schaar, *Escape from Authority*, p. 6.
195. For an illustration of Fromm's habit of presenting his assertions on the true needs and values of people as objectively valid, see Fromm, *Gesellschaft und Seele*, pp. 99–109.
196. Eysenck, 'Utopia in Dreamland'.
197. Berlin, *Four Essays on Liberty*, pp. 149–50.
198. E. Fromm, 'Prophets and Priests' (1967), in Fromm, *On Disobedience*, pp. 41–57, on p. 43.
199. Fromm, *The Revolution of Hope*, p. 79. On Fromm's late views on the 'New Man' and the 'New Society', see Fromm, *To Have or To Be?*, pp. 133–202.
200. Ibid., p. 115. Fromm refers here to 'shared enjoyment' as 'one of the deepest forms of human happiness'.
201. For an insightful (and influential) account of reciprocal altruism from an evolutionary perspective, see Trivers, 'Reciprocal Altruism', pp. 35–55.
202. Fromm, *Man for Himself*, p. 101.
203. For a defence of utopianism in political thought, see Goodwin and Taylor, *The Politics of Utopia*.
204. Fromm, *To Have or To Be?*, p. 201.

Conclusion

1. D. C. Dennett, *Darwin's Dangerous Idea* (New York: Simon & Schuster, 1995), p. 75.
2. S. E. Taylor, *Positive Illusions: Creative Self-Deception and the Healthy Mind* (New York: Basic Books, 1989); Taylor and Brown, 'Illusion and Well-Being'; Taylor and Brown, 'Positive Illusions'; Taylor and Armor, 'Positive Illusions'.
3. Taylor and Brown, 'Illusion and Well-Being', p. 204.
4. In addition to Taylor and Brown, there have been other social psychologists whose studies have corroborated the theory of 'depressive realism'. For an overview, see S. Fisher and R. P. Greenberg, *Freud Scientifically Reappraised* (New York: John Wiley & Sons, 1996), pp. 58–60.
5. Taylor and Brown, 'Positive Illusions', p. 25. Cf. Taylor and Armor, 'Positive Illusions', p. 888.
6. Trivers, 'Self-Deception in Service of Deceit', p. 290.
7. Pinker, *The Blank Slate*, p. 265.
8. Trivers, 'Self-Deception in Service of Deceit', p. 271.
9. North Americans 'are able to think they are more competent than they really are without encountering many negative consequences for holding these positive illusions', S. J. Heine, D. R. Lehman, H. R. Markus and S. Kitayama, 'Is There a Universal Need for Self-Regard?' *Psychological Review*, 106:4 (1999), pp. 766–94, on p. 773.
10. Ibid.
11. Kivivuori, *Paha Tieto*.

12. For a conceptual analysis of ideology, see M. Freeden, *Ideologies and Political Theory: A Conceptual Approach* (Oxford: Clarendon Press, 1996).
13. S. Milgram, *Obedience to Authority* (New York: HarperPerennial, 1975), p. 145.
14. K. Mannheim, *Ideology and Utopia: An Introduction to the Sociology of Knowledge* (1936; London: Routledge & Kegan Paul, 1960), pp. 84–7.
15. H. Arendt, *The Origins of Totalitarianism* (1951; Cleveland, OH: Meridian Books, 1964), pp. 470–1.
16. Gellner, *The Psychoanalytic Movement*, p. xiii.
17. M. H. Stein, 'Panel on "Aggression" (opening remarks)', *International Journal of Psychoanalysis*, 53 (1972), p. 13.
18. E. Voegelin, *Autobiographical Reflections*, ed. E. Sandoz (Baton Rouge, LA: Louisiana State University Press, 1989), p. 18.
19. R. Musil, 'On Stupidity' (1937), in *Precision and Soul: Essays and Addresses*, ed. and trans. B. Pike and D. S. Luft (Chicago, IL: Chicago University Press, 1990), pp. 268–86, on pp. 283–4.
20. D. S. Luft, *Robert Musil and the Crisis of European Culture, 1880–1942* (Berkeley, CA: University of California Press, 1980), p. 283.
21. R. Musil, *Tagebücher*, ed. A. Frisé (Reinbek bei Hamburg: Rowohlt, 1976), pp. 787, 896, 967–8.
22. E. Voegelin, *Hitler and the Germans*, ed. and trans. D. Clemens and B. Purcell (Columbia, MO: University of Missouri Press, 1999), pp. 249, 252.
23. Ibid., pp. 241–2.
24. Fromm, *To Have or To Be?*, p. 128.
25. Ibid., p. 129.
26. Mannheim, *Ideology and Utopia*, p. 236.
27. Quoted in Sargent, 'The Three Faces of Utopianism', p. 1.

WORKS CITED

Archival Sources

Sigmund Freud Collection, Library of Congress Manuscript Division, Washington, DC, United States.

The Erich Fromm Archives, c/o Rainer Funk, Ursrainer Ring 24, D-72076 Tübingen, Germany.

C. G. Jung Biographical Archive, Francis A. Countway Library of Medicine, Harvard Medical School, Boston, MA, United States.

Trotsky Archive, Houghton Library, Harvard University, Cambridge, MA, United States.

Original works by Gross, Jung, Reich and Fromm:

Otto Gross

Several of Gross's writings have been published on the website of the International Otto Gross Society. See http://www.ottogross.org/english/works/works.html

'Affective Rejection' (1902), in *Collected Works*, pp. 93–101. Originally published as 'Die Affektlage der Ablehnung', *Monatsschrift für Psychiatrie und Neurologie*, 12 (1902), pp. 359–70.

'The Cerebral Second Function', in *Collected Works*, pp. 73–92. Originally published as *Die cerebrale Sekundärfunction* (Leipzig: Verlag von F. C. W. Vogel, 1902).

Collected Works 1901–1907: The Graz Years, ed. and trans. L. Madison (Hamilton, NY: Mindpiece, 2000).

'Disintegration of Consciousness', in *Collected Works*, pp. 107–11. Originally published as 'Über Vorstellungszerfall', *Monatsschrift für Psychiatrie*, 11 (1902), pp. 205–12.

Drei Aufsätze über den inneren Konflikt (Bonn: A. Marcus & E. Webers Verlag, 1920).

'Elterngewalt' (1908), in *Von geschlechtlicher Not*, pp. 9–13.

'Freud's Idiogenetic Element and its Significance in Kraepelin's Manic-Depressiviness', in *Collected Works*, pp. 162–92. Originally published as *Das Freud'sche Ideogenitätsmoment und seine Bedeutung im manisch-depressiven Irresein Kraepelins* (Leipzig: Vogel, 1907).

'Die kommunistische Grundidee in der Paradiessymbolik' (1919), in *Von geschlechtlicher Not*, pp. 41–54.

'Ludwig Rubiner's "Psychoanalyse"', *Die Aktion*, 3:20 (1913), pp. 506–7.

'Offener Brief an Maximilian Harden' (1914), *Von geschlechtlicher Not zur sozialen Katastrophe*, pp. 24–6.

'On the Biology of Language Apparatus', in *Collected Works*, pp. 139–61. Originally published as 'Zur Biologie des Sprachapparatus', *Allgemeine Zeitschrift für Psychiatrie und psychisch-gerichtliche Medizin*, 61 (1904), pp. 795–835.

'On the Phylogenetic Origin of Ethics', in *Collected Works*, pp. 65–7. Originally published as 'Zur Phyllogenese der Ethik', *Archiv für Kriminal-Anthropologie und Kriminalistik*, 9 (1902), pp. 101–3.

'On the Question of Socially Repressive Images', in *Collected Works*, pp. 59–64. Originally published as 'Zur Frage der socialen Hemmungsvorstellungen', *Archiv für Kriminal-Anthropologie und Kriminalistik*, 7 (1901), pp. 123–31.

'Orienterung der Geistigen' (1919), in *Von geschlechtlicher Not*, pp. 32–5.

'Protest and Morality in the Unconscious' (1919), *New German Critique*, 10 (1977), pp. 105–9. Also included as 'Protest und Moral im Unbewussten', in *Von geschlechtlicher Not zur sozialen Katastrophe*, pp. 55–60.

'Themen der revolutionären Psychologie', in von Olenhusen and Heuer (eds), *Die Gesetze des Vaters*, pp. 421–3.

'Über Bewusstseinszerfall', *Monatsschrift für Psychiatrie und Neurologie*, 15 (1904), pp. 45–51.

'Über Destruktionssymbolik', *Zentralblatt für Psychoanalyse und Psychotherapie*, 4 (1914), pp. 524–34.

'Über Einsamkeit', in *Drei Aufsätze über den inneren Konflikt*, pp. 21–5.

'Über Konflikt und Beziehung', in *Drei Aufsätze über den inneren Konflikte*, pp. 3–20.

Über psychopathische Minderwertigkeiten (Wien: Wilhelm Braumüller, 1909).

'Vom Konflikt des Eigenen und Fremden' (1916), in *Von geschlechtlicher Not*, pp. 27–31.

Von geschlechtlicher Not zur sozialen Katastrophe, ed. K. Kreiler (Frankfurt am Main: Robinson Verlag, 1980).

'Zum Problem: Parlamentarismus' (1919), in *Von geschlechtlicher Not*, pp. 60–3.

'Zum Solidaritätsproblem im Klassenkampf', in von Olenhusen and Heuer (eds), *Die Gesetze des Vaters*, pp. 415–21.

'Zur Differentialdiagnostik negativistischer Phänomene', *Psychiatrisch-Neurologische Wochenschrift*, 37 (1904), pp. 345–53, and 38 (1904), pp. 357–63.

'Zur funktionellen Geistesbildung des Revolutionärs' (1919), in *Von geschlechtlicher Not*, pp. 64–70.

'Zur neuerlichen Vorarbeit: vom Unterricht' (1919), in *Von geschlechtlicher Not*, pp. 35–41.

'Zur Nomenklatur "Dementia sejunctiva"', *Neurologisches Centralblatt*, 23:24 (1904), pp. 1144–6.

'Zur Überwindung der kulturellen Krise' (1913), in *Von geschlechtlicher Not*, pp. 13–16.

Turner, J., with C. Rumpf-Worthen and R. Jenkins (eds and trans.), 'The Otto Gross – Frieda Weekley Correspondence', *D.H. Lawrence Review*, 22:2 (1990), pp. 137–227.

Whimster, S., with G. Heuer, 'Otto Gross and Else Jaffé and Max Weber', *Theory, Culture and Society*, 15:3–4 (1998), pp. 129–60 [containing Gross's correspondence with Else Jaffé].

Carl G. Jung

Aion (1951), in *Collected Works*, vol. 9/ii.

Analytical Psychology: Notes of the Seminar Given in 1925 by C. G. Jung, ed. W. McGuire (London: Routledge, 1989).

'Brother Klaus' (1933), in *Collected Works*, vol. 11, pp. 316–23.

'Child Development and Education' (1928), in *Collected Works*, vol. 17, pp. 47–62.

'Circular Letter' (1934), in *Collected Works*, vol. 10, pp. 545–6.

Collected Papers on Analytical Psychology, ed. and trans. C. E. Long (London: Baillière, Tindall and Cox, 1917).

The Collected Works of C. G. Jung, trans. R. F. C. Hull (except vol. 2), 18 vols (London: Routledge & Kegan Paul, 1953–81).

Dream Analysis: Notes of the Seminar Given in 1928–1930 by C. G. Jung, ed. W. McGuire (London: Routledge & Kegan Paul, 1984).

Experimental Researches, *Collected Works*, vol. 2.

'The Fight with the Shadow' (1946), in *Collected Works*, vol. 10, pp. 218–26.

The Freud/Jung Letters: The Correspondence between Sigmund Freud and C. G. Jung, ed. W. McGuire, trans. R. Manheim and R. F. C. Hull (Princeton, NJ: Princeton University Press, 1974).

'Instinct and the Unconscious' (1919), in *Collected Works*, vol. 8, pp. 129–38.

C. G. Jung Speaking: Interviews and Encounters, ed. R. F. C. Hull and W. McGuire (Princeton, NJ: Princeton University Press, 1977).

Letters, ed. G. Adler, with A. Jaffé, trans. R. F. C. Hull, 2 vols (London: Routledge & Kegan Paul, 1973).

Memories, Dreams, Reflections, recorded and ed. A. Jaffé, trans. R. and C. Winston (1963; London: Fontana Paperbacks, 1983).

Nietzsche's Zarathustra: Notes of the Seminar Given in 1934–1939 by C. G. Jung, ed. J .L. Jarrett, 2 vols (Princeton, NJ: Princeton University Press, 1988).

'On Psychic Energy' (1928), in *Collected Works*, vol. 8, pp. 3–66.

On the Psychology and Pathology of So-Called Occult Phenomena (1902), in *Collected Works*, vol. 1, pp. 3–88.

'On the Psychology of the Unconscious' (1917/43), in *Collected Works*, vol. 7, pp. 3–119.

'Picasso' (1932), in *Collected Works*, vol. 15, pp. 135–41.

Psychological Types (1921), in *Collected Works*, vol. 6.

The Psychology of Dementia Praecox (1907), in *Collected Works*, vol. 3, pp. 1–151.

'The Psychology of the Transference' (1946), in *Collected Works*, vol. 16, pp. 163–323.

Psychology of the Unconscious: A Study of the Transformations and Symbolisms of the Libido (1916; New York: Dodd, Mead and Company, 1925).

'Psychology of the Unconscious Processes' (1916), in *Collected Papers on Analytical Psychology*, pp. 354–444.

'Return to Simple Life' (1941), in *Collected Works*, vol. 18, pp. 582–8.

'The Significance of the Father in the Destiny of the Individual' (1909), in *Collected Papers on Analytical Psychology*, pp. 156–75.

'The Significance of the Father in the Destiny of the Individual' (1949), in *Collected Works*, vol. 4, pp. 301–23.

'The Structure of the Unconscious' (1916), in *Collected Works*, vol. 7, pp. 269–304.

'The Swiss Line in the European Spectrum' (1928), in *Collected Works*, vol. 10, pp. 479–88.

Synchronicity: An Acausal Connecting Principle (1952), in *Collected Works*, vol. 8, pp. 417–519.

'The Transcendent Function' ([1916]/1957), in *Collected Works*, vol. 8, pp. 67–91.

The Undiscovered Self (1957), in *Collected Works*, vol. 10, pp. 245–305.

Visions: Notes of the Seminar Given in 1930–1934 by C. G. Jung, ed. C. Douglas (London: Routledge, 1998).

'Wotan' (1936), in *Collected Works*, vol. 10, pp. 179–93.

Wilhelm Reich

American Odyssey: Letters and Journals 1940–1947, ed. M. B. Higgins (New York: Farrar, Straus and Giroux, 1999).

The Bioelectrical Investigation of Sexuality and Anxiety (1934–7), ed. M. Higgins and C. M. Raphael, trans. M. Faber with D. and I. Jordan (New York: Farrar, Straus and Giroux, 1982).

The Bion Experiments on the Origin of Life (1938; New York: Octagon Books, 1979).

Cancer Biopathy, Vol. 2 of The Discovery of the Orgone (1948), trans. A. White with M. Higgins and C. M. Raphael (New York: Farrar, Straus and Giroux, 1973).

Character Analysis (1933), trans. V. R. Carfagno (London: Vision Press, 1973).

Children of the Future, ed. M. Higgins and C. M. Raphael, trans. D. and I. Jordan and B. Placzek (New York: Farrar, Straus and Giroux, 1984).

Contact with Space, ORANUR Second Report: OROP Desert Ea 1954–55 (New York: Core Pilot Press, 1957).

Cosmic Superimposition, in *Ether, God and Devil* (1949) / *Cosmic Superimposition* (1951) (New York: Farrar, Straus and Giroux, 1973).

'The Developmental History of Orgonomic Functionalism', *Orgonomic Functionalism: A Journal Devoted to the Work of Wilhelm Reich*, 1 (1990), pp. 1–29.

Dialectical Materialism and Psychoanalysis (1929; London: Socialist Reproduction, 1972).

Early Writings, trans. P. Schmitz (New York: Farrar, Straus and Giroux, 1975).

Der Einbruch der sexuellen Zwangsmoral (1932; Köln: Kiepenheuer & Witsch, 1972).

Ether, God and Devil (1949) / *Cosmic Superimposition* (1951) (New York: Farrar, Straus and Giroux, 1973).

Function of the Orgasm: Sex-Economic Problems of Biological Energy (1942), trans. V. R. Carfagno (London: Souvenir Press, 1973).

Jenseits der Psychologie: Briefe und Tagebücher 1934–1939, ed. M. B. Higgins (Köln: Kiepenheuer & Witsch, 1997).

Listen, Little Man! (1948; Harmondsworth: Penguin Books, 1975).

Mass Psychology of Fascism (1933), trans. V. R. Carfagno (London: Souvenir Press, 1972).

Menschen im Staat (Frankfurt am Main: Stroemfeld, 1995).

The Murder of Christ: Vol. 1 of The Emotional Plague of Mankind (1953; New York: The Noonday Press/ Farrar, Straus and Giroux, 1974).

'New Goals on the Horizon', *Orgone Energy Bulletin*, 3:2 (1951), p. 116.

'The Oranur Experiment' (1951), in *Selected Writings*, pp. 357–434.

Passion of Youth: An Autobiography, 1897–1922, ed. M. B. Higgins and C. M. Raphael, trans. P. Schmitz and J. Tompkins (New York: Farrar, Straus and Giroux, 1988).

Reich Speaks of Freud, ed. M. Higgins and C. M. Raphael, trans. T. Pol (New York: Farrar, Straus and Giroux, 1974).

Selected Sex-Pol Writings: 1934-37: Articles from the 'Zeitschrift für Politische Psychologie und Sexualökonomie' (London: Socialist Reproduction, 1973).

Selected Writings: An Introduction to Orgonomy (London: Vision Press, 1973).

Die sexuelle Revolution: Zur charakterlichen Selbststeuerung des Menschen (1936; Frankfurt am Main: Europäische Verlagsanstalt, 1971) [originally titled *Die Sexualität im Kulturkampf*].

What is Class Consciousness? (1934; London: Socialist Reproduction, 1973) [originally published as a series of articles under the pseudonym Ernst Parell].

Reich, W., and A. S. Neill, *Record of a Friendship: The Correspondence between Wilhelm Reich and A. S. Neill 1936–1957*, ed. B. R. Placzek (London: Victor Gollanz, 1982).

Erich Fromm

The Anatomy of Human Destructiveness (1973; Harmondsworth: Penguin Books, 1987).

'The Application of Humanist Psychoanalysis to Marx's Theory' (1965), in *Socialist Humanism*, pp. 228–45.

The Art of Listening (New York: Continuum, 1994).

The Art of Loving (1956; London: George Allen & Unwin, 1975).

Beyond the Chains of Illusion (1962; London: Abacus, 1980).

The Crisis of Psychoanalysis (New York: Holt, Rinehart, and Winston, 1970).

The Dogma of Christ and Other Essays on Religion, Psychology and Culture (New York: Holt, Rinehart, and Winston, 1963).

Escape from Freedom (1941; New York: Holt, Rinehart and Winston, 1961).

Ethik und Politik: Antworten auf aktuelle politische Fragen, ed. R.Funk (Weinhem and Basel: Beltz, 1990).

'Foreword', in H. Brandt, *The Search For a Third Way* (New York: Doubleday & Co., 1970), pp. xi–xvii.

Gesamtausgabe, 12 vols, ed. R. Funk (Stuttgart: Deutsche Verlags-Anstalt, 1999).

Die Gesellschaft als Gegenstand der Psychoanalyse, ed. R. Funk (Frankfurt am Main: Suhrkamp, 1993).

Gesellschaft und Seele: Beiträge zur Sozialpsychologie und zur psychoanalytischen Praxis, ed. R. Funk (Weinheim and Basel: Beltz Verlag, 1992).

Greatness and Limitations of Freud's Thought (London: Abacus, 1982).

The Heart of Man (1964; New York: Harper & Row, 1968).

Humanismus als reale Utopie, ed. R. Funk (Weinheim and Basel: Beltz Verlag, 1992).

'Introduction' (1965), in *Socialist Humanism*, pp. vii–xii.

'Das Jüdische Gesetz' (1922), in *Gesamtausgabe*, vol. 11, pp. 19–126.

'Let Man Prevail' (1960), in *On Disobedience*, pp. 58–74.

Love, Sexuality, and Matriarchy: About Gender, ed. R. Funk (New York: Fromm International Publishing Corporation, 1997).

Man for Himself: An Inquiry into the Psychology of Ethics (1947; London: Routledge & Kegan Paul, 1967).

Marx's Concept of Man (1961; New York: Frederick Ungar Publishing, 1983).

'Marx's Contribution to the Knowledge of Man' (1968), in *The Crisis of Psychoanalysis*, pp. 46–58.

May Man Prevail? An Inquiry into the Facts and Fictions of Foreign Policy (New York: Doubleday & Co., 1961).

'Medicine and the Ethical Problem of Modern Man' (1957), in *The Dogma of Christ*, pp. 169–90.

'Meister Eckhart und Karl Marx: Die reale Utopie der Orientierung am Sein' (1974), in *Gesamtausgabe*, vol. 12, pp. 485–526.

'Nachwort zu George Orwell "1984"' (1961), in *Gesamtausgabe*, vol. 5, pp. 285–93.

On Disobedience and Other Essays (New York: Seabury Press, 1981).

Die Pathologie der Normalität: Zur Wissenschaft vom Menschen, ed. R. Funk (Weinheim and Basel: Beltz Verlag, 1991).

'The Present Human Condition' (1955–), in *The Dogma of Christ*, pp. 95–106.

'Prophets and Priests' (1967), in *On Disobedience*, pp. 41–57.

'Psychoanalysis – Science or Party Line?' (1958), in *The Dogma of Christ*, pp. 131–46.

'The Psychological Aspects of the Guaranteed Income' (1966), in *On Disobedience*, pp. 91–101.

'Reminiscences of Shlomo Barukh Rabinkow', in L. Jung (ed.), *Sages and Saints* (Hoboken: Ktav Publishing House, 1987), pp. 99–105.

The Revision of Psychoanalysis, ed. R. Funk (Boulder, CO: Westview Press, 1992).

The Revolution of Hope (New York: Harper & Row, 1968).

'The Revolutionary Character' (1963), in *The Dogma of Christ*, pp. 147–68.

The Sane Society (1955; New York: Holt, Rinehart and Winston, 1969).

Sigmund Freud's Mission: An Analysis of his Personality and Influence (New York: Harper, 1959).

'The Significance of the Theory of Mother Right for Today' (1970), in *The Crisis of Psychoanalysis*, pp. 79–83.

(ed.), *Socialist Humanism: An International Symposium* (New York: Anchor Books, 1966).

'The Theory of Mother Right and its Relevance for Social Psychology' (1934), in *The Crisis of Psychoanalysis*, pp. 84–109.

To Have or To Be? (1976; London: Cape, 1979).

'Values, Psychology, and Human Existence' (1959), in *On Disobedience*, pp. 1–15.

'Vorwort zu Edward Bellamy "Looking Backward"' (1960), in *Gesamtausgabe*, vol. 5, pp. 273–84.

The Working Class in Weimar Germany: A Psychological and Sociological Study, ed. W. Bonss, trans. B. Weinberger (London: Berg Publishers, 1984).

You Shall Be as Gods (New York: Holt, Rinehart and Winston, 1966).

Suzuki, D. T., and E. Fromm, *Zen Buddhism and Psychoanalysis* (New York: Harper & Row, 1960).

Primary Sources

Adorno, T., et al., *The Authoritarian Personality* (New York: Harper & Row, 1950).

Alexander, F., and S. T. Selesnick, 'Freud-Bleuler Correspondence', *Archives of General Psychiatry*, 12 (1965), pp. 1–9.

Arendt, H., *The Origins of Totalitarianism* (1951; Cleveland, OH: Meridian Books, 1964).

Bachofen, J. J., *Myth, Religion, and Mother Right: Selected Writings of J. J. Bachofen*, trans. R. Manheim (Princeton, NJ: Princeton University Press, 1967).

Berlin, I., *Karl Marx: His Life and Environment* (London: T. Butterworth, 1939).

—, *Four Essays on Liberty* (Oxford: Oxford University Press, 1969).

Bleuler, E., *Die Psychoide als Prinzip der organischen Entwicklung* (Berlin: J. Springer, 1925).

Brod, M., *Das grosse Wagnis* (Leipzig: Kurt Wolff, 1918).

Carol, H., 'Man and His Environment' (1950), in *C. G. Jung Speaking*, pp. 201–4.

Cassirer, E., *The Myth of the State* (New Haven, CT: Yale University Press, 1946).

Collingwood, R. G., *An Autobiography* (1939; Oxford: Clarendon Press, 2002).

—, *The Idea of History*, rev. edn, intro. J. van der Dussen (Oxford: Oxford University Press, 1994).

—, *An Essay on Metaphysics*, rev. edn, ed. R. Martin (Oxford: Oxford University Press, 1998).

Driesch, H., *The Science and Philosophy of the Organism* (London: A. and C. Black, 1908).

—, *The History and Theory of Vitalism* (London: Macmillan, 1914).

Eliade, M., *The Myth of the Eternal Return* (1949), trans. W. R. Trask (Princeton, NJ: Princeton University Press, 1971).

Engels, F., *The Origin of the Family, Private Property, and the State* (1884; Moscow: Progress Publishers, 1968).

Evans, R. I., *Dialogue with Erich Fromm* (1966; New York: Praeger, 1981).

Fenichel, O., *119 Rundbriefe* (1934–45), ed. E. Mühlleitner and J. Reichmayr, 2 vols (Frankfurt am Main: Stroemfeld-Verlag, 1998).

Freud, S., *Totem and Taboo* (1912–13), trans. J. Strachey, in *The Standard Edition of the Complete Psychological Works of Sigmund Freud*, Vol. 13 (London: Hogarth Press, 1981), pp. 1–162.

—, *The Future of an Illusion* (1927), trans. J. Strachey, in *Civilization, Society and Religion*.

—, *Civilization and its Discontents* (1930), trans. J. Strachey, in *Civilization, Society and Religion*.

—, *Civilization, Society and Religion*, The Penguin Freud Library, Vol. 12 (London: Penguin Books, 1991).

Freud, S., and K. Abraham, *The Complete Correspondence of S. Freud and K. Abraham, 1907–1925*, ed. E. Falzeder, trans. C. Schwarzacher (London: Karnac, 2002).

Freud, S., and L. Andreas-Salomé, *Letters*, ed. E. Pfeifer (New York: W. W. Norton, 1985).

Freud, S., and E. Jones, *The Complete Correspondence of Sigmund Freud and Ernest Jones 1908–1939*, ed. R. A. Paskauskas (Cambridge, MA: Belknap Press of Harvard University Press, 1993).

Freud, S., and C. G. Jung, *The Freud/Jung Letters: The Correspondence between Sigmund Freud and C. G. Jung*, ed. W. McGuire, trans. R. Manheim and R. F. C. Hull. Princeton, Princeton University Press, 1974).

Gerster, G., 'Jung and the Christmas Tree' (1957), in *C. G. Jung Speaking*, pp. 353–8.

Gross, H., 'Degeneration und Deportation', *Politische-Anthropologische Revue*, 6:5 (1905), also published in H. Gross, *Gesammelte Kriminalistische Aufsätze*, 2 vols (Leipzig: Vogel, 1902–8), vol. 2, pp. 70–7.

Hauschka, T. 'The Cancer Biopathy of Wilhelm Reich', MS (1949–50), The Wilhelm Reich Microfiche Collection, Reel 5, No. 228E, Helsinki University Library.

Hegel, G. W. F., *Reason in History: A General Introduction to the Philosophy of History*, trans. R. S. Hartman (Indianapolis, IN: Bobbs-Merrill, 1953).

Jung, F., 'Von geschlechtlicher Not zur sozialen Katastrophe (Introduction)', in Michaels, *Anarchy and Eros*, pp. 183–219.

Koestler, A., in R. Crossman (ed.), *The God that Failed* (New York: Harper & Brothers, 1949), pp. 15–75.

Kropotkin, P., *Mutual Aid: A Factor of Evolution* (1902; Mineola, NY: Dover Publications, 2006).

Lindner, T., 'Review of C. G. Jung, *Seelenprobleme der Gegenwart*', *Nordisk Medicinsk Tidskrift*, 5 (1933), pp. 1013–14.

Malinowski, B., *The Sexual Life of Savages in North-Western Melanesia* (London: Routledge, 1932).

Marx, K., *Capital, Vol. 1* (1867; London: Lawrence and Wishart, 1983).

Maslow, A. H., *The Farther Reaches of Human Nature* (Harmondsworth: Penguin Books, 1973).

More, T., *Utopia* (1516), trans. P. Turner (London: Penguin Books, 1965).

Musil, R., 'On Stupidity' (1937), in *Precision and Soul: Essays and Addresses*, ed. and trans. B. Pike and D. S. Luft (Chicago, IL: Chicago University Press, 1990), pp. 268–86.

—, *Tagebücher*, ed. A. Frisé (Reinbek bei Hamburg: Rowohlt, 1976).

Neill, A. N., *Summerhill: A Radical Approach to Child Rearing* (New York: Hart, 1960).

Nietzsche, F., *The Birth of Tragedy* (1872; Garden City, NY: Doubleday Anchor Books, 1956).

Nordenstreng, K., 'Kompleksien profeetta' ('The Prophet of Complexes'), *Suomen Kuvalehti*, 25 (24 June 1961), pp. 26–7.

Ollendorff Reich, I., *Wilhelm Reich: A Personal Biography* (New York: St Martin's Press, 1969).

Orwell, G., *Nineteen Eighty-Four* (1949; Harmondsworth: Penguin Books, 1983).

Otto, R., *The Idea of the Holy* (1917), trans. J. W. Harvey (Oxford: Oxford University Press, 1990).

Popper, K., *Conjectures and Refutations* (London: Routledge & Kegan Paul, 1963).

Rank, O., 'Bericht über die I. Private Psychoanalytische Vereinigung in Salzburg am 27. April 1908', *Zentralblatt für Psychoanalyse*, 1:1 (1911–12), pp. 125–9.

Reich, P., *Book of Dreams* (New York: Harper & Row, 1973).

Semon, R., *Mnemic Psychology* (1904; New York: Macmillan, 1923).

Skinner, B. F., *Beyond Freedom and Dignity* (Toronto, Bantam Books, 1972).

Skinner, Q., *Visions of Politics*, 3 vols (Cambridge: Cambridge University Press, 2002).

Stärcke, A., 'Geisteskrankheit und Gesellschaft', in A. J. Storfer (ed.), *Almanach für das Jahr 1926* (Wien: Internationaler Psychoanalytischer Verlag, 1926), pp. 93–112.

Stekel, W., *The Autobiography of Wilhelm Stekel: The Life Story of a Pioneer Psychoanalyst*, ed. E. A. Gutheil (New York: Liveright, 1950).

Trotsky, L., *The Struggle Against Fascism in Germany* (New York: Pathfinder Press, 1971).

—, *Problems of Everyday Life and Other Writings on Culture and Science* (New York: Monad Press, 1973).

Voegelin, E., *Autobiographical Reflections*, ed. E. Sandoz (Baton Rouge, LA: Louisiana State University Press, 1989).

—, *Hitler and the Germans*, ed. and trans. D. Clemens and B. Purcell (Columbia, MO: University of Missouri Press, 1999).

Voloshinov, V. N., *Freudianism: A Marxist Critique* (1927), ed. N. H. Bruss, trans. I. R. Titunik (New York: Academic Press, 1976).

Westermarck, E., *The History of Human Marriage* (London: Macmillan, 1891).

—, *A Short History of Marriage* (London: Macmillan, 1926).

—, *Three Essays on Sex and Marriage* (London: Macmillan, 1934).

—, *The Future of Marriage in Western Civilisation* (London: Macmillan, 1936).

Wittgenstein, L., *Philosophical Investigations*, trans. G. E. M. Anscombe (Oxford: Blackwell, 1953).

Secondary Sources

Akeret, R. U., *Tales from a Traveling Couch* (New York: W. W. Norton & Co., 1996).

Allen, R. F., *Literary Life in German Expressionism and the Berlin Circles* (Ann Arbor, MI: UMI Research Press, 1983).

Anderson, K., 'Erich Fromm and the Frankfurt School Critique of Criminal Justice', in Anderson and Quinney (eds), *Erich Fromm and Critical Criminology*, pp. 83–119.

Anderson, K., and R. Quinney (eds), *Erich Fromm and Critical Criminology* (Urbana and Chicago, IL: University of Illinois Press, 2000).

Anthony, M., *The Valkyries: The Women Around Jung* (Longmead: Element Books, 1990).

Ash, M. G., *Gestalt Psychology in German Culture, 1890–1967: Holism and the Quest for Objectivity* (Cambridge: Cambridge University Press, 1995).

Bair, D., *Jung: A Biography* (Boston, MA: Little, Brown and Company, 2003).

Balaban, A., *Mourning a Father Lost: A Kibbutz Childhood Remembered*, trans. Y. Lotan (Lanham, MD: Rowman & Littlefield, 2004).

Barclay, M., 'Utopia and Psychological Theory', *Theory and Psychology*, 3:2 (1993), pp. 173–90.

Beckner, M. O., 'Vitalism', in P. Edwards (ed.), *The Encyclopedia of Philosophy*, 8 vols (New York: Macmillan Company & Free Press, 1967), vol. 8, pp. 253–6.

Bennet, E. A., *What Jung Really Said* (London: Mcdonald & Co, 1966).

van den Berg, H., *Avantgarde und Anarchismus: Dada in Zürich und Berlin* (Heidelberg: Universitätsverlag C. Winter, 1999).

Bergmann, A., 'Sexualhygiene, Rassenhygiene und der rationalisierte Tod. Wilhelm Reichs "sexuelle Massenhygiene" und seine Vision einer "freien" Sexualität', in Fallend and Nitzschke (eds), *Der 'Fall' Wilhelm Reich*, pp. 270–96.

Berman, E., 'Psychoanalysis, Rescue and Utopia', *Utopian Studies*, 4:2 (1993), pp. 44–56.

—, 'The Utopian Fantasy of a New Person and the Danger of a False Analytic Self', *Psychoanalytic Psychology*, 17 (2000), pp. 38–60.

Bernstein, F., 'Visions of Sexual Health and Illness in Revolutionary Russia', in R. Davidson and L. A. Hall (eds), *Sex, Sin and Suffering: Venereal Disease and European Society since 1870* (London: Routledge, 2001), pp. 93–117.

Bertschinger-Joos, E., 'Frieda Gross – Briefe aus Graz 1882–1906', in von Olenhusen and Heuer (eds), *Die Gesetze des Vaters*, pp. 310–19.

Berze, J., and D. K. Stelzer, 'Befund und Gutachten über den Geisteszustand des am 15. Dezember 1913 über Auftrag des k.k. Bezirkgerichtes Tulln untersuchten Dr. Otto Gross', ed. A. Hansen, *Gegner*, 3 (1999/2000), pp. 24–36.

Betz, B., 'An Analysis of the Prophetic Character of the Dialectical Rhetoric of Erich Fromm' (unpublished PhD thesis, Northwestern University, 1974).

Bishop, P., *The Dionysian Self: C. G. Jung's Reception of Friedrich Nietzsche* (Berlin: Walter de Gruyter, 1995).

— (ed.), *Jung in Contexts* (London: Routledge, 1999).

—, *Synchronicity and Intellectual Intuition in Kant, Swedenborg, and Jung* (Lewiston, ME: Edwin Mellen Press, 2000).

Blank, H. R., 'Review of Erich Fromm, *The Sane Society*', *Psychoanalytic Quarterly*, 25 (1956), pp. 270–2.

Boadella, D., *Wilhelm Reich: The Evolution of his Work* (1973; London: Arena, 1985).

Bochsler, R., 'Der Überfall auf die Zürcher Polizeikaserne 1907, Oder: Welche Rolle spielte Hans Gross im Anarchistenprozess 1912?', in Dehmlow and Heuer (eds), *Bohème, Psychoanalyse und Revolution*, pp. 105–24.

Bos, J. 'A Silent Antipode: The Making and Breaking of Psychoanalyst Wilhelm Stekel', *History of Psychology*, 6:4 (2003), pp. 331–61.

Bos, J., D. Park and P. Pietikainen, 'Strategic Self-Marginalization: The Case of Psychoanalysis', *Journal of the History of the Behavioral Sciences*, 41:3 (2005), pp. 207-24.

Bottomore, T., 'Fromm, Erich', in T. Bottomore (ed.), *A Dictionary of Marxist Thought* (Oxford: Blackwell, 1991, p. 213).

Breil, R. (ed.), *Naturphilosophie* (München: Verlag Karl Alber Freiburg, 2000).

Brinton, C., 'Utopia and Democracy', in Manuel (ed.), *Utopias*, pp. 50–68.

Bronner, S. E., 'Fromm in America', in Kessler and Funk (eds), *Erich Fromm und die Frankfurter Schule*, pp. 41–60.

—, *Of Critical Theory and its Theorists* (Oxford: Blackwell, 1994).

Brown, D. E., *Human Universals* (New York: McGraw-Gill, 1991).

Brumlik, M., 'Messianic Thinking in the Jewish Intelligentsia of the Twenties', in *Wissenschaft vom Menschen / Science of Man, Yearbook of the International Erich Fromm Society*, 2 (1991), pp. 20–32.

Buhle, M. J., P. Buhle and D. Georgakas (eds), *Encyclopedia of the American Left* (New York and Oxford: Oxford University Press, 1998).

Buhle, P., *Marxism in the United States* (London: Verso, 1987).

—, 'Peace Movements', in Buhle et al. (eds), *Encyclopedia of the American Left*, pp. 592–8.

Burckhardt, P., *Geschichte der Stadt Basel* (Basel: Helbing & Lichtenhahn, 1942).

Burnham, J., *Suicide of the West* (New York: John Day Co., 1965).

Burston, D., *The Legacy of Erich Fromm* (Cambridge, MA: Harvard University Press, 1991).

Caruteneto, A., *A Secret Symmetry: Sabina Spielrein between Jung and Freud*, trans. A. Pomerans, J. Shepley and K. Winston (London: Routledge & Kegan Paul, 1982).

Chasseguet-Smirgel, J., and B. Grunberger, *Freud or Reich? Psychoanalysis and Illusion*, trans. C. Pajaczkowska (New Haven, CT: Yale University Press, 1986).

Claeys, G. C., and L. T. Sargent (eds), *The Utopia Reader* (New York: New York University Press, 1999).

Cocks, G., *Psychotherapy in the Third Reich: The Göring Institute*, 2nd rev. edn (New Brunswick, NJ: Transaction Publishers, 1997).

Conger, J. P., *Jung and Reich: The Body as Shadow* (Berkeley, CA: North Atlantic Books, 1988).

Conti, C., *Abschied vom Bürgertum: Alternative Bewegungen in Deutschland von 1890 bis heute* (Reinbek bei Hamburg: Rowohlt, 1984).

Corrington, R. S., *Wilhelm Reich: Psychoanalyst and Radical Naturalist* (New York: Farrar, Straus and Giroux, 2003).

Cortina, M., and M. Maccoby (eds), *A Prophetic Analyst: Erich Fromm's Contribution to Psychoanalysis* (Northvale, NJ: Jason Aronson, 1996).

Coser, L. A., *Refugee Scholars in America* (New Haven, CT: Yale University Press, 1984).

Coute, D., *The Illusion: An Essay on Politics, Theatre and the Novel* (London: Deutsch, 1971).

Crowder, G., *Classical Anarchism: The Political Thought of Godwin, Proudhon, Bakunin, and Kropotkin* (Oxford: Clarendon Press, 1991).

Dahmer, H., *Libido und Gesellschaft: Studien über Freud und die Freudsche Linke* (Frankfurt: Suhrkamp, 1973).

Danto, E. A., *Freud's Free Clinics: Psychoanalysis and Social Justice, 1918–1938* (New York: Columbia University Press, 2005).

Danziger, K., *Constructing the Subject: Historical Origins of Psychologhical Research* (Cambridge: Cambridge University Press, 1990).

Degler, C. N., *In Search of Human Nature* (Oxford: Oxford University Press, 1991).

Dehmlow, R., and G. Heuer (eds), *1. Internationaler Otto Gross Kongress* (Marburg an der Lahn: LiteraturWissenschaft.de; Hannover: Laurentius, 2000).

— (eds), *Bohème, Psychoanalyse und Revolution: 3. Internationaler Otto Gross Kongress* (Marburg an der Lahn: Literatur Wissenschaft.de, 2003).

Dennett, D. C., *Darwin's Dangerous Idea* (New York: Simon & Schuster, 1995).

Deutscher, I., *The Prophet Armed: Trotsky 1879–1921* (1954; Oxford: Oxford University Press, 1987).

—, *The Prophet Unarmed: Trotsky 1921–1929* (1959; Oxford: Oxford University Press, 1987).

—, *The Prophet Outcast: Trotsky 1929–1940* (1963; Oxford: Oxford University Press, 1987).

Dixon, A., *Primate Sexuality* (Oxford: Oxford University Press, 1998).

Dolnick, E., *Madness on the Couch: Blaming the Victim in the Heyday of Psychoanalysis* (New York: Simon & Schuster, 1998).

Dowbiggin, I., *Inheriting Madness: Professionalization and Psychiatric Knowledge in Nineteenth-Century France* (Berkeley, CA: University of California Press, 1991).

Eilittä, L., *Approaches to Personal Identity in Kafka's Short Fiction* (Helsinki: Finnish Academy of Science and Letters, 1999).

Eklöf, M., *Läkarens ethos: Studier i den svenska läkarkårens identiteter, intressen och ideal 1890–1960* (Linköping: Linköpings Universitet, 2000).

Elboim-Dror, R., *Yesterday's Tomorrow*, 2 vols (Jerusalem: Yad Izhak Ben-Zvi, 1993) [in Hebrew].

—, *Clean Death in Tel Aviv* (Lincoln, NE: iUniverse, 2003).

Elias, N., *The Germans: Power Struggles and the Development of Habitus in the Nineteenth and Twentieth Centuries*, ed. M. Schroter (Cambridge: Polity Press, 1996).

Eller, C., *The Myth of Matriarchal Prehistory* (Boston, MA: Beacon Press, 2000).

Ellwood, R., *The Politics of Myth: A Study of C. G. Jung, Mircea Eliade, and Joseph Campbell* (Albany, NY: State University of New York Press, 1999).

Encyclopaedia Judaica, 16 vols (Jerusalem: Keter Publishing House, 1971–2).

Erös, F., 'Fromm's Theory and the Problems of "Real Existing" Socialism', *Wissenschaft vom Menschen / Science of Man: Yearbook of the International Erich Fromm Society*, 2 (1991), pp. 315–23.

Etkind, A., *Eros of the Impossible: The History of Psychoanalysis in Russia* (1993), trans. N. and M. Rubins (Boulder, CO: Westview Press, 1997).

—, 'There Are No Naked Thoughts: Psychoanalysis, Psychotherapy and Medical Psychology in Russia', in E. L. Grigorenko, P. Ruzgis and R. J. Sternberg (eds), *Psychology of Russia: Past, Present, Future* (Commack, NY: Nova Science, 1997), pp. 59–77.

—, 'The Fate of Psychoanalysis in the Soviet Utopia', unpublished presentation at the Conference on Psychological Utopias, Avesta, Sweden, 18 June 2000.

Eysenck, H. J., 'Utopia in Dreamland', review of E. Fromm, *The Anatomy of Human Destructiveness*, *The Spectator*, 26 October 1974.

Faivre, A., *Philosophie de la nature: physique sacrée et théosophie XVIIIe–XIXe siècle* (Paris: A. Michel, 1997).

Fallend, K., *Wilhelm Reich in Wien* (Wien: Geyer-Edition, 1988).

Fallend, K., and B. Nitzschke (eds), *Der 'Fall' Wilhelm Reich: Beiträge zum Verhältnis von Psychoanalyse und Politik* (Frankfurt am Main: Suhrkamp, 1997).

Federn, P., *Witnessing Psychoanalysis* (London: Karnac Books, 1990).

Fisher, D. J., *Cultural Theory and Psychoanalytic Tradition* (New Brunswick, NJ: Transaction Publishers, 1991).

Fisher, S., and R. P. Greenberg, *Freud Scientifically Reappraised* (New York: John Wiley & Sons, 1996).

Freeden, M., *Ideologies and Political Theory: A Conceptual Approach* (Oxford: Clarendon Press, 1996).

Friedman, M., *Martin Buber's Life and Work: The Later Years, 1945–1965* (New York: E. P. Dutton, 1983).

Frosh, S., *The Politics of Psychoanalysis* (Houndsmills: Macmillan, 1987).

Funk, R., *Erich Fromm: His Life and Ideas* (New York: Continuum, 2000).

—, 'Erich Fromm's Life and Work', in Anderson and Quinney (eds), *Erich Fromm and Critical Criminology*, pp. 3–18.

Furedi, F., *Therapy Culture: Cultivating Vulnerability in an Uncertain Age* (London: Routledge, 2003).

Furet, F., *The Passing of an Illusion: The Idea of Communism in the Twentieth Century*, trans. D. Furet (Chicago, IL: University of Chicago Press, 1999).

Gabriel, Y., *Freud and Society* (London: Routledge & Kegan Paul, 1983).

Gay, P., *Freud: A Life for our Time* (New York: Norton, 1988).

Gellner, E., *The Psychoanalytic Movement: The Cunning of Unreason* (1985; London: Fontana Press, 1993).

Gente, H.-P. (ed.), *Marxismus, Psychoanalyse, Sexpol*, 2 vols (Frankfurt am Main: Fischer Bücherei, 1970).

Geoghegan, V., *Utopianism and Marxism* (London: Methuen, 1987).

Geritz, A. J., *Thomas More: An Annotated Bibliography of Criticism, 1935–1997* (Westport, CT: Greenwood Press, 1998).

Gess, H., *Vom Faschismus zum Neuen Denken – C. G. Jungs Theorie im Wandeln der Zeit* (Luneburg: Zu Klampen, 1994).

Giddens, A., *Modernity and Self-Identity: Self and Society in the Late Modern Age* (Stanford, CA: Stanford University Press, 1991).

Glen, J. S., *Erich Fromm: A Protestant Critique* (Philadelphia, PA: Westminster Press, 1966).

Goffman, E., *The Representation of Self in Everyday Life* (New York: Doubleday, 1959).

—, *Stigma: Notes on the Management of Spoiled Identity* (1963; New York: Simon & Schuster, 1986).

Goldstein, K., 'Carl Wernicke', in W. Haymaker (ed.), *The Founders of Neurology* (Springfield, IL: Charles C. Thomas, 1953), pp. 406–9.

Goldstein, W., 'Messianism and Marxism: Walter Benjamin and Ernst Bloch's Dialectical Theories of Secularisation', *Critical Sociology*, 27 (2002), pp. 246–81.

Goodway, D. (ed.), *For Anarchism: History, Theory, and Practice* (London: Routledge, 1989).

Goodwin, B. (ed.), *The Philosophy of Utopia* (London: Frank Cass, 2001).

Goodwin, B., and K. Taylor, *The Politics of Utopia* (London: Hutchinson, 1982).

Gould, S. J., *Ontogeny and Phylogeny* (Cambridge, MA: Belknap Press of Harvard University Press, 1977).

—, *The Mismeasure of Man* (Norton: New York, 1981).

Graham, R., 'The Role of Contract in Anarchist Ideology', in D. Goodway (ed.), *For Anarchism: History, Theory, and Practice* (London: Routledge, 1989), pp. 150–75.

Gray, J., *Isaiah Berlin* (Princeton, NJ: Princeton University Press, 1996).

Green, M., *The von Richthofen Sisters: The Triumphant and the Tragic Modes of Love* (New York: Basic Books, 1974).

—, *Mountain of Truth: The Counterculture Begins – Ascona, 1900–1920* (Hanover, NH: University Press of New England, 1986).

—, *Otto Gross: Freudian Psychoanalyst, 1877–1920* (Lewiston, NY: Edwin Mellen Press, 1999).

—, 'The Recurrence of New Age Mythology', in Heuer (ed.), *2. Internationaler Otto Gross Kongress*, pp. 331–6.

Greenfield, J., *Wilhelm Reich versus the U.S.A.* (New York: Norton, 1974).

Griffin, R., *The Nature of Fascism* (London: Pinter Publishers, 1991).

Gross, M. L., *The Psychological Society* (New York: Random House, 1978).

Grossman, S., 'C. G. Jung and National Socialism', in Bishop (ed.), *Jung in Contexts*, pp. 92–121.

Grotjahn, M., *My Favorite Patient: The Memoirs of a Psychoanalyst* (Frankfurt am Main: Peter Lang, 1987).

Gruber, H., *Red Vienna: Experiment in Working-Class Culture 1919–1934* (Oxford: Oxford University Press, 1991).

Gunter, P. A. Y., 'Bergson and Jung', in Bishop (ed.), *Jung in Contexts*, pp. 265–82.

Hanegraaff, W., *New Age Religion and Western Culture* (Leiden: E. J. Brill, 1996).

Hannah, B., *Jung – His Life and Work: A Biographical Memoir* (New York: G. P. Putnam's Sons, 1976).

Hansen, A., 'Eine "Art von innerlich revolutionärer Vorarbeit": Koordinaten bei der Begegnung zwischen Franz Jung und Otto Gross', in Dehmlow and Heuer (eds), *1. Internationaler Otto Gross Kongress*, pp. 74–87.

Harrington, A., *Reenchanted Science: Holism in German Culture from Wilhelm II to Hitler* (Princeton, NJ: Princeton University Press, 1996).

Harris, B., and A. Brock, 'Freudian Psychopolitics: The Rivalry of Wilhelm Reich and Otto Fenichel', *Bulletin of the History of Medicine*, 66 (1992), pp. 578–612.

Haule, J. R., 'From Somnambulism to the Archetypes: The French Roots of Jung's Split with Freud', in Bishop (ed.), *Jung in Contexts*, pp. 242–64.

Heine, S. J., D. R. Lehman, H. R. Markus and S. Kitayama, 'Is There a Universal Need for Self-Regard?' *Psychological Review*, 106:4 (1999), pp. 766–94.

Hell, D., C. Scharfetter and A. Möller, *Eugen Bleuler, Leben und Werk* (Bern: Huber, 2001).

Heller [Geller], M., *Cogs in the Soviet Wheel: The Formation of Soviet Man*, trans. D. Floyd (London: Collins Harvill, 1988).

Heller [Geller], M., and A. Nekrich, *Utopia in Power: The History of the Soviet Union from 1917 to the Present* (New York: Summit Books, 1986).

Heuer, G., 'Jung's Twin Brother: Otto Gross and Carl Gustav Jung', *Journal of Analytical Psychology*, 46:4 (2001), pp. 655-88.

— (ed.), *2. Internationaler Otto Gross Kongress* (Marburg: LiteraturWissenschaft.de, 2002).

—, 'Die Wiederkehr des Verdrängten: Revolution und Konterrevolution in der Psychoanalyse', in Heuer (ed.), *2. Internationaler Otto Gross Kongress*, pp. 77–104.

—, '"Der Skorpion im Messkelch" und "der Teufel unter der Couch": Oskar Panizza und Otto Gross – eine Seelenverwandtschaft', in Dehmlow and Heuer (eds), *Bohème, Psychoanalyse und Revolution*, pp. 163–95.

—, '"Ganz Wien in die Luft sprengen? ... Das wäre ja wunderbar!" Otto Gross und der Anarchismus', in von Olenhusen and Heuer (eds), *Die Gesetze des Vaters*, pp. 223-39

—, 'The Influence of the Life and Ideas of Otto Gross on the Life and Ideas of C. G. Jung' (unpublished PhD thesis, University of Essex, 2004).

Hirte, C., et al., 'Anarchismus und Psychoanalyse zu Beginn des 20. Jahrhunderts', special issue of *Schriften der Erich-Mühsam-Gesellschaft*, 19 (2002).

Hobsbawm, E., *The Age of Extremes: A History of the World, 1914–1991* (New York: Vintage Books, 1996).

—, *Interesting Times* (London: Allen Lane, 2002).

Hollander, P., *Political Pilgrims: Travels of Western Intellectuals to the Soviet Union, China, and Cuba* (New York: Harper & Row, 1983).

Hosking, G., *The First Socialist Society: A History of the Soviet Union from Within*, 2nd edn (Cambridge, MA: Harvard University Press, 1996).

Hornstein, G. A., *To Redeem One Person is to Redeem the World* (New York: Free Press, 2000).

Howitt, D., and J. Owusu-Bempah, *The Racism of Psychology* (New York: Harvester Wheatsheaf, 1994).

Hurwitz, E., *Otto Gross: 'Paradies'-Sucher zwischen Freud und Jung* (Zürich: Suhrkamp Verlag, 1979).

—, 'Hans und Otto Gross', in von Olenhusen and Heuer (eds), *Die Gesetze des Vaters*, pp. 33–44

Jack, H. A., 'Die Friedensbewegung und Erich Fromm', in L. von Werder (ed.), *Der unbekannte Fromm: Biographische Studien* (Frankfurt: Haag und Herchen Verlag, 1987), pp. 61–70.

Jacoby, R., *The Repression of Psychoanalysis: Otto Fenichel and the Political Freudians* (New York: Basic Books, 1983).

Jaffé, A., *From the Life and Work of C. G. Jung*, trans. R. F. C. Hull (New York: Harper & Row, 1971).

Johnston, W. M., *The Austrian Mind: An Intellectual and Social History* (1972; Berkeley, CA: University of California Press, 1983).

Jones, E., *Sigmund Freud, Life and Work*, 2 vols (London: Hogarth Press, 1955).

—, *Free Associations* (London: Hogarth Press, 1959).

Joravsky, D., 'The Construction of the Stalinist Psyche', in S. Fitzpatrick (ed.), *Cultural Revolution in Russia, 1928–1931* (Bloomington, IN: Indiana University Press, 1978), pp. 105–28.

—, *The Lysenko Affair* (Chicago, IL: University of Chicago Press, 1986).

—, *Russian Psychology* (Oxford: Basil Blackwell, 1989).

Jung, C., and T. Anz (eds), *Der Fall Otto Gross: Eine Pressekampagne deutscher Intellektueller im Winter 1913/14* (Marburg an der Lahn: Literatur Wissenschaft.de, 2002).

Kanz, C., 'Mütterlichkeitskonzepte und Geschlechterdebatten Anfang des 20. Jahrhunderts. Otto Gross – ein Vorreiter der "Gender Studies"?', in Heuer (ed.), *2. Internationaler Otto Gross Kongress*, pp. 279–89.

Kätzel, S., *Marxismus und Psychoanalyse: Eine ideologiegeschichtliche Studie zur Diskussion in Deutschland und der UdSSR 1919–1933* (Berlin: Deutscher Verlag der Wissenschaften, 1987).

Kerr, J., *A Most Dangerous Method: The Story of Jung, Freud and Sabina Spielrein* (New York: Vintage Books, 1993).

Kessler, M. and R. Funk (eds), *Erich Fromm und die Frankfurter Schule* (Tübingen: Francke Verlag, 1992).

Kirsch, T. B., *The Jungians: A Comparative and Historical Perspective* (London: Routledge, 2000).

Kivivuori, J., *Paha Tieto* [*Evil Knowledge*] (Helsinki: Nemo, 2003).

Klein-Landskron, E., 'Max Horkheimer und Erich Fromm', in Kessler and Funk (eds), *Erich Fromm und die Frankfurter Schule*, pp. 161–80.

Kohn, H., *Nationalism and Liberty: The Swiss Example* (New York: G. Allen & Unwin, 1956).

Kozulin, A., *Psychology in Utopia: Toward a Social History of Soviet Psychology* (Cambridge, MA: MIT Press, 1984).

Kumar, K., *Utopia and Anti-Utopia in Modern Times* (Oxford: Basil Blackwell, 1987).

—, *Utopianism* (Minneapolis, MN: University of Minnesota Press, 1991).

Kurzweil, E., *The Freudians* (New Haven, CT: Yale University Press, 1989).

Laland, K. N., and G. R. Brown, *Sense and Nonsense: Evolutionary Perspectives on Human Behaviour* (Oxford: Oxford University Press, 2003).

Laska, B. A., *Wilhelm Reich* (Hamburg: Rowohlt, 1981).

—, 'Otto Gross zwischen Max Stirner und Wilhelm Reich', in Dehmlow and Heuer, (eds), *Bohème, Psychoanalyse und Revolution*, pp. 125–62.

Lemov, R., *World as Laboratory: Experiments with Mice, Mazes and Men* (New York: Hill and Wang, 2005).

Levitas, R., *The Concept of Utopia* (New York: Philip Allan, 1990).

Lewis, J., *Fascism and the Working Class in Austria, 1918–1934: The Failure of Labour in the First Republic* (New York: Berg, 1991).

Lieberman, D., J. Tooby and L. Cosmides, 'Does Morality have a Biological Basis? An Empirical Test of the Factors Governing Moral Sentiments Relating to Incest', *Proceedings of the Royal Society of London: Series B, Biological Sciences*, 270 (2003), pp. 819–26.

Lilla, M., *The Reckless Mind: Intellectuals in Politics* (New York: New York Review of Books, 2001).

Linke, H.-J., *Das Kultische in der Dichtung Stefan Georges und seiner Schule* (München: Helmut Küpper vormals George Bondi, 1960).

Lobkowics, N., 'Alienation', in C. D. Kernig (ed.), *Marxism, Communism and Western Society*, 8 vols (New York: Herder and Herder, 1972–3), vol. 1, pp. 88–109.

Loewenstein, R. M., 'Review of Erich Fromm, *Man for Himself*, *Psychoanalytic Quarterly*, 17 (1948), pp. 534–5.

Lothane, Z., 'Tender Love and Transference: Unpublished Letters of C. G. Jung and Sabina Spielrein', *International Journal of Psychoanalysis*, 80:6 (1999), pp. 1189–204.

Luft, D. S., *Robert Musil and the Crisis of European Culture, 1880–1942* (Berkeley, CA: University of California Press, 1980).

Maccoby, M., 'The Two Voices of Erich Fromm: The Prophetic and the Analytic', in Cortina and Maccoby (eds), *A Prophetic Analyst*, pp. 61–92.

MacIntyre, A., *After Virtue* (Notre Dame: University of Notre Dame Press, 1984).

McLaughlin, N., 'How to Become a Forgotten Intellectual: Intellectual Movements and the Rise and Fall of Erich Fromm', *Sociological Forum*, 13 (1998), pp. 215–46.

—, 'Optimal Marginality: Innovation and Orthodoxy in Fromm's Revision of Psychoanalysis', *Sociological Quarterly*, 42:2 (2001), pp. 271–88.

McLeish, J., *Soviet Psychology: History, Theory, Content* (London: Methuen & Co., 1975).

McLynn, F., *Carl Gustav Jung* (New York: St Martin's Griffin, 1997).

Madison, L., 'Introduction', in O. Gross, *Collected Works 1901–1907: The Graz Years*, ed. and trans. L. Madison (Hamilton, NY: Mindpiece, 2000), pp. 1–58.

Maidenbaum, A., and S. A. Martin (eds), *Lingering Shadows: Jungians, Freudians, and Anti-Semitism* (Boston, MA: Shambhala, 1991).

Mann, E. W., and E. Hoffman, *Wilhelm Reich: The Man who Dreamed of Tomorrow* (Wellingborough: Crucible, 1980).

Mannheim, K., *Ideology and Utopia: An Introduction to the Sociology of Knowledge* (1936; London: Routledge & Kegan Paul, 1960).

Manuel, F. E. (ed.). *Utopias and Utopian Thought* (1966; London: Souvenir Press, 1973).

Manuel, F. E., and F. P. Manuel, *Utopian Thought in the Western World* (Cambridge, MA: Belknap Press of Harvard University Press, 1979).

Marshall, P., 'Human Nature and Anarchism', in D. Goodway (ed.) *For Anarchism: History, Theory, and Practice* (London: Routledge, 1989), pp. 127-49.

—, *Demanding the Impossible: A History of Anarchism* (London: HarperCollins, 1992).

Martin, J., *Wilhelm Reich and the Cold War* (Fort Bragg, CA: Flatland Books, 2000).

Martin, R., and J. Barresi, *The Rise and Fall of Soul and Self* (New York: Columbia University Press, 2006).

Mayr, E., *The Growth of Biological Thought* (Cambridge, MA: Belknap Press of Harvard University Press, 1982).

Mazlish, B., *A New Science* (Oxford: Oxford University Press, 1989).

Menaker, E., *Appointment in Vienna* (New York: St Martin's Press, 1989).

Michaels, J., *Anarchy and Eros: Otto Gross' Impact on German Expressionist Writers* (New York: Peter Lang, 1983).

—, 'Otto Gross und das Konzept des Matriarchats', in Heuer (ed.), *2. Internationaler Otto Gross Kongress*, pp. 105–15.

Miele, F., 'The Imperial Animals 25 Years Later: An Interview with Lionel Tiger and Robin Fox', *Skeptic*, 4:1 (1996), pp. 78–85.

Milgram, S., *Obedience to Authority* (New York: HarperPerennial, 1975).

Miller, M. A., *Freud and the Bolsheviks* (New Haven, CT: Yale University Press, 1998).

Mitzman, A., 'Anarchism, Expressionism and Psychoanalysis', *New German Critique*, 10 (1977), pp. 77–109.

Morawski, J. G. 'Assessing Psychology's Moral Heritage through our Neglected Utopias', *American Psychologist*, 37:10 (1982), pp. 1082–95.

Mosse, G., *The Crisis of German Ideology: Intellectual Origins of the Third Reich* (London: Weidenfeld and Nicholson, 1964).

—, *Masses and Man: Nationalist and Fascist Perceptions of Reality* (New York: Howard Fertig, 1980).

Müller, H., 'Der Mauersprung von Zürich. Otto Gross, C. G. Jung und die Anarchisten von Zürich-Ascona', in Heuer (ed.), *2. Internationaler Otto Gross Kongress*, pp. 27–48.

Nagy, M., *Philosophical Issues in the Psychology of C. G. Jung* (Albany, NY: State University of New York Press, 1991).

Nanko, U., *Die Deutsche Glaubensbewegung: Eine historische und soziologische Untersuchung* (Marburg: Diagonal Verlag, 1993).

Neumann, E., *The Great Mother: An Analysis of the Archetype*, trans. R. Manheim (London: Routledge & Kegan Paul, 1955).

Neundörfer, G., 'Otto Gross und die Königliche Psychiatrische Klinik in München', in Dehmlow and Heuer, *Bohème, Psychoanalyse und Revolution*, pp. 47–52.

Nitzschke, B., '"Ich muss mich dagegen wehren, still kaltgestellt zu werden". Voraussetzungen, Umstände und Konsequenzen des Ausschlusses Wilhelm Reich's aus der DPG/IPV in den Jahren 1933/34', in Fallend and Nitzschke (eds), *Der 'Fall' Wilhelm Reich*, pp. 68–130.

—, 'Verinnerlichung äusserer Konflikte – Entäusserung innerer Konflikte: Über einige Gemeinsamkeiten und Differenzen zwischen Otto Gross, Wilhelm Reich und Sigmund Freud', in Dehmlow and Heuer (eds), *1. Internationaler Otto Gross Kongress*, pp. 39–54.

Noll, R., *The Jung Cult: Origins of a Charismatic Movement* (Princeton, NJ: Princeton University Press, 1994).

—, *The Aryan Christ: The Secret Life of Carl Jung* (New York: Random House, 1997).

Nye, R. A., *Crime, Madness and Politics in Modern France: The Medical Concept of National Decline* (Princeton, NJ: Princeton University Press, 1984).

Ohlander, A.-S., *Kvinnor, barn och arbete i Sverige 1850–1993*, Statens Offentliga Utredningar 38 (Stockholm: Fritzes, 1994).

von Olenhusen, A. G., '"Il poeta bello" oder der Mann, der immer dabei war: Der Anarchist, Literat und Psychologe Johannes Nohl (1882–1963) und Erich Mühsam, Otto Gross und Hermann Hesse', in Dehmlow and Heuer (eds), *1. Internationaler Otto Gross Kongress*, pp. 101–10.

—, 'Wahnsinn in den Zeiten des Krieges: Otto Gross, Franz Jung und das Kriegsrecht', in von Olenhusen and Heuer (eds), *Die Gesetze des Vaters*, pp. 82–128

von Olenhusen, A. G., and G. Heuer (eds), *Die Gesetze des Vaters: 4. Internationaler Otto Gross Kongress* (Marburg an der Lahn: Literatur Wissenschaft.de, 2005).

Otis, L. 'Organic Memory and Psychoanalysis', *History of Psychiatry*, 4 (1993), pp. 349–72.

Ovcharenko, V., 'Love, Psychoanalysis and Destruction', *Journal of Analytical Psychology*, 44:3 (1999), pp. 355–74.

Paget, H., 'Erich Fromm', in Buhle et al. (eds), *Encyclopedia of the American Left*, pp. 248–9.

Pells, R., *The Liberal Mind in a Conservative Age: American Intellectuals in the 1940s and the 1950s* (New York: Harper & Row, 1985).

Perusek, G., 'Shifting Terrain: Styles of Liberalism, Periodization, and Levels of Analysis', *International Journal of Politics, Culture and Society*, 15:3 (2002), pp. 405–26.

Pick, D., *Faces of Degeneration: A European Disorder, c. 1848–c. 1918* (Cambridge: Cambridge University Press, 1989).

Pietikainen, P., 'National Typologies, Races, and Mentalities in C. G. Jung's Psychology', *History of European Ideas*, 24:6 (1998), pp. 359–73.

—, *C. G. Jung and the Psychology of Symbolic Forms* (Helsinki: Finnish Academy of Science and Letters, 1999).

—, 'Jung's Psychology in the Light of his "Personal Myth"', *Psychoanalysis and History*, 1:2 (1999), pp. 237–51.

—, 'The *Volk* and its Unconscious: Jung, Hauer, and the "German Revolution"', *Journal of Contemporary History*, 35:4 (2000), pp. 523–39.

—, 'Dynamic Psychology, Utopia, and Escape from History: The Case of C. G. Jung', *Utopian Studies*, 12:1 (2001), pp. 41–55.

—, 'Soul Man Meets the Blind Watchmaker: C. G. Jung and Neo- Darwinism', *Psychoanalysis and History*, 5:2 (2003), pp. 195–212.

— (ed.), *Modernity and its Discontents: Sceptical Essays on the Psychomedical Management of Malaise* (Stockholm: Ax:son Johnson Foundation, 2005).

Pinker, S., *The Blank Slate: The Modern Denial of Human Nature* (New York: Viking, 2002).

Porter, R., 'Mood Disorders – Social Section', in G. E. Berrios and R. Porter (eds), *A History of Clinical Psychiatry: The Origin and History of Psychiatric Disorders* (London: Athlone, 1995), pp. 409–20.

Pressman, N., *Last Resort: Psychosurgery and the Limits of Medicine* (Cambridge: Cambridge University Press, 1998).

Quarta, C., 'Homo Utopicus: On the Need for Utopia', *Utopian Studies*, 7:2 (1996), pp. 153–66.

Read, J., L. R. Mosher and R. P. Bentall, *Models of Madness: Psychological, Social and Biological Approaches to Schizophrenia* (Hove: Brunner-Routledge, 2004).

Rice, J. L., *Freud's Russia: National Identity in the Evolution of Psychoanalysis* (New Brunswick, NJ: Transaction Publishers, 1993).

Ricoeur, P., *Freud and Philosophy: An Essay on Interpretation* (1965), trans. D. Savage (New Haven, CT: Yale University Press, 1970).

Rieff, P., *The Triumph of the Therapeutic* (New York: Harper & Row, 1968).

Riess, C., *Ascona: Geschichte des seltsamsten Dorfes der Welt* (Zürich: Europa Verlag, 1964).

Roazen, P., *Political Theory and the Psychology of the Unconscious* (London: Open Gate Press, 2000).

—, 'The Exclusion of Erich Fromm from the IPA', *Contemporary Psychoanalysis*, 37:1 (2001), pp. 5–42.

Roazen, P., and B. Swerdloff, *Heresy: Sandor Rado and the Psychoanalytic Movement* (Northvale, NJ: Jason Aronson, 1995).

Robinson, P. A., *The Freudian Left: Wilhelm Reich, Geza Roheim, Herbert Marcuse* (New York: Harper & Row, 1969).

Roll-Hansen, N., *The Lysenko Effect: The Politics of Science* (Amherst, NY: Humanity Books, 2005).

Roochnik, D., *Beautiful City: The Dialectical Character of Plato's Republic* (Ithaca, NY: Cornell University Press, 2003).

Rycroft, C., *Reich* (London: Fontana/Collins, 1971).

de Salis, J.-R., *Switzerland and Europe: Essays and Reflections* (Alabama: University of Alabama Press, 1971).

Samelson, F., 'The Authoritarian Character from Berlin to Berkeley and Beyond: The Odyssey of a Problem', in W. F. Stone, G. Lederer and R. Christie (eds), *Strength and Weakness: The Authoritarian Personality Today* (New York: Springer Verlag, 1993), pp. 22–43.

Samuels, A., *The Political Psyche* (London: Routledge, 1993).

Sargent, L. T., 'The Three Faces of Utopianism Revisited', *Utopian Studies*, 5:1 (1994), pp. 1–37.

Sassoon, D., *One Hundred Years of Socialism: The West European Left in the Twentieth Century* (London: I. B. Tauris, 1996).

Saul, L. J., 'Review of Erich Fromm, *Escape from Freedom*', *Psychoanalytic Quarterly*, 11:2 (1943), p. 245–8.

Schaar, J. H., *Escape from Authority: The Perspectives of Erich Fromm* (New York: Basic Books, 1961).

Schachter, D. L., *Searching for Memory* (New York: Basic Books, 1996).

Segerstråle, U., *Defenders of the Truth* (Oxford: Oxford University Press, 2001).

Sennett, R., *The Fall of Public Man* (New York: Vintage Books, 1978).

Service, R., *A History of Twentieth-Century Russia* (Cambridge, MA: Harvard University Press, 1998).

Shamdasani, S., 'From Geneva to Zürich: Jung and French Switzerland', *Journal of Analytical Psychology*, 43 (1998), pp. 115–26.

—, *Jung and the Making of Modern Psychology* (Cambridge: Cambridge University Press, 2003).

—, *Jung Stripped Bare, by his Biographers, Even* (London: Karnac Books, 2005).

Sharaf, M., *Fury on Earth: A Biography of Wilhelm Reich* (New York: Da Capo Press, 1983).

Siltala, J., *Työelämän huonontumisen lyhyt historia* (Helsinki: Kustannusosakeyhtiö Otava, 2004).

Smirnov, G., *The Soviet Man: The Making of a Socialist Type of Personality*, trans. R. Daglish (Moscow: Progress Publishers, 1973).

Smith, C. D., *Jung's Quest for Wholeness: A Religious and Historical Perspective* (Albany, NY: State University of New York Press, 1990).

Smith, R. C., *The Wounded Jung* (Evanston, IL: Northwestern University Press, 1996).

von Soden, K., *Die Sexualberatungsstellen der Weimarer Republik 1919–1933* (Berlin: Edition Hentrich, 1988).

Stack, D. A., 'The First Darwinian Left: Radical and Socialist Responses to Darwin, 1859–1914', *History of Political Thought*, 21:4 (2000), pp. 682–710.

Steele, R. S., *Freud and Jung: Conflicts of Interpretation* (London: Routledge & Kegan Paul, 1982).

Stein, M. H., 'Panel on "Aggression" (opening remarks)', *International Journal of Psychoanalysis*, 53 (1972), p. 13.

Storr, A., *Human Destructiveness* (New York: Ballantine Books, 1992).

Struve, W., *Elites Against Democracy: Leadership Ideals in Bourgeoisie Political Thought in Germany, 1890–1933* (Princeton, NJ: Princeton University Press, 1973).

Sulloway, F., *Freud, Biologist of the Mind* (1979; Cambridge, MA: Harvard University Press, 1992).

Tarr, Z., and J. Marcus, 'Erich Fromm und das Judentum', in Kessler and Funk (eds), *Erich Fromm und die Frankfurter Schule*, pp. 211–20.

Taylor, C., *Sources of the Self* (Cambridge: Cambridge University Press, 1992).

Taylor, S. E., *Positive Illusions: Creative Self-Deception and the Healthy Mind* (New York: Basic Books, 1989).

Taylor, S. E., and D. A. Armor, 'Positive Illusions and Coping with Adversity', *Journal of Personality*, 64:4 (1996), pp. 873–97.

Taylor, S. E., and J. D. Brown, 'Illusion and Well-Being: A Social Psychological Perspective on Mental Health', *Psychological Bulletin*, 103 (1988), pp. 193–210.

—, 'Positive Illusions and Well-Being Revisited: Separating Fact from Fiction', *Psychological Bulletin*, 116:1 (1994), pp. 21–7.

Thomas, J.-F., 'Le Suisse Est-Il Utopiste?' in G. Slusser, P. Alkon, R. Gaillard and D. Chatelain (eds), *Transformations of Utopia* (New York: AMS Press, 1999), pp. 89–97.

Trautman, T. R., *Lewis Henry Morgan and the Invention of Kinship* (Berkeley, CA: University of California Press, 1987).

Trivers, R., 'Reciprocal Altruism' (1971), in R. Trivers, *Natural Selection*, pp. 3–55.

—, 'Parent-Offspring Conflict' (1974), in R. Trivers, *Natural Selection*, pp. 123–53.

—, 'Self-Deception in Service of Deceit' (2002), in R. Trivers, *Natural Selection*, pp. 255–93.

—, *Natural Selection and Social Theory: Selected Papers of Robert Trivers* (Oxford: Oxford University Press, 2002).

Tugaybayeva, B. N., 'Comments on the History of Psychoanalysis in Russia', in V.A. Koltsova et al (eds), *Post-Soviet Perspectives on Russian Psychology* (Westport, CT: Greenwood Press, 1996), pp. 253–66.

Tully, J. (ed.), *Meaning and Context: Quentin Skinner and his Critics* (Cambridge: Cambridge University Press, 1988).

Valsiner, J., 'Social Utopias and Knowledge Construction in Psychology', in V. A. Koltsova et al. (eds), *Post-Soviet Perspectives on Russian Psychology* (Westport, CN: Greenwood Press, 1996), pp. 70–84.

Vandermeersch, P., *Unresolved Questions in the Freud/Jung Debate* (Leuven: Leuven University Press, 1991).

Volkogonov, D., *Trotsky: The Eternal Revolutionary*, trans. and ed. H. Shukman (London: HarperCollins, 1997).

de Waal, F., *The Ape and the Sushi Master* (New York: Basic Books, 2001).

Wehr, G., *Jung: A Biography*, trans. D. M. Weeks (Boston, MA: Shambhala, 1987).

White, E. W., 'Otto Gross: The Taos Connection', in von Olenhusen and Heuer (eds), *Die Gesetze des Vaters*, pp. 375–402.

Whitebook, J., *Perversion and Utopia: A Study in Psychoanalysis and Critical Theory* (Cambridge, MA: The MIT Press, 1996).

Wild, P., *Sointula: Island Utopia* (Madeira Park: Harbour, 1995).

Wolf, S., '"[...] ich werde noch einmal unter euch fahren, dass euch Hören und Sehen vergeht": – Gustav Landauer, Otto Gross und die Psychoanalyse', in von Olenhusen and Heuer (eds), *Die Gesetze des Vaters*, pp. 240–85.

Wolf, W., *Faschismus in der Schweiz* (Zürich: Flamberg, 1969).

Wood, D. K., *Men Against Time: Nicolas Berdyaev, T. S. Eliot, Aldous Huxley and C .G. Jung* (Lawrence, KS: University Press of Kansas, 1982).

Woodcock, G., 'Anarchism: A Historical Introduction', in G. Woodcock (ed.), *The Anarchist Reader* (Hassocks: Harvester Press/Humanities Press, 1977), pp. 11–56.

— (ed.), *The Anarchist Reader* (Hassocks: Harvester Press/Humanities Press, 1977).

Wortis, J., *My Analysis with Freud* (Northvale, NJ: Jason Aronson, 1994).

Zilbersheid, U., *Jenseits der Arbeit. Der vergessene sozialistische Traum von Marx, Fromm und Marcuse* (Frankfurt am Main: Peter Lang, 1999).

—, 'The Idea of Abolition of Labor in Socialist Utopian Thought', *Utopian Studies*, 13:1 (2002), pp. 21–42.

Zimmer, O., '"A Unique Fusion of the Natural and the Man-Made": The Trajectory of Swiss Nationalism', *Journal of Contemporary History*, 39:1 (2004), pp. 5–24.

INDEX

For Product Safety Concerns and Information please contact our EU
representative GPSR@taylorandfrancis.com
Taylor & Francis Verlag GmbH, Kaufingerstraße 24, 80331 München, Germany

www.ingramcontent.com/pod-product-compliance
Ingram Content Group UK Ltd.
Pitfield, Milton Keynes, MK11 3LW, UK
UKHW020015200926
475702UK00014B/1902
9781138663572